BERNARDO DE GÁLVEZ IN LOUISIANA

BERNARDO DE GÁLVEZ

BERNARDO DE GÁLVEZ IN LOUISIANA

1776-1783

BY

JOHN WALTON CAUGHEY

Foreword by Jack D. L. Holmes

A FIREBIRD PRESS BOOK

PELICAN PUBLISHING COMPANY
Gretna 1998

Copyright © 1934
Regents of the University of California

Copyright © 1972
Pelican Publishing Company, Inc.
ISBN: 1-565545-17-6
LCN: 72–86562

Published August, 1972

Manufactured in the United States of America
Published by Pelican Publishing Company, Inc.
1000 Burmaster Street, Gretna, Louisiana 70053

CONTENTS

	PAGE
PORTRAIT OF BERNARDO DE GÁLVEZ	*Frontispiece*
LIST OF ABBREVIATIONS	vi
FOREWORD	vii
PREFACE	xii

PART ONE: THE BACKGROUND

CHAPTER		
I.	THE ESTABLISHMENT OF SPANISH CONTROL	1
II.	O'REILLY'S CONSTRUCTIVE STATESMANSHIP	29
III.	UNZAGA AND LOCAL PROBLEMS	43

PART TWO: GÁLVEZ' ADMINISTRATION

IV.	THE COMMENCEMENT OF GÁLVEZ' CAREER	61
V.	TRADE REGULATION AND COLONIAL DEVELOPMENT	70
VI.	AID FOR THE AMERICANS	85
VII.	WILLING'S EXPEDITION	102
VIII.	PREPARATIONS FOR WAR	135
IX.	THE STRUGGLE FOR THE MISSISSIPPI	149
X.	THE CAPTURE OF MOBILE	171
XI.	PREPARATIONS FOR THE SIEGE OF PENSACOLA	187
XII.	"YO SOLO"	200
XIII.	THE NATCHEZ REBELLION	215
XIV.	THE CLOSE OF GÁLVEZ' CAREER	243
	BIBLIOGRAPHY	259
	INDEX	273

LIST OF ABBREVIATIONS
INDICATING ARCHIVAL LOCATION

A.G.I. . . . . . Archivo General de Indias, at Seville, and its several sections:

Cuba . . . . . . Papeles procedentes de la Isla de Cuba

Guad. . . . . . . Audiencia de Guadalajara

Ind. Gen. . . . . Indiferente General

Mexico . . . . . Audiencia de Mexico

Sto. Dom. . . . Audiencia de Santo Domingo

The following number is that of the *legajo* or bundle which contains the specific document.

A.H.N. . . . . Archivo Histórico Nacional, at Madrid

B.L., La.Coll. . Bancroft Library, at Berkeley, Louisiana Collection

H.L. . . . . . . Henry E. Huntington Library, at San Marino, California

L.C. . . . . . . Library of Congress

Foreword

Given the current renewed interest in the Spanish Borderlands by historians from both sides of the Atlantic, the reprinting of a recognized "classic" for Spanish Louisiana should be greeted with enthusiasm. Those of us who have chosen this field of historical research pay homage to the host of scholars who were first led from the wilderness of erroneous and legendary interpretation of Spain's role in the dominion of portions of the United States by the "Moses of the Spanish Borderlands," the late *maestro* of the University of California in Berkeley—Herbert Eugene Bolton.

Certainly, one of the greatest of Bolton's students was John Walton Caughey. From the plains of Kansas he journeyed to the University of Texas for his undergraduate degree and then turned his sights westward to complete his graduate studies at the Berkeley campus. "Louisiana Under Spain, 1762–1783" was the title of his 1928 doctoral dissertation, written from primary sources obtained in the archives of Spain under the capable direction of Bolton.

Six years later, after some revision, Caughey published his thesis under the title, *Bernardo de Gálvez in Louisiana, 1776–1783*. Four years later, he carved his initials again in the tree of knowledge by publishing a documentary study of Alexander McGillivray, the redoubtable half-breed Creek leader whom another historian once labelled "The Talleyrand of Alabama." Several chapters of the Gálvez study were also published in *New Spain and the Anglo-American West*, the *Hispanic American Historical Review* and the *Louisiana Historical Quarterly*.

Unfortunately for serious scholars of Spanish Louisiana, Dr. Caughey has abandoned his earlier field of interest in favor of new fields. He has followed, perhaps too closely, Horace Greeley's injunction, "Go West, young man," and, as editor of the *Pacific Historical Review* and the *Chronicles of California* series, he is considered an authority on California, the Indian tribes of that region and the gold rushes. In the fifth edition of the *Dictionary of American Scholars, Vol. I: History* (New York: 1969; p. 82) he does not even list his important historical publications on Spanish Louisiana.

Yet, in his seventieth year it is fitting that the Pelican Publishing Company reprint what must be his "first love," and no man can ever forget the poignancy, tears and heartache of those early days. Even as David Bjork, Sister Mary A. M. O'Callaghan, Lawrence Kinnard, and Abraham P. Nasatir—all Bolton students who chose Spanish Louisiana as their metier—Caughey will be renowned in Louisiana historical circles as long as the name of Bernardo de Gálvez is remembered.

In analyzing Caughey's study, it is important to realize that he has attempted too much. Gálvez requires a full-length study in his own right. Yet Caughey chose to trace the background of Spain's role in Louisiana prior to January 1, 1777, when Gálvez was sworn in as governor-general. This forms the first part of Caughey's study and embraces three chapters. Part two, beginning with the fourth chapter, is the study of Gálvez's career.

In his 1952 study of Bernardo de Gálvez, the eminent Spanish historian, Guillermo Porrás Muñoz, quotes a popular child's refrain commonly heard about the Gálvez family:

¿Quién manda en este mundo?	Who commands on this globe?
José, el primero,	José, the first,
Matías, el segundo,	Matías, the second,
y Bernardo, el tercero.	and Bernardo, the third.
Fiscal . . . Virrey,	Attorney-general . . . Viceroy,
Virrey . . . Ministro,	Viceroy . . . Minister,
y Ministro . . . Rey.	and Minister . . . King.
El Padre, aquí,	The Father, here,
el Hijo, en La Habana,	the Son, in Havana,
y el Espíritu en España.	and the Holy Ghost in Spain.

Although the slightly blasphemous ditty implies nepotism among the Gálvez family, it also recognizes the brilliant accomplishments of an extraordinary Málaga family, which served Spain in much the same way that the Adams family of Massachusetts, the Roosevelts of

New York and the Kennedys of Massachusetts have served the United States. José de Gálvez, a former *visitador* to New Spain who was Minister of the Indies, enjoyed power, as Caughey notes, "second only to that of King Carlos himself." His elder brother, Matías, former captain-general of Guatemala, had been elevated to the vice-royalty of New Spain. Bernardo, who was Matías's son and José's favorite nephew, while an unexperienced youth of twenty-four, led Spanish troops against the Apache along the banks of the little Colorado River in Texas. Despite several arrow and spear wounds, young Bernardo continued to lead his men to a victorious conclusion of the campaign.

Although some ministers in Spain felt that Gálvez had fought too well and had incited the Indians to new uprisings, he was well received when he returned to Spain and began the swift climb through the military ranks. He again saw battle and resulting wounds in the disastrous Spanish attack at Algiers in July, 1775. After a brief tour of duty as lieutenant-colonel at the Ávila Military Academy, he was named colonel and commanding officer of the Louisiana Infantry Regiment at New Orleans. Less than a year later he was sworn in as governor-general by Luis de Unzaga y Amezaga. He was thirty years old, charged with the awesome responsibility of ruling a province, which stretched from the Gulf of Mexico to upper Missouri and from British West Florida to the hazy borders of Texas.

Gálvez received explicit orders from Uncle José governing his myriad duties. He was to record accurate census records for the province; maintain annual debit and credit accounts; make official visits to the far-flung posts of his command; supervise the drawing of accurate maps and charts of Louisiana; develop new frontier settlements composed of loyal, Catholic immigrants; take strong steps to eliminate the customary contraband trade which had been allowed to flourish under Unzaga; encourage agricultural production; maintain the friendship of the Southern Indian nations; follow the relatively mild Spanish treatment of Negro slaves, but do all he could to prevent an uprising among the blacks; serve as vice-patron of the Catholic Church in Louisiana by creating new parishes and appointing their priests; command the regular and militia organizations and keep a watchful eye on his English neighbors.

Gálvez performed his duties to the full satisfaction of his superiors, and so gallantly had he fought during the American Revolutionary campaigns of 1779–1780, that he was exempted from the customary *residencia*—the judicial inquiry into his previous term of office as governor-general. It is difficult to place Gálvez in his proper ranking among the nine governors-general who were appointed regularly for Spanish Louisiana. Certainly, he was near the top. Moreover, he earned the loyalty and affection of the people of Louisiana and helped erase the unfortunate memory of "Bloody O'Reilly" and the early Hispanophobia of the colony. His marriage in 1779 to Felicité de St. Maxent d'Estréhan, the daughter of the wealthy Gilbert Antoine de St. Maxent, did much to cement the Franco-Spanish alliance in Louisiana.

Much of the popularity of Gálvez may be traced to his vigorous and capable leadership during the American Revolution. Even before Spain entered that fray as an ally of France against England, the Spanish government was aiding the American colonists with money and supplies from New Orleans, a fact which most American history texts have forgotten to mention. He led a motley force of Louisiana settlers—black, white and mulatto—and the regular military and naval forces against Baton Rouge in 1779. This victory added the Natchez District to Spain's possessions.

The following year, he led his men from certain defeat after most of his fleet was shipwrecked off the Mobile bar and lay siege to the British at Fort Charlotte. The Mobile District was added to his conquests, after which he conducted a determined siege of the British capital at Pensacola. By the end of 1781, it was clear that all of West Florida would be returned to Spain, and the British also ceded East Florida to the former owners in the peace treaty of 1783. Descendants of those who fought for Spain during the Gálvez campaigns have been recognized as being entitled to membership in the Sons and in the Daughters of the American Revolution.

After the American Revolution, Gálvez ordered José de Evia to make a complete reconnaissance of the Gulf of Mexico from the Florida Keys all the way to Támpico, Mexico, and he took special interest in the mission as it progressed through 1783–1786. In the latter year, he died at Mexico City, having arrived only a short time before as viceroy, the same post his father once held. One wonders what the course of Mexican history might have been had he lived to employ the same vigorous measures that established his rule in Louisiana as one of the best.

JACK D. L. HOLMES
Professor of History
University of Alabama in Birmingham

May 29, 1972

Preface

THE LOUISIANA CAREER of Bernardo de Gálvez, though it spanned only half a dozen years in his early thirties, embraced his most significant achievements. As governor of the colony he dealt with the regular problems of a frontier province, those of regulating trade, controlling the Indians, encouraging settlement and agriculture, and strengthening the military defenses. His administration illustrates the vigor with which Spain held the frontier during the reign of Carlos III.

Gálvez also had an important rôle in the struggle between Spain and England, the major contest in the series of international rivalries in colonial America. As a friendly neutral, he lent liberal assistance to the American Revolutionists, particularly to those operating in the West. After Spain entered the war against England in 1779, he conquered the British posts on the lower Mississippi, at Mobile, and at Pensacola; as the Spanish chief of operations in America he directed the capture of the Bahama Islands and made elaborate preparations for an assault on Jamaica. His victories inclined England toward greater generosity to the United States with respect to the Trans-Alleghany West; and in recovering the Floridas he had the distinction of gaining for Spain her maximum territorial extent in North America.

Gálvez has received passing mention in many works on the American Revolution and on Spanish Louisiana, but no biography has ever been published and few shorter monographs have dealt with episodes in his life. This book represents the first attempt at a comprehensive study of his career. It sketches the earlier and later phases of his life in Nueva Vizcaya, Europe, Havana, and Mexico City, but attention is concentrated upon the years in Louisiana—Gálvez' real career.

Parts of the material of Chapters V and VIII have been presented in two articles in the *Hispanic American Historical Review*. Chapters

VII and XIII appeared in substantially their present form in the *Louisiana Historical Quarterly*.

In pursuing this study I have incurred many obligations of gratitude. The greatest is to Professor Herbert Eugene Bolton, who has fathered my interest in historical research generally, as well as in the life of Gálvez. A fellowship from the Native Sons of the Golden West made possible my work in the Spanish archives. The staffs of the Bancroft Library, the Archivo General de Indias at Seville, the Archivo Histórico Nacional at Madrid, the Library of Congress, the Howard Memorial Library at New Orleans, and the Henry E. Huntington Library gave me essential assistance. For all manner of help, especially in matters of literary style, I am indebted to my wife, LaRee, and finally to Nancy, who tiptoed that I might finish "her book."

J. W. C.

Los Angeles, California
December, 1932

PART ONE

The Background

Chapter I

THE ESTABLISHMENT OF SPANISH CONTROL

LOUISIANA'S HISTORICAL DRAMA begins with a prologue of Spanish exploration. During the second generation of European activity in the New World, from 1519 to 1543, Spanish energy, credulity, greed, and ambition led to a series of penetrations into the heart of North America. Pineda skirted the Gulf Coast and reported a great river, most probably the Mississippi; the journey of Narváez and De Vaca was even more adventurous; De Soto, with the most pretentious attempt at colonization ever directed toward the Mississippi Valley, ranged from Florida to Arkansas and from the Carolinas to Texas pursuing phantom wealth and wonders. These Spaniards sought gold and pearls; they expected another Mexico. Lured on by Indian tales, they followed visions of a terrestrial paradise, but hardships, disappointments, and death were their lot. Their glamorous and far-flung explorations had no issue in colonies planted; instead, Spain turned back to more attractive lands farther south, and for a century and a half Louisiana was left to its Indian denizens.

Revival of interest in the great Mississippi basin came through the French. The approach this time was from the north, from the St. Lawrence and the Great Lakes. Joliet the trader and Marquette the missionary began, and La Salle completed, this rediscovery of the Father of Waters. La Salle, who had pioneered in the fur trade in the Illinois country, was the first person to descend the Mississippi to its mouth. He projected a French colony on the Gulf, but shipwreck, dissension, desertion, disease, and Indian hostility caused the colony's disintegration, while his own imperiousness invited the commander's assassination.

La Salle's colony failed, but the idea did not die. His plans were taken over and his aims voiced anew by a number of applicants for his grant, whose petitions reminded Louis XIV of the advantage of French frontage on the Gulf and of access to the mines of Mexico. During the War of the Palatinate the French court shelved plans for the new colony, but after the Treaty of Ryswick the king looked more favorably upon the project and found an added incentive in the rumor that the English were about to occupy the mouth of the Mississippi. The Minister of Marine, Count de Pontchartrain, thereupon sent Iberville to establish settlements on the lower Mississippi. One is tempted to dwell on Iberville. Of the illustrious Le Moyne family of Canada, already distinguished through his victories over the British on Hudson Bay and in Newfoundland, and in addition a practiced woodsman, he was a happy choice for the founding of Louisiana. With him came his brother, Bienville, whose lifetime was to span the entire period of French control in Louisiana.

Under these two brothers the lower course of the Mississippi was explored, but the center of activities was in the Alabama Basin, first at Biloxi and then at Mobile. Pestilence, famine, and hurricane ravaged the infant colony, already distracted by bickerings among the colonists. The home government neglected the colony in essential matters and burdened the governor with absurd orders, such as directions to domesticate the wild cattle for the sake of their wool, to search for pearl fisheries on the Gulf, above all to discover mines, and to employ the Indian girls in raising silkworms. Bienville was indefatigable in ingratiating himself with the neighboring Indians, but he was at a disadvantage in competing with English traders from the Carolinas, who offered better goods at lower prices. An investigation, in 1710, revealed only 125 men, 28 women, and 25 children in the whole colony, and their condition was anything but prosperous.

Pontchartrain therefore welcomed an opportunity in 1712 to shift responsibility for the colony to Antoine Cruzat. A fifteen-year contract was signed with terms that promised to be most advantageous to the proprietor. The new régime brought temporary invigoration in the shape of supplies and a few new settlers. But Cruzat made his trade monopoly too severe. The consequent stagnation, together with the heavy expense incident to a war against the Natchez, ruined the once wealthy proprietor, and in 1717 he asked to be released from his contract. Natchitoches was established in the Red River region, Fort Toulouse on the Alabama, and Fort Rosalie at Natchez under Cruzat's rule, but otherwise Louisiana profited little.

After the proprietorship, the destinies of Louisiana fell under the sway of that prince of speculators, John Law. Capitalizing the reputed resources of Louisiana, this Scotch precursor of high finance dazzled all France with the prospect of perpetual prosperity. The bubble burst; Law was ruined; the Mississippi Company went to the wall; and France herself narrowly escaped bankruptcy. But however much economists and the French may execrate John Law, Louisianians should remember him with a measure of gratitude. His boom put new life into an all but defunct colony. Population jumped from a scant 700 to more than 5000.[1] The Illinois district was transferred from Canadian control, and received a notable influx of settlers. Settlement of the German Coast and the Yazoo district was begun and New Orleans was founded. At about the same time the Black Code, usually thought of as barbarously severe but in reality remarkable for its humanity, was imported from Sainte Domingue.

The final three decades of French domination can be passed over rather hurriedly. Bienville closed his career in Louisiana in an inglorious and disastrous attack on the Chickasaws. English influence over the Indian allies increased steadily. "The Choctaws and Alibamons," wrote Kerlérec in 1761, "harass us daily, to have supplies and merchandise. They threaten to go over to the English, if we cannot relieve them, and, in the meantime, during their frequent visits they devour the little that remains of our provisions and exhaust our meager stock of merchandise. We have just ground to fear and to expect hostilities from them."[2] D'Abbadie reported that the colony was "in a state of complete destitution; that it was a chaos of iniquities," that the inhabitants were characterized by drunkenness, laziness, and insubordination, three-fourths of them being in a state of insolvency.[3]

---

[1] Bolton and Marshall, *The Colonization of North America, 1492-1783*, 278-279. Chambers' figures are 400 and 7020, *Mississippi Valley Beginnings*, 68.

[2] Quoted in Gayarré, *History of Louisiana*, II, 88.

[3] Quoted, *ibid.*, II, 105-106, 108.

France was ready, after sixty years of endeavor, to admit her failure in colonizing Louisiana. The colony was notorious as a financial liability. Pontchartrain had encountered expenses without profits, Cruzat had lost his fortune, Law's company had gone bankrupt, and in later years the French treasury had subsidized the colony to the extent of 800,000 livres annually. Gayarré estimates that altogether seventy or eighty million livres had been disbursed on the colony, without return and without the prospect of any reduction in expense.[4]

Military reverses augmented France's dissatisfaction with the Louisiana burden. The colony was not captured, it is true, but Canada was lost and likewise the sugar islands, and as the price for the return of St. Lucia the English insisted upon the Mississippi as a boundary. Even though the island of New Orleans was retained, the remnant of Louisiana seemed a miserable empire, a most inconvenient colonial unit. Wedged in between the English and the Spaniards the colony's existence would be precarious, its sure defense impossible, and its administrative expense but slightly diminished by lopping off the eastern watershed of the Mississippi. Consequently, France's willingness to cede the remainder of Louisiana to Spain is readily understandable. To France the colony was worse than valueless. By the cession appreciation would be shown for Spain's belated assistance in the Seven Years' War, and it might help to perpetuate the cordiality embodied in the Family Compact, which thus far had redounded chiefly to the benefit of France. There was justice, furthermore, in offering recompense for Florida, which Spain had been forced to surrender to the English as ransom for Havana.

The traditional view has been that Spain fathomed this French "generosity," recognized Louisiana as a "white elephant," and that, when Carlos III couched his reluctance to accept in the polite protest, "My cousin is losing altogether too much," he really meant "My cousin is giving me something that will cost me altogether too much." Though corroborated by Spain's delay in taking charge of Louisiana

---

[4] This sketch of early Louisiana history is based on: Bolton and Marshall, *op. cit.,* 40-42, 78-102, 275-288; Gayarré, *op. cit.,* I and II; Phelps, *Louisiana, a Record of Expansion,* 1-105; Reynolds, *The Alabama-Tombigbee Basin in International Relations, 1701-1763* (MS, Ph.D. thesis, University of California).

after the cession, this interpretation has been something of a paradox in view of Carlos' full appreciation of the northern borderlands as a buffer to insulate Spanish America proper. On the eve of the occupation of Alta California and the organization of the Provincias Internas, we might have expected a more enthusiastic Spanish welcome for Louisiana.

Recent research in the diplomatic archives vindicates Spanish perspicacity. As early as 1760, it now appears, Carlos had broached the matter thus to the French ambassador, "I must arrange with France after the peace for Louisiana by means of some exchange." In subsequent negotiations France, mindful of the strategic value of Louisiana to Spain, proffered it as a bribe for Spain's agreement to the Family Compact, for a Spanish loan to France, and for Spain's prompt entrance into the war against England. Then in the peace negotiations the offer was renewed, but more as a peace bribe than as recompense for Florida. The purpose of the cession as finally made was to reconcile Spain to an early peace with England and to English possession of the Gulf Coast east of New Orleans. Thus is recorded history made more logical—both France and Spain looked askance at Louisiana as an expensive colony, but both nations recognized its strategic value as a part of the barrier against the English which Spain was erecting along the northern fringe of her American empire.[5]

Nevertheless, Spain was in no hurry to take possession; the cession was kept a secret, and a lack of zeal is evident in the assumption of Louisiana's expense. The French government, anxious to be rid of the encumbrance, prepared a notice of the cession for the governor of Louisiana in January, 1763, but in compliance with Spain's request for delay did not forward it. Instead, instructions were sent, on February 10, relative to the surrender of eastern Louisiana to the English. This letter definitely gave the impression that western Louisiana was to remain French, a piece of "duplicity" which probably had a good deal to do with the migrations of French settlers and friendly Indian

---

[5] The interpretation in Shepherd, "The Cession of Louisiana to Spain," *Political Science Quarterly*, XIX (1904), 439–458, is revised and supplemented by Aiton, "The Diplomacy of the Louisiana Cession," *American Historical Review*, XXXVI (1931), 701–720.

tribes across the Mississippi. In December, 1763, the French minister at Madrid urged that Spain take action, and, lest Spain be made still more reluctant to occupy Louisiana, the French minister recommended that Kerlérec's memorial concerning the colony "be recast to produce a more favorable impression."[6] But notwithstanding all this urging, three years elapsed after the cession before Spain's representative arrived at New Orleans.

In the meantime a commensurate lack of enthusiasm had been evinced in the colony. Rumors of the impending transfer disturbed the colonists in the summer of 1764. On September 10 of that year, D'Abbadie received official notice from the King of France, with instructions concerning his procedure toward the Spaniards when they should arrive. The act of cession, therewith transmitted, was recorded with the Superior Council and published in October. Champigny reports that the consternation in Louisiana was only tempered by the illusion that France might be induced to reconsider her abrogation.[7]

With this purpose in view, a meeting was called for January 4, 1765. It was attended by the Superior Council and a number of prominent citizens. After listening to an impassioned speech by Lafrénière, the Attorney-General, in which he advocated that the King of France be implored to rescind the cession to Spain, the gathering endorsed the proposition by unanimous vote. Jean Milhet, the wealthiest merchant of New Orleans, was selected to convey the petition to the king. Milhet journeyed to Paris, and in company with Bienville, the Father of Louisiana, called on the Duke de Choiseul. Bienville's pathetic appeal for his beloved colony is said to have moved Choiseul greatly, but it did not alter his resolution concerning the transfer. To him the cession was a closed issue.[8]

Eventually Spain moved to possess her new colony. As its governor, Carlos III appointed one of the most distinguished of his subjects, Antonio de Ulloa, "who had made himself illustrious in the republic

---

[6] Villiers du Terrage, *Les Dernières Années de la Louisiane française*, 156–159, 195–197; Bjork, *The Establishment of Spanish Rule in the Province of Louisiana, 1762–1770* (MS, Ph.D. thesis, University of California), 52.

[7] "Memoir of the Present State of Louisiana," *in* French, ed., *Historical Collections of Louisiana*, V, 144–145.

[8] Martin, *The History of Louisiana*, I, 348–349; Gayarré, *op. cit.*, II, 128–129.

of letters, and who was one of the brightest ornaments of Spain in the eighteenth century by his scientific labors and travels, and by his long and useful services as a naval officer and an administrator."[9]

Ulloa was born in Seville in 1716. Because of his exceptional scholarship in the Royal Academy of Midshipmen he was chosen, at the age of nineteen, to escort and coöperate with an expedition sponsored by the Academy of Sciences of Paris, the purpose of which was to measure an arc of the meridian at the equator. After ten strenuous years in Peru the observations were completed. Ulloa had distinguished himself, not only by tireless devotion to the scientific labors, but also by organizing the naval defenses of Peru and Chile against Anson's fleet. The home voyage from Callao and around the Horn was eventful. His ship survived an attack by English privateers, but to elude pursuit headed for Louisbourg on Cape Breton Island instead of for Brest. Entering Louisbourg, the voyagers found themselves prisoners to the New Englanders, who, after their capture of the French Fortress of the North, had kept the French flag flying as a decoy.

A prisoner of war, Ulloa was sent to England. But fellow-scientists there came to his rescue, secured his release and recovered his papers, and elected him to membership in the Royal Society of London.[10] In 1748, having returned to Spain, he published at royal expense his *Historical Relation of a Voyage Made to South America,* including with the account of the scientific operations, observations on natural history and the customs of the people, and a summary of Peruvian history.[11] He was also an associate member of the academies of Berlin and Stockholm, an active member of the Academy of Madrid, and a correspondent of the Academy of Science of Paris. He was responsible for Spain's first cabinet of natural history and for her first laboratory of metallurgy. He planned the canal of Old Castile. He supervised the

---

[9] *Ibid.,* 141.
[10] See the comparison with modern scientific ethics in Robert H. Lowie, *Are We Civilized?,* 289.
[11] Other publications were: *Noticias Americanas, entretenimientos physico-históricos sobre la América Meridional y la Septentrional Oriental* (1772), a work on the naval forces of Africa and Europe (1773), and his observations on an eclipse of the sun (1778).

drafting of an accurate map of the Peninsula. He fostered improvements in printing and in cloth making.

But notwithstanding his erudition and his versatility, he was occasionally the theorist, bungling practicalities. In 1779, for example, when sent with a squadron to capture eight English vessels off the Azores, he became so engrossed in astronomical observations that he forgot to open his instructions and the ships escaped. As governor of Louisiana also, his scholarly proclivities were not to prove advantageous. His scientific detachment seemed to the creoles aloofness; his preoccupation, sulking; his indifference to environment, lack of feeling. Misinterpreting his every action, the Louisianians were disappointed and irritated by this governor whose distinction they did not appreciate.[12]

Ulloa was appointed governor of Louisiana at the zenith of his career. But his actual arrival, on March 5, 1766, was not at all auspicious; he was ushered into the colony by a severe thunderstorm. This may not have been prophetic of the trouble that lay ahead of him, but certainly the habitants recalled it later as an ill omen.

In person Ulloa was mild and unimposing, not of the prepossessing type whose every attitude carries conviction of power. His retinue was correspondingly unimpressive; a mere handful of soldiers, about ninety in all, travel worn and drenched by the rains, forming an escort utterly inadequate for a triumphal entry. The impression was rather that the Spanish nation had reached senility and could take only a faltering hold upon Louisiana. On the very day of his arrival Ulloa gave offense by brusquely refusing a request of the Superior Council, thus wounding the pride of those petty functionaries and setting to smoulder the fires of discontent that were eventually to drive him from the colony.

Ulloa's difficulties in Louisiana were largely the result of misunderstandings. Had the colonists known the governor's actual instructions, they might have been less apprehensive of the change, for Spain apparently realized that Louisiana presented a new problem in colonial

---

[12] This biographical sketch is based on the following: Gayarré, *op. cit.*, II, 141–152, 173–178; Bolton, *Athanase de Mézières and the Louisiana-Texas Frontier*, I, 127–128 n.; French, *op. cit.*, V, 151–152 n.; Villiers du Terrage, *op. cit.*, 228.

THE ESTABLISHMENT OF SPANISH CONTROL 9

administration to which Spain's customary methods were hardly applicable. Ulloa, therefore, was directed to alter existing conditions as little as possible. Local laws and customs were to continue. The colony was not to be integrated with the rest of Spanish America, but was to be directly under the king. These instructions, however, were not fully announced in New Orleans. Had Spain provided an adequate escort, the colonists would have had a more wholesome respect for Spanish power. Had Ulloa's great reputation preceded him into Louisiana, the colonists might have excused some of his vagaries.

But none of these foundations was properly laid. The colonists deplored the coming of the Spaniards. They expected in Spanish rule a blight to their prosperity and happiness. Their disapproval of the imposition of Spanish control was ingrained, and could only be overcome by the exercise of consummate tact on the part of the new governor, by promises and proof that as Spanish colonists they would be better off than they had been under France, or by a great display of force that would quell rebellious spirits, over-awe malcontents, and win the admiration of the populace. Unfortunately Ulloa was not endowed by nature or equipped by his king to win the allegiance of the colonists by any of these methods. His cold reception offended him, and the more he saw of New Orleans and its inhabitants the more contemptuous he became. The creoles felt this and closed the doors of their hearts against reconciliation through the personality of the governor. Nor were they inclined to listen to his promises.[13]

Ulloa's two and a half years in Louisiana were fraught with perplexing problems. The first was how to control the colony with a handful of soldiers, the ninety with which he arrived being reduced by death and desertion to seventy-nine. At first blush Spain seems open to harsh criticism for providing her representative with a force so inadequate. But there was an understanding with France which led Spain to believe that the French soldiers stationed in Louisiana could be induced to enter the service of Spain, thereby saving unnecessary transportation charges for both governments.[14] Ulloa invited the

---
[13] Gayarré, *op. cit.*, II, Lectures 3 and 4.
[14] Grimaldi to Ulloa, May 24, 1766, A. G. I., Cuba, 174.

soldiers to enlist under the Spanish flag, but in spite of the urging of their officers, they were practically unanimous in declining. Perhaps the chief reason for their refusal was that Ulloa reduced the pay of Spanish soldiers from thirty-five to seven livres a month. This action was in consonance with his instructions, "not to change existing conditions in Louisiana" (seven livres having been the regular pay of French soldiers), and it put the soldiers of the two nations on an equal footing. Notwithstanding these theoretical advantages, the actual results were the refusal of the French troops to enter the Spanish service, and almost mutinous discontent on the part of the Spanish troops. Gayarré is of the opinion that if Ulloa, by a less literal interpretation of his instructions, had raised the French pay to the Spanish level, most of the French troops would have succumbed to the allurement.[15]

The depreciated paper currency of the colony was another grave problem. Though recognized officially by the French government at three-fourths of its face value, this currency actually circulated at about one-fourth. Ulloa's policy was probably a more liberal one than the French government would have followed. He proposed to make the paper legal tender at 65 per cent, and he tried to buy up a supply at 75 per cent, but the people clamored for assumption at par. He got into further difficulty by trying to pay the Spanish troops in the French currency. Additional complications arose when the French government suspended payment on all bills of exchange drawn since 1762, when Spain accepted Louisiana. A protest by Foucault and Aubry, that such a retraction was morally impossible, together with a protest from the Spanish government, induced France to retract this decree. The immediate expenses of the French officials in Louisiana, however, were met by an advance of 241,250 francs from Ulloa.[16] Whereas the failure to enlist French soldiers was mainly due to Ulloa's blunder, the lack of harmony on the currency question seems chiefly chargeable to the unreasonableness of the colonists. They failed to meet Ulloa halfway.

Commercial regulations also occasioned commotion. Under France, New Orleans had exported large quantities of furs, mostly to the

---

[15] Gayarré, *op. cit.*, II, 161–162.   [16] Villiers du Terrage, *op. cit.*, 229–236, 245.

mother country. There had also been much trade with New England, particularly the importation of meal. After the English established themselves at Natchez and Manchac, contraband trade became so common that the phrase, "going to Little Manchac," was coined to denote smuggling. According to Ulloa's original instructions Louisiana was to have no commerce with the rest of Spanish America, but, by a decree of May 6, 1766, the Spanish government permitted such trade under certain conditions. On September 6, Aubry made public announcement of Spain's new requirement that French ships have their passports and price lists approved by Ulloa before discharging their cargoes. English merchants could trade under the same restrictions. Although this regulation was designed to protect the inhabitants from exploitation by the merchants, or perhaps because that was its effect, it was severely criticized by the merchants of New Orleans and by the captains of vessels then in the river, so much so that Aubry promised unofficially not to enforce the rule. Ulloa was not in a position to insist.[17]

In 1768 Ulloa received another commercial decree from the Spanish court restricting the colony's commerce to Spanish ships and certain Spanish ports.[18] Strictly enforced, this measure would have wrought havoc with most of the trade of the colony; for example, with the lumber exports directed almost entirely to the French islands, and with the import of slaves from Sainte Domingue. Trade with Spain, furthermore, had no prospect of satisfaction; Spain had little use for furs, one of the leading Louisiana exports, and could get indigo, sugar, and lumber from other colonies more advantageously than from Louisiana. There was such widespread dissatisfaction and such great alarm that Ulloa might proceed to enforce this commercial decree of 1768 that some writers insist that this ordinance was what brought the animosity toward Ulloa to a head.[19] Yet oddly, if this deduction be

---

[17] *Ibid.*, 236–238.

[18] Royal cédula, May 3, 1768, A. G. I., Sto. Dom., 1215; Grimaldi to Loyola, June 20, 1768, A. G. I., Cuba, 2357.

[19] Fortier, *A History of Louisiana*, I, 190–195; Brown, "Anglo-Spanish Relations in America," *Hispanic American Historical Review*, V (1925), 348; Winston, "The Cause and Results of the Revolution of 1768 in Louisiana," *Louisiana Historical Quarterly*, XV (1932), 188–190.

correct, the memorial of the colonists and the decree of the Superior Council marshaling the complaints against Ulloa stress the decree of 1766 and refer only vaguely to the one of 1768.[20]

As a counterirritant to his disputes with the French colonists, Ulloa had the Indian problem. Notwithstanding the economic advantages which the English traders enjoyed, the French had cultivated the friendship of many Indian tribes on both sides of the Mississippi. The French method, emphasizing the trader and annual presents, differed radically from the Spanish mission-presidio system. In Louisiana Spain perforce adopted the French method. Soon after Ulloa's arrival he was visited by delegates from tribes as far away as eighty leagues. Everything possible was done, by Spanish and French alike, to ingratiate these Indians toward their new masters. That he might have first-hand information upon which to base his actions toward the Indians, Ulloa, in company with Aubry, made an extended tour through Lower Louisiana in the summer of 1766. He held conferences with the Indians, examined sites for forts, and surveyed trade possibilities, spending some time at Natchitoches investigating communications with Texas and New Mexico. Plans for a personal visit to Illinois had to be abandoned, but a special expedition was sent there to make observations and to report a plan of defense.[21]

But however pressing the problems of the French inhabitants, and however urgent the exigencies of Indian relations, Ulloa seems to have kept uppermost in his mind the menace of the English. Aubry's memorial for the use of the Spanish governor, dated August 12, 1765, had emphasized this danger. Ulloa kept it in view during his journey of inspection in 1766. And when a small reënforcement arrived later in the year, he stationed the soldiers where they would be effective checks on the English: at Balize, in two new forts at the mouth of the Missouri, at the Red River opposite Natchez, and at the Iberville River opposite Fort Bute.[22]

---

[20] Gayarré, *op. cit.*, II, 367–383.
[21] Villiers du Terrage, *op. cit.*, 235; Bjork, *op. cit.*, 94.
[22] Ulloa to Grimaldi, October 6, 1768, A. G. I., Sto. Dom., 2542; Villiers du Terrage, *op. cit.*, 219; Houck, *The Spanish Régime in Missouri*, I, 1–3, 20–28.

Handicapped by the inadequacy of his military retinue, Ulloa was unable to take formal possession of Louisiana. On his arrival the Superior Council requested that he exhibit his powers, but he declined. By word and by action (in preferring to deal with the French governor, Aubry) he offended the Superior Council. A royal order to suppress the Superior Council and to appoint in its place an assessor and two secretaries, one French and one Spanish, threatened to add injury to insult for the councilors.[23] An anomalous situation ensued; Ulloa financed the colony, but his orders became effective only as they were announced through Aubry. At Balize on January 20, 1767, Ulloa and Aubry prepared a document whereby possession was taken for Spain, and the Spanish flag was hoisted there. Nevertheless, it is evident that this was not considered a complete transfer, for a year later Aubry wrote to his government, "I am still waiting for the arrival of the Spanish troops, without which it is absolutely impossible that Ulloa should take possession of the colony."[24]

Spain was dilatory, however, in sending additional troops to Ulloa. On June 7, 1768, Bucareli wrote that 5 sergeants, 4 corporals, and 81 soldiers had arrived at Havana destined for Louisiana and that 250 more were to be sent from Cádiz whenever there was room in the packet boats. The ninety, though, were not dispatched immediately to New Orleans because they were not officered or disciplined and because Grimaldi had ordered them employed in Cuba until all arrived.[25] This delay unquestionably made possible the insurrection of October, 1768.

Allusion has already been made to several reasons for discontent with the Spanish régime in Louisiana. A half-century of intermittent warfare on the Texas frontier had accentuated antipathy toward Spain, even though not toward the Texans. Ulloa's alienation of the troops, the nonredemption of the paper currency, the interference with free trade and smuggling, the snubbing of the Superior Council, the devious method of government through Aubry, the refusal of Ulloa to exhibit his powers—all these contributed to diminish Spanish

---

[23] Bucareli to Ulloa, June 7, 1768, A. G. I., Cuba, 1054.
[24] French, *op. cit.*, V, 158; Gayarré, *op. cit.*, II, 185.
[25] Bucareli to Ulloa, June 7, 1768, A. G. I., Cuba, 1054.

prestige. Another list of grievances can be ascribed to Ulloa's personality. Portraits of Ulloa are rather contradictory, colored by the prejudices of his observers, or reflecting the fluctuations in his own temperament. By one report a charming conversationalist, combining sparkling wit and deep learning, by another he is described as peevish, haughty, excitable, tactless, unsympathetic.[26] His wintering at Balize offended New Orleans' civic pride. His marriage to the Peruvian Marchioness d'Abrado still further antagonized the populace. Her beauty excited the jealousy of the Louisiana women. Her intimacy with her cortège of Peruvian girls provided the wherewithal for gossip. Their marriage by Ulloa's chaplain created another scandal.[27]

Intrigue and agitation fanned the smouldering discontent into open rebellion. Idealistic motives doubtless played a great part in producing the insurrection, yet it is worth noting that almost without exception the leaders in the movement to purge Louisiana of the Spaniards had some personal grievance. By diligent propaganda their feelings of righteous indignation had been disseminated to most of the people of Lower Louisiana, and to assure their success they circulated a few exaggerations and misrepresentations. Ulloa was charged with threatening certain Acadians with slavery; with forcing the inhabitants of New Orleans to go six miles out of town to punish their slaves, merely because his wife was shocked by the cries of the blacks; with threatening to reduce the French to a diet of tortillas; with procuring a Spanish nurse for his child. The conspirators also stooped to subterfuge in order to hold the support of the planters along the German Coast, whose discontent was a result of Ulloa's failure to pay for corn and wheat he had got from them. On the very eve of the uprising, St. Maxent was sent from New Orleans with the money to satisfy this debt, but the insurgents secretly intercepted him, and prevented his quenching the revolutionary ardor of the Germans.[28]

The actual insurrection was worthy of comic opera. First, a petition was circulated, which more than five hundred signed, demanding

---

[26] Gayarré, *op. cit.*, II, 184; French, *op. cit.*, V, 151-152.
[27] Gayarré, *op. cit.*, II, 173-186.
[28] Esteban Gayarré, Certificación de lo Acaecido en la Sublevación de Los Franceses, October 30, 1768, *in* Serrano y Sanz, *Documentos Históricos de la Florida y la Luisiana*, 272; Gayarré, *op. cit.*, II, 187, 218-224.

Ulloa's banishment, restoration of former privileges, and freedom of trade. Then, on the night of the 27th, the guns at the gate of New Orleans were spiked. The next morning, the petition having been presented to the Superior Council and referred to committee, the membership of the council was increased by the addition of half a dozen of the insurgents. In the afternoon Villieré entered New Orleans with a mob of four hundred Germans, Acadians, and other agriculturists. Seeing that "all was in a state of cumbustion," Aubry advised Ulloa to take refuge on the Spanish frigate anchored in the river, and Ulloa gathered up his family and his official papers and followed this advice. "The insurgents," he reported to Grimaldi, "proposing to attack my house during the night and to carry off everything of value that they found there, gave me a receipt so that I might be reimbursed by His Majesty's treasurer." The Spaniards who had remained at headquarters, however, made such a show of resistance that the attack did not materialize.[29]

The following morning, October 29, found the mob ready for another demonstration. So turbulent did it become that Ulloa had the Spanish frigate move a little farther from the bank, whereupon the rumor spread that he was about to bombard the town. The Superior Council also became apprehensive and refused to consider the petition until the inhabitants quieted down. Lafrénière then addressed an oration to the Council, reciting the grievances against Ulloa and the harmful effects of the Spanish commercial regulations, making much of Louis XV's polite wishes for the colony, and of the implied promises in Ulloa's word of greeting from Havana. Enthusiastically the Council ordered Ulloa to leave, and petitioned Louis XV to retract the cession. Aubry courageously appended a note of protest against this action of the Council.

The insurgents sacrificed consistency for pecuniary gain when they permitted the Spanish treasurer to remain. But tradition has it that pecuniary interest, in turn, fell a victim to enthusiasm. Petit, returning from a wedding celebration early in the morning of November 1, cut

---

[29] [Account of the Louisiana Insurrection, 1768], A. G. I., Sto. Dom., 2543; Villiers du Terrage, *op. cit.*, 255–257; Gayarré, *op. cit.*, II, 190–191.

the mooring cables of Ulloa's ship and sent it drifting toward Balize and Cuba and Spain with the Spanish treasury on board as well as Governor Ulloa. Sober historians spoil the drama by striking out the story of this grand flourish, eliminating thus the only act of violence of the entire insurrection. Had Petit perpetrated the deed, it certainly would have been mentioned in Ulloa's elaborate report and in the evidence used against Petit in the subsequent trial. The truth seems to be that the pronouncement of the Superior Council sufficed to bring about the expulsion of Ulloa. Aboard a French vessel he dropped down to Balize, waited a few days for favorable weather, and sailed for Cuba on November 16.

A population which hardly numbered eighteen hundred men able to carry arms, and which had in its bosom several thousands of black slaves, whom it was necessary to intimidate into subjection, had rebelled against the will of France, had flung the gauntlet at the Spanish monarchy, and was bearding a powerful nation, whose distinguished [sic] trait of character did not consist in forgiveness of injuries particularly when her pride was wounded.[30]

All factions, after their hasty action, had leisure to justify their positions in voluminous reports. Aubry forwarded to France several letters which gave the impression that his position was not much more pleasant than Ulloa's had been. The Council justified itself in two pamphlets.[31] One breathes the spirit of Lafrénière, whose fulminations were much like the inspiring tirades that Patrick Henry delivered a few years later. The other goes so far as to deny that Ulloa's departure was the result of any undue persuasion. Father Dagobert made deposition that Ulloa had caused a white man and a black woman to be married secretly, and that his own marriage was clandestine. But the most important report and the only one directed to Spain was that of Ulloa. On December 4 he wrote a detailed report from Havana, and on February 14, 1769, he arrived in Spain to report in person to the king.[32]

---

[30] Gayarré, *op. cit.*, II, 228.

[31] Manifeste des Habitants . . . , A. G. I., Cuba, 1054, and in French, *op. cit.*, V, 218–230; Petition of the colonists and merchants to the king, *ibid.*, V, 178–179.

[32] Ulloa to Grimaldi, December 4, 1768, A. G. I., Sto. Dom., 2542; Nota de Personas de que se componía la familia con que se transportó á España dn. Antonio de Ulloa, December 14, 1768, *ibid*.

Meanwhile, the more radical leaders of the insurgents were anxious to follow up the advantage gained through the departure of Ulloa. First, they made sure that he was really gone. Supposing that he had fortified himself at the mouth of the Mississippi, they sent a party of one hundred and thirty or forty men in four boats to dislodge him. The party went down fourteen leagues, but, hearing that Ulloa had gone, it returned to New Orleans.

The insurgents also despatched three men to represent to the French court the causes and aims of the revolution. Their sailing was delayed; after a false start on December 17 their vessel had to return to Balize for repairs and did not set out again until January 19. When they finally reached France, information about the insurrection had preceded them through Spanish channels. Consequently—though the result might easily have been the same without any delay in their passage—France declined to interfere in a problem which she regarded as belonging entirely to Spain.

In January, also, there was an effort to align the Indians against the Spaniards, but Trudeau, Laussel, Macarti, Amelot, Grand Pré, Rocheblave, St. Maxent, and other conservatives in the colony interfered.[33]

The ire of the insurgents was aroused particularly against the Spanish frigate "Volante." Early in December the Superior Council considered a resolution calling for the expulsion of the frigate, and on the fourteenth voted "to solicit the captain of the frigate to accelerate his departure in the shortest possible delay" and to relieve the Spanish officers of command of the forts which Ulloa had garrisoned. Foucault, though simulating reluctance, seems to have been in sympathy with this step, but Aubry again exhibited his courage by protesting vigorously against "this great indecency," which, he suggested, "would draw down upon this province the indignation and the vengeance of the two greatest monarchs of Europe and make this colony the object of the contempt and odium of all nations." Aubry's

---

[33] Joseph Melchor de Acosta, captain of the "Volante," left an illuminating account of New Orleans in the months following Ulloa's departure in his Relación diaria..., May 22, 1769, A. G. I., Sto. Dom., 1221. See also Champigny, "Memoir," in French, op. cit., V, 178–183.

expressed readiness to shed the last drop of his blood to prevent the execution of this order thwarted its operation in December and likewise in February, when the Superior Council again debated action.[34]

There were loyalists, one should note, among the French in Louisiana in 1768 and 1769. Aubry exaggerated somewhat in ascribing all the disturbance to ten or a dozen firebrands, but it is obvious that his stand against the excesses proposed was not entirely the lonely one that is sometimes represented. He could count on the soldiers under his immediate command and on many substantial citizens such as Trudeau, Laussel, Macarti, Amelot, Grand Pré, Rocheblave, Fleurian, Boüe, Vilard, Molino, Lassois, and St. Maxent. Even the men of the German Coast, when called together to force the departure of the "Volante," excused themselves almost in the fashion of the parable of the unwilling wedding guests.

Some declared that they could not abandon their crops and labors, which were very important; others, that they would have to leave their negroes, who in their absence would not work; others, that they should be paid a certain stipend each day while thus employed; and others finally, that having been deceived the first time they did not wish to risk another fraud.

The consternation occasioned on February 28, 1769, by the arrival of the Spanish packet boat "Nuestra Señora de los Remedios" illustrates the insecure ascendancy of the insurgents. When it appeared at Bayou St. Jean, they supposed that it was a war vessel with two companies of soldiers and were much alarmed.[35]

Confusion was the chief characteristic of the situation in Louisiana during the ten months following Ulloa's departure. Aubry, who had opposed the expulsion, became the nominal head of the colony. There were a number of flare-ups of the revolutionary impulse directed especially against the Spanish frigate, and these are recorded by Aubry and Acosta. But general support for the defiance of Spain seems to have waned as the months passed, and even the rebellious leaders modulated their radicalism. It was discouraging that the solici-

---

[34] Acosta, *loc. cit.;* Aubry to Bucareli, February 24, 1769, A. G. I., Cuba, 1054.
[35] Acosta, *loc. cit.*

tation for help from the English at Pensacola met with a rebuff.[36] In spite of the rebellion Spain retained some contact with the colony and extended financial support. On June 22, 1769, for example, there was a remittance of 12,782 pesos, 3 reales, to Loyola at New Orleans, 8000 pesos to be disbursed with Aubry's approval to support the Spanish subjects in the colony, to succor the French troops, and to get presents for the Indians, and the remainder to satisfy a bill for similar expenses.[37] Spanish rule in the Illinois country (Missouri) was not interrupted.[38] The insurrection, it would seem, then, did not affect the whole colony nor go the whole length of severing all dependence on Spain, but was fitfully burning itself out.

Some writers hail the Louisiana insurrection as the first American Revolution, and its leaders as the "first political victims upon the altar of American liberty." Chambers calls it "the Latin Echo to America's Liberty Call," though this time the echo preceded the call.[39] The principles enunciated by Lafrénière support these impressions:

> The right of the people to decide any act touching their welfare.... Parliaments and Superior Councils are the depositories of the laws under whose sanction the people may live in happiness; they are the natural protectors by law of honest citizens.[40]

American revolutions, in their full form, however, seem to pass through two stages. The English colonists were fighting at first for their rights as Englishmen and later for independence. The Spanish Americans, likewise, rallied first to the slogan, "Old King or None," and later shortened it to "No King." The Louisiana revolt did not get past the first stage. Expulsion of the Spaniards was the aim of the movement, and restoration of French control its highest goal. Some of the more volatile spirits, it is true, did propose the expulsion of Aubry and the French troops and the erection of a Creole Republic.

---

[36] Champigny, "Memoir," in French, op. cit., V, 182–183.
[37] Bucareli to Aubry, June 22, 1769, draft, A. G. I., Cuba, 1054.
[38] Houck, op. cit., I, 35–52.
[39] Mississippi Valley Beginnings, 87, 99.
[40] Expression of such sentiments in Louisiana is, after all, hardly surprising since we know that the writings of Locke, Rousseau, Voltaire, and Montesquieu were available in the colony. See the list of titles in Prevost's library in E. D. Price and H. H. Cruzat, eds., "Inventory of the Estate of Sieur Jean Baptiste Prevost, 1769," Louisiana Historical Quarterly, IX (1926), 411–498.

Marquis, himself a Swiss, even went so far as to draft a frame of government on the Swiss model. This quixotic scheme, however, was overwhelmed by practical considerations, embodied in a "Memoir against the Republicans," published in New Orleans in 1769, and Marquis' "rosy colored bubble of the imagination" vanished. Aubry was not molested, and even the Spanish officials who remained met with increasing cordiality.[41]

Reports of the insurrection reached France, as has been described, but the French government seems not to have taken official cognizance of them. Grimaldi, on the part of Spain, remonstrated with France for this flagrant indifference to the insult to Spain. In the latter country, however, the Council of the Indies pondered the problem. There were two alternatives. Spain might let the erring child depart in peace, or might vindicate her honor by a vigorous repression of the revolt. The Council of the Indies recognized once more the cost of maintenance of Louisiana; it saw the expense of resuming control. But it realized the usefulness of the barrier against the English and the advisability of avenging the insult to Spanish honor. Hence, for reasons of policy, the most important of which had to do with the effect that would be produced on the rest of the Spanish colonies, the Council settled on the suppression of the revolt and the establishment of Spanish control.[42]

Responsibility for the task was assigned to Don Alejandro O'Reilly, one of the many Irish Catholics driven by persecution at home to service under a foreign but sympathetic monarch. He was forty-seven years of age when sent to Louisiana. Most of those forty-seven years had been devoted to military service for Spain in the War of the Austrian Succession; for Austria, 1757–1759; for France, 1759–1760; for Spain again in the war with Portugal and in the Seven Years' War. At the close of this last-named war he was given an opportunity to drill the Spanish army in Austrian tactics, and was sent to Havana to restore the defenses of Cuba. Returning to Spain, he had the good fortune to save the life of Carlos III in the Madrid riot of 1765. Later in

---

[41] Gayarré, *op. cit.*, II, 281–282; Villiers du Terrage, *op. cit.*, 285.

[42] A summary of the written opinions of the members of the Council is given in Gayarré, *op. cit.*, II, 249–264.

life his prestige suffered a decline, particularly because of his disastrous defeat at Algiers in 1774. But in 1769, when sent to Louisiana, he was recognized as Spain's best general.

Mild in manner, courteous, suave, O'Reilly was nevertheless a man of determination. His gentle demeanor clothed an indomitable will. As a soldier he had made unquestioning obedience his creed; and as a corollary to this he held inexorable justice to be the surest avenue to mild and respected government. Convinced that prompt punishment of malefactors was in the long run the most lenient course to pursue, he had no qualms of conscience in administering it.[43]

Although probably not any more distinguished than Ulloa, O'Reilly was of a different fiber. Whereas Ulloa was preëminent in scholarship, only incidentally a naval commander, and deficient in tact, O'Reilly was Spain's foremost military figure, and as capable an administrator as a general. He became dictator of Louisiana. Comparison of the achievements of these two men, nevertheless, is bound to be unfair to Ulloa. For in contrast to the ninety soldiers that had composed the first Spanish force of occupation, O'Reilly brought 2056 of the flower of the Spanish army. Even had the Louisianians been without dissent in their opposition to Spain, they could have mustered no more than 1800 men.[44]

Unfavorable weather detained O'Reilly for a time at Balize, and Lafrénière, Marquis, and Milhet, three of the chief insurrectionists, seized the opportunity to intercede with him for leniency. They came away from the conference with the impression that they had been promised clemency. But O'Reilly's exact words to them guaranteed merely justice, and his report of the meeting implied that he looked upon them as spies.

Three deputies came to the entrance of the river to compliment me, where I was detained to collect my convoy, but this formality had for its object the reconnoitering of my true forces and the penetration of my intentions. I succeeded in persuading them that all the habitants and Indians

---

[43] This biographical sketch is based on the following: Gayarré, *op. cit.*, II, 285–289, 245–251, III, 39–41; Bjork, *op. cit.*, 127–128, 142–245; French, *op. cit.*, V, 188, 193–196; O'Hart, *Irish Pedigrees*.

[44] Bucareli to Arriaga, July 7, 1769, A. G. I., Sto. Dom., 1220.

of this province, though fanatical and united, could not resist the troops, artillery, and other preparations I had brought. Without compromising my honor I explained my desire to do good and my great repugnance to doing evil, and that I would never do anything unless it was just and also necessary.[45]

On August 17, 1769, the Spanish fleet of twenty-four sails anchored at New Orleans. At five o'clock the next afternoon the flagship fired a signal gun and the Spanish troops poured out of the ships. With splendid precision they marched, two thousand strong, to their appointed posts on opposite sides of the square. Then the artillery of fifty pieces and the cavalry contingent stationed themselves on the side of the square next to the river, and opposite the French troops drawn up in front of the church. Suddenly the sailors on the Spanish ships shouted, "*Viva el Rey, Viva el Rey, Viva el Rey,*" and the Spanish troops replied with gusto. While the echoes were still ringing, the guns of the ships thundered a salute. The fifty cannon on the square roared out an answer, augmented by the simultaneous discharge of the Spanish muskets. The reverberations announced the landing of General O'Reilly.

To the beating of drums he descended from his ship. An imposing escort of Spain's finest soldiers, in smart uniforms and bearing silver maces as the symbol of his authority, preceded the general, and behind him came the other officers in their full regalia. With the greatest pomp, made even more impressive by the general's slight limp, they advanced to the flagpole near which were gathered Aubry and the other prominent colonists. At O'Reilly's request Aubry read aloud the proclamations of the French and Spanish monarchs concerning the transfer. O'Reilly received the keys of the town. As the French flag was lowered and that of Spain raised, the French soldiery shouted "*Viva el Rey,*" the Spaniards responded, and another salute was fired.

O'Reilly then went to the cathedral, exchanged cordial greetings with the Vicar-General, and received his blessing. They entered the church, where a *Te Deum* was sung as conclusion to the ceremony of taking possession. O'Reilly had treated the creoles to a spectacle the

---

[45] O'Reilly to Munian, August 31, 1769, *ibid.; Louisiana Historical Quarterly,* V (1922), 17.

like of which New Orleans had never witnessed. His entry was the antithesis of Ulloa's apologetic coming. Thus was accomplished the first step in establishing Spanish control over Louisiana. O'Reilly had displayed most effectively the military force under his command, and through the pageantry of his dramatic entry had inspired the respect of the colonists.[46]

The second step was taken without any ostentation. The general invited the twelve foremost leaders in the insurrection to gather at his quarters on the morning of August 21, and then quietly arrested them. He acquainted them at once with his purpose to have them tried according to (Spanish) law as the king had ordered, and introduced the judges who would hear the defenses and decide the verdict.[47] The general forebodings roused throughout New Orleans by this preliminary of retribution for the revolt were allayed by the following proclamation of amnesty for all participants in the uprising other than the twelve under arrest.

IN THE NAME OF THE KING

Don Alexandro O'Reilly

>Commander of Benfayen in the Order of Alcántara, Lieutenant General and Inspector General of the Armies of His Catholic Majesty, Captain General and Governor of the Province of Louisiana.

By virtue of the orders and powers with which we are entrusted by His Catholic Majesty, we declare to all the inhabitants of the province of Louisiana, that, although recent events have given His Majesty just cause to make them feel his indignation, he proposes now to show only clemency toward the populace, persuaded that it did not do wrong, except in allowing itself to be seduced by the intrigues of ambitious men, fanatic and wrongfully intentioned, who had the temerity to take advantage of ignorance and excessive credulity. These individuals alone will answer for their crimes and will be judged according to the laws.

An act so generous must assure His Majesty that his new subjects will strive each day of their lives to merit by their fidelity, zeal, and obedience

---

[46] Relación de Como D. Alejandro O'Reilly Pacificó la Ciudad de Nueva Orleans, August 30, 1769, *in* Serrano y Sanz, *op. cit.*, 299–301; O'Reilly to Arriaga, August 31, 1769, *loc. cit.*, 307–308; Gayarré, *op. cit.*, II, 295–299.

[47] O'Reilly to Munian, August 31, 1769, A. G. I., Sto. Dom., 1220.

the grace which he now bestows upon them and the protection which he accords them from this moment.

At New Orleans, the twenty-first of August, one thousand seven hundred sixty-nine.[48]

Aubry is usually made to bear the onus of blame for nominating the twelve to be prosecuted. His report on the insurrection and its leaders, presented with alacrity in answer to O'Reilly's request for information, was one basis for the selection. But O'Reilly had other informers. Ulloa's report mentioned some of the leaders by name, and Acosta, the captain of the "Volante," had supplied a list of "individuals who merit the royal displeasure." Judging from Acosta's list, the result would have been almost the same if Aubry had refused to give any information.[49]

Meanwhile the trial began. The taking of testimony was inquisitorial rather than in open court; the defendants did not hear the testimony offered against them; they were not granted as full an opportunity to present their defense as is the rule in modern American courts; and their fate was decided by a magistrate rather than a jury —which is to say that their trial was in the Spanish mode, and consequently less advantageous for the defense than English and American court procedure. But apart from the shortcomings of Spanish jurisprudence the trial apparently was fair, and the defendants were denied none of the regular means of establishing their innocence.

The issue of the trial hinged on whether Louisiana had become a Spanish colony and whether the colonists owed allegiance to Spain. If the answer to these questions was affirmative, the accused were technically guilty of treason. Don Felix del Rey, who acted as the prosecuting attorney, summed up the state's case on October 20. His argument in its essence was that many of Ulloa's acts were tantamount to a formal possessing of the colony and that Spain's title to the province was perfect even without such a ceremony. He asked, therefore, the due penalties for high treason: death sentences and confiscation of property. The defendants held that since Ulloa had not taken formal

---

[48] O'Reilly, proclamation (printed), A. G. I., Sto. Dom., 2656.

[49] Acosta, Yndividuos que merecen el Rl. Desagrado, May 22, 1769, A. G. I., Cuba, 1054; Aubry to O'Reilly, August 20, 1769, A. G. I., Sto. Dom., 1221.

possession the colonists had not become Spanish subjects and so could not have committed treason. The question is a delicate one, though the principles of international law apparently support the prosecution. Nevertheless, the court's verdict, pronounced on October 24 by O'Reilly, though determined by his legal advisors, the judge and the assessor, was a surprise. The defendants were declared guilty of treason; five were condemned to the gallows and six to prison, the twelfth defendant having died before the trial was ended (perhaps being killed in a struggle with his guards, as Martin affirms); the property of the twelve was confiscated. To quote from the court record:

> From the merits of the case tried in New Orleans before His Excellency Don Alexandro O'Reilly against the principal instigators of the recent rebellion which occurred in this province there resulted the penalties which are detailed below:
> > Sentenced to the gallows: Lafrésnière, Noyan, Villeret, Marquis, Carrezes, Joseph Milhet.
> > Sentenced to prison in a fort: Masan for ten years, Hardi de Boisblanc for six years, Petit for life, Poupé for six years, Milhet for six years, Doucet for ten years.
> > NOTE.
> That those sentenced to the gallows, for lack of a hangman, were executed by a firing squad on the twenty-fifth of this month.
> On the twenty-sixth the Memorial of the Habitants and other papers seditious and offensive to the authority and government of the King and to the entire Spanish nation were burned in the Plaza de Armas by the hand of a slave (in the absence of a hangman).
> All the property of the twelve above named was confiscated.[50]

The community was greatly shocked at the severity of the sentence. It was generally realized that the insurgents had done wrong in bringing about the banishment of Ulloa; but no blood had been shed, and there were so many extenuating circumstances in the just grievances against the former governor that the misdeeds of even the worst offenders seemed something short of crimes—certainly they were not capital offenses. The colonists, too, had relied on the promises of

---

[50] Affidavit by Rodríguez, October 29, 1769, A. G. I., Sto. Dom., 2543; Testimonio sacado por ... Rodríguez, A. G. I., Cuba, 81. See also Winston, "The Cause and Results of the Revolution of 1768 in Louisiana," *Louisiana Historical Quarterly*, XV (1932), 198–213; and Gayarré, *op. cit.*, II, 315–343.

O'Reilly—or rather, on what they thought were promises—that justice would be tempered with mercy. Passionate appeals were addressed to O'Reilly, therefore, begging him to grant pardons to the culprits, or at least to commute their sentences. But the general was inflexible. The king had ordered him "to inflict summary punishment, in strict conformity to the laws, on the exciters of the insurrection"; and with this explicit command before him O'Reilly could not see his way clear to follow a more lenient course. And so, with practically no delay, the sentences were executed.[51]

Two other participants in the revolt were sentenced by O'Reilly. Arensburg, Ulloa's seventy-seven-year-old commander at the German Coast, was ordered to move to New Orleans, and his property was sequestered. De Sasier, one of the emissaries of the Superior Council to France, was denominated "hombre muy malo," and his return to Louisiana was forbidden.[52]

The six sentenced to prison arrived at the Castillo del Morro at Havana, November 11, 1769. The archives yield just a faint suggestion of their experiences there. On November 14 three of them humbly petitioned the authorities for an increase in the allowance for their subsistence, since "the two bits a day for each would not procure the half of their most modest necessities." Later, Petit prayed that his three-year-old son be allowed to visit him, and Mazan that his wife be permitted to come to Cuba. After slightly more than a year's incarceration all six were released, on December 4, 1770, and sent to Puerto Rico. They were not permitted to return to Louisiana, however, and in spite of Bernardo de Gálvez' urging, in 1782, that Milhet's sequestered property be restored to his widow and three daughters, the official reply was that no refunds would be made in connection with O'Reilly's fines. Royal clemency apparently did not imply disapproval of O'Reilly's actions.[53]

---

[51] O'Reilly to Bucareli, December (?), 1769, A. G. I., Mexico, 1242; Gayarré, *op. cit.*, II, 339–341.

[52] O'Reilly to Grimaldi, December 10, 1769, A. G. I., Sto. Dom., 2543.

[53] Bucareli to O'Reilly, November 11, 1769, A. G. I., Cuba, 1054; Milhet, Hardy de Boysblanc, and Poupet to ———, November 14, 1769, A. G. I., Cuba, 1109; Petit to ———, August 16, 1770, *ibid.*; Mazan to ———, August 16, 1770, *ibid.*; Bucareli to Unzaga, December 27, 1770, A. G. I., Cuba, 1054; Gálvez to José de Gálvez, November 30, 1782, and draft of reply, January 31, 1784, A. G. I., Sto. Dom., 2543.

During Reconstruction days in the South there developed in the popular phraseology a strong adhesion between the words "damned" and "Yankee." Louisiana furnishes a parallel in the expression "Bloody O'Reilly." François-Xavier Martin stigmatized O'Reilly's sentence thus bitterly:

> Posterity, the judge of men in power, will doom this act to public execration. No necessity demanded, no policy justified it. Ulloa's conduct had provoked the measures to which the inhabitants had resorted. During nearly two years he had haunted the province as a phantom of dubious authority. The efforts of the colonists to prevent the transfer of their natal soil to a foreign prince originated in their attachment to their own, and the Catholic king ought to have beheld in their conduct a pledge of their future devotion to himself. They had but lately seen their country severed, and a part of it added to the dominion of Great Britain; they had bewailed their separation from their friends and kindred; and were afterwards to be alienated, without their consent, and subjected to a foreign yoke. If the indiscretion of a few of them needed an apology, the common misfortune afforded it.[54]

Measured by modern standards, O'Reilly does appear a harsh judge; yet there is some injustice in expecting a man to anticipate the more refined moral standards of a future generation. Measured by eighteenth-century standards, his actions seem less repulsive. Spain's customary response to rebellions at that time was to put to death the leading instigators. José de Gálvez in 1767 revenged a bloodless rebellion in Guanajuato by having eighty-five alleged culprits executed, seventy-three lashed, one hundred and seventeen banished, and six hundred and seventy-four imprisoned.[55] Such a comparison, while it does not clear O'Reilly of all stigma of inhumanity, suggests the customs of his generation. But in the last analysis, if justification for O'Reilly's conduct is to be found, it must be sought in the instructions which bound him and in the king's reaction to the report of the trial and sentences. "I have resolved," reads the king's command, "that... you organize legal proceedings, and punish in accordance with the

---

[54] Martin, *op. cit.*, II, 7–8.
[55] Priestley, *José de Gálvez, Visitor-General of New Spain*, 226–232; Chapman, *A History of California, the Spanish Period*, 212.

laws the exciters and accomplices of the insurrection."⁵⁶ O'Reilly apparently felt that he had complied with these directions.

> I have exacted satisfaction for the affront to the sovereign respect and authority of the king in this province; the punishment was indispensable because of the very bad example of letting such grave transgression go unpunished....
> I am convinced that the accomplishment of my commission and everything done here will afford great satisfaction to our court and likewise to that of France....
> I hope that I have carried out his royal intentions, and if this is gained, it will be my complete satisfaction.⁵⁷

Immediately upon his return to Spain, O'Reilly had a long interview with the king, Grimaldi, and Arriaga. The king's commendation was not merely verbal.

> His Majesty, finding himself entirely satisfied with your distinguished zeal, talent, and military skill, and also with the ability and perfections demonstrated in the repeated important commissions which it has been convenient to confide to you, *especially in that which was just concluded in Louisiana, in which you were able to fulfill his Royal desire;* His Majesty has seen fit to place in your charge the inspection of all the infantry....⁵⁸

The promotion to this highly influential and remunerative office is an even surer indication of the king's approval than the words in praise of O'Reilly's efficiency and moderation. From the royal viewpoint, O'Reilly had been a good and faithful servant; he had obeyed his orders; he had not been guilty of unseemly harshness: he had established Spanish control over Louisiana.

---

⁵⁶ Grimaldi to O'Reilly (the king's instructions), April 16, 1769, A. H. N., Consejos, 20,854; another copy in A. G. I., Cuba, 2357. Attention should be directed to the excellent piece of historical reconstruction performed by Gayarré. Lacking a copy of O'Reilly's instructions, he was able to infer their nature by reasoning from O'Reilly's reports, Aubry's reports, etc. (Gayarré, *op. cit.*, 345-350). His inference has been corroborated by Professor David K. Bjork, who brought to light the actual instructions, as well as the king's congratulatory note on the moderation that O'Reilly had shown (Bjork, *op. cit.*, 129, 145, 149).

⁵⁷ O'Reilly to Bucareli, December (?), 1769, A. G. I., Mexico, 1242.

⁵⁸ Munian to O'Reilly, June 19, 1770, *ibid.*, italics mine; Royal cédula, August 17, 1772, A. G. I., Cuba, 2357; O'Reilly to Bucareli, June 15, 1770, A. G. I., Mexico, 1242.

Chapter II

O'REILLY'S CONSTRUCTIVE STATESMANSHIP

IN MOST ACCOUNTS of O'Reilly's administration the tragic episodes of the trial and executions are unduly emphasized. His vindication of Spain's honor was significant, yet the subsequent acts of his administration, though less spectacular, were more important to the colony. The punishment of the leading insurrectionists quelled the revolutionary impulse; but O'Reilly's later conduct mollified the French creoles and won their loyalty to Spain. In addition, O'Reilly sketched the plans and laid the foundations for Spain's activities in Louisiana for the next thirty years. This phase of his sojourn in Louisiana should certainly be considered in any appraisal of his achievements in the colony, yet customarily his administration has been viewed from the wrong perspective, and the importance of his administrative labors has been overlooked.[1]

An understanding of O'Reilly's activities in Louisiana will be facilitated if his fundamental purposes are kept in mind. His first concern, of course, was to serve the interest of his sovereign—to make Louisiana subservient and profitable to the king. This dominant motive did not exclude all others, but they were subordinate to it. He was anxious, for example, to bring prosperity and contentment to the Louisianians for their own sakes but more especially because he knew that the king would have a better, more loyal, more profitable colony under such circumstances. Consequently we find him recommending and instituting many reforms for the benefit of the populace. A third compelling motive, subordinate again to the service of Carlos III, was his constant concern to prevent encroachments by the English, to exclude

---

[1] The latter part of O'Reilly's administration is described at greatest length in Bjork, *op. cit.*, 150–255.

them from commerce in Lower Louisiana, to prevent their intrusions into Spanish Illinois and the Arkansas region, to forestall any occasion for English aggression because of undue Spanish activity east of the Mississippi. A true picture of O'Reilly would show him devoted primarily to the interests of his king, but not unconcerned about the welfare of the colonists, and always on the alert against the English.

It will be convenient also to characterize the methods he employed. Whenever possible he followed the orthodox patterns already employed in the rest of Spanish America. Frequently the transition from French to Spanish practices seemed to the colonists a cataclysmal change. This was not so much because France and Spain labored under different political and economic theories; it was rather because of different degrees of enforcement. Especially in the latter part of the French régime there had been little interposition of royal control. Under Spain, on the contrary, enforcement of regulations was the rule.

Wherever peculiar conditions made French methods more suitable than the Spanish devices, O'Reilly retained them. Thus the French Black Code was kept and the French Indian policy adopted. He evinced, likewise, a confidence in the Louisiana creoles. He turned the municipal offices over to them; he relied on them almost exclusively for his Indian agents; and, after having sent away the bulk of his Spanish soldiery, he enrolled and armed French colonists in the militia.

O'Reilly habitually prefaced action by investigation. The punishment of the insurrectionists was handled with so much dispatch that one gets the impression of hastiness and snap judgment. Even here, however, O'Reilly had gathered a great deal of information before acting: it was his customary procedure. Reference need only be made to the reports required from Aubry, Acosta, De Mézières, Rui, Piernas, Nugent, and Kelly, and to his own journey of investigation to Pointe Coupée. Louisiana, as he reorganized it, combined much that was characteristic of all Spanish colonies with some worthy survivals of the old French system. His policies were the fruit of careful consideration, and once determined upon were energetically enforced. But in spite of the military precision that was ingrained in his character, he convinced the creoles that they could rely on him and he expressed his confidence in them by placing them in positions of responsibility.

Limitations of space, and perhaps of interest, preclude the inclusion of a detailed account of O'Reilly's administration. It will suffice to indicate by a brief summary what he set out to do and what he accomplished in the various matters that came to his attention.

Spain's first intention had been to alter Louisiana as little as possible, to hoist the Spanish flag in place of the French but in all other respects to leave the colony virtually French. Ulloa's reports on the inefficiency of some of the French methods, followed as those reports were by the insurrection, persuaded the court that a change of policy was advisable. O'Reilly was directed, therefore, to reorganize the institutions of Louisiana, establishing "that form of political government and administration of justice prescribed by our wise laws, and by which all the states of his majesty in America have been maintained in the most perfect tranquillity, content, and subordination."[2]

For the political reorganization of New Orleans O'Reilly applied the orthodox Spanish pattern, which called for an indigenous local government, officered by resident landowners responsive to local interests, and supported by local sources of revenue.[3] The Superior Council of the French régime, in disrepute because of its activities in the insurrection, was abolished and a *cabildo* erected in its stead. The six *regidores* composing the cabildo were French, and they in turn chose four Frenchmen to be the two *alcaldes,* the *síndico procurador general,* and the *mayordomo de propios.*[4] After these officers were sworn in, plans were matured for the Cabildo Building—one of the chief attractions of the present "French" quarter of New Orleans.[5] Specified rev-

---

[2] French, *op. cit.,* V, 254.

[3] Jones, "Local Government in the Spanish Colonies as Provided by the Recopilación de Leyes de Los Reynos de las Indias," *Southwestern Historical Quarterly,* XIX (1915), 88.

[4] O'Reilly, Instrucciones que he dejado en la Luisiana, November 25, 1769, A. G. I., Cuba, 1055, and printed in French, *op. cit.,* V, 254–268. The procedure parallels almost exactly that at San Fernando de Béxar in 1731, an account of which is given in Austin, "The Municipal Government of San Fernando de Béxar," *Texas State Historical Quarterly,* VIII (1905), 297–299. Villiers du Terrage, *op. cit.,* 319; O'Reilly to Arriaga, December 10, 1769, A. G. I., Sto. Dom., 1223; the regidores to Unzaga (pledge of faithful conduct in their office). December 31, 1769, *ibid.,* 1221.

[5] O'Reilly to Arriaga, December 10, 1769, A. G. I., Sto. Dom., 1223; Bolton, *The Spanish Borderlands,* 249.

enues were allocated to the cabildo. The anchorage charge which the French had collected for harbor upkeep was continued. License fees were levied on taverns, inns, shops, and gaming houses. A few import duties, such as a tax of one peso on each sixty-gallon cask of brandy, were instituted. The municipality received the rent on two tracts of government land facing the plaza. And the butchers of the city volunteered to pay three hundred and seventy-five pesos to the cabildo annually, promising, moreover, not to shift this burden to the consumers by increased prices. New Orleans was thus assured a yearly income of about two thousand pesos, which was considered adequate. Royal approbation was given.[6]

Inasmuch as the province had been accustomed to French legal practices, O'Reilly attached to the proclamation creating the cabildo, another indicating the salient features of Spanish law. This statement, which came to be known as the "Code O'Reilly," was substantially an abridgement of the *Recopilación de Leyes de las Indias*. With the French Black Code it was declared the law of the colony.[7] French and Spanish law were not very different from each other, both being derived largely from Roman law. The change in Louisiana was drastic, however, because a system of enforcement was set up where the absence of enforcement had been conspicuous. "O'Reilly," Aubry wrote with a measure of accuracy, "enforced all those wise and beneficent laws of which the impotence of our government had prevented the observance for several years."[8] By the end of the year (1769) Spanish courts and justice had replaced the haphazard justice of the French system. "It has been my great satisfaction," O'Reilly reported, "to see the new laws as well as the political government well received, and I am persuaded that with prudence and equity on the part of my successor they will establish favorable impressions on the minds of the people."[9]

---

[6] O'Reilly, Instrucciones que he dejado en la Luisiana, November 25, 1769, A. G. I., Cuba, 1055; O'Reilly to Arriaga, December 10, 1769, A. G. I., Sto. Dom., 1223; Royal cédula, August 17, 1772, *ibid.*, 2530.

[7] O'Reilly, Instrucción del modo de substanciar y determinar, November 25, 1769, A. G. I., Cuba, 1055, and printed in French, *op. cit.*, V, 269-288.

[8] Quoted in Villiers du Terrage, *op. cit.*, 319-320.

[9] O'Reilly to Arriaga, December 10, 1769, A.G.I., Sto. Dom., 1223.

In addition to the purely local officials such as those of the cabildo, Spanish political theory recognized another class, the provincial officers. These were ordinarily *peninsulares* (Spanish-born Spaniards) appointed by the crown or the governor and detached as much as possible from local ties and support. Their attachment, it was hoped, would be to the crown rather than to the colonists. In Louisiana an exceptional circumstance dictated departure from this pattern. Frenchmen, it was conceded, were better fitted to govern the parishes and to deal with the Indians than were any Spaniards available. All the parishes, therefore, were placed under French lieutenants, and a French commandant was appointed for the Natchitoches district. Only in the Illinois district did a Spaniard receive an important provincial commission from O'Reilly; Pedro Piernas, who had held the same position under Ulloa, was sent to St. Louis as commandant.[10]

O'Reilly's reform of trade regulation represents probably the most drastic change that he produced in the colony. The change was not so much the introduction of new theory as the tightening of enforcement. Both France and Spain, and for that matter, all Europe, stood committed to the mercantilist theory, and their trade regulations aimed at an exclusive policy. Under France this control had been so very loose that the greater part of the trade fell to ships from the English colonies. In Ulloa's term as governor some changes were announced, but Ulloa's authority, even when supplemented by Aubry's, was not sufficient to secure enforcement. O'Reilly had enough soldiers to command respect for mercantilism.

He forbade commercial intercourse with foreign ports and with the rest of the Spanish colonies, Havana excepted, and limited the trade with Spain and Havana to Spanish ships. Envisioning the danger of contraband trade with Mexico from Natchitoches and Opelousas, he recommended that the officials at these posts should be relieved "with sufficient frequency so that they would not have time to corrupt themselves with illicit gains."[11] He banished from the colony two Genevans, the Duraldes brothers, and likewise three Jews because their

---

[10] O'Reilly (list of appointees), February 4, 1770, A. G. I., Cuba, 1055.

[11] O'Reilly to Arriaga, October 17, 1769, No. 3, A. G. I., Sto. Dom., 1221.

stocks of diamonds, watches, and jewelry far exceeded the capacity of the local market and were intended apparently for smuggling into Vera Cruz and Campeche, where these merchants had correspondents. His report lists the names of sixteen others banished because of their commercial proclivities. Among them we notice such English names as Elias Hughes and Juan Vincent.[12]

He subjected to severer scrutiny the right of the English to navigate the Mississippi, denying them any right to "anchor in port or to cross plank on shore without the governor's permission."[13] His purpose of course was to prevent smuggling from vessels proceeding through Spanish territory to Manchac and Natchez, but, since warping and tacking was the only feasible means of ascending the river, his order practically annulled the English right to navigate the Mississippi.

While O'Reilly remained, smuggling was distinctly on the wane, yet it is a mistake to think that trade with the English was done away with entirely, or that the interruption was of long duration. At least one Anglo-American merchant, Oliver Pollock, was not expelled from New Orleans. He had ingratiated himself with O'Reilly by refusing to profiteer on a shipload of flour when New Orleans was suffering a shortage, offering it instead to the governor at the latter's price. Reporting the transaction to the king, O'Reilly recommended that Pollock be allowed free trade at New Orleans thenceforth.[14] Then, too, O'Reilly remained in Louisiana only a few months; when he departed with most of the troops, smuggling was resumed.

Although enough of a soldier to believe that laws should be rigorously enforced, O'Reilly was not fully in sympathy with mercantilism. He recognized the vital necessity of foreign trade for Louisiana. The colonists needed flour, wine, tools, arms, ammunition, and clothing, in return for which they could export lumber, indigo, tobacco, and furs. O'Reilly therefore recommended to the court that free trade in certain specified commodities be allowed between Louisiana and

---

[12] *Ibid.*

[13] O'Reilly to Browne, September 24, 1769. Quoted in Brown, "Anglo-Spanish Relations in America," *loc. cit.*, 370–371.

[14] Deposition of Oliver Pollock, June 8, 1808, *in* Wilkinson, *Memoirs of My Own Times*, II, appendix I.

Havana as well as the ports of Spain. His friend Bucareli, who was Captain General of Cuba, endorsed this recommendation, and the court accepted it.[15] Because Louisiana tobacco was of inferior quality, O'Reilly forbade its exportation to Havana, but he suggested that vessels importing red wine from Catalonia should take a cargo of lumber to Havana, and thence carry sugar to Spain.[16] To promote the trade with Havana, he appointed a commission to submit log books indicating the best summer course from Havana to Balize, the best winter course for the same voyage, and the best return route.[17] For the further encouragement of commerce no duties were to be charged at New Orleans except the nominal anchorage fee.[18] O'Reilly, it would appear, was interested not merely in securing a more profitable trade for Spain and in stamping out the English trade with the colony but also in promoting the prosperity of Louisiana.

Anthropologists have directed attention to the tendency for continuity of certain cultural traits in a given area, nothwithstanding the intrusion of a new racial element. The Indian policy in Louisiana might be cited as an example. Because the local tribes had become accustomed to control by traders and had acquired an insistent craving for the trade goods, there was no attempt to establish missions. Perhaps it is just as well, for these Indians were of the aggressive, warlike sort that had not proved very susceptible to mission control. Moreover, after their experiences with French traders, they were certainly spoiled for the mission system. At any rate, Spain followed the line of least resistance by continuing the French system.[19] The experiment, for experiment it was for Spain, had been launched by Ulloa, who had held parleys with the Indians of Lower Louisiana, assuring them that Spain would grant annual presents just as the French had done.

---

[15] O'Reilly to Arriaga, October 17, 1769, No. 4, A. G. I., Sto. Dom., 1221; Bucareli to Arriaga, April 1, 1770, A. G. I., Ind. Gen., 1630; O'Reilly to Bucareli, April 3, 1770, No. 93, A. G. I., Cuba, 1055; Grimaldi to Bucareli, June 23, 1770, A. G. I., Ind. Gen., 1630.

[16] O'Reilly to Bucareli, April 3, 1770, A. G. I., Cuba, 174; O'Reilly to Arriaga, October 17, 1770, No. 4, A. G. I., Sto. Dom., 1221.

[17] O'Reilly to Arriaga, October 17, 1769, No. 10, *ibid.*, 2543.

[18] Grimaldi to O'Reilly, January 27, 1770, No. 13, A. G. I., Cuba, 174.

[19] Bolton, *Athanase de Mézières*, I, 70.

O'Reilly continued this deviation from the customary Spanish method. One of his first moves was to convene an Indian council[20] at New Orleans, in which he tried his hand at French Indian diplomacy. He called together the chiefs of all the tribes within a radius of seventy leagues of New Orleans. At eleven thirty on the morning of the appointed day nine chiefs, accompanied by interpreters and a number of warriors, presented themselves at O'Reilly's house. They found the general seated under a canopy in front of his house, surrounded by officers of the garrison and some of the principal citizens of New Orleans. Laying down their weapons at O'Reilly's feet, the chiefs saluted him with *banderas* (small painted sticks with fans of feathers), which they waved around their heads, tapped four times against their breasts, and then presented to O'Reilly. A pipe was lighted and circulated to everyone in the council, and O'Reilly participated in this ceremony, "not to depreciate their customs." Finally, each chief gave his hand to the general, "their principal sign of friendship."

These ceremonies concluded, the chief of the Bayagoulas as spokesman for the Indians made the following harangue:

> Red men, Chiefs, and Warriors, I speak in your name to the Great Chief whom the great King of Spain has sent to take possession of these lands. Father and Great Chief, we hope that you will have pity on these your sons, and that you will concede to us the same favors and the same benefactions that the French used to, and that you will deign now to furnish us arms and utensils, and give us some small succor in order that we may live the rest of the year. I am reluctant, Great Chief of the Chiefs, to trouble you, and therefore I desist, assuring you, however, that all these Red Men, Warriors and Chiefs of the nations will be inviolably faithful to you, not only here but in all places where there are people under your orders.

When he concluded, all the other Indians raised their voices, beat upon their breasts, and indicated by signs and gestures that they indorsed his sentiments.

After the ejaculations and gesticulations had subsided, O'Reilly replied. He dwelt on the Bourbon kinship and the alliance between

---

[20] The description which follows is based on O'Reilly to Arriaga, October 17, 1769, No. 3, enclosure B, A. G. I., Sto. Dom., 1221.

the kings of France and Spain, in consequence of which anyone who was the friend of one automatically became the friend of the other. "Yours is the supreme happiness," he said, "of being subjects of the greatest monarch in the world, who is not only the possessor of many kingdoms and more than thirty million vassals, but is also great, heroic, just, and faithful to his friends and allies." He adjured them to avoid hostilities and to treat the English well. Finally, he promised that the annual presents would be delivered with punctuality, that nothing but their constant faithfulness would be required of them, and that the king would always be ready to protect them.

Medals bearing the royal image were then conferred on the nine chiefs. After the medals had been kissed by the chiefs, O'Reilly drew his sword, touched each one on the shoulder and breast, made the sign of the cross above their heads, and embraced and shook hands with them all. There were also presents for them. So astounding was the ceremony that the usually immobile faces of the chiefs lighted up with pleasure and surprise. Their awe-struck admiration was renewed in the afternoon when they witnessed a spectacular sham battle staged by the Spanish soldiers. Superior showmanship captivated the Indians just as it had impressed the French colonists at the possession-taking formalities. The chiefs departed with such manifestations of gratitude and admiration as the interpreters and the French officials still in the colony had never before seen. O'Reilly's actions at this council are reminiscent of Bienville, or of Frontenac at Lake Ontario; they are a far cry from those of the typical Spanish missionary.

Winning the support of the Indians along the lower Mississippi required merely a transfer of the affection already felt toward the French. For other tribes, particularly for those along the old Red River border, a conversion was required. Hatred of the Spaniards, inculcated by the French traders, must be transmuted into friendliness. Here in the Red River region lived the *Norteños,* the Indians of the North, who had been such an abomination to the Texas colony. Athanase de Mézières—a Frenchman who possessed the double advantage of friendship with the Indians and familiarity with the French system, and in whom, moreover, the Indians would see living proof that the accession of Spain meant continued friendly interest on the part of the Louisiana whites—Athanase de Mézières was made commandant at Natchitoches.[21] "By this," O'Reilly reported to his government, "I hope to obtain for the presidios of Mexico [i.e., those of Texas] a quietude which they have not hitherto enjoyed, and to make it very difficult for anyone to introduce illicit trade at these posts."[22]

Toward the accomplishment of these two ends, diverse yet interrelated, De Mézières put forth every effort. Presents to the Cadodacho and other friendly tribes were continued. Bonded traders were appointed to deal with them, and a contract was made with Juan Piseros of New Orleans to furnish the trade goods, for which he was to be paid in bear's fat at twenty-five sous a pot, buffalo hides at ten livres each, or deerskins at thirty-five sous each. All trade with the unfriendly Norteños was cut off, in order to coerce them into friendship. If this coercion was to be effective, unlicensed traders, vagabonds, and outlaws had to be expelled from the district; at least six such characters were expelled from Natchitoches. Two herds of horses and mules were confiscated, as were other goods of unauthorized traders, including four Indian slaves. By May, 1770, De Mézières was able to report that no unlicensed traders were living with the Indians.[23]

While these two duties of De Mézières's were the most significant, they were by no means his only responsibilities. His was a multiplicity of functions. He exercised executive, legislative, judicial, and administrative powers at Natchitoches, not to mention his diplomatic services with the Indian nations.

In Upper Louisiana the Indian problem was in one respect the reverse of that at Natchitoches. In the Red River region there was a lacuna in the list of friendly tribes, a gap which De Mézières was expected to fill by winning over the Norteños. In Spanish Illinois, on the contrary, there was a plethora of friendly tribes, many of them resid-

---

[21] For information about the man, the region, the problem and its solution, see Bolton, *Athanase de Mézières*.

[22] O'Reilly to Arriaga, December 10, 1769, No. 18, A. G. I., Sto. Dom., 1223, quoted in Bjork, "Documents Relating to Alexandro O'Reilly," *Louisiana Historical Quarterly*, VII (1924), 21-22.

[23] Bolton, *op. cit.*, I, 90-92.

ing in English territory east of the Mississippi.[24] Now Spain was glad to have the friendship and the trade of these tribes, but she did not care to give England legitimate cause for complaint about undue Spanish influence among them. The commander at St. Louis therefore had to walk circumspectly. In the instructions which O'Reilly sent to that officer he enjoined him to take special precautions against offending the English. Presents were not to be given to tribes east of the Mississippi, and the Indians in Spanish territory were to be urged not to molest the English and not to interfere with their navigation of the river. The commandant was to regulate strictly, however, the commerce of Spanish Illinois. All traders and hunters had to be licensed by him, and on returning to St. Louis were to make a report. English merchants or traders were denied access to the territory, and, theoretically at least, there was to be no communication with them.[25]

Another interior post of importance was at the mouth of the Arkansas. It was a stopping point for expeditions journeying between New Orleans and Spanish Illinois and a strategic point for control of the tribes of the Arkansas valley. It was also a danger point for English contraband trade. When O'Reilly sent Piernas to Upper Louisiana, he had him establish a lieutenant and six soldiers at Arkansas Post. This officer's instructions suggest the purpose of the establishment. He was to cultivate the friendship of the Indians, foster Spanish trade, and do all that he could to prevent illicit trade with the English.[26]

Spain had accepted Louisiana because she saw in it the means of insulating the rest of Spanish America against the English. Acquisition of the province, it is true, made possible the abandonment of the struggling outposts on the old Louisiana-Texas border, and in accordance with one of Rubí's recommendations for a general reorganization of the northern frontier that retrenchment was undertaken;[27] but a new frontier had been acquired, and new frontier problems were

---

[24] In 1769 St. Ange listed twenty-three tribes that were accustomed to come to St. Louis annually for presents. A dozen of them resided east of the Mississippi. Houck, *op. cit.*, I, 44-45.
[25] *Ibid.*, I, 77-82.
[26] O'Reilly to Arriaga, March 1, 1770, No. 31, A. G. I., Sto. Dom., 1223.
[27] Bolton, *Texas in the Middle Eighteenth Century*, 378-383.

the price for relief from old ones. If Louisiana was to be a barrier at all, it was necessary to stop the English at the Mississippi. A threefold resistance was organized by O'Reilly: penetration of English traders and settlers into Louisiana and commercial intercourse across the Mississippi were forbidden; a line of forts was built along the river; and a citizen militia was created.

Of the first of these defenses mention has been made, especially in connection with the regulation for the control of foreign trade and for the Illinois and Arkansas regions. O'Reilly apparently made a sincere attempt to keep the English out. He was not completely successful, to be sure, but he could report:

> I found the English in complete possession of the commerce of the colony. They had in this town their merchants and traders with open stores and shops, and I can safely assert that they pocketed nine-tenths of the money spent here. The commerce of France used to receive the productions of the colony in payment of the articles imported into it from the mother country; but the English, selling their goods much cheaper, had the gathering of all the money. I drove off all the English traders and the other individuals of that Nation whom I found in this town, and I shall admit none of their vessels.[28]

All along the extended frontier, precautions were taken to avoid friction. Work on the second defensive measure, a series of forts on the Mississippi, had been started by Ulloa, but much of his work seems to have been wasted effort. His fort on an island at Balize, on which he had expended 25,000 pesos, was investigated by O'Reilly's captain of engineers and by a junta at New Orleans. When they reported that this fort, Real Católica, was exposed to the elements, costly to maintain, and strategically useless, O'Reilly had it evacuated. A small garrison was reëstablished at French Balize, chiefly to furnish river pilots. Fort San Luis de Natchez was likewise abandoned, and the Acadian settlers in the neighborhood were permitted to join their compatriots in the Iberville district. Since the Acadian settlers in this latter locality were a sufficient defense against any English attack that might be launched from Fort Bute, and because the Choctaw Indians from the

---

[28] Quoted in Gayarré, *op. cit.*, III, 28; Pittman, *The Present State of the European Settlements on the Mississippi*, 55.

English territory had come to expect too expensive hospitality from the Spanish fort here, O'Reilly had it evacuated also. The fortifications he maintained were, from south to north: Balize, New Orleans, Pointe Coupée, Arkansas, Ste. Geneviève, St. Louis, and the fort at the mouth of the Missouri. The heaviest garrison of regular soldiers was maintained at New Orleans. The other garrisons ranged from half a dozen soldiers at Balize and at the mouth of the Arkansas to thirty-odd at St. Louis.[29]

Statistics are not conveniently available to indicate the exact number of regular soldiers that O'Reilly kept in Louisiana. One hundred and seventy-nine men of the Regiment of Lisbon volunteered for enrollment in the Battalion of Louisiana,[30] and apparently this approximates the full roster of regulars retained. At any rate it is obvious that the chief bulwark of defense against the English was to be the citizen militia. O'Reilly gave proof of his confidence in the Louisianians by sending the rest of his regulars back to Havana almost as rapidly as the ships could accommodate them. The process began as early as September of 1769 and continued throughout the following months.[31] Thirteen militia companies, comprising 1040 men, were organized under native officers paid by the government. They were armed from the king's stores and drilled by regular army officers.[32] So impressive was this organization that the English across the river began to be suspicious.[33] But O'Reilly made overtures to Gage for harmonious relations between the two colonies, and Gage replied that "nothing could be more agreeable to the king than the knowledge of the orders your Excellency has given."[34]

---

[29] O'Reilly to Arriaga, December 29, 1769, and March 1, 1770, A. G. I., Sto. Dom., 1223.

[30] O'Reilly to Bucareli, November 10, 1769, No. 83, A. G. I., Cuba, 1055.

[31] *Idem* to *idem*, September 10, 1769, A. G. I., Mexico, 1242; O'Reilly to Grimaldi, October 17, 1769, No. 10, A. G. I., Sto. Dom., 2543; O'Reilly to Munian, November 10, 1769, *ibid*.

[32] O'Reilly [statement of militia officers], February 12, 1770, A. G. I., Cuba, 2357; also March 1, 1770, *ibid.*, 1055.

[33] Haldimand to Gage, June 12, 1770, *in* Carter, *Great Britain and the Illinois Country*, 143.

[34] Quoted in Bjork, *The Establishment of Spanish Rule in the Province of Louisiana*, 247–249.

Louisiana's defenses were thus organized, not as an impregnable bulwark against the English, but as a sort of obstacle that would delay them, at least temporarily, in their attempts to get at the mines of Mexico, and to tap the equally profitable trade with Spanish America proper.

O'Reilly instituted other reforms. He established titles to agricultural land and set the requirements for "homesteading." He investigated the church in Louisiana and recommended provision for eighteen priests. When he left for Havana in March, 1770, he had reënforced Spain's formal title to the province by transforming it, so far as was possible, into a Spanish colony.[35] The Hispaniolizing of Louisiana was never to be completed, but O'Reilly made a good beginning, and succeeding governors augmented his efforts. In this transformation the subjugation of the insurrectionists was not the consummation but merely the preliminary thereto. In the last analysis, then, O'Reilly's administration is not to be regarded as coterminous with the proceedings against the insurgents but as beginning, in its full significance, after that ordeal.

---

[35] French, *op. cit.*, V, 289–291; O'Reilly to Arriaga, February 14, 1770, A. G. I., Cuba, 1055.

Chapter III

UNZAGA AND LOCAL PROBLEMS

UNZAGA'S GOVERNORSHIP of Louisiana was to a very marked degree a continuation of O'Reilly's control, modified in many particulars, however, by the personality of the new governor. Unzaga was a native of Málaga. Since 1735 he had been serving in the Spanish army, the first eight years in Spain, Italy, and Africa, and the last twenty-six in America, where he had risen to the rank of colonel of the Regiment of Havana. In 1769, when O'Reilly set out for Louisiana, he brought Unzaga along to be governor of the province, a capacity in which the latter served for approximately seven years.[1]

Introduced to the Louisianians as a protégé of O'Reilly, subordinate to the latter's orders until his departure, Unzaga, nevertheless, was in sharp contrast to his chief. As an older man, he might have been expected to be less impetuous; in addition, he seems to have been by nature milder, more conciliatory. These qualities fitted him well to serve as a mollifying influence upon the French creoles. He was not exactly an antidote for O'Reilly, for that was not needed. O'Reilly's good work in Louisiana was not entirely unappreciated at the time, though later generations have lost sight of it. But Unzaga carried on the work he had started, the work of reconciling the creoles to Spanish rule; and, because of his gentler nature, he did it more effectively, perhaps, than O'Reilly himself could have.

Some confusion has arisen about the date when Unzaga's administration began. On the one hand is the assertion that O'Reilly was never governor of Louisiana,[2] a misapprehension possibly due to the fact that Unzaga had been designated as O'Reilly's successor even before O'Reilly started from Spain.[3] Yet O'Reilly was addressed as Gov-

---
[1] Gayarré, *op. cit.*, III, 44, 102–104; Bolton, *Athanase de Mézières*, I, 136–137, n.
[2] Phelps, *Louisiana*, 127.
[3] Mention of this is to be found in O'Reilly to Arriaga, December 10, 1769, No. 17, A. G. I., Sto. Dom., 1223. Referred to by Bjork, "Documents Relating to the Establishment of Schools in Louisiana, 1771," *Mississippi Valley Historical Review*, XI (1925), 562.

ernor and made official use of the title.⁴ On the other hand is the statement that it was not until October 29, 1770, that O'Reilly "delivered up the government of the province" to Unzaga.⁵ As a matter of fact Unzaga's administration began officially on December 1, 1769, when O'Reilly installed him as presiding officer of the cabildo and announced his appointment as governor.⁶

For the sake of the new governor's prestige, O'Reilly was careful not to infringe upon Unzaga's prerogatives. On their tour of inspection to Pointe Coupée, for example, he was punctilious in according to Unzaga all the deference his official position deserved. Nevertheless, everyone realized that as long as O'Reilly was in the colony the governor was definitely subordinate to him, and it was not until the general embarked for Havana that Unzaga became governor indeed. Then his governorship took on new significance; he assumed full responsibility for defense of the colony and full power for its control. The exact date of O'Reilly's departure thus acquires additional significance. It was early in March, 1770, rather than October 29 of that year as is usually given. From February 18 to 28 O'Reilly was writing farewell letters to the various provincial officers; he arrived at Havana on March 23, at Cádiz on May 31, and at court on June 9.⁷

Early in Unzaga's administration there was danger that war between Spain and England might arise out of the Falkland Islands dispute, and the British commanders, Gage and Haldimand, laid plans for an attack on Louisiana, should war eventuate.⁸ On June 8, 1770, Unzaga reported that Pensacola had been reënforced by one thousand men; and the governor of Havana, being appraised of this reënforcement, informed his government of the danger of an English attack on

---

⁴ See above, p. 23; also Dart, "The Oath of Allegiance to Spain." *Louisiana Historical Quarterly*, IV (1921), 211.

⁵ Gayarré, *op. cit.*, III, 37; Villiers du Terrage, *op. cit.*, 351.

⁶ O'Reilly wrote to Bucareli, December 10, that Unzaga had been invested with "el govierno militar y politico de esta ciudad y su distrito, que exerce desde 1º del corriente mes."—A. G. I., Cuba, 1055.

⁷ Copies of farewell letters, A. G. I., Cuba, 134 A; Bucareli to Arriaga, April 1, 1770, draft, A. G. I., Ind. Gen., 1630; O'Reilly to Bucareli, June 15, 1770, A. G. I., Mexico, 1242.

⁸ Carter, *Great Britain and the Illinois Country*, 142-144.

Louisiana or Havana. O'Reilly recommended that one hundred men and additional military supplies be sent to Louisiana. This was done, and Unzaga was ordered to defend Louisiana as best he could with the small force of regulars and with the militia; but if attacked by a strong force, he was to retreat to Mexico. The detachment at Arkansas, similarly, was to withdraw to Natchitoches if necessary, and the Illinois garrisons were to retire to the friendly Indian villages along the Missouri.[9] There was real danger of an attack. General Gage was ordered, on January 2, 1771, to mobilize an army for the purpose.[10] But though the fires of war were all ready to be kindled, the match flickered out: the Falkland Islands dispute was settled amicably; Louisiana and the English colonies might relax their vigilance.

Religious contentions impinged upon the consciousness of the colony much more forcefully than apprehension of an English attack. Similar ecclesiastical disturbances had enlivened the closing days of the French régime when Jesuits and Capuchins wrangled for supremacy. When the Capuchins prevailed, partly because of the world-wide movement against the Jesuits, they proceeded to fulfill some of the dire predictions of their former rivals. Spiritual atrophy ensued; the fathers grew lax in the oversight of their parishes and began to neglect the priestly functions, whose significance, the Jesuits charged, they did not understand.

Soon after the establishment of Spanish domination, the criticisms were renewed, this time by Spanish Capuchins. Father Cirilo penned virulent tirades to his superior at Havana denouncing the ignorance, laziness, and corruption of the Louisiana Capuchins. Father Dagobert, it must be admitted, was an easy-going old fellow, well liked by the people, but not a strict shepherd, blissfully ignorant of the finer points of Catholic doctrine, and inclined to be overconfident of God's forgiving grace—at least, Father Cirilo thought such confidence unwarranted. Father Dagobert and his fellow-priests lived in luxurious comfort, set the best table in New Orleans, and were ministered to by

---

[9] Unzaga to Grimaldi, June 8, 1770; A. G. I., Sto. Dom., 2543; Bucareli to Arriaga, August 17, 1770, *ibid.;* O'Reilly to Grimaldi, September 30, 1770, *ibid.;* Grimaldi to Unzaga, October 24, 1770, *ibid.*

[10] Carter, *op. cit.*, 182–183.

black wenches, whose morals Father Cirilo questioned. But Bishop Echevarria, on the advice of Unzaga, resolved to continue Father Dagobert as vicar-general. The latter's acknowledgment of the appointment "is written with great propriety, with dignified subordination and Christian meekness, and is not such a document as could be expected from the individual described by Father Cirilo."

Unzaga hesitated to offend either faction in this clerical squabble. Father Cirilo got the impression from conferences with him that the governor was opposed to the French Capuchins and anxious for the removal of Father Dagobert. But, as Father Cirilo's diatribes grew more and more caustic, Unzaga asserted himself in favor of the French Capuchins. Political considerations doubtless had great influence on his decision. Father Dagobert was very popular with the Louisianians and his expulsion would have disaffected the colonists, though probably not so seriously as some maintained. Yet the governor's arguments took cognizance chiefly of the scurrility of the persecution and the imprudence of Father Cirilo. As far as personalities were concerned, the balance was all in favor of Father Dagobert.[11]

Although outward serenity now prevailed, Father Cirilo continued his complaints. The bishop accused Unzaga of indolence in the matter and asked the captain general of Cuba to remonstrate with him. Unzaga defended his original position in a long letter to the captain general, and justified himself further in a letter to Arriaga, minister of the king. Finally the whole question was submitted to the king, who supported the bishop, but without censuring Unzaga, and recommended that harmony be attained by mutual concessions. Thus the matter blew over.[12] We find Father Cirilo admitting, in 1775, notwithstanding his fulminations against the French Capuchins, "that the French are best fitted to bear fruit among these people [the Louisianians], because they alone preach in French."[13] Following his suggestion, the bishop recommended that six French priests be sent to Loui-

---

[11] Gayarré, *op. cit.*, III, 49–65, 83–85, 90–91; Houck, *op. cit.*, I, 114–120.

[12] Bispham, "Contest for Ecclesiastical Supremacy in the Valley of the Mississippi," *Louisiana Historical Quarterly*, I (1917), 184–185; Para el Consejo, March 15, 1775, A. G. I., Sto. Dom., 2583.

[13] Cirilo to the bishop of Havana, December 18, 1775, *ibid.*

siana to bring the total to eighteen, as O'Reilly had advised, and that four Spanish priests be sent to take the place of four French priests who were too old for active service. Unzaga seconded the request, and the Council of the Indies recognized the need of this spiritual reënforcement of the colony.[14]

Inasmuch as the king did not pronounce judgment against either party in this dispute, it may suffice, by way of conclusion, to indorse Unzaga's statement, "I know how difficult it is to come to a correct appreciation of the true merits of men of that sacred calling, when they choose to quarrel among themselves." More interesting possibly than the altercation was Unzaga's fearlessness in opposing the bishop of Havana and the boldness with which he argued for liberal policies.

It is not always that the laws made for one region can be safely adapted to another.... You should take into consideration the difficulty which there is in eradicating practices, usages and customs.... The people here will remain quiet as long as they are gently treated; but the use of the rod would produce confusion and ruin. Their dispositions are the result of the happy state of liberty to which they have been accustomed from the cradle, and in which they ought to be maintained, so far as is consistent with the laws of the kingdom.[15]

In passing, we might notice another fruitless effort to make Spanish the Louisiana French. Elaborate plans were laid for the establishment of a school at New Orleans to introduce the Spanish language and to inculcate loyalty to Spain. Four teachers were employed and a select library of books was provided, but in spite of various official attempts to encourage this school and to persuade the creoles to enroll their children in it, the attendance was never satisfactory and finally dwindled to six. Unzaga's words directing attention to the difficulty "in eradicating practices, usages and customs" are again pertinent.[16]

Under Unzaga justice was administered in accordance with the forms outlined by O'Reilly. Some cases were tried before the alcaldes; others were taken to the governor's court. In this latter court, Unzaga,

---

[14] The bishop, February 8, 1776, *ibid.*; Unzaga to Valdellano, June 19, 1776, *ibid.*; Para el Consejo, November 5, 1776, *ibid.*

[15] Unzaga to the Bishop and to Torre, quoted in Gayarré, *op. cit.*, III, 84–91.

[16] Bjork, "Documents Relating to the Establishment of Schools in Louisiana, 1771," *op. cit.*, 561–569.

not being a lawyer by profession, relied largely on the advice of Don Cecilio Odoardo, his *assessor* or *auditor*.[17] Court procedure embodied some peculiarities. Witnesses did not ordinarily appear in court, but their sworn depositions were introduced as evidence. The defendant in a criminal case, likewise, had an examination in jail instead of a "day in court," and his confession or protestation of innocence was entered in the record. Torture was applied to some suspects who were reluctant to testify. Capable counsel was provided, however, even for negroes charged with crimes against whites. Appeals were provided for from these courts of first instance to the cabildo and thence to a special tribunal at Havana. In at least one litigation such appeals were made.[18]

All evidence possible was collected in criminal cases. But where the evidence was clear the court acted rapidly. For example, Juan Baptiste Cezaire Lebreton was murdered on the night of May 31, 1771. The next morning the court appointed two doctors to examine the body. Testimony was taken from all who knew anything of the murder, and suspects were jailed. When it was seen that the accusations of the various witnesses were corroborated by several independent bits of evidence, an accused negro was tortured on the rack, a confession was extracted, and along with it the implication of a partner in his crime. Under torture this second negro confessed. Just three weeks after the murder these two slaves were hanged, and their heads and hands were cut off and nailed up on the public roads. An accomplice received one hundred lashes and her ears were cut off, and another was tarred and feathered and ridden on a pack animal. But because a third was so ill that the two hundred lashes decreed for him would then have resulted in his death, the attorney for the defense got the punishment suspended until he should have recovered from his illness.[19] Punishment was prompt, versatile, and rigorous, but not

---

[17] These terms are used in the sense of "one who sits beside" and "one who hears"; in other words, a legal adviser. Porteous, "A Suit for Debt in the Governor's Court, New Orleans, 1770," *Louisiana Historical Quarterly*, VIII (1925), 240–241.

[18] "Index to the Spanish Judicial Records," *Louisiana Historical Quarterly*, VI– (1923–), *passim;* Joseph Loppinot vs. Juan Villeneuve, April 15, 1774, *ibid.*, X (1927), 438.

[19] Porteous, "Torture in Spanish Criminal Procedure in Louisiana, 1771," *Louisiana Historical Quarterly*, VIII (1925), 5–22.

without a touch of compassion—or perhaps, since the slave was merely a piece of property, it would be more nearly correct to say that the court tempered justice with business acumen.

In cases in which the evidence was not conclusive the court was more cautious. A negro named Pedro was accused, on July 16, 1774, of having poisoned his overseer. After an autopsy, testimony was taken, the accused was examined, a prosecuting attorney and a counsel for the defense were appointed, and the trial proceeded. Judgment was not given, however, until more than three years later, when Governor Gálvez, on Odoardo's advice, found Pedro not guilty of murder, but in order "to avoid the scandal that the memory of such a crime would occasion to the public," sentenced him "to ten years hard labor, with shackles on his feet."[20]

The Spanish courts were available for the protection of foreigners. On February 28, 1771, Carlos Blanchard, owner of an English ship on the Mississippi, was robbed of trade goods valued at 415 piastres. Pablo Rocheblave, a Louisiana planter, was suspected. Prosecution by the state resulted in the conviction of Rocheblave, and Unzaga condemned him to five years' banishment from the province and its environs.[21]

Royal interests were also served by the courts. Late in 1773 one of the regidores, Dionisio Braud, was deprived of his office for having gone to France without getting a royal permit. His property in New Orleans was attached, and the office of regidor, thus forfeited to the royal treasury, was sold at auction on February 23 of the following year to Daniel Fagot for 1202 pesos.[22]

The majority of the cases tried, however, were civil actions between various colonists for collection of debts, collection of alimony, dissolution of partnerships, division of estates, etc. Frequently these cases, "for the service of God, and the uncertainty of law suits," were settled out of court.[23] The courts also acted in a notarial capacity. By proclamation of November 3, 1770, Unzaga had forbidden the sale or trans-

---

[20] "Index, etc.," *op. cit.,* 455–462.
[21] Porteous, "Trial of Pablo Rocheblave before Governor Unzaga, 1771," *Louisiana Historical Quarterly,* VIII (1925), 372–381.
[22] "Index, etc.," *op. cit.,* 147–148, 293–295. [23] *Ibid.,* VI (1923), 711.

fer of "negroes, plantations, houses, or seacraft" without the formal execution of the deed before a notary public. Consequently, a large part of the court records is given over to recording sales of negroes, real estate, and other property; to recording contracts for the construction of houses and boats; to recording apprenticeships, wills, appointments of legal representatives, manumissions. Manumission seems to have been fairly frequent.[24]

By comparison with the administration of justice in the preceding French régime, that of the Spanish period was highly efficient. The court records are fuller and pay more attention to detail. The decisions rendered are determined, not merely upon the opinion of the magistrate, but also by reference to a codified law, the essentials of which had been made known to the colonists. The court, furthermore, was no respecter of persons. Mention has been made of the case in which a transient Englishman was given the verdict over a colonist. Unzaga showed no favoritism even toward his own father-in-law, pronouncing a decision against him in 1773.[25]

However rigorous Unzaga was in the enforcement of local laws in Louisiana, he was discreet enough to close his eyes to brazen infractions of Spain's commercial regulations for the colony. Although O'Reilly had obtained some modifications in Spain's exclusive policy and had recommended still further liberality, he was too much a military man not to enforce the restrictions until they were repealed. The effect was to stifle Louisiana's trade. For the colony's available exports, chiefly furs and peltries and lumber, there was little demand in Spain and Havana. France, England, and the English colonies, however, provided ready markets, while West Florida abounded in depots where manufactured goods were offered in exchange. English ships on the Mississippi were handier still. The Spanish restrictions ran counter to economic law, and through the connivance of Unzaga the latter triumphed. With his tacit consent trade with the English recovered from its temporary lethargy. The English converted two large vessels into floating warehouses and employed them exclusively

---

[24] Gayarré, *op. cit.*, III, 631–632; "Index, etc.," *ibid.*, VI– (1923–), *passim*.
[25] Gayarré, *op. cit.*, III, 98–99.

in the contraband trade, and practically the entire sum that the Louisianians mustered annually to pay for imported goods found its way into English hands.[26]

Unzaga was obliged, of course, to make a pretense of preventing smuggling. "The small boats," he wrote in 1771, "that from time to time pass before this city, under pretext of going to their posts at Manchac and Natchez, have no other object than the commerce which they can enjoy on this river." Occasionally action was brought against an over-bold English smuggler, as, for example, against Joseph Nach in 1774. But such actions were perfunctory and did not interfere materially with the English monopoly.[27] To the colonists, appreciative though they were of Unzaga's protection of the French Capuchins and of his impartial dispensation of justice, the crowning proof of their governor's concern for their welfare was his leniency toward the contraband trade. A few of the French habitants felt that their position was intolerable. In 1773 Colonel Israel Putnam reported encountering a schooner at the mouth of the Mississippi "that had about 40 Passengers one borde of french pepel that was going to Hispanyolow to Cape france they being tiered of Spannish government."[28] But by far the greater number of the Louisianians, thanks to Unzaga's propitiating influence, found contentment under Spain's rule.

Under Unzaga's administration the policy that O'Reilly had outlined for the Natchitoches district began to bear fruit. Although De Mézières never received from the Spaniards the full confidence that he deserved, he made a success of the tasks assigned him. In 1770 he went to Cadodacho and held conferences with the chiefs of the Taovayas, Tawakoni, Yscanis, and Kichai (Tribes of the North), as a result of which, in the following year, treaties were concluded with these tribes as well as with the Cainiones and Tonkawa. After coercing these tribes into submission by cutting off their trade, it was now ad-

---

[26] Phelps, *op. cit.*, 136–137; Martin, *op. cit.*, II, 26–27.

[27] Unzaga to Bucareli, January 22, 1771, A. G. I., Cuba, 1055; Unzaga to Arriaga, September 7, 1774, No. 127, A. G. I., Sto. Dom., 2582; Testimonio del proceso contra Jph. Nach & Co., *ibid.*; Fortier, *op. cit.*, II, 38–40.

[28] Israel Putnam, Journal of an exploring expedition to the Natchez—in the year 1773, L.C., copy made in 1845 from the original in the hands of Lemuel Grosvenor of Pomfret, Conn.

visable to retain their friendship by extending to them the system of bonded traders. Unzaga gave De Mézières permission to appoint the traders. Governor Ripperda of Texas appreciated De Mézières's service to Texas in pacifying the Norteños without destroying their hostility toward the Apaches. He objected, however, to the penetration of traders into Texas on the ground that this trade indirectly supplied the Apaches with arms and ammunition. But the traders were not withdrawn.[29]

The correspondence of Ripperda, Unzaga, and De Mézières in the early seventies indicates that the Louisiana-Texas border was almost as serious an intercolonial problem as it had been an international one. Ripperda saw the advantages of French methods as exemplified by Louisiana's efficient agent, De Mézières, but his superiors in Mexico "stood firmly by the time honored Indian policy of New Spain," forbidding trade and presents and the furnishing of arms.[30] As a consequence, the influence of Louisiana traders extended farther into Texas than it had in the period before the cession, giving a certain proof that the French trader system was better suited to the local problem than the orthodox Spanish system. The Spaniards of Texas did not relish the encroachments of the Louisiana "French," but they feared to move against them because of the Apache peril and because to oust the traders would drive the tribes to the English.[31]

That the Natchitoches district flourished under Unzaga's governorship is borne out by the census report of February 16, 1776. Population had risen from 800 to more than 1000. There were sizable herds of horses, cattle, and hogs. Some indigo was raised and much tobacco. But economically the Indian trade was the leading business, its profits being computed in deerskins and bear oil. The fort had been rebuilt and was in good condition. De Mézières's particular pride, however, was the splendid parochial church which he had been instrumental in building. The church received annually 400 pesos. The post, inci-

---

[29] Unzaga to De Mézières, October 4, 1771; Bolton, *Athanase de Mézières*, I, 254–255; Ripperda to Unzaga, September 8, 1772, *ibid.*, I, 344–349.

[30] *Ibid.*, I, 107; Bolton, "The Mission as a Frontier Institution in the Spanish-American Colonies," *American Historical Review*, XXIII (1917), 42–61.

[31] Bolton, *Athanase de Mézières*, I, 110.

dentally, received a like sum from the brandy sellers, "to secure the closing of the wineshops which have been attempted," and an equal amount was paid by the gaming houses.[82]

Peace and prosperity went hand in hand also in Spanish Illinois. French Illinois, of course, had been a rich colony, at least agriculturally; so rich, in fact, as to deserve the name "the Garden of New France." Farm products such as flour, corn, pork products, and tobacco supplemented the fruits of the chase such as furs, hides, bear hams, bear oil, and venison as export commodities. With the cession to England, many of the French settlers joined the trek across the river to what turned out to be Spanish Illinois. There they found conditions quite as favorable as those they had left, and in a short time they were living in comfort. Francisco Vallé, the richest habitant of Ste. Geneviève, raised quantities of provisions and had 100 negroes besides hired white help.[83] The tide of French migrations to Spanish Illinois subsided before Unzaga's governorship.

An official report for 1770-1771 gives Ste. Geneviève a population of 605, including slaves, and St. Louis, 497.[84] This report verifies Piernas' estimate of the preceding year, in which he gave Ste. Geneviève's population as about six hundred, and that of St. Louis somewhat less. Pittman gave substantially the same report.[85] Gayarré and Phelps, however, indicate that there were 33 whites and 18 blacks in St. Louis in 1770 and exactly the same number in Ste. Geneviève. Apparently these writers have mistaken for an actual census report a *sample* census report form, which O'Reilly sent to Piernas in February, 1770.[86] It is essential to realize the actual size of the Spanish Illinois settlements in 1770; otherwise one would get the impression that there was a large immigration of Frenchmen from across the river during the period 1770 to 1776. Most of the moving took place when the western bank of the Mississippi was presumed to be French. There was a grad-

---

[82] De Mézières to Unzaga, February 16, 1776, *ibid.*, II, 120-121.
[83] Pittman, *op. cit.*, 95-96; Houck, *op. cit.*, I, 85-107.
[84] Census of Louisiana, September 2, 1772, A. G. I., Cuba, 2357.
[85] Houck, *op. cit.*, I, 70-72; Pittman, *op. cit.*, 94-96.
[86] Gayarré, *op. cit.*, III, 23; Phelps, *op. cit.*, 133. This *sample* census report is included with O'Reilly to Arriaga, March 1, 1770, A. G. I., Sto. Dom., 1223. Also printed but with some ambiguity in Houck, *op. cit.*, I, 84.

ual increase in the population of Spanish Illinois under Unzaga's governorship, particularly at St. Louis, which became the Spanish headquarters for the district. The younger village, in fact, almost caught up in size with Ste. Geneviève.[37]

Indian slavery seems to have been a common practice in this region, most of the slaves being women or children who were used as domestic servants. In the summer of 1770 the citizens of St. Louis and Ste. Geneviève were required to make formal declaration of all such "savage slaves." Twelve citizens of the latter village reported that they possessed twenty-eight Indian slaves, while at St. Louis thirty-seven citizens reported the possession of sixty-nine Indian slaves.[38]

Farm production showed a healthy growth, the lead mines near Ste. Geneviève supplied the district with bullets, and the salt works continued to run, though there were complaints that the surplus was being "dumped" at lower prices on the English market across the river. But, all things considered, the most encouraging fact about Spanish Illinois was that most of the Indian tribes over which the French had had influence were committed now to friendship to the Spaniards. Many tribes east of the Mississippi were included in the group.[39]

The English settlements on the east bank of the Mississippi, especially those in the Natchez and Manchac districts, were increasing even more rapidly than the settlements in Spanish Louisiana. The English government did nothing to encourage the populating of this region, but the New England and to a lesser extent the other Atlantic

---

[37] The actual figures are:

Years	St. Louis	Ste. Geneviève	Years	St. Louis	Ste. Geneviève
1770–1771	497	605	1773	637	676
1772	597	691	1779	689	698

Census of Louisiana, A. G. I., Cuba, 2357; Houck, *op. cit.*, I, 53–54, 61; Viles, "Population and Extent of Settlement in Missouri before 1804," *Missouri Historical Review*, V (1911), 202, 206–207; Nasatir, *Indian Trade and Diplomacy in the Spanish Illinois* (MS, Ph.D. thesis, University of California), 119.

[38] Declaration of Indian slaves at Ste. Geneviève, May 26, 1770, B.L., La. Coll.; declaration of Indian slaves at St. Louis, July 12, 1770, *ibid*.

[39] Piernas to O'Reilly, October 31, 1769, *in* Houck, *op. cit.*, I, 71–72. Compare the reports of St. Ange for 1769 and Cruzat for 1777, *ibid.*, I, 44–45, 141–148.

Coast colonies contributed individualistic immigrants.[40] In their coming Unzaga saw a menace to Spanish control west of the river. "If they possess these establishments fronting on the kingdom of Mexico without any other interposition than the Mississippi River, they will introduce to us commerce in time of peace and armies in time of war."[41]

With the outbreak of the American Revolution this chronic concern of Unzaga's became acute. Ordered "to investigate with all discretion and secrecy not only the success of the English armies and of the revolted colonies but also the intentions of both sides, using every means that he could," he launched a number of inquiries, including the sending of a ship to Philadelphia, "ostensibly to look for flour, but also to endeavor to discover their designs."[42] The reports that he received were alarming, and a survey of the defenses of Louisiana was not reassuring. He wrote that there were "neither troops to defend the colony, nor forts to contain them, nor means to march on land," and characterized the militia aside from the question of its reliability as "neither skilled nor sufficient." His conclusion was that, if he were attacked, he would follow the advice that had been given him in 1770 and fall back to Mexico.[43]

The state of war in the English colonies also forced Unzaga to face certain problems of neutrality. Various Revolutionary leaders, encouraged by Spain's hints of interest in the colonial cause, importuned the governor of Louisiana to lend assistance to the Revolutionists. They buttressed their requests for arms and military supplies with embarrassing arguments and uncomfortable predictions. In May, 1776, for example, Charles Lee, then second in command to Washington, pointed out that, if Great Britain subjugated the colonies, the Spanish West Indies and even Mexico itself would be at the mercy of Great Britain. If, on the contrary, the colonies won independence, Spain would have nothing to fear from them as neighbors. "The genius of the people, their situation and their circumstances engage them by preference in agriculture and free trade, which are most suited to their

---

[40] Winsor, *The Westward Movement*, 110.
[41] Unzaga to Torre, February 27, 1772, No. 18, A. G. I., Cuba, 1145.
[42] Unzaga to Arriaga, June 19, 1776, No. 160, A. G. I., Sto. Dom., 2547.
[43] Unzaga to José de Gálvez, June 19, 1776, No. 159, *ibid.*, 2656.

interests and inclination." In the present tense this statement seems quite incongruous; nevertheless, Lee believed that he had diagnosed the thirteen states for some time to come, and he summed up his case with the assertion that success in the Revolution would be as advantageous to Spain as to America, and defeat as disastrous.[44]

Unzaga preferred not to commit himself. He conferred with George Gibson, who brought Lee's letter, and, encouraged by Oliver Pollock, of whom more later, even went so far as to have Gibson arrested (temporarily) to allay suspicion long enough for Lieutenant Linn to start north with nine thousand pounds of powder for the Revolutionists.[45] But when Gibson made certain pointed inquiries about Spanish policy and his own attitude, the governor put him off without an answer and referred the queries to the court.[46] Unzaga was uneasy about Louisiana's exposure to attack but he was not convinced that the surest defense of the province was through aiding the Americans.

Of one thing he was convinced, however, and that was his desire to retire from the governorship. Poor health, advanced age, and impaired eyesight handicapped him in his work, and after forty-one years in American service he was homesick for his native Málaga. His reiterated requests for permission to retire were answered eventually not with the coveted recall but with promotion to the captaincy general of Caracas. On the first of January in 1777 he relinquished the governorship of Louisiana and in March embarked for his new responsibility. In Gayarré's words:

> He had won the esteem and affection of the population, and his departure caused unbounded regrets. His administration had been that of a gentle and indulgent father, and his having dared to connive at the breach by the British of the fiscal and commercial laws of Spain, a strict observance of which would have been fatal, materially increased the prosperity of the colony.[47]

---

[44] Charles Lee to the Governor of New Orleans, May, 1776, *ibid.*, 2596.

[45] Unzaga to José de Gálvez, September 7, 1776, No. 181, *ibid.*; Winsor, *op. cit.*, 147-148.

[46] Unzaga to José de Gálvez, September 30, 1776, No. 184, *ibid.*

[47] Gayarré, *op. cit.*, III, 104.

By the end of 1776 three Spanish governors had administered Louisiana. Each one had played a part: Ulloa in bringing on the insurrection, O'Reilly in establishing and formulating Spanish control, Unzaga in reconciling the colonists to Spanish rule. The stage was set for the new governor, Bernardo de Gálvez. He was not perfect; in intellectual attainment he must bow to Ulloa, in military reputation to O'Reilly, in executive experience to Unzaga. Nevertheless, Gálvez had certain attributes of greatness appropriate to the serious crises that were to arise in his governorship, and these abilities enabled him to make his administration one of greater moment than any of his predecessors'.

PART TWO

Gálvez' Administration

Chapter IV

THE COMMENCEMENT OF GÁLVEZ' CAREER

THE YOUNG MAN to whom Unzaga relinquished his office on January 1, 1777, had come to the colony just a few months earlier as commandant of the troops in Louisiana. He had been introduced, of course, by the usual formal notice, that "Lieutenant Colonel Don Bernardo de Gálvez, Captain of Grenadiers in the Regiment of Infantry of Seville, has been named by the King Colonel of the permanent Battalion of your city [New Orleans]." More illuminating is the postscript that O'Reilly subscribed in his own hand:

> The aforesaid bears his instructions and will present them shortly. He is an individual whom I esteem highly, and his uncle, the minister of the Indies, is my particular friend, wherefore I will thank you for any attentions you can show him.[1]

The word "wherefore" probably should be underlined, for his family connections were worth much to Bernardo de Gálvez; they were possibly an even greater advantage than his dynamic and attractive personality. He was not only the nephew but also the favorite protégé of José de Gálvez, formerly visitor-general of New Spain and now minister of the Indies; and this in an age when nepotism was a virtue rather than a scandal. José de Gálvez, enjoying power second only to that of King Carlos himself, showered favors on all his relatives, but the greatest honors went to his elder brother, Matías, who was elevated to the viceroyalty of New Spain, and to Matías' son Bernardo.[2]

When he came to New Orleans, Bernardo de Gálvez already had a long service record. In the war with Portugal in 1762 he served as lieutenant, after which his uncle obtained for him a captain's commission in the Regiment of Corunna. He came to New Spain as part

---
[1] O'Reilly to Unzaga, June 15, 1776, A. G. I., Cuba, 181.
[2] Priestley, *José de Gálvez*, 9-10.

of his uncle's *entourage* in the visitation of that viceroyalty. In April, 1769, he was attached as captain and second in command in an expedition against the Apaches on the frontier of Nueva Vizcaya. In reporting this appointment to José de Gálvez, Lope de Cuellar stated quite frankly, "I hope that you will recognize my motives to provide the greatest satisfaction for Don Bernardo, and to manifest to your excellency my constant recognition."[3] Protesting against Cuellar's "excess of gratefulness or kindness," José de Gálvez remarked that his nephew showed "promise of valor and leadership," but because of his extreme youth had not yet acquired "steadiness and experience." He questioned, therefore, the wisdom of ranking him ahead of the seasoned and distinguished soldier, Lieutenant Diego Becerril. But though he deplored the "excessive honor" bestowed upon his nephew, he did not countermand it, and Bernardo not only continued in this capacity but was soon made commander of the Nueva Vizcaya and Sonora frontier.[4]

At least one frontier official expressed misgivings about the appointment of an untried youth to such an important position. "Although he is a spirited lad, at his age of twenty-two or twenty-four he has not acquired the experience and maturity that the methods of fighting against these enemies [the Apaches] requires."[5] Such misgivings, however, turned out to be poor prophecy. As commandant of this frontier Gálvez led several major expeditions against the Apaches. On the first of these, in the fall of 1770, he demonstrated the qualities of leadership that he possessed. With about one hundred and thirty-five frontier soldiers and Indian allies he set out from Chihuahua in mid-October. Not until they reached the Pecos River were the elusive Apaches located, but by this time supplies had run short, the men were discouraged, and prudence seemed to dictate an immediate return to Chihuahua. But on the morning of November 2, after all were on horse, the young commander spoke to his soldiers and Indians "more or less in this tone":

---

[3] Cuellar to José de Gálvez, April 28, 1769, No. 342, copy, Huntington Library, Gálvez Papers.

[4] José de Gálvez to Cuellar, May 17, 1769, No. 2, copy, *ibid*.

[5] Fayni to Arriaga, October 12, 1770, A. G. I., Guad., 512.

My comrades: the time has come to deliver the final blow and to give proof of our constancy. Cold and ice! already I have seen the light-heartedness with which you know how to endure them. Hunger! which is worse than all inclemencies of weather, we have known, not through my fault, but because Heaven with much water destroyed our provisions. Our enemies do not know the day or the month when we expect to encounter them; to return to get provisions would be to give time for the Indians to give us the slip, after which, it is my feeling, it will be impossible to catch them. You will go to Chihuahua with the sorrow of having spent time and money without accomplishing a thing. It is not for one to have shame, nor is ignominy in harmony with my way of thinking. Alone I would go without having anyone to accompany me; and I will either take a scalp to Chihuahua and perform my duty or pay with my life for the king's bread that I have eaten. There is the road from our land, follow it those of you who have faint hearts; but follow me those of you who wish to take part in my glorious hardships, follow me on the assumption that I can give you nothing but thanks for this fineness, but that it will live always in my memory and recollection.[6]

Having given this challenge, Gálvez struck spurs to his horse and started to ford the Pecos. With one accord his men followed, shouting "that they would follow until they died; that they would eat horses, and after that stones, and would never forsake him."

"I had that day the eternal satisfaction," Gálvez reported, "of seeing one hundred and thirty-five men, with nothing as a promise of reward, follow far more contentedly than when they left Chihuahua. May God strengthen the good desires which they have of sacrificing themselves in His service and in that of the king."

All day the cavalcade followed the Apache trail, and late in the afternoon the scouts discovered the village. They made a fireless camp, changed to fresh horses, and an hour before dawn set out to make a surprise attack. The commander gave the *Santiago,* at which cry the soldiers, vying with each other to be first, rushed in upon the Indian village "with such fury as not to give the enemy time to be frightened, and, having scarcely time to suffer death, left no chance to fear it." The Indians had no chance to resist. Some avoided death by surrendering; others sought to escape by jumping into the river, but Gálvez,

---

[6] Relación que en Extracto . . . , November 23, 1770, *ibid.,* 416.

setting an example which his soldiers followed, plunged his horse into the stream to attack the Indians in the water, "where they perished miserably between the two elements."

"And finally," as Gálvez concluded his narrative,

> out of God's great compassion the day was ended; in which only one of ours was slightly wounded, and there were counted twenty-eight Apaches killed without including those who died in the river. Thirty-six were taken prisoners, men and women, and only three escaped of the first who had risen early to bring in the horses and were not in the village when I entered it.

The pillage included 204 animals, which were divided among the Indian auxiliaries, and many buffalo hides and antelope skins to the value of 2000 pesos, "with which one and all were content."[7]

The episode is only too typical of Indian fighting in the American West and along Spain's northern frontier. The purpose of the expedition—to gain for the Spanish frontier settlements at least temporary security against Apache raids—was achieved with uncommon success. Apart from the ethical objections that may be made to the entire attitude of Caucasians toward the Indian, we must notice that Gálvez acquitted himself well. He succeeded; he justified his appointment as commandant of this frontier, not so much through brilliant military stratagem as through compelling and persuasive leadership. He was able to play upon the emotions of his men and to raise them to a high pitch of enthusiasm, under which they were willing to persevere in the face of hardships and hunger. He was intrepid and indifferent to personal danger, dashing into the thick of the fight and setting his men a valorous example.

Viceroy Croix, a very close friend of the Gálvez family (though perhaps the intimacy should not be stressed), was enthusiastic over the "glorious action" of his young friend. He took no chances that the authorities in Spain might overlook it. "I believe it my obligation," he wrote to the minister of the Indies, "to pray your excellency to see to it that the distinguished merit of Don Bernardo de Gálvez is presented to the king so that he may reap the benefits of the royal gratitude."[8]

---

[7] *Ibid..* [8] Croix to Arriaga, December 27, 1770, No. 93, *ibid.,* 512.

Six months later, after Gálvez had led a second successful expedition against the Apaches—an expedition notable because for the first time Apache captives (from the preceding foray) were persuaded to accompany the Spanish toops as guides and auxiliaries—the viceroy reiterated his request that the king's attention be directed to Gálvez' "particular merits and conduct" and recommended his promotion to the rank and pay of lieutenant colonel.[9] In September of that same year Croix complimented Gálvez on the salutary effects of his wise handling of Apache captives. Tidings of this good treatment had penetrated to the tribes and impelled them to propose to Gálvez a cessation of hostilities throughout *Apachería*.[10]

Congratulations were premature, however, for peace did not prevail. Gálvez' first report to the new viceroy, Bucareli, told of a Gila Apache raid on Chihuahua in which he was severely wounded. The Indians ran off a herd of horses and mules; they were overtaken by a corporal and fourteen men, but in the clash which followed ten of these men lost their lives and four were wounded. Twenty-four soldieds had been despatched to support the first group but had not arrived in time. Meanwhile there had been some delay in appraising Gálvez of the raid and pursuit, because he was in the parochial church where the town's patron saint was being honored with an *octavario*.[11] As soon as he learned of the crisis he hurried forth to participate.

> Notwithstanding the fact that I was convalescing from a serious illness [he wrote], and that my slight or negligible strength would have excused me from mounting a horse, as soon as the function was over and I learned that my men were after the Indians, although no soldier remained to accompany me, I set out alone to join them. It was my misfortune, however, before meeting my soldiers to encounter five Indians, who, after a long while, left me wounded, struck in the arm by an arrow and with two lance thrusts in the chest.[12]

In November of the same year Gálvez attempted to lead another expedition into the land of the Apaches, this time toward the Gila

---
[9] Croix to Arriaga, June 27, 1771, No. 1028, *ibid*. Extracto de los Diarios..., *ibid*.
[10] Croix to Arriaga, September 19, 1771, No. 1090, *ibid*.
[11] A festival lasting a week.
[12] Gálvez to Bucareli, October 18, 1771, A. G. I., Guad., 512.

region, but, receiving "a heavy blow on the chest" when thrown by his horse, he found it almost impossible to continue the campaign.[13] Even before this accident the visitor-general had asked that his nephew be relieved and allowed to return to Spain.[14] Hugo Oconor was sent to take his place, arriving at Chihuahua in December only to find that Gálvez was off on a last campaign, "from which it seems that he returned with only the gain of having captured one horse."[15] Gálvez returned to Mexico in February, escorting fourteen Apache captives, who were enrolled in the *Colegio de San Gregorio*.[16] José de Gálvez sent a courier from Vera Cruz requesting that his nephew be given special permission to hurry to the coast to sail with him for Spain.[17] The viceroy acquiesced.

Bernardo de Gálvez' career in New Spain obviously ended in somewhat less of a blaze of glory than had enhaloed him after his first Apache campaign. His persistent critic, Fayni, attributed the failure of the final campaign to poor leadership.[18] O'Reilly, though far away, also had some words of censure. "It seems to me that they [Cuellar and Gálvez] have emboldened and incited the Indians too much, and that we must now exert ourselves to the utmost to inflict exemplary punishment on them and eventually to regain their friendship."[19] Yet O'Reilly seems not to have realized what formidable antagonists the Apaches were. He expected more effective control by Oconor, but as a matter of fact the new commander's first few Apache expeditions were practically barren of results.[20]

An impartial estimate of Gálvez' work on the Chihuahua frontier must recognize that he was not so successful toward the last as earlier. It must also recognize, however, that he was handicapped in the fall

---

[13] Gálvez to Bucareli, November 29, 1771, *ibid*.

[14] Bucareli to O'Reilly, October 27, 1771, draft, mentioning the request of José de Gálvez and the designation of Hugo Oconor to relieve Bernardo de Gálvez, A. G. I., Mexico, 1242.

[15] Bucareli to Arriaga, December 27, 1771, draft, A. G. I., Ind. Gen., 1630.

[16] *Idem* to *idem*, February 23, 1772, No. 212, A. G. I., Guad., 512.

[17] José de Gálvez to Bucareli, February 17, 1772, Huntington Library, Gálvez Papers.

[18] Fayni to Pedro Garcia Mayoral, December 28, 1771, A. G. I., Guad., 338.

[19] O'Reilly to Bucareli, ———, 1772, A. G. I., Mexico, 1242.

[20] *Idem* to *idem*, February 22, 1772, *ibid*.; Bucareli to O'Reilly, October 27, November 27, December 27, 1772, drafts, *ibid*.

THE COMMENCEMENT OF GÁLVEZ' CAREER

of 1771 by impaired physical condition, chiefly the result of wounds of battle. It must reckon also with the foe, for whose fortitude and skill Gálvez expressed unfeigned admiration.[21] Viewed as a whole, Gálvez' frontier defense compares very favorably with that of more experienced men to whom Spain intrusted this knotty problem. Certainly it brought him to the attention of the court; unmistakable influences of this frontier training seem apparent in the way that he met military and Indian problems in Louisiana; and when later he became viceroy of New Spain, the jurisdiction of that office was extended again over the frontier because of his knowledge of the problem. Biographically speaking, these are the three principal fruits of his experience on the frontier.

Soon after his return to Spain, Gálvez obtained a leave of absence from Spanish service, went to France, and enrolled in the Regiment of Cantabria "to perfect himself in military science." He earned promotion to the rank of lieutenant in this organization and then returned to Spain in 1775.[22] As captain of infantry under O'Reilly in that same year, he was a member of the unfortunate landing party at Algiers and received another severe wound. By way of reward he was made a lieutenant colonel and attached to the military school at Ávila. Then in 1776 he came to Louisiana as colonel of the regiment.

He had hardly time to familiarize himself with the duties of this position before new responsibilities were thrust upon him. A royal order of September 19, 1776, instructed him to succeed Unzaga as acting governor of the colony.[23] On January 1, 1777, he took over the office.[24] On January 9 Unzaga made an inventory of the papers turned over to the new governor, and on March 22 he sailed for Caracas on the frigate "La Luisiana."[25]

---

[21] Gálvez to Bucareli, November 1, 1771, copy, A. G. I., Guad., 512.

[22] *Appleton's Cyclopaedia of American Biography*, II, 584–585.

[23] Quoted in De la Torre to José de Gálvez, December 1, 1776, No. 1282, A. G. I., Sto. Dom., 1211.

[24] Gayarré and others following him give February 1 as the date. Gayarré, *op. cit.*, III, 105; A. P. Whitaker, in *Dictionary of American Biography*, VII, 119–120. But Unzaga and Gálvez give January 1, Unzaga to Torre, January 15, 1777, No. 247, A. G. I., Cuba, 1146; Gálvez to Torre, January 28, 1777, No. 249, *ibid.*

[25] Unzaga, inventory of papers, January 9, 1777, A. G. I., Cuba, 134 A. Gálvez, statement of sailings, May 12, 1777, A. G. I., Cuba, 1146.

The authorities do not agree on Gálvez' age when he became governor of Louisiana. Gayarré and others following him say that he was twenty-one,[26] but if so he could not have been more than seven when a lieutenant in the war with Portugal and only fifteen or sixteen when fighting the Apaches. The first assumption is a bare possibility, since the lieutenant's commission was probably mostly honorary, but the second is untenable. Twenty-nine or thirty-one are more reasonable suggestions, agreeing with Fayni's statement that he was twenty-two or twenty-four in 1770,[27] and corroborated, the one by the assertion that he died at the age of thirty-eight in 1786,[28] and the other by the statement that he was born on July 23, 1746.[29] Reconciliation of all these assertions is impossible, but reasonable accuracy is served by saying in the Spanish fashion that he was about thirty, "poco mas ó menos."

With a dozen years of military service behind him the new governor was not the callow stripling that some writers indicate. But though maturity of experience was his, he was still imbued with the enthusiasm of youth. His personality, as well as his just and enlightened policies, make it easy to understand why he became so popular both as governor at New Orleans and later as viceroy at Mexico City.[30]

Gálvez' initial duties as governor are conveniently summarized in a letter that his uncle wrote on November 25, 1776.[31] A recapitulation follows. He was to require censuses at New Orleans and at the other posts, and likewise statements of annual expenses. He was to visit the provincial districts, going as far as Natchitoches, Opelousas, and Attacapas, and should obtain full written accounts of affairs at the posts beyond the Arkansas, giving special attention to the English frontier. He was to get maps of the Mississippi and of the coast from Balize to Bahía del Espíritu Santo. He was to welcome foreigners into the

---

[26] Gayarré, *op. cit.*, III, 104; Winsor, *The Westward Movement*, 149.

[27] Fayni to Arriaga, October 12, 1770, A. G. I., Guad., 512.

[28] Rivera, *Los Gobernantes de Mexico*, I, 454–458.

[29] Whitaker, in *Dictionary of American Biography*, VII, 119, following *Diccionario Geográfico, Estadístico, Histórico, de la Isla de Cuba*, II, 381–382.

[30] Bancroft, *History of Mexico*, III, 391–392; Beleña, *Recopilación Sumaria de Todos los Autos Acordados*, I, pp. i-x. Valdes, *Gazetas de Mexico*, II, 3–4.

[31] José de Gálvez to Gálvez, November 25, 1776, A. G. I., Cuba, 174.

province on condition that they be Catholics and take the oath of allegiance.

He was to take strong measures against illicit commerce, pardoning past offenders but proclaiming that future offenders would be punished severely. Trade with foreign vessels should be similarly curtailed. He was to encourage tobacco raising and was to inflict severe punishment for fraudulent packing of tobacco.

He was to cultivate the friendship of the Indians. He was instructed concerning court procedure and his relations with other colonial officials. He was urged to foster immigration and agriculture, and the minister advised an annual visitation throughout the colony.

He was to take measures to keep the slaves in subjection and to have them treated humanely. Congregation of slaves was not to be permitted, especially after dark, and precautions concerning free mulattoes were urged.

He was to organize a better-disciplined militia. Reports were requested on the religious situation, salt mines, roads, woodworkers, and on foreign money in circulation. Finally, he was to collect information about affairs in the English colonies and to send secret commissioners for the purpose.

Some of these tasks were mere routine matters, but others led to complications that are discussed in the chapters that follow.

Chapter V

TRADE REGULATION AND COLONIAL DEVELOPMENT

TRADE REGULATION was a persistent problem for the Spanish governors of Louisiana. Ulloa had incurred colonial displeasure when he endeavored to control commerce; O'Reilly attacked the problem directly by curtailing English trade and opening the door for trade with Havana; Unzaga avoided the issue by closing his eyes to smuggling;[1] Gálvez inherited the perplexity and it was one of the first that he was compelled to face.

His administration began with a prospect of hearty approval from the Louisianians, because new commercial regulations arrived almost simultaneously permitting trade with France and the French colonies, on condition merely that it be conducted through two duly appointed French commissioners, that a 5 per cent export duty be paid, that guards be put on the ships to prevent smuggling, and that the ships load only at New Orleans.[2] Villars and Favre d'Aunoy were installed as the French commissioners on February 12, 1777. The new regulations, even if strictly enforced, would have diverted much of Louisiana's trade from the English to the French. Governor Gálvez went further, interpreting the convention liberally, making the inspections of cargoes perfunctory, and permitting French ships to load anywhere on the river instead of just at New Orleans, with the result that the French commissioners could report, as early as March 30, that trade between Louisiana and the French islands was waxing prosperous.[3] At the same time Gálvez was continuing his predecessor's policy of noninterference with the illicit trade that English merchants were

---

[1] See my "Bernardo de Gálvez and the English Smugglers on the Mississippi, 1777," *Hispanic American Historical Review*, XII (1932), 46–50.

[2] The French text of the regulations is given in Villiers du Terrage, *op. cit.*, 353–354.

[3] Gayarré, *op. cit.*, III, 106.

carrying on. "Their audacity had come to such an extreme," Navarro reported, when Unzaga was governor, "that forgetting, or despising perhaps, the sacred immunity of the territory they built a dock on the land in order to facilitate the passage of the floating warehouses of their vessels."[4] Of Gálvez' first few months some of these merchants related that they "were treated with the greatest indulgence," and that every coveted privilege "was on the slightest application granted."[5]

On the night of April 17, 1777, however, Gálvez astounded these English merchants by seizing eleven boats engaged in the contraband trade, and followed up this action with a proclamation on April 18 ordering all English subjects to leave Louisiana within a fortnight.[6] In view of Spain's desire to substitute French commerce with Louisiana for English, it was logical to strike directly at the latter. Included among Gálvez' instructions when he assumed the governorship had been a strict injunction to stop smuggling.[7] Yet, if the confiscations were made because Gálvez was zealous in carrying out the royal instructions, it is difficult to explain why action was delayed until April 17. Official orders do not appear to have been the immediate cause. "Since no ships have arrived from Spain," one Englishman reasoned, "he [Gálvez] must not have been ordered to make the seizures."[8]

In his report to the king, Gálvez explained his actions in the following terms:

> I had slight hopes of being able to confiscate the English boats engaged in illicit commerce on this river. Because their merchandise is of better quality than ours for trade with the Indians, who are so accustomed to French and English goods, and since the inhabitants are deeply interested in protecting them with great secrecy, I could not believe that the natives would ever appear as accusers to their own disadvantage. But because an English ship of war seized three of our boats, which were bringing tar from their land to send from here to Havana, the people began to clamor against this inconsiderate and ungrateful nation, which through the free navigation of the river has obtained the best products of this province.

---

[4] Robertson, *Louisiana under the Rule of Spain, France, and the United States*, I, 246.
[5] British merchants to Lloyd, April 26, 1777, A. G. I., Cuba, 188–3.
[6] *Ibid.;* Gálvez to José de Gálvez, May 12, 1777, No. 40, A. G. I., Sto. Dom., 2596.
[7] José de Gálvez to Gálvez, November 25, 1776, A. G. I., Cuba, 174.
[8] Historical Manuscripts Commission, *Report on American Manuscripts*, I, 112–113.

Their resentment showed me that it would be possible to find accusers, though without this occurrence it would have been impossible, and in fact, taking advantage of the coincidence, I took the most energetic measures to manifest to his Majesty the willingness that I have pledged in fulfillment of his royal orders. Within twenty-four hours after the three mentioned boats of ours had been taken, I confiscated eleven which were employed in the contraband trade in this jurisdiction, and although most of these are entirely useless for navigation and only serve to store goods which have not a quick sale, nevertheless I have dealt them a blow which not only has thrown them into a panic, but which, I believe, is such that for some time they will not think of returning to carry on their clandestine commerce.[9]

In short, Gálvez explained that the violence done by the British frigate "West Florida" was merely a convenient pretext upon which he could gratify his long cherished desire to enforce the king's regulation against smuggling. But the British inclined to the opinion that the "West Florida" insult was the whole cause, one Pensacola officer writing that Gálvez made the seizures in anger over this incident, and that later he was sorry but could not revoke his proclamation.[10] One cannot be certain which of these two explanations is the true one, the motive of administrative zeal or of personal pique, but since some three months of Gálvez' governorship elapsed before he took any action against the smugglers, administrative zeal does not seem to have been the whole cause.

Very shortly after the confiscation of the smugglers' boats the British frigate "Atlanta," captained by Thomas Lloyd, arrived in the Mississippi on the way to the British posts at Manchac and Baton Rouge. While still seven leagues below New Orleans, Lloyd addressed a polite letter of protest to Gálvez anent the recent confiscations.[11] In reply, Gálvez reproached Lloyd for interfering with Spanish shipping on the Mississippi. On the evening of April 21, according to the testi-

---

[9] Gálvez to José de Gálvez, May 12, 1777, No. 40, A. G. I., Sto. Dom., 2596.

[10] Stiell to Howe, June 3, 1777, Historical Manuscripts Commission, *op. cit.*, I, 115-116.

[11] "On my arriving in the River, to my great surprise heard that you had seized the Vessels belonging to his Britannick Maj's. Subjects, and put the Masters with their Crews in confinement, I must Beg that your Excellency will give me your reasons for this unexpected proceeding, as it is my duty (having the Honour to Command one of His Majs. Ships of War) to inquire into the particulars, that His Subjects may get redress."—Lloyd to Gálvez, April, 1777, A. G. I., Cuba, 188-3.

mony of a passenger, the French boat "Margarita" and the Spanish boat "Marie" were stopped by the "Atlanta," two loaded cannon being fired at the "Marie." The "Margarita" was boarded "with pistols and sabres," and both boats were detained some time.[12] Lloyd replied to the governor that he suspected that the boats belonged to the Rebels and that after discovering his error he allowed them to proceed.[13]

Several letters were exchanged concerning the confiscations. While thanking Gálvez for his friendship and for past favors to the British, Lloyd pointed out that the treaty of 1763 permitted British ships to navigate the Mississippi, and he claimed that they were "exempt from visitation."[14] The Spanish governor admitted that navigation of the Mississippi was permissible, but not contraband trade. He made much' of the fact that the vessels seized were tied to the Spanish shore, and reminded Lloyd that two of the eleven boats seized were American, not British.[15]

Nevertheless, Gálvez realized that he was in an awkward predicament. He boasted to the captain general of Cuba, "I received them with match in hand, not to allow any violence, and I believe that this precaution is what checked them." In the next breath, however, he added, "But I have been assured that they have requested another frigate from Pensacola, doubtless with the hope of undertaking with stronger forces that which they do not dare alone." And realizing that two frigates would almost suffice for the capture of his capital, Gálvez concluded his letter with an appeal for reënforcements, both naval and military.[16]

On May 12 the fears of Governor Gálvez were allayed unexpectedly when Lloyd departed from New Orleans, sending a letter with

---

[12] Gálvez to Lloyd, April 26, 1777, draft, A. G. I., Cuba, 188-3; affidavit of James Willing before Gálvez, April 25, 1777, *ibid.*

[13] Lloyd to Gálvez, April, 1777, *ibid.*

[14] Lloyd to Gálvez, May 4, 1777, *ibid.* O'Reilly had limited this right of navigation very seriously, however, and although Great Britain had protested, the Spanish government had approved his policy. Brown, "Anglo-Spanish Relations in America," *loc. cit.*, 370-371.

[15] Gálvez to Lloyd, May, 1777, draft, A. G. I., Cuba, 188-3

[16] Gálvez to De la Torre, May 6, 1777, No. 261, *ibid.*, 1146.

the word that he was going to investigate the report of an American privateer at the mouth of the Mississippi.[17]

Although Lloyd might explain his departure by the appearance of the American privateer, and though Gálvez might claim that his determined stand "with match in hand" had dissuaded the Englishman from making more strenuous protests, some of the credit for the peaceful termination of Lloyd's visit should go to the English merchants of New Orleans, who had advised Lloyd as follows:

We had the honor to receive your letter 24th Instant, informing us of the motive of your voyage hither, and requiring us to wait on you in order to communicate the particulars of the late Seizure of the British·vessells in this river.

In the fear of offending his Excellency the Spanish Governor, we must decline at present the Honor of waiting on you, but shall lay before you a brief narrative of the matter.

From the time that the present Governor The Count de Galvez, took possession of his Government, the British subjects here were treated with the greatest indulgence; every priviledge we could wish for, was on the Slightest application granted to us and from the known Generosity & humanity of that Gentleman we had reason to hope for a long duration of these advantages.

It was therefore with much surprise that on the night of the 17th Instant we found the British Vessells seized on, and a proclamation issued out next day ordering all British subjects to quit the Spanish territories in fifteen days.

It appears that the Governor was induced to proceed to these extremities by the Seizure of a small Schooner and two Canoes in Lake Pontchertrain by His Majestys Armed Schooner the West Florida. These it seems were said to be Spanish property, and he accordingly resented the act as an insult to his nation. Whether they were really Spanish property, or that the matter was misrepresented to him, we are yet uncertain.

At any rate the Governor considers the Seizure of that Craft which had nothing on board save a few Barrells of tar as an ungenerous act, the advantages reaped by the English in consequence of his indulgence being out

---

[17] "My duty requires me to leave you so abruptly, having received more information last night, which obliges me to drop down the River to receive one of the Privateers belonging to His Brittanick Majs. Rebellious Subjects, I am informed that she is now in the Mississippi and mounts thirty Six Guns, called the Columbus commanded by one Barry. it is the Vessel that you mentioned to me yesterday of her being an English Frigate."—Lloyd to Gálvez, May 12, 1777, *ibid.*, 188–3.

of all proportion to the trivial benefit his province received by drawing its Tar from the English Lands.

The Masters and Crews of the Vessells are in prison and their tryal is now carrying on. Several of the Vessells will probably be Condemned, supposing to have committed Acts of Contraband, but some of them have circumstances greatly in their favour, and against which nothing can be urged, save their having a plank or Stage from the Gunnell to the shore, a matter which in the tryal is said to be regarded as of much consequence. In other respects the Governor has relaxed from the Severity we were threatened with, and has consented to our Staying with the usual priviledges for the collection of our Debts and settlement of our Affairs, and indeed in every other particular seems to be inclinable to put matters on their ancient footing.[18]

It is from the Confiscation of the Vessells alone that any loss is to be dreaded; on that subject you will probably be applied to by the individuals who suffer, in that case, should you think it necessary to interfere, we beg leave to recommend to you moderate measures, for it is in the power of Mr. Galvez to hurt the British Merchants here far beyond the value of the Shipping seized.[19]

The departure of the "Atlanta" was not quite the end of the matter. The owners of the two American ships confiscated asked special consideration, "since the subjects of those provinces are so highly favored by our sovereign in their actual revolution." Gálvez replied that commerce was "prohibited as much for them as for the European English," but promised to submit the matter to the king for his consideration.[20] According to Gayarré these American boats were secretly released after a short while.[21]

In August two commissioners from Pensacola appeared in New Orleans to intercede for the British merchants. Their arguments were those of Lloyd elaborated. They asserted that the seizures of the British boat crews were illegal, they being not amenable to Spanish contraband laws because of the right of British ships to navigate the Missis-

---

[18] This action indicates that Gálvez was impelled somewhat less by administrative zeal than would appear from his report to José de Gálvez. The confiscations were apparently an impetuous act that Gálvez sought to justify on the basis of Spain's exclusive policy.
[19] British merchants of New Orleans to Lloyd, April 26, 1777, A. G. I., Cuba, 188–3.
[20] Gálvez to José de Gálvez, May 12, 1777, No. 40, A. G. I., Sto. Dom., 2596.
[21] Gayarré, *op. cit.*, III, 107.

sippi. They objected also to the Spanish method of taking testimony in jail, alleging that some of the sailors had sworn falsely in order to get out of prison with their personal effects. They insisted that Spanish officials had no right to search English vessels, even though they were moored to the Spanish bank.[22]

Their protests were fruitless. Just two days after the commissioners lodged their complaints at New Orleans, the Spanish court approved Gálvez' confiscations.[23] Patrick Morgan, owner of one of the vessels, petitioned the king for its release on the ground that he was a resident of New Orleans and merely had commercial relations with a London firm. But the *fiscal,* to whom the question was referred, thought this even worse.[24] Ten years later the question of the seizures was reviewed by the Council of the Indies, but no action was taken in favor of the British merchants.[25]

In the meantime Gálvez obligingly again closed his eyes to the English smuggling, and trade was resumed "on its ancient footing," greatly to the satisfaction of all concerned. Commerce with the English, however, enjoyed only a temporary revival. By a series of proclamations in that same year, 1777, Louisiana was given freedom of commerce with Yucatan and Cuba, the export duty at New Orleans was reduced to 2 per cent, and permission to import Guinea negroes was given once more to the French.[26] The result was complete destruction of British trade. "The British flag," the French commissioners reported on July 18, 1778, "has not appeared on this river for more than three months.... The duties to be paid by our ships... are reduced every day.... The whole trade of the Mississippi is now in our hands."[27] As a consequence of the new Spanish commercial policy as interpreted by Gálvez, English contraband trade with Louisiana

---

[22] Alexander Dickson and Stephenson to Gálvez, August 2, and August 17, 1777, A. G. I., Cuba, 188-3.

[23] José de Gálvez to Gálvez, August 19, 1777, *ibid.,* 174.

[24] *Respuesta del Sor. Fiscal,* November 21, 1779, copy, A. G. I., Sto. Dom., 2652.

[25] *Ibid.* This entire *legajo* concerns Gálvez' confiscations. There are *testimonios* concerning the vessels of "Juan Waugk, Norton, Juan Cambel, P. Morgan, Ros y Compa., Thomas Collar, and Jphn. Calvert."

[26] Proclamations of Gálvez, April 18, 1777, A. G. I., Cuba, 1232; July 15, 1777, *ibid.;* November 21, 1777, B. L., La. Coll.

[27] Gayarré, *op. cit.,* III, 117-118.

was almost extinguished even before Spain's entrance in the war against Great Britain in 1779 put a final stop to it.

Gálvez sought to encourage agriculture as well as commerce. The Spanish government had agreed to make annual purchases of tobacco to the amount of $800,000 in the hope of stimulating the Louisiana planters and of acquiring a cheap supply for the tobacco monopoly in Mexico and for sale to France.[28] Gálvez convened a meeting of the planters to deliberate upon a fair price, and they agreed upon seven livres a pound for leaf tobacco and ten for tobacco in *carottes*. A proclamation to that effect was issued on June 15, 1777.[29] After having made arrangements with the viceroy of New Spain about prices, methods of grading, packing, shipping, etc., Gálvez promised to buy the entire crop of the colony.[30] The French commissioners were very optimistic about the future of tobacco culture in Louisiana. "Enjoying a better climate than Maryland and Virginia," they wrote, "Louisiana, on account of its extent and fertility, could furnish the world with tobacco."[31] Although production fell considerably short of this rosy estimate, the export to Mexico in 1777 sold for more than 50,000 pesos.[32]

The strongest deterrent to tobacco culture and to agricultural development in general was a shortage of labor. When the government urged, for example, the cultivation of hemp and flax, the colonists of Upper Louisiana replied "that they were going to make all possible efforts" but could not "expect a large crop," and petitioned the king to "make easier for them the method by which they might acquire some negro slaves."[33] The king ordered that negroes be supplied them on credit. And on November 21, 1777, Gálvez published a proclamation authorizing the introduction of Guinea negroes. The embargo against negroes from the islands, however, was expressly reaffirmed.[34]

---

[28] Gayarré, *op. cit.*, III, 107.
[29] Proclamation of Gálvez, June 15, 1777, A. G. I., Cuba, 1232.
[30] Bucareli to José de Gálvez, September 25, 1777, No. 3325, A. G. I., Mexico, 89-4-9; Gayarré, *op. cit.*, III, 107.
[31] Quoted in Gayarré, *loc. cit.*
[32] Bucareli to José de Gálvez, September 25, 1777, No. 3325, A. G. I., Mexico, 89-4-9.
[33] Houck, *op. cit.*, I, 158-159.
[34] Proclamation of Gálvez, November 21, 1777, B. L., La. Coll.

A census taken shortly after Gálvez became governor revealed that population had increased but slightly since the close of the French period. The figures were:[85]

District of New Orleans			
Balize	42	Whites	8381
New Orleans	3202	Free Mulattoes	273
Right Bank	1747	Free Negroes	263
Left Bank	3206	Mulatto Slaves	545
Bayou Gentilly	411	Negro Slaves	8464
Total	8428	Total	17926
		Able to bear arms	1956
[Other Districts]			
German Coast	2617		
Acadian Coast	1363		
Iberville	437		
Pointe Coupée	1635		
Opelousas and Attakapas	1072		
Natchitoches and Rapide	740		
Arkansas	81		
Illinois	1448		
Capuchins	10		
Nuns	15		
Hunters	80		
[Total	9498]		
Total	17926		

It is apparent, therefore, that importation of slaves was only a partial remedy; for the sake of prosperity and strengthened defenses Louisiana needed more white settlers. Spain redoubled her efforts to attract settlers by promises of paternalistic protection. Advertising was the first artificial stimulant employed. French coasting vessels were requested to broadcast the inducements of Louisiana to the inhabitants of the French West Indies. Learning of this attempt to proselyte colonists, the French commissioners were inspired to write, "If it be Frenchmen who are to be relied upon for the cultivation of Louisi-

---

[85] Census report, May 12, 1777, certified copy, A. G. I., Cuba, 2351.

ana, it seems to us more natural that his most Christian Majesty should resume the possession of the colony."[36]

Immigrants received actual assistance as well as invitations. By order of the governor families were to be located in the most suitable places, were to receive plots of ground five arpents in frontage, as well as rations of maize during the first year at the rate of a barrel a head for adults and half a barrel for children. In addition each family was given "an axe, a hoe, a scythe or a sickle, a spade, two hens, a cock, and a pig of two months, with which they may easily found and establish a household which will provide them a living, or may even make their fortune."[37]

Early in 1778, a considerable number of people was brought over at the king's expense from the Canary Islands. Some of these families, under the command of Marigny de Mandeville, Gálvez' brother-in-law, formed a new settlement at Terre-aux-Boeufs, to the east of the Mississippi about twelve miles below New Orleans. Others went to Bayou Lafourche, about eighty miles above New Orleans, where they formed the village of Valenzuela. The rest, directed by St. Maxent, Gálvez' father-in-law, settled opposite the mouth of the Amite River, some twenty-four miles below Baton Rouge.[38] Royal aid was given to these settlers in the building of their houses and the erection of a church in each settlement, in addition to gifts of implements and stock.

Meanwhile, English and American refugees from the disturbances of the American Revolution had discovered and occupied a site in Spanish territory about sixty miles northwest of New Orleans. These refugees "formed a small village," Gálvez wrote, "to which they gave the name of Gálveztown [villa de Gálvez], asking me not to change the name, since in consideration of their having gathered at this refuge during my governorship they wished by the said name to give an indication of their gratitude and a notice of the period of its foundation."[39] Their attachment to Spain found other expression. "To demonstrate

---

[36] Quoted in Gayarré, *op. cit.*, III, 108.
[37] Proclamation of Gálvez, February 19, 1778, *in* Houck, *op. cit.*, I, 155-157.
[38] Martin, *op. cit.*, II, 43.
[39] Gálvez to José de Gálvez, January 15, 1779, A. G. I., Sto. Dom., 2574.

the love and affection that the habitants of this place have toward the Spanish nation," wrote Collell, the commandant of the district, "they asked me to give each one of their houses a Spanish name; to which request I acceded and gave the following names." A list of seventeen settlers is given, together with the names given to their houses in honor of the various members of the Spanish royal family, of José and Bernardo de Gálvez, and of several of Spain's officers in Louisiana.[40]

Gálvez recommended this site at the confluence of the Amite and Iberville for the settlement of a third group of poor colonists from the Canary Islands. He described it as the only elevated region on the island of New Orleans,[41] and pointed out that its occupation would protect New Orleans against an English or Indian surprise attack, that it would have excellent communications with New Orleans by land and water, and that it was athwart the only practicable route between the English stations, Mobile and Manchac. The governor, however, was limited to a written description of the location, because the death of Luis Andry, "the only person in the country who could make exact maps," gave him the embarrassment of being unable to send a map showing the site of the colony.[42]

For the Canary Islanders brought into Louisiana, Gálvez had not much admiration but a great deal of compassion. He reported of the 1582 who had arrived up to July 7, 1779, that 329 were married recruits with 1100 dependents, women and children, and only 153 were unmarried recruits. Since the soldier's pay was only a peso and a half a day in silver, married soldiers found is practically impossible to support their families, "much less these 329, most of whom had families of five or six persons, and some of nine or ten." Consequently he deemed it advisable to excuse these married recruits from military

---

[40] In the list some of the English names are recognizable even after the attempt to render them into Spanish: Luis Deves (Davis), Leandro Deves, Wet (West), Moris (Morris), Bernat, Quenti, Reeli (Riley), Gulvi, Guillermo (William), Nikolson, Gre (Gray), Huescat, Escot (Scott), Reynals (Reynolds), Paquer (Packer), Simon. Collell to Gálvez, January 15, 1779, A. G. I., Cuba, 2351.

[41] The triangle between the Iberville, the Mississippi, and the Gulf.

[42] Gálvez to José de Gálvez, January 19, 1779, A. G. I., Sto. Dom., 2574; Scramuzza, "Gálveztown, a Spanish Settlement of Colonial Louisiana," *Louisiana Historical Quarterly*, XIII (1930), 553–609; Plan of the Costa de Iberville, August 14, 1779, A. G. I., Cuba, 2351.

service, though this was the condition of their transportation to Louisiana, and to establish them simply as agricultural settlers. The 153 bachelors, along with 106 men from Mexico, would suffice to complete the battalion.[43]

Almost five hundred settlers from Málaga arrived in 1779. Francisco Bouligny conducted them to Bayou Teche, a region already occupied by a few Acadians. A settlement called New Iberia was founded. The new immigrants were treated even more liberally than their predecessors. They received cattle and money, as well as lands, implements, and houses.[44] The new settlers, at the instigation of the government, made serious attempts to raise flax and hemp, but finding the culture difficult they concentrated on cattle raising, an industry for which the region was ideal.[45] The populating of Louisiana proved an expensive undertaking. In 1779, for example, the Louisiana Division of Immigration and Indian Affairs expended 128,568 pesos instead of the 40,000 allowed by the royal budget, and the excess was due chiefly to the influx of settlers.[46]

At the same time methods of procuring settlers for Spanish Illinois were being considered. Cruzat asked permission to dangle inducements before the French Canadians, whom he considered desirable citizens because they were good farmers and good Catholics. Aid was necessary, however, "because they are so poor that when they arrive in these settlements they come burdened with a family, but have not a shirt to wear." He believed they could be persuaded to move because "in being forced to bear arms against the *Bostoneses* and in having the labor needed to support their families cut off, they are much irritated."[47] Gálvez immediately ordered that announcement be made

---

[43] Gálvez to José de Gálvez, July 7, 1779, No. 304, A. G. I., Sto. Dom., 2662.

[44] Hatcher, "The Louisiana Background of the Colonization of Texas," *Southwestern Historical Quarterly*, XXIII (1920), 170; Gálvez to José de Gálvez, January 15, 1779, No. 233, A. G. I., Sto. Dom., 2574; Robertson, *op. cit.*, I, 248; Martin, *op. cit.*, II, 46.

[45] Gayarré, *op. cit.*, III 120.

[46] "Ramao de Población y Amistad de Indios: items as usual, augmented by the extra expenditures on account of the arrival of settlers, transportation of Indians, Indian gifts, etc. . . . . . . 1,028,544 reales de plata." (A peso was worth eight silver reales.)— Cunningham, "Financial Reports Relating to Louisiana," *Mississippi Valley Historical Review*, VI (1919), 385.

[47] Cruzat to Gálvez, December 8, 1777, *in* Houck, *op. cit.*, I, 153-154.

that such immigrants would "receive the assistance necessary to make a beginning in establishing themselves," and the king signified his approval. Regulations for the dispensing of royal aid were sent to Illinois.[48] Reports on the population of Spanish Illinois, however, do not give the impression that many French Canadians took advantage of this opportunity to move across the Mississippi.[49]

The Marquis de Croix, as commander of the Provincias Internas, was planning a compaign against the Apaches at this time, and hoped to have his forces augmented by three or four hundred Louisiana hunters under Gálvez in person. But Croix and Gálvez, who had campaigned together in Nueva Vizcaya, missed out on this reunion, because the English menace in Louisiana was too insistent to permit Gálvez to leave.[50] Although he was denied the thrill of the Apache foray, Gálvez had a great deal to do in Indian affairs in his province, and until military duties monopolized his attention he kept in close touch with De Mézières at Natchitoches, with Cruzat and De Leyba at St. Louis, and with the other Indian agents of the colony.[51]

In a characteristic communication dealing with relations with the Indians, Gálvez reported that the chiefs of two tribes that had recently abandoned the English territory and moved across the river surrendered to him three medals and a gollet with which they had been decorated by the English. They requested similar insignia from Gálvez, and he promised to present them as soon as received from the king.

> These people are sensitive, and it is necessary to receive them and entertain them and even to bear their impertinences, though at the same time without allowing them to forget our superiority and the respect that they owe us. I have the patience to treat them thus for the sake of the king's service, and seat the chiefs at my table when they come to see me in order to receive favors.[52]

---

[48] Gálvez to José de Gálvez, January 27, 1778, *ibid.*, I, 152–157.
[49] Viles, *op. cit.*, 189–213.
[50] Bolton, *Athanase de Mézières*, I, 111, II, 171, 218–224. Gálvez to José de Gálvez, June 9, 1778, A. G. I., Sto. Dom., 2547.
[51] Bolton, *op. cit.*, II, 122–336; Houck, *op. cit.*, I, 134–252.
[52] Gálvez to José de Gálvez, April 12, 1778, No. 141, A. G. I., Sto. Dom., 2596.

Gálvez was the first Spanish governor of Louisiana who had a background of experience on the old northern frontier of New Spain. On the basis, therefore, of his personal experience as commandant of the Nueva Vizcaya and Sonora frontier, he was as well qualified as any Spaniard to compare the Spanish and French methods of Indian control. An exhaustive study of his judgments of the French trader system, particularly in the Red River region which reached out toward the Apache country, would prove interesting and instructive. Here it will suffice to quote a paragraph in which he weighed the merits of the two systems.

The knowledge which I have acquired since I have been in this colony of the way in which the English and French treat or have treated their Indians impels me to desire that in our other establishments they should be treated in the same way. I do not know whether under the present circumstances the method could be installed of keeping them friendly by means of presents; if it should be possible to do so, the King would keep them very contented for ten years with what he now spends in one year in making war upon them; in addition to this advantage and the innumerable advantages which our Internal Provinces would gain, the Indians would forget how to make war upon us; and, a sort of luxury being introduced among them by means of commerce, they would reach the point, as have all in this province, of being unable to do without us, because they have learned sundry conveniences of life of whose existence they previously knew nothing, and which they now look on as indispensable. Moreover, they would have the same experience as the Indians here, who, becoming accustomed to guns and powder, have forgotten the use and construction of their bows and arrows, knowing no other arms than those we give them, living exposed to the danger of being disarmed and dying of hunger from any moment when in common accord we European nations should cease to give them the powder they need. I know that years would pass before the frontier Indians of New Spain would reach this point, and that we should not see them do so in our own time. But the life of kingdoms is long; and so long as the glorious house of Bourbon shall reign and the ministry be held by men so devoted to their sovereign and to their country as Your Excellency, we must hope that the kingdom of Spain may continue for many centuries in splendor, and that this system may contribute greatly to the security and happiness of her vassals.[53]

---

[53] Gálvez to José de Gálvez, October 24, 1778, quoted in West, "The Indian Policy of Bernardo de Gálvez," *Mississippi Valley Historical Association, Proceedings,* VIII (1914–1915), 100–101.

Other developments in Gálvez' civil administration cannot be taken up in detail, but one deserves special mention. Some of the Spanish officers at New Orleans quite understandably succumbed to the charms of the creole beauties. Jacinto Panis, the adjutant major, implored the king's permission to marry Margarethe Wiltz, widow of Joseph Milhet, one of the men put to death in punishment of the insurrection.[54] Likewise Estevan Miró, sergeant major of the battalion and future governor of the colony, sought and received the king's permission to marry Marie Céleste Elénore de Macarty.[55] Following the good example of his brother officers, Governor Gálvez married Félicie de St. Maxent d'Estréhan, the widow of Jean Baptiste Honoré d'Estréhan.[56]

By all accounts they were a very happy couple; certainly the marriage enhanced Gálvez' popularity and political appeal as well as his financial standing. The Louisianians were flattered that their governor selected a daughter of the colony to be his wife. Nor was the charm and winsomeness of Doña Félicie of merely local appeal; she won just as enthusiastic approval in Mexico City and was one of the chief factors in her husband's great popularity there as viceroy.

In administering the domestic affairs of Louisiana, Gálvez deserves credit for a few outstanding accomplishments. The various measures by which the commerce of the colony was taken out of English hands and turned over in large part to the French constituted an important reform. As superintendent of immigration he brought about a more enduring improvement. His most noteworthy service to Spain, however, was the intangible one of captivating the creoles by his policies, his marriage, and his personal charm. According to Navarro, the "mildness of the laws and the graciousness and humanity" of the governor contributed in great part to the happiness of the Louisianians and to their loyalty to Spain.[57]

---

[54] Jacinto Panis to the king, petition endorsed by Unzaga, February 15, 1776, A. G. I., Sto. Dom., 2547; Arthur and Kernion, *Old Families of Louisiana*, 231.

[55] In remitting Miró's memorial Gálvez vouched for the young lady's nobility and dowry. Gálvez to José de Gálvez, May 27, 1779, No. 284, draft, A. G. I., Cuba, 223C; Arthur and Kernion, *op. cit.*, 333.

[56] *Ibid.*, 414.

[57] Robertson, *op. cit.*, I, 247.

CHAPTER VI

AID FOR THE AMERICAN REVOLUTIONISTS

THROUGHOUT THE YEARS in which he sought solutions for Louisiana's domestic problems, Gálvez was rendering important though unostentatious assistance to the patriots in the American Revolution. In view of the spectacular campaigns of George Rogers Clark, and of the inconspicuous but momentous work of Oliver Pollock, the two Americans most instrumental in securing the trans-Alleghany region for the United States, it would be folly to claim for Gálvez entire credit for the success of the Revolution in the West. It is justifiable, however, to include him with Clark and Pollock in a triumvirate to which the honors are due. Much of Gálvez' assistance was given before Spain had entered the war against England.

Of course Spain took a lively interest in the Revolution from the start. Her Louisiana officials in particular were directed to submit in full and frequent reports whatever echoes of the struggle reached them. Her policy, nevertheless, was not very clearly defined; and Unzaga, lacking specific instructions, was in a quandary about how he ought to treat the various Tories and Rebels with whom he came in contact. In all probability he would have followed a policy of strict neutrality had it not been for the influence of Oliver Pollock, an Irish-American who deserves further introduction.

In Louisiana Pollock had the initial advantage of a personal friendship with O'Reilly. He had met the general at Havana, being introduced by Father Butler, and their mutual Irish extraction and Pollock's mastery of the Spanish language had done the rest.[1] Their friendship was cemented, after both had come to New Orleans, by the

---
[1] Deposition of Oliver Pollock, June 8, 1808, *in* Wilkinson, *Memoirs of My Own Times*, II, appendix I.

American's generosity in relieving the danger of famine there. Pollock's favorable position continued after O'Reilly's departure. "It is notorious," General Wilkinson stated some years later, "that Mr. Pollock's connection with the Spanish officers, at New Orleans, was the most intimate, and his influence boundless, from the administration of Governor O'Reilly to that of Governor Miro."[2] Concerning his relations with Unzaga, Pollock himself said, "I was introduced to him by General O'Reilly, just before he left the colony, and the same intimacy subsisted with him, that I before enjoyed with O'Reilly; and during the whole of his government, I supplied the country frequently with provisions, dry goods and negroes."[3]

From the outset of hostilities between England and her colonies Pollock was an ardent partisan of the latter. His first opportunity to serve the cause came in the summer of 1776 when Captain George Gibson and Lieutenant Linn arrived at New Orleans. Disguised as traders these officers had journeyed down the Ohio and Mississippi from Fort Pitt, bringing to the "Governor of New Orleans" a letter from Charles Lee and a note of introduction from the "Committee of Safety."[4] In a fashion that may have been characteristic, Lee explained the sending of these emissaries. He began by sketching his own biography and wrote with feeling on the causes of the Revolution. Then, after mentioning the "generosity of Spaniards," he sought to demonstrate that Spain had a real interest in the Revolution and should assist the Americans as a means of insuring Spanish America against English invasion. He concluded:

> Consequently, they [the Americans] flatter themselves that not only humanity and generosity but also interest, honor, and the security of your soverign will dictate to your excellency the means to supply us the articles we lack, which consist of muskets, blankets, and medicinal drugs, particularly quinine.[5]

---

[2] Wilkinson, *op. cit.*, II, 150.

[3] Deposition of Oliver Pollock, June 8, 1808, *ibid.*

[4] Edmd. Pendleton, John Page, Dudley Digges, P. Carrington, Jas. Mercer, Thos. Lud: Lee, W. Cabell, and John Tabb to the "Governor of New Orleans," May 22, 1776, A. G. I., Sto. Dom., 2596; Lee to the governor of Louisiana, May —, 1776, *ibid.*

[5] *Ibid.*

The American need for powder was the thing that Gibson stressed in his conversations with Unzaga, and it was in terms of powder that his voyage had its greatest effectiveness. Only through Pollock's intercession was the governor persuaded to accede to the request.[6] "Unzaga ... privately delivered me gunpowder out of the King's store," Pollock stated, "which I delivered to Colonel Gibson, in the American service."[7] Gibson paid for the powder with a draft on the "Grand Council of Virginia" for the "sum of One Thousand Eight Hundred and Fifty Spanish mill'd Dollars ... for value received."[8]

Linn took three-fourths of the powder up the river, getting it to Forts Pitt and Wheeling just in time to save those posts from falling into the hands of the British and Indians. Gibson submitted to arrest at New Orleans so that British West Florida would not have grounds to question Louisiana's neutrality, but he was released shortly and sent with the rest of the powder and other supplies by boat to Philadelphia.[9] "Gunpowder was actually shipp'd and sent up the River Mississippi to be forwarded by way of the Ohio to the Americans," according to an anonymous commentator, "and ... was also sent to Philadelphia by a vessel fitted out by one Pollock from New Orleans, to Welling and Morris, which vessel arrived safe."[10] These two shipments of powder were the only ones sent to the Revolutionists during the governorship of Unzaga, but the latter had become sufficiently acquainted with Pollock to suggest to his successor "that if the court of Spain was going to take part with Great Britain, Oliver Pollock should not remain in the country twenty-four hours," but if, on the contrary, "they were going to take part with France, Oliver Pollock was the only man he could confide in, in the colony, meaning [the only] English merchant."[11]

---

[6] Winsor, *op. cit.*, 148.
[7] Deposition of Oliver Pollock, June 8, 1808, *loc. cit.*
[8] Gibson to Unzaga, September 21, 1776, A. G. I., Cuba, 573.
[9] Thwaites and Kellogg, *Frontier Defense on the Upper Ohio*, 226; Deposition of Oliver Pollock, June 8, 1808, *loc. cit.*
[10] "Commerce Up Ye Mississippi," *in* Historical Manuscripts Commission, *op. cit.*, I, 113.
[11] Deposition of Oliver Pollock, June 8, 1808, *loc. cit.*

From the outset the new governor displayed his partiality toward the Americans. He disrupted English contraband commerce, it will be recalled, while at the same time he granted favors to American shipping. New Orleans was opened to American privateers for the sale of prizes. In 1777, when the captain of a British frigate protested against the harboring of Captain Barry and the American privateer "Columbus," Gálvez promptly replied that his king had accorded immunity on the river to all such ships. "Whoever fights on the river," he warned, "will incur the disapproval of my sovereign, and in consideration of my duty I would have to oppose to the extent of my power."[12] The British prudently refrained from molesting American ships at New Orleans.

The contrast between the vigorous pro-Americanism of Gálvez and the lukewarmness of Unzaga is usually explained by their contrasting personalities. The old governor was cautious and conservative, the new governor daring and impetuous. Personalities help elucidation, but an order from the court deserves mention.

On February 20, 1777, two royal orders were despatched to the governor of Louisiana. The first read: "the bearer will be a commissioner or factor of a Spanish merchant who sends various effects to your province for sale there; they are to be deposited in warehouses, which must be furnished, and are to be entered free of duty."[13] An invoice revealed that these goods consisted of

6 cases of quinine, 8 cases of other medicines, 108 bolts of woolen cloth and serge, 100 hundredweights of powder in 100 barrels, and 300 muskets with bayonets in 30 boxes.[14]

Obviously, trade goods such as these were not for an ordinary market. A secret despatch of the same date explained that these goods belonged to the king, but since it would be "inconvenient to send them in his royal name to the succor of the English colonies," they were entrusted to a merchant who would be the nominal owner. He would "sell"

---

[12] Lloyd to Gálvez, May 12, 1777, A. G. I., Sto. Dom., 2661; Gálvez to Lloyd, May 12, 1777, *ibid*.

[13] Royal order to the governor of Louisiana, February 20, 1777, draft, A. G. I., Sto. Dom., 1598.

[14] Torre, Noticia de los efectos remitidos á la Nueva Orleans..., May 9, 1777, *ibid*.

AID FOR THE AMERICANS

them to General Lee's agent, but Gálvez and the other colonial officials were to shun all connection with the transaction, "so that England could never argue that Spain had aided her insurgent foes, and that the most she could charge would be that our merchants sold them the necessary goods."[15]

Since Gálvez, because of his short residence in New Orleans, might not know a local merchant who could be entrusted with such delicate business, one was to be sent from Spain or Havana—the final choice being Miguel Eduardo of Havana.[16] The king entrusted direction of this important secret commission to Gálvez, hoping that he would perform it with sagacity, tact, and maturity as well as with vigor and zeal.[17] Gálvez reported Eduardo's arrival on May 13 and pledged his most earnest efforts to carry out the king's orders.[18]

But difficulties arose almost at once. Having held other commissions in the king's service, Eduardo was immediately an object of suspicion, and it was soon noised abroad that the goods he was managing belonged to the king. The method prescribed for delivering the supplies to the Revolutionists being thus quite discredited, Gálvez took the responsibility of suggesting another plan characterized by complicated artifice. First, Eduardo must be sent back to Havana, his presence having prejudiced the commission enough already. Secondly, it would be best to admit what had become notorious, that these goods belonged to the king. Gálvez would say that the powder was to replace some that had deteriorated in the warehouse, that the muskets were for the battalion, the woolen cloth to clothe the same corps, and the quinine for the king's hospital. Nothing would remain to be done then except to transfer these supplies to the Americans without rousing suspicion.

In this incident a single true statement, instead of the proverbial lie, was to entail a whole series of falsehoods. Concerning the cloth Gálvez proposed to pretend that it had been rejected for the regiments of Havana, that it was moth-eaten and of bad quality, and that since the

---

[15] Royal order to the governor of Louisiana, February 20, 1777, reservada, draft, *ibid*.
[16] Royal order to the governor of Louisiana, February 22, 1777, draft, *ibid*.
[17] Royal order to the governor of Louisiana, February 20, 1777, reservada, draft, *ibid*.
[18] Gálvez to José de Gálvez, May 13, 1777, No. 52, *ibid*.

king wanted his troops well clad it would be sold. A reliable merchant of New Orleans, sworn to secrecy, would purchase the cloth and forward it clandestinely to its destination. For the powder he proposed that this same merchant should apply for "some barrels of whatever other commodity has about the same weight" as powder, that the head of one barrel should be knocked in, revealing nonexplosive contents, after which the barrels of powder should be taken away without a voucher from the superintendent of the warehouse. The same method was to be utilized for the quinine and muskets.

These pretenses might dissemble sufficiently this shipment of supplies for the Revolutionists, but Gálvez was dubious about his ability to avoid English suspicion of subsequent shipments unless they were better managed at Havana. He urged that the captain general be more cautious and that there be no official registry or bills of lading, such as had betrayed the king's connection with this shipment. He advocated that later consignments of this sort ought to be smuggled into Louisiana, since they would attract less notice thus than if brought in openly without payment of duties.[19] The king approved Gálvez' complicated *modus operandi* and authorized him "to proceed as it might seem most proper and convenient in this so interesting and delicate matter."[20]

Later in the summer Gálvez received a letter from George Morgan, the American commander at Fort Pitt, importuning various sorts of Spanish assistance. Morgan had in mind an expedition against Pensacola and Mobile, provided Gálvez approved and provided he could count on getting transports, artillery, powder, and provisions at New Orleans. Whether or not this remarkable request should be met, Morgan hoped that Gálvez would at least permit the Americans "to trade freely with New Orleans."[21]

Although Gálvez had been ordered "to endeavor to incite them [the Americans] by secret confidences to the conquest of Pensacola and

---

[19] Gálvez to José de Gálvez, June 2, 1777, No. 61, A. G. I., Sto. Dom., 1598.

[20] Royal order to Gálvez, October 13, 1777, copy, *ibid.*

[21] Morgan to Gálvez, April 22, 1777, enclosed in Gálvez to José de Gálvez, August 9, 1777, No. 78, A. G. I., Sto. Dom., 2596; Morgan's letter is quoted in Gayarré, *op. cit.*, III, 109–110.

the other posts which the English have on the right bank of the river and in the neighborhood,"[22] yet he was not anxious to encourage military activity in the purlieus of New Orleans. His response to Morgan, therefore, was equivocal. "Although it would please me greatly," he wrote, "I cannot enter into it." But his attitude toward the project of an American attack on Pensacola was not so inimical as some writers imply,[23] for his letter continued, "You may rest assured that I will extend my permission and whatever assistance I can, but it must appear that I am ignorant of it all."[24]

Sometimes it is asserted that Gálvez wanted the English to retain Pensacola until he could conquer it himself, and that on this account he discouraged Morgan, an interpretation which credits him with phenomenal foresight. A simpler interpretation places more stress on the inconveniences to Louisiana if the two English factions should clash just beyond the Mississippi. Gálvez expressed a disinclination for the rôle of being "the witness of a thousand hostilities and exposed to suffer them," and he conceived it his duty to forestall the coming of an American army because of "the excesses with which troops are apt to be managed in foreign countries."[25]

It is significant, also, that he closed his letter to Morgan with a practical guaranty that American trade with New Orleans would be permitted and assisted.

> The commerce that you desire with this province can be established from whatever point is desired or convenient, assured that those who carry it on will be well received and protected by me, holding me responsible for all.[26]

The flotilla that brought Morgan's letter returned laden with arms, ammunitions, and provisions. Such goods to the value of $70,000 had

---

[22] Royal order to the governor of Louisiana, February 20, 1777, reservada, draft, A. G. I., Sto. Dom., 1598.

[23] Gayarré, *op. cit.*, III, 110; James, "Spanish Influence in the West during the American Revolution," *Mississippi Valley Historical Review*, IV (1917), 197–198.

[24] Gálvez to Morgan, August 9, 1777, certified copy, A. G. I., Sto. Dom., 2596.

[25] Gálvez to José de Gálvez, June 2, 1777, *in* Serrano y Sanz, *Documentos Históricos de la Florida y la Luisiana*, 313.

[26] Gálvez to Morgan, August 9, 1777, certified copy, A. G. I., Sto. Dom., 2596.

been sent to the upper Ohio by the end of Gálvez' first year as governor of Louisiana.[27]

Although this aid was supposedly secret, it was not carried on surreptitiously enough to deceive the English in West Florida. As early as March, 1777, Governor Chester protested against the transmission of arms and ammunition up the river under the protection of the Spanish flag, and the English commander in chief labeled the conduct of the Spanish governor "very Extraordinary."[28] Responding to the English complaint, Gálvez insisted that he was only being hospitable to the Americans, and that if the "rebels" had been assisted at New Orleans, it was because Unzaga and he "did not know them as such."[29]

Patrick Henry, then governor of Virginia, used his rhetorical talents as had Lee and Morgan in urging upon Gálvez the policy of aiding the Revolutionists. A paragraph from his letter of October 24, 1777, is typical:

> I humbly conceive that it is an object worthy the attention of your Excellency and of the Ministers of Spain, although the grandeur of your nation does not depend on Commerce, to secure the Trade at least of the Southern States of America, and thereby deprive their ancient and natural Enemy the English of all those vast supplies of Naval Stores, and many other articles, which have enabled them to become so powerful on the Seas; Immense Quantities of Hemp, Flax, Skins, Furrs, Beef, Pork, Flower Staves, Shingles, etc. the produce of our back country might be easily carried down the Mississippi to New Orleans, which place if it were made a free port, would be resorted to by the French, and Dutch, who might take off the Tobacco and other articles, which Spain would not want for her own consumption. Indeed if you were once more in posession of the two Floridas, you might enjoy a great part of the Trade of our Northern States. If Your Excellency should think it would be worthy the attention of your court to cultivate a correspondence with these States through the Mississippi, we would establish a post at the mouth of the Ohio, to facilitate the necessary intercourse between us.[30]

---

[27] Gayarré, *op. cit.*, III, 113.

[28] James, "Spanish Influence in the West during the American Revolution," *op. cit.*, 199; Howe to Stiell, April 22, 1778, *in* Historical Manuscripts Commission, *op. cit.*, I, 237.

[29] Gálvez to Chester, April 4, 1777, certified copy, A. G. I., Sto. Dom., 2596.

[30] Henry to Gálvez, October 20, 1777, A. G. I., Cuba, 2370.

The same expertly deferential approach is evident in another of Henry's letters a few months later. Mentioning the English "Cruizers" that were making communication by sea with New Orleans precarious, he adverted to the "easy and safe communication with the Gulph of Mexico," which, he said, invited "Intercourse & correspondence between the Subjects of his Catholic Majesty & the good people of this Commonwealth." Sensible of the favors the patriots had received from Gálvez and his nation, Governor Henry sought some means of making returns. He inquired first if American annexation of West Florida would not "greatly distress the English West India Settlements, & hinder the progress of their Rivalship to Spain." His second suggestion started with the idea of an American post near the mouth of the Ohio for the protection of Spanish-American commerce on the river, proceeded to discuss the patriots' crying need for military stores, and ended with a request for a loan of 150,000 pistoles. Anticipating the question of what Spain could expect in exchange for these additional advances, Henry supplied the answer: "the Gratitude of this Free & Independent Country, the Trade in any, or all of its valuable productions, & the Friendship of its warlike Inhabitants."[81]

Early in 1778 English resentment at Gálvez' pro-American activities was paradoxically overshadowed by anger toward James Willing and yet intensified because of the hospitality extended to him and his followers. As the high light of Gálvez' direct assistance to the Revolutionists Willing's expedition is reserved for treatment in a separate chapter.[82] In principle, the aid given to Willing was the same as that given earlier, in 1777, and the same as that given subsequently to George Rogers Clark and others.

The exploits of George Rogers Clark are a familiar story.[83] Weary of the constant danger of British-Indian attacks on the trans-Alleghany settlements of Virginia, Clark had journeyed to the state capital to get permission to strike at the root of the trouble. On Janu-

---

[81] *Idem* to *idem*, January 14, 1778, *ibid*.

[82] See below, Chapter VII; also my "Willing's Expedition down the Mississippi, 1778," *Louisiana Historical Quarterly*, XV (1932), 5–36.

[83] Except as otherwise noted the account of Clark's work is drawn from James, *George Rogers Clark Papers, 1771–1781*, and his *George Rogers Clark*.

ary 2, 1778, Governor Patrick Henry gave him a colonel's commission and secretly authorized him to raise a force of three hundred and fifty men for an attack on Kaskaskia. Returning to the frontier, Clark set about recruiting his troops. The results were not very encouraging. By May 15 he had only one hundred and fifty men. He set out from Fort Pitt, however, descending to the falls of the Ohio, where he was reënforced by a small contingent from the Holston settlement and a few Kentucky frontiersmen.

On June 24, after a day of rejoicing over the news of the French alliance, they shot the falls and proceeded toward the mouth of the Tennessee, from which point they marched overland to Kaskaskia. It was a strenuous six-day march, the last two days of it negotiated without anything to eat; but on the night of July 4 they took Kaskaskia by surprise. While one division surrounded the town, Clark and the rest of the troops entered the open gate of the fort, captured in his bedroom the Frenchman Rocheblave, commander for the English, and without firing a shot secured the town's submission. By daylight all the inhabitants were disarmed.

The French villagers, who had been "taught to expect nothing but Savage treatment from the Americans," begged for their lives "with the greatest fervency," and were "willing to be Slaves to save their Families." Clark explained to them that the Americans were not so ferocious as they had imagined and offered them the full privileges of American citizenship if they should take oath of allegiance. By this promise, along with the announcement of the French alliance, they were induced to espouse the American cause. Finally, as a result of the assurance of full protection for their Catholic religion, "in a few Minutes the scean of mourning and distress was turned to an excess of Joy."[84]

When the true disposition of the American "Big Knives" was communicated to the French at Cahokia, they likewise "submitted to their happier fate with very little hesitation." At Cahokia, Clark held powwows with the Indians from far and near, and in these he got into sev-

---

[84] Clark to Mason, November 19, 1779, *in* James, *George Rogers Clark Papers, 1771–1781*, 120.

eral hazardous predicaments, but by bluff and bluster, argument and luck, he was able to extricate himself. Of his achievements he wrote modestly, "This Speech had a greater effect than I could have imagined, and did more service than a Regiment of Men cou'd have done."[35] If their solemn promises could be believed, the tribes had been won over.

Vincennes was the next objective. Doubting his ability to take the place by force, Clark resorted to a ruse. "I pretended," he admitted later, "that I was about to send an Express to the falls of the Ohio for a Body of Troops to Join me at a certain place in order to attact it."[36] The French of Kaskaskia, not knowing there were only ten men at the falls, were anxious to save their neighbors and kinsmen from injury. Father Gibault offered to go in person to persuade them to accept American control. Clark consented; and so did the people of Vincennes. Thus, without a single life being lost, Clark had secured control of the region north of the Ohio.

The conquest was ardently welcomed in Spanish Illinois. "If the affairs of government, of which I have been in charge only a few days, would permit," Leyba wrote to Clark from St. Louis, "I would go in person to congratulate you on your happy arrival at Kaskaskias."[37] And to the governor of Louisiana he reported, "Colonel Clark merits the best attentions of all the people in his jurisdiction, who are indebted to him for his affability, clemency, and upright administration of justice."[38] The cordial feeling was reciprocated. From Clark's pen we have this statement:

> An intamacy had commenced between Don Leybrau Lieut. Governour of Western Illinois and myself he omitted nothing in his Power to prove his Attachment to the Americans with such openness as left no room for doubt; as I was never before in Compy. of any Spanish gent. I was much surprised in my expectations; for instead of finding that reserve thought peculiar to that Nation, I here saw not the least symptoms of it.[39]

---

[35] *Ibid.*, 125.
[36] *Ibid.*, 122.
[37] Leyba to Clark, July 8, 1778, A. G. I., Cuba, 1.
[38] Leyba to Gálvez, July 21, 1778, *ibid*. Similar sentiments were expressed in Leyba's letter to Patrick Henry, April 23, 1779, copy, *ibid*.
[39] Clark to Mason, November 19, 1779, *in* James, *op. cit.*, 129.

Not without importance, too, is Clark's habit of adding postscripts to his letters, such as this: "My compliments to Madm. Lebau and my two favourites the little Misses."[40]

Immediately upon learning of the fall of the Illinois posts, Colonel Hamilton began preparations at Detroit for their recovery. Friendly Indians were mobilized, aid was solicited from the commanders at St. Joseph and Michilimackinac, and provisions and military supplies were collected. In October the force started for Vincennes. A gale and rough water threatened them on Lake Erie, their passage up the Maumee was hindered by the lowness of the water, and low water and ice interfered with their progress down the Wabash. Nevertheless, Hamilton reached Vincennes on December 17 with a force of more than five hundred men.[41] In the face of such opposition Lieutenant Helm had no choice but to surrender, though the usual story of his marching out with one man seems questionable.[42]

Winter now put a period to English activities. Hamilton dismissed his Indian allies, sent the Detroit militia back home, and settled down with a garrison of ninety men to wait for spring, meanwhile communicating to the authorities at Pensacola his plans for a joint attack upon the Americans in the West. He also sent letters to various Louisiana officials, protesting against the sending of gunpowder up the Mississippi to the Rebels. If this traffic were continued, he warned that his savages and the "native Inhabitants of the Banks of the Ohio" might forget the instructions he had given them concerning the subjects of the king of Spain. He warned the Spaniards also not to give asylum to the Rebels whom he intended shortly to drive out of Kaskaskia.[43]

At this juncture Clark saw an opportunity for a master stroke. François Vigo, a St. Louis merchant with pro-American proclivities, had been taken prisoner at Vincennes. Hamilton released him after exacting a promise that he would do nothing prejudicial to the Eng-

---

[40] Clark to Leyba, October 26, 1778, A. G. I., Cuba, 1.

[41] One hundred and seventy-five white, the rest Indians. James, *op. cit.*, pp. lxxi-lxxii.

[42] Winsor, *op. cit.*, 131.

[43] Hamilton to the governor of New Orleans, January 13, 1779, A. G. I., Cuba, 2370.

AID FOR THE AMERICANS

lish cause on his way to St. Louis. Vigo was true to his word, but immediately upon reaching St. Louis he set out for Kaskaskia to give Clark complete information about Hamilton's forces and a fair indication of his plans.[44]

With some seventy Americans and sixty French volunteers Clark set out for Vincennes. The weather was mild for February, but much of the way was flooded, and in the last part of the journey the men were wading in water waist deep or worse much of the time. After enduring unbelievable hardships, they arrived at the outskirts of the town. Clark then performed the seemingly impossible feat of warning the townspeople of his arrival while keeping the British unaware of it. In the evening he marched into town, was enthusiastically received by the habitants, and proceeded to the investment of the fort. "I never saw a Much pritier fire than Keep up on Both Sides for Eighteen Hours," Clark wrote. "Governor Hamilton being ordered to Surrender he thought proper to Comply."[45] From this time on the Americans were fairly secure in their possession of the region north of the Ohio.

A great deal of Clark's success is attributable to his intrepid leadership and to the fortitude of his followers. His men endured many hardships; they got along at times on very short rations; they suffered for lack of clothing, being "often barefoot, and at times almost naked."[46] But there is an irreducible minimum of food and clothing that soldiers must have. Clark was frequently sore put to meet it. Besides, he had to have a great variety of military supplies, not to mention the wherewithal for Indian presents. For such sustenance Clark had to depend on others.

Virginia had sponsored his expedition, but her resources were so depleted by the burden of supplying Washington's army that she could give to Clark little more than moral assistance. The French creoles of Illinois helped considerably by donating supplies; the

---

[44] Leyba to Gálvez, February 5, 1779, A. G. I., Cuba, 1; Thompson, "Penalties of Patriotism," *Journal of the Illinois State Historical Society,* IX (1916–1917), 404–412.

[45] Clark to Leyba, March 1, 1779, A. G. I., Cuba, 1.

[46] Randall, "George Rogers Clark's Service of Supply," *Mississippi Valley Historical Review,* VIII (1921), 254.

Cahokians contributed one-fifth of their live stock, and the people of Vincennes furnished powder for the assault on the fort.[47] But Clark's chief reliance was upon Pollock and Gálvez at New Orleans. The powder from Fort Pitt with which he first outfitted his men was part of that obtained by Gibson and Linn. On August 6, 1778, he acknowledged the receipt of "a large Assortment of Goods." "I hope," he continued, "that you will send me an Assortment of Five thousand Dollars worth of Goods most Suitable for Soldiers and Indians.... I am in great want of Ammunition for this and other Garrisons in the Illinois Country.... I should be glad to have you send me four thousand Pounds of Powder." During September Pollock sent Clark goods amounting to $7200, and just before the attack on Vincennes five hundred pounds of powder and some swivels were received.[48]

Not only did Clark receive essential supplies from Pollock and Gálvez; he also depended on them for credit to meet most of the bills of his commissary department. This financial support enabled the Americans to retain control of the territory north of the Ohio. Clark did not begrudge Pollock recognition of this essential aid. "The invoice Mr. Pollock rendered upon all occasions in paying those bills," he declared, "I considered at the Time and now to be one of the happy circumstances that enabled me to keep Possession of that Country."[49] This dependence upon Pollock, who in turn was supported by Gálvez, integrates Clark's expedition with Louisiana history. Although aid from New Orleans was perhaps not a *sine qua non* for the success of the Americans in the West, they relied on it heavily.

Pollock's rôle in the Revolution and his relations with Gálvez deserve additional notice. He has been likened to Robert Morris and called the western Financier of the Revolution. He faced herculean tasks in establishing American credit at New Orleans so that there would be financial support for the three major American activities in the West: the supply service, Willing's expedition, and Clark in Illi-

---

[47] *Ibid.*, 251 n.; Eckenrode, *The Revolution in Virginia, passim;* James, *op. cit.*, 327, p. lxxxii.

[48] *Ibid.*, p. lxvii; Clark to Pollock, August 6, 1778, *ibid.*, 64–65.

[49] *Ibid.*, p. xcvii.

nois. It would be difficult to overestimate Pollock's contributions to the success of the Revolution.[50]

To meet Clark's drafts proved to be Pollock's most difficult problem. Though theoretically upon the state of Virginia, they proved negotiable only as Pollock could devise means to cover them. His first recourse was to the governor of Louisiana, and Gálvez was generous in putting government funds at his disposal. On August 26, 1779, Pollock gave receipt for treasury loans to the amount of $74,087,[51] and on June 9, 1781, there was an additional loan of $5000.[52] These funds, Pollock testified later, were received "as very secret service money" for the use of the United States but chiefly on his own credit, and they were delivered usually at night by Juan Morales, Gálvez' private secretary.[53]

Liberal though Gálvez was in advancing government funds, American needs could not have been met if Pollock had not made use of his personal fortune and credit. He did so without stint so long as he possessed either, and he succeeded in paying Clark's drafts at par in New Orleans when Continental currency was worth only twelve cents on the dollar in the East.[54] Frequently the difficulties seemed insurmountable. On one occasion he had to borrow at $12\frac{1}{2}$ per cent discount to meet a $12,000 draft.[55] Shortly thereafter he was called upon for $10,000. Refused a loan by every merchant of New Orleans because of "the little probability there was of getting paid . . . in any reasonable time," he finally got it by mortgaging part of his own property.[56]

---

[50] Professor James Alton James is preparing a volume on Pollock that will undoubtedly secure for the latter the recognition he so richly deserves. There is much material on his career in the Spanish archives and the Pollock Papers in the Library of Congress. See also: Deposition of Oliver Pollock, June 8, 1808, *loc. cit.;* Gayarré, *op. cit.,* III, *passim;* James, "Oliver Pollock, Financier of the Revolution in the West," *Mississippi Valley Historical Review,* XVI (1929), 67–80.

[51] Receipt signed by Pollock, August 26, 1779, itemized as follows: $24,023, June 9, 1778; $15,948, October 24, 1778; $22,640, July 3, 1779; $11,476, June 5, 1780. A. G. I., Cuba, 569.

[52] Approved in José de Gálvez to Gálvez, November 17, 1781, A. G. I., Cuba, 175; José de Gálvez to the intendant of Louisiana, March 12, 1782, *ibid,* 569.

[53] Deposition of Oliver Pollock, June 8, 1808, *loc. cit.*

[54] James, "Spanish Influence in the West during the American Revolution," *op. cit.,* 207.

[55] Winsor, *op. cit.,* 121.   [56] James, *George Rogers Clark Papers, 1771–1781,* p. xcvii.

Besides the sum obtained from Gálvez, Pollock placed $136,466.85 in use for the American cause. This was technically an obligation of the state of Virginia through Pollock her agent, and the Virginia House of Delegates recognized it officially as a state indebtedness.[57] Yet it is quite obvious that the loans were made because of Pollock's good standing and that he was considered personally responsible for their payment. His personal responsibility was impressed upon him in 1784 when he was arrested at Havana to satisfy the debts still due at New Orleans,[58] and again in 1792 when bills due him to the amount of "$9,574¼" were attached at Havana for the same purpose.[59]

When Pollock laid his fortune on the altar of the Revolution, it was almost a donation. The patriotic service was most noble but the investment exceedingly doubtful. Eventually he did recover from both Virginia and the United States, but only after more than a decade of vexatious delay and uncertainty. Of his efforts to arrange with his creditors at Havana and New Orleans, of his negotiations at Philadelphia and Williamsburg and New York, of his contemplated trip to Spain, of how his private business was completely upset during this decade of uncertitude—the story is long and perhaps beside the point. He deserves an additional encomium for having endured this tardiness of recompense, yet quite apart from it, his contribution to the success of the Revolution in the West must be recognized as great.

In the course of his efforts to collect his credits and satisfy his creditors, Pollock met Gálvez again. In 1785, Gálvez came to Havana at the opportune time to secure Pollock's release and permit his return to Philadelphia as a more efficacious means of securing satisfaction for his creditors.[60] Previously, Pollock had persuaded Gálvez to represent to Congress that he held Pollock "personally responsible" for the loan of $74,087 in the hope that this would expedite payment by the United

---

[57] Virginia House of Delegates, copy of resolution, December 27, 1782, A. G. I., Cuba, 1393; Pollock to the president of Congress, February 24, 1783, L. C., Papers of the Continental Congress, L.

[58] Unzaga to Pollock and to Thomas Mifflin, President of Congress, August 26, 1784, drafts, A. G. I., Cuba, 1354; Pollock to the "Financier General," August 24, 1778, L. C., Pollock Papers.

[59] Pollock's affidavit, January 27, 1792, A. G. I., Cuba, 1469; Thomas Jefferson to Viar and Jaudenes, March 2, 1792, copy, *ibid*.

[60] Gálvez to José de Gálvez, April 30, 1785, A. G. I., Sto. Dom., 1243.

States.⁶¹ Gálvez seems to have gone a step farther, possibly with the court's approval, though perhaps as a peculation. At any rate, thereafter the debt is mentioned as due to Gálvez instead of to the Spanish treasury, though the loan had not come from Gálvez' personal fortune, and when settlement was finally made, the payment was to Gálvez' estate.⁶²

While Spain was still neutral, Gálvez played an important part in the American Revolution. He facilitated American shipping by sea and up the river. He coöperated with Pollock in sending essential supplies to Washington's army and to the army of the West. In conjunction with Pollock he was the financial backer of the expedition that won the Northwest. To assistance from New Orleans is largely attributable the establishment of American control west of the Alleghanies. American appreciation of Gálvez' help was expressed several times but never more happily than when Pollock, because of Gálvez' services dating from January, 1777, expressed a desire to have his portrait made for Congress "in order to perpetuate your memory in the united States of America, as ranking in your Exalted Nation, as a Soldier and a Gentleman with those that have been of Singular Service in the Glorious Contest of Liberty."⁶³

In relation to the history of the United States, it suffices perhaps to know that this assistance was given, but in relation to the history of Louisiana the motive for the aid is of importance. Most emphatically the aid was not an end in itself. Had this been so we would be compelled to label it a quixotic action—the purposeless encouragement of a revolution that was to be an inspiration for the revolt of the Spanish colonies. Rather it was a by-product of Spain's persistent policy of opposing the English along the Mississippi frontier. In the Revolutionary War Spain saw an opportunity to make a new application of the *divide et impera* principle, a principle that she had occasionally used with good effect in Indian control. This was the spirit that prompted Gálvez to assist the Americans.

---

⁶¹ Pollock to Gálvez, August 9, 1783, reservada, A. G. I., Cuba, 1377.
⁶² Pollock to "Baron de Caron De Let" (Carondelet), May 3, 1792, copy, A. G. I., Cuba, 184.
⁶³ Pollock to Gálvez, December 18, 1779, copy, *ibid.*, 112.

Chapter VII

WILLING'S EXPEDITION

ALTHOUGH GÁLVEZ rendered vital assistance to the Revolutionists through Pollock's supply service and in financing George Rogers Clark in Illinois, his most direct contact with the Americans was in connection with Willing's expedition. James Willing, who styled himself "Captain in the service of the united Independent States of America," raided the Loyalist settlements along the lower Mississippi in February of 1778. Regional histories sketch the general outline of this raid: Willing's departure from Fort Pitt, his sudden descent upon Natchez, a convocation of the settlers, their oath of neutrality, the seizure of certain Loyalists, plantations raided, slaves carried off, buildings burned, boats on the river captured, English refugees fleeing across the river into Spanish territory. Then the sequel: Willing welcomed into New Orleans, the plunder auctioned off, English protests to Governor Gálvez, his refusal to surrender Willing, the revival of Loyalism at Natchez, and the interruption of American traffic on the river. Only recently, however, has more detailed information come to light, making possible definite conclusions on such essential points as Willing's instructions from the Continental Congress, the terms upon which he guaranteed inviolability to the Natchez people, his relations with Pollock, the attitude of Gálvez, and the effects of the raid.[1]

There is not much to write of Willing before his expedition down the Mississippi. He belonged to a prominent Philadelphia family, his elder brother being a partner of Robert Morris and a member of the first Continental Congress. Since 1774 he had resided at Natchez, doing an indifferent business as a merchant and frittering away his fortune in dissolute living. Apparently Willing, like Samuel Adams, Pat-

---

[1] See my "Willing's Expedition down the Mississippi, 1778," *Louisiana Historical Quarterly*, XV (1932), 5-36.

rick Henry, and others of his contemporaries, was not a success in business. "Should Mr. Willing's out standing Debts come in by Next Aprill," reads a letter to one of his New Orleans creditors, "you may depend on a Remitance on that Gen'ts. Acct. of About three or four Thousand Dollars, but as I am Apprehensive there is little dependance on a great Amt. of his Debts to be Colected by that time would not advise to lay any great dependance."[2] Like Adams and Henry, furthermore, Willing was an agitator for the Revolution. As soon as news of the Revolution reached Natchez, he tried to stir up interest in the cause of the colonies but without success.[3]

Willing returned to Pennsylvania in 1777, and early in the fall of that year he had several conferences with the Commerce Committee of the Continental Congress. Just what was said in those conferences is not known. It has been asserted that Willing drew a vivid picture of the probability of Loyalist activity in the Natchez district, warned the committee that the Mississippi would be closed to American boats and particularly to the shipment of war supplies north from New Orleans, and advocated an expedition to the lower Mississippi to enlist or compel the support of West Florida. Undoubtedly the committee had something of the sort in mind, although in July Congress had disapproved George Morgan's plan for an American attack on Pensacola and Mobile. The Commerce Committee decided to send a less pretentious expedition and commissioned Willing captain in the navy for the purpose.[4] Apparently the commission was granted without the general knowledge of Congress.[5]

Willing's instructions have since been lost and forgotten. They can be reconstructed, however, with fair accuracy from bits of indirect evidence. His letter of introduction to Hand, the commander of Fort Pitt, for example, states that he "is charged with some (Public) dispatches for New Orleans," and that "it is of great Importance that Mr. Willing

---

[2] Blommart to Pollock, January 29, 1775, L. C., Pollock Papers.

[3] Martin, *op. cit.*, II, 40; Thwaites and Kellogg, *Frontier Defense on the Upper Ohio*, 191 *n*.

[4] Burnett, *Letters of Members of the Continental Congress*, II, 421–423, 443–447; Claiborne, *op. cit.*, 115–116.

[5] Burnett, *op. cit.*, II, p. iv; III, 96.

get speedily down, and that he has truly faithful People with him."[6] A letter of the same date to Oliver Pollock indicates that Willing was not only entrusted with certain despatches for New Orleans, but was also expected to bring up the Mississippi and Ohio part of the stores which Spain had agreed to deliver at New Orleans for the use of the United States. "Mr. James Willing will return with these Boats and to him you may commit your Dispatches, also the superintending Care of the Goods."[7] The point is corroborated by a request that Hand received from Willing before his departure from Fort Pitt.

> As I expect to bring at least five boats from New Orleans laden with dry goods, and navigated by 20 or 25 men each, I request the favor of you to give the necessary orders for a sufficient quantity of flour & pork to be lodged for me by the beginning of April next at the Arkansas. Not less than 60 or 70 barrels of flour, of 250 to 350 lbs. each, & 20 or 30 bbls of pork.[8]

From Willing's action at Natchez one would gather that he was expected to attempt to secure the neutrality of the people of West Florida. In addition, he asserted, three years later, that he had "instructions to capture whatever british property he might meet with."[9] The claim is substantiated by several statements already in print. De Mézières reported that Willing had a commission "to expel the English whom he might meet"; Dunbar stated that there was authorization "to make capture of British property on the river"; and Rocheblave wrote from the Illinois country that the instructions had been to capture "whatever British property he might meet with on the river."[10] Because these statements are either *ex parte* or by men who probably did not have access to the actual instructions, it is only natural that historians, even when aware of them, have been inclined to discount their conclusiveness. Believing that Willing disregarded his instructions and resorted to force where he was expected to be peaceful, they denounce him as

---

[6] *Ibid.*, II, 565.
[7] Commerce Committee to Pollock, November 21, 1777, L. C., Pollock Papers.
[8] Thwaites and Kellogg, *op. cit.*, 198–199.
[9] Burnett, *op. cit.*, II, 565 n.
[10] Bolton, *op. cit.*, II, 235; "Journal of Sir William Dunbar," *in* Claiborne, *op. cit.*, 119–120; Rocheblave to Haldimand, July 4, 1778, *Report of Canadian Archives, 1890*, State Papers, 106.

cruel, brutal, wanton, rapacious, more like an Indian than a civilized warrior.

But in another letter written by Willing and preserved in the Archivo General de Indias at Seville there is evidence that his orders were of the sort indicated. On May 30, 1778, he began a letter to Pollock in this fashion:

> In the first place to Begin with my Instructions; the following Extracts will serve to specify their Tenour—After being ordered to make prize of all British Property on the Mississippi River I was instructed to apply to the Governor of this Province for Liberty to make Sale of them. That obtained I am again Instructed to pay One moiety of the Net proceeds into Your hands as Agent for the Congress.[11]

Inasmuch as this reference to the order to seize English property is entirely incidental to a dispute over the disposition of the prizes, I see no reason to charge inaccuracy in the quoting of the instructions. This letter, together with the several statements quoted above, would seem to be acceptable evidence that Willing was instructed "to make prize of all British Property on the Mississippi River." Whether this expression should be interpreted strictly to affect merely property afloat on the river or loosely to comprehend property along the shore as well, is another question. But certainly Willing was expected not only to bear despatches to New Orleans, convey supplies back north, and solicit the support, or at least the neutrality, of West Florida, but also to lay violent hands on English property.

Armed with the instructions whose general import has just been outlined, Willing proceeded to Fort Pitt. The armed boat "Rattletrap" was assigned to his command, and on January 10, 1778, with a volunteer crew of about thirty men he set out. The Frenchman Rocheblave, commander for the English at Kaskaskia, was filled with consternation when he heard of the expedition, believing that Illinois was to be attacked. And on his way down the Ohio Willing did seize the Becquet brothers and their peltries as well as Mr. la Chance and a cargo of brandy.[12] Rocheblave interpreted these seizures as an earnest of what

---
[11] Willing to Pollock, May 30, 1778, A. G. I., Cuba, 2370.
[12] Thwaites and Kellogg, *op. cit.*, 302–303, 287–288.

might be expected should the Americans come to the Illinois in greater force. It may help to explain his distrust of Clark when the latter promised him honorable treatment. Or he may have guessed Willing's aversion toward him expressed later in a letter to George Rogers Clark. "I am well acquainted with the Kaskaskia Gentry. they are damn'd Rogues as well as their ancient Leader RocheBlave God send him a sight of Williamsburgh, Govr Henry won't be displeased to see one of these *Hair Buyers*."[13]

Willing, at any rate, achieved sufficient notoriety along the Ohio that when Hamilton heard of Clark's capture of Kaskaskia he supposed the captors to be from Willing's flotilla, assisted, perhaps, by the Spaniards.[14] But the objective was not Illinois. The "Rattletrap" drifted on down the Ohio and the Mississippi. Somewhere along the Ohio a message to George Morgan from Cruzat, commander for the Spaniards at St. Louis, was intercepted and endorsed, "Recvd and Examined this 17 Jany 1778 J. Willing."[15] The next record of the expedition is from the Spanish post at the mouth of the Arkansas.

The Petition of Sundry American families arrived since the departure of James Willing, Esq. Captain in the Army of the United States of America Shewith, that your Petitioners upon their arrival at the English side found the Place called Concord abandend and understand that Captain Willing left Orders that nobody should remain there: In consequence whereof as well as from the fear they have of being disturbed by Savages in the Royal Interest of Great Britain and also not chosing to go further down the River until certain Intelligence be had from below, Your Petitioners humbly request that you will take them under your Protection.[16]

On the sixteenth or seventeenth of February the expedition reached the plantation of Anthony Hutchins, a short distance above Natchez. Hutchins was made prisoner, and his negroes and some other property were seized. The expedition went on to Natchez, where the proceedings are best described in the words of the settlers.

---

[13] Willing to Clark, September 1, 1778, *in* James, *op. cit.*, 67–68.

[14] Winsor, *op. cit.*, 129.

[15] Burnett, *op. cit.*, III, 144 *n.*; United States, *Journals of the Continental Congress*, X, 275.

[16] Petition of fourteen Americans, February 2, 1778, A. G. I., Cuba, 191.

On the afternoon of Friday the 19th of this month, James Willing, Captain in the service of the United States of America, from which he arrived with a detachment of troops under his command, disembarked at Natchez, and early on the following morning sent orders to all parts for us to convene in order that at the same time that we should be made prisoners of war to the United States he might take possession in their name of this jurisdiction. The inhabitants, mindful of the unfortunate state of their very great remoteness from protection and fearful of the confiscation of their property, felt it necessary to go to the said Captain Willing to propose measures ... and the inhabitants unanimously delegated four of their number to treat in their name for a capitulation, which should be formed in the best terms possible.[17]

The committee proposed the following:

That we will not in any fashion take arms against the United States of America, or help to supply, or give any assistance to the enemies of said States.

That our persons, slaves, and other property of whatever description shall be left secure and without the least molestation during our neutrality.[18]

And on February 21 Willing signified his approval in these words:

Approved in full by me in the name of the United States of America (every public official of the crown of Great Britain who holds property in this district being excepted) and those who have held commission and signed the oath of neutrality contained in the preceding articles.

The property of all British subjects who are not resident in this district is likewise excepted as belonging to enemies of the before mentioned states.[19]

Virtually every account of Willing's expedition has it that the temptation to loot overrode his promise in this Natchez oath of neutrality, and that he embarked on a "career of confiscation and cruelty," ransacking homes in which he had been a guest, seizing slaves and other movable property, burning dwellings, and forcing most of the inhabitants to flee across the river to the "unfriendly but humane Louisianians." In the contemporary documents, however, there seems to be no indication that anything of the sort was done to the people

---

[17] Capitulation at Natchez, February 21, 1778, Spanish translation, A. G. I., Cuba, 2351.
[18] *Ibid.* [19] *Ibid.*

guaranteed protection by the Natchez oath *in the Natchez District*. The violence to Anthony Hutchins is the nearest approach to such a breach of faith. And contrary to the impression that most secondary accounts give, Hutchins was not molested after this oath of neutrality, but before. He was not even included in it. It is true that Willing allowed him to take a similar oath a few days later, and that Hutchins was disappointed that this action did not result in his property being restored to him, but it was not necessarily a breach of faith on Willing's part not to make the guaranty of protection retroactive. Perhaps the blot of breach of contract has been laid unjustly on Willing's escutcheon.[20]

However this may be, a few days later Willing committed the sort of depredations charged, but south of the Natchez district. At Manchac, on February 23, an advance party captured the "Rebecca," "mounted with sixteen Guns, four pounders, besides Swivels," which with the "Hinchenbrook" had been sent to "Scour the inland passage and frustrate the designs of the Rebels."[21] The Americans went on to seize other boats; they raided plantations along the Mississippi and likewise on Thompson's Creek and the Amite. Some of the settlers were even followed into Spanish territory and despoiled of their property there. Excesses and wanton destruction accompanied the seizures, but the plundering was not indiscriminate. Friends of the American cause were not molested, and there was some attempt at justice, as when "they divided the property at Castle's taking one half for his partner's share, but leaving the other unhurt for himself."[22]

Willing's victims later became quite vociferous in complaining about his depredations to Governor Gálvez. Of many reports of this plundering there follows just one paragraph telling of the seizure of a boat in which Stephen Shakespear was taking most of his movable belongings into Spanish sanctuary.

> The Bateau being fastened Head and Stearn to the Spanish Shore, and we had laid ourselves down to rest, we were awakened by a sudden Noise,

---

[20] Hutchins to Gálvez, March 14, 1778, A. G. I., Cuba, 191.

[21] Historical Manuscripts Commission, *op. cit.*, I, 213, 221.

[22] "Private Journal of Sir William Dunbar," *in* Claiborne, *op. cit.*, 119.

which we found to be occasioned by one Colbert [Calvert] and some armed Men under his Command on the Spanish Shore casting off the Ropes, who immediately ordered me down into the Cabin and not speak a word. I not immediately complying Calvert ordered one of the Men to Blow my Brains out, on which the Man presented his gun and said he would blow hell through me, upon which I haveing obeyed they pushed off from Shore for New Orleans.[23]

From the laments of the despoiled, one can piece together a long and damning account of the American activities. Part of the evidence indicates the hatred of the settlers for Willing rather than proves his malevolence; for example, the report that Mary Blommart, having taken a dose of "Red Precipitate" prescribed by "François Dolony Surgeon to the Rebels commanded by Mr. James Willing," as she was dying "cried out with a most lamentable voice, Oh! *Willing! Willing! Willing!* and expired in excruciating pain;"[24] but there is too much unanimity in the reports that the Americans shot hogs, killed cattle, broke bottled wine, burned dwellings, and in other ways laid waste and destroyed, for anyone to exonerate Willing entirely. Yet it should be remembered that these reports give a one-sided story; and a reputation is not often enhanced by the testimony of adversaries. Furthermore, the unfortunate settlers were prone to overlook the facts that the Natchez oath protected only the Natchez district and that Willing had been instructed to make prizes.[25]

Consternation spread among the Loyalists of West Florida because of the depredations at Manchac. With a certain diabolical astuteness the American captain fostered the impression that a large army was advancing on the colony. Instead of the thirty men who had started out on the "Rattletrap," instead of the hundred or more to which his force had been augmented by the enlistment of plunder-seeking

---

[23] Frederick Spell, affidavit at New Orleans, July 25, 1778, A. G. I., Cuba, 191; Stephen Shakespear to Gálvez, March 12, 1778, *ibid.;* Stephen Shakespear, affidavit at Pensacola, May 6, 1778, A. G. I., Cuba, 2370.

[24] Francis Farrell, M.D., affidavit at Natchez, June 20, 1778, A. G. I., Cuba, 191.

[25] Most accounts of Willing's expedition have been based on evidence provided by his victims; for example, Dunbar's journal *in* Claiborne, *op. cit.,* 119–121. I utilize much additional material of the same sort, contained in petitions to Governor Gálvez, *in* A. G. I., Cuba, 191, 2351, 2370, and other legajos; but I also use documents in the same repository from American and Spanish pens.

adventurers, the West Floridians estimated the American force at five or even eight thousand. Willing represented that he commanded only the advance guard, and that General Clark followed with the main army. He overawed opposition by advancing in front of Spanish bateaux coming peaceably down the river. Recognition, if not approbation, is due this skill in allaying opposition. In addition he was an able orator. At the mouth of the Big Black more than one hundred settlers listened to his "seventh of March speech." "Willing was a good speaker," one of them reported, "and he represented the cause of the colonies, and the certainty of their ultimate success, in very persuasive terms." Exaggeration of Willing's strength, uncertainty about the loyalism of their neighbors, apprehension of Indian attacks, and the intimidation of Willing's plundering and speaking militated against any organized resistance by the West Floridians.[26]

Along the lower Mississippi, volunteers from New Orleans coöperated with Willing's men in plundering the English. Pollock led in the organization of these supplementary forces and laid some of the plans for American operations, as, for example, in the seizure of the "Rebecca." His nephew, Thomas Pollock, was sent upstream with fifteen men for this purpose, and although Willing's lieutenant McIntyre had already accomplished the capture, the New Orleans detachment participated in some of the other depredations.[27]

Under Captain Lafitte another group of twenty-six boatmen was enlisted at New Orleans, ostensibly with the purpose of going to Manchac to bring down endangered English property. Instead of proceeding to this work, however, they floated down the river by night and joined two canoes manned by a slightly larger group of Americans. Continuing downstream they came to the English brig "Neptune." The Americans tried to persuade the New Orleans boatmen to join in an attack on the ship. Two of the boatmen, disapproving of the project into which they had been drawn unsuspectingly, "went on shore and left the party," but the others joined the Americans in

---

[26] "Journal of Captain Phelps," *in* Claiborne, *op. cit.*, 118; McCarty to Askin, June 7, 1778, *in* Alvord, *Kaskaskia Records,* 45.

[27] Pollock to the president of Congress, September 18, 1782, L. C., Papers of the Continental Congress, L.

boarding and seizing the "Neptune." Four passengers were put off in a boat manned by sixteen or seventeen French and Spanish boatmen, who, according to their description, were "armed with Cutlasses and wore either Cockades or Deer Tails in their Hats."[28] Another English ship managed to make its escape, but the "Despatch," when near the mouth of the Mississippi, fell a victim to the Americans under Calvert. The captain of the "Despatch" disappeared, and its owner was inclined to suspect foul work on the part of Calvert and his Americans.[29]

Reports of Willing's depredations circulated rapidly throughout West Florida, and the uncertainty and uneasiness which had prevented any armed resistance to the Americans prompted an emigration to the haven of Spanish Louisiana. Houses were locked up, negroes, cattle, and valuables were hustled across the river or hastily put on skiffs and barges and started for New Orleans. Carlos Grand Pré and Juan Delavilleheuvre, the first Spanish officials encountered by these refugees, granted them a provisional welcome and wrote to the governor for further instructions. Gálvez confirmed their hospitality and issued a proclamation affirming Spain's "perfect neutrality" in the struggle between England and her colonies, and conceding "without distinction to the one or to the other the sacred right of hospitality whenever the necessity to claim it should arise."[30]

No exact enumeration exists of the West Floridians who availed themselves of the refuge offered by the governor of Louisiana. Some took the trouble to give written expression of their appreciation. Henry Stuart, who had escaped "in his Shirt," wrote to Gálvez, "It is impossible that I can ever forget the humane and generous treatment I have met with."[31] Another refugee wrote, "It is our duty to proclaim to all the world ... the Beneficient [sic] part which you have

---

[28] Peter Sellier, affidavit at Pensacola, May 4, 1778, A. G. I., Cuba, 191.

[29] Benjamin Hodgdon, affidavit at Pensacola, May 3, 1778, A. G. I., Cuba, 191; David Ross and Company to Gálvez, April 11, 1778, with supporting statements by Pierre Demoriulle, April 13, by Guillaume Terbonne, April 13, and by La Martinière, April 15, *ibid.*, 2370.

[30] Gálvez, proclamation, March 3, 1778, A. G. I., Sto. Dom., 2596; Gálvez to Grand Pré, March 1 and 20, 1778, B. L., La. Coll.

[31] Stuart to Gálvez, March 8, 1778, copy, A. G. I., Sto. Dom., 2596.

so generously and Seasonably taken."[82] Thirty-six others attached their names or marks to a letter expressing "very gratefull thanks for the Succor you have had the goodness to afford us."[33] Judging from these letters, appreciation of Gálvez' kindness seems to have been warm and sincere, and if we may infer that here, as is generally true, the majority did not bother to express its gratitude, the movement across the river becomes an important migration. Some of the refugees, furthermore, made the move permanent. Permission to stay and plant crops was granted tentatively by Governor Gálvez, and the Spanish court later confirmed the permission.[84]

Gálvez extended a comparable welcome to the American party. This cordiality was due in part to the chronic dislike of the Louisianians for the English, a dislike which had been aggravated recently by English interference with Louisiana shipping.[85] It was due also to the influence of Oliver Pollock. Chiefly because of his intimacy with the Spanish governors, Pollock had been named Virginia's agent at New Orleans, and now in a letter brought by Willing he was similarly commissioned by the Continental Congress. Pollock's work has been touched upon above.[86] Again he comes toward the center of the stage, for in the six months following Willing's arrival the stories of his work, of Willing's activities, and of Gálvez' actions merge.

Even before Willing reached New Orleans, Pollock prepared for his coming. "In February 1778," to quote his own account, "I receiv'd intelligence of Capt Willings approch, and immediately I waited on his Excellency the Governor & took every necessary arrangement with him."[87] Pollock persuaded Governor Gálvez to extend to the Americans the freedom of the city. A public building was assigned them for a barrack, and Pollock was permitted to auction off their

---

[82] Harry Alexander to Gálvez, March 15, 1778, copy, *ibid*.

[83] J. Blommart and thirty-five British refugees to Gálvez, no date, *ibid*.

[84] Gálvez to José de Gálvez, April 12, 1778, A. G. I., Sto. Dom., 2596; José de Gálvez to Gálvez, July 24, 1778, A. G. I., Cuba, 174.

[85] See my "The Panis Mission to Pensacola, 1778," *Hispanic American Historical Review*, X (1930), 480.

[86] Chapter VI.

[87] Pollock to the president of Congress, September 18, 1782, L. C., Papers of the Continental Congress, L.

plunder, which consisted mostly of negro slaves. Although Spanish law forbade commerce with foreigners, Gálvez justified his action as follows:

> By this policy I hope to secure great advantages for the king and for this province. To the first because all the things such as indigo, peltries, etc., which they have salvaged and introduced into our territories, are not brought in without my license and consequently not without paying the regular duties. And to the second because the captured negroes, as well as those who have been brought for safekeeping into our domain whose owners are planning to return to Europe, will be purchased by these inhabitants at less than half their value.[38]

In the absence of documentary evidence to fix the amount obtained from these sales, estimates of the plunder have varied considerably, ranging from $15,000 to $1,500,000.[29] Pollock's figures ought to be the most reliable. On April 1 he reported that Willing had got 100 slaves worth 140 pesos each, and that the net proceeds from these and the other plunder amounted to $25,000; and on July 6 he reported $37,500 in addition to the "Rebecca," which had been armed as a war vessel instead of being sold.[40] Nor did this total include the several prizes which Gálvez ordered returned to the English. Obviously, the damage done was much greater than the rather meager profits obtained. Considering the difference between the sale price and the actual value of the slaves and other prizes, and adding the value of the buildings burned, the live stock killed, the crops destroyed, the wine spilled, the household goods ruined, the shipping disturbed, and the agricultural activity interrupted, one comes to a surprisingly high figure and to the conclusion that the pillaging was done on a grand scale.

Although the English had been most appreciative of the favors received from Gálvez, they entered strenuous protests against the welcome accorded to Willing and especially against the disposal of the plunder in New Orleans. By March 15 at least fifteen petitions had

---

[38] Gálvez to José de Gálvez, March 11, 1778, A. G. I., Sto. Dom., 2596.

[39] James, "Spanish Influence in the West during the American Revolution," *Mississippi Valley Historical Review*, IV (1917), 205; Alvord, *Kaskaskia Records*, 45; Winsor, *op. cit.*, 156.

[40] Pollock to Continental Congress, April 1 and July 6, 1778, L. C., Papers of the Continental Congress, L.

been sent to Gálvez, and more were to follow. These petitions recited in detail the damage done by Willing and asserted that the Americans had seized English property even after it had been taken into Spanish territory for safekeeping, that they had violated Spanish sovereignty by making off with boats moored to the Spanish shore, and that they had captured other ships farther downstream where the river was entirely Spanish. Since Willing and the plunder were at New Orleans, the injured Loyalists petitioned Gálvez to see to it that appropriate restitution was made.[41] To consider these cases the governor appointed a commission of three, which eventually decided that the claims against the Americans were just.[42]

These petitions caused Gálvez some concern but no serious alarms until the "Sylph," an English naval vessel commanded by John Fergusson, arrived in the Mississippi. On March 14 Fergusson took up the cause of Willing's victims and wrote vigorously to Gálvez in their behalf. The governor replied with equal vehemence, and the correspondence continued, sometimes technical, sometimes acrimonious, sometimes delving deep into the mazes of international law, frequently trivial, but always spirited. In the course of this disputing Gálvez found it advisable to address certain messages to Willing and Pollock, who replied at length, and thus a full airing resulted, not only of what had been done by the Americans and the Spaniards and the English, but also of the justification which each faction saw for its actions.

The points at issue were really those raised by Willing's victims in their petitions to Gálvez and related to the legality of the American captures of boats tied to the Spanish bank of the Mississippi above Manchac, of boats south of Manchac where both banks were Spanish, and of property which had been carried over into Spanish territory. The English questioned also the propriety of Galvez' conduct in admitting Willing to New Orleans, in allowing him so much freedom there, and in permitting the sale of the plunder. In restating these

---

[41] Fifteen such petitions, dated March 7 to 15, 1778, are to be found in A. G. I., Cuba, 191.

[42] Diario general de todas las ocurrencias, A. G. I., Cuba, 2351; Pollock to Gálvez, July 10, 1778, A. G. I., Cuba, 2370.

points Fergusson added some new arguments. He quoted Gálvez' letter of the preceding year to Captain Lloyd of the "Atlanta," in which Gálvez had asserted that the Mississippi was not a proper theater for hostilities. At that time Gálvez would not allow the English to seize American ships on the lower Mississippi; now he had permitted the very reverse.[43]

In the course of the correspondence certain minutiae were very much magnified and assumed the proportions of major issues. From a study of the letters one might get the impression that Gálvez seized with avidity upon some of these incidentals for the purpose of prolonging the discussions and delaying a settlement. Certainly it was to his interest to maintain the *status quo* and to postpone the termination of negotiations. But Fergusson made the first descent to trivialities, and throughout the controversy was most assiduous in dwelling on points extraneous to the main issues but which might serve to embarrass his correspondent. There is the temptation in a debate, of course, to concede no point that may possibly favor the opponent, and furthermore, a contestant is apt to be infected with an enthusiasm which carries his quibbling to unjustified and uncontemplated lengths. Gálvez and Fergusson often enlivened their sound arguments on the merits of the case by spirited paragraphs on a variety of nonessentials.

Fergusson's letter of greeting to the Spanish governor included a complaint against McIntyre, one of Willing's lieutenants, "who placed himself opposite to His Majesty's Ship under my command, and made use of several threats and provoking speeches." The English officer asked prompt satisfaction "to prevent the fatal consequences that may attend your giving more countenance to a lawless Banditti, than you seem to do to His Britannic Majesty's Servants and liege Subjects."[44]

Gálvez' reply was not exactly soothing:

The complaint which you have made to me against the American officer is just, though it would be much more just, if to the simple cry which he made to the frigate he had not been answered with hard and offensive

---
[43] Fergusson to Gálvez, March 15, 1778, A. G. I., Cuba, 191.
[44] *Idem* to *idem*, March 14, 1778, *ibid*.

words, which provided a motive for his reply. In consequence of knowing this I will make said officer apologize to me for having made threats in the territory of His Catholic Majesty as well as for his impudence to you, and for this purpose I hope that you will see fit to send an officer of your frigate, so that in my presence the American can make adequate reparation, and the officer can convey it to you for your satisfaction and that of His British Majesty's flag.[45]

Later, when Fergusson declined to send an officer to receive this apology and demanded that McIntyre be surrendered for appropriate punishment, Gálvez declined on the ground that the offense was primarily against himself and the Spanish flag. For this violation of Spanish hospitality "complete satisfaction" in the form of an apology was exacted. Then Gálvez went on to draw an interesting distinction between an insult which was merely verbal and an affront which involved actual damage. The distinction is perhaps not usually recognized where libel or slander are concerned, but the governor made the most of it.

You surely are ready to admit that the insult was by word, and by words only the satisfaction must be given; if it had been by act, the satisfaction would have been with his person. This is justice, and any other pretension is useless.[46]

Not content with having frustrated the British attempt to bring McIntyre to punishment for his vocal outburst, Gálvez embraced the opportunity to ruffle Fergusson's feelings still further. Knowing full well that national pride would not permit acceptance, he offered to send on board the frigate a Spanish flag and a corporal's guard (at Fergusson's expense) to insure the English against any possible molestation from the Americans in New Orleans. The reply was the inevitable one—Fergusson felt able to protect himself and his vessel without the assistance of the seven grenadiers. Whereupon Gálvez protested that he had not intended to provide a force capable of defending the frigate, which he knew to be well manned, nor even to reënforce it, but that he had hoped to prevent a conflict through the presence of a flag "which the Americans respect." Without the protection of the

---

[45] Gálvez to Fergusson, March 15, 1778, certified copy, A. G. I., Cuba, 1232.
[46] *Idem* to *idem*, March 20, 1778, certified copy, *ibid*.

Spanish flag there was real danger of attack, he asserted, "since the Americans allege that having suffered captures on the river, on the same river they have the right to make reprisals."⁴⁷

In the same letter Gálvez reminded the English captain that he had neglected to salute the Spanish flag in the customary manner, and requested that he should not refer to any person under the protection of the Spanish government as a "Rebel." Fergusson, explaining his inability to salute the Spanish flag, wrote:

> I cannot ... whilst there is a Flag—displayed under your Guns, which is not acknowledged by Great Britain, and ought not to be by any Power upon Earth, and particularly by Nations that are possessed of Colonies, who should be cautious of setting a pernicious example in abetting, favoring or assisting by any means, directly or indirectly, such Subjects united in direct and open rebellion.⁴⁸

Not all the correspondence dealt with matters of punctilio, however. There was some careful reasoning on the propriety of Gálvez' recent actions, on the legality of Willing's plundering, and on his status in New Orleans. Gálvez professed an inability to understand why Fergusson accused him of "a declaration of war, a violation of the treaties of peace, the law of nations, and the rights of mankind," since his action in admitting to Spanish Louisiana both the English (the refugees) and the Americans (the expeditionary force under Willing) was in accord with the practice in Europe. Asserting his desire to preserve an "exact neutrality," Gálvez warned that, if the slightest hostility were committed on the Mississippi below Manchac toward Spanish subjects or toward any of the individuals under the king's protection, he would consider himself obligated to suppress it with force. The wording of this sentence is such that it appears to have been intended as a caution to Fergusson not to attempt any stroke of violence against Willing or his men while they were under the protection of Gálvez. Gálvez later claimed credit for rattling the saber to shield the Americans.⁴⁹

---

⁴⁷ *Idem* to *idem*, March 14, 15, 18, and 20, 1778, certified copies, *ibid.;* Fergusson to Gálvez, March 15, 1778, A. G. I., Cuba, 191.

⁴⁸ Fergusson to Gálvez, March 15, 1778, *ibid.*

⁴⁹ Gálvez to Fergusson, March 15, 1778, certified copy, *ibid.*, 1232; Gálvez to Gardoqui, Havana, April 28, 1785, A. G. I., Sto. Dom., 1243.

Fergusson, however, put a different interpretation upon Gálvez' statement, treating it as an acknowledgment that the captures which the Americans had made in the part of the river mentioned were improper. The governor's approval of these seizures, as expressed in the permission that Willing and Pollock had received to bring such plunder into New Orleans and to dispose of it there, he branded as inconsistent, not only with the sentiments expressed in Gálvez' last letter, but also with the stand that Gálvez had taken in the preceding spring. He referred to the letter to Captain Lloyd, of May 12, 1777, in which Gálvez had asserted that the Mississippi was not a proper theater for hostilities between the English and the Americans and had said that he would not allow Lloyd to seize American ships. Fergusson asked, therefore, that Gálvez order the restitution of all property captured on the Mississippi.[50]

On March 18, Gálvez replied that his earlier correspondence with Lloyd was being misinterpreted, that it had referred only to the lower Mississippi where both banks were Spanish, and that if he had written "en todo el Rio," the reference was clearly to that part of it. As to the river above Manchac he maintained that the Spanish-English boundary was explicitly defined by treaty as "in the middle of the Mississippi," and asked if the English wanted to cede all the river to Spain. The argument continued, correctly, it would seem, that since the Spanish and English shared control of the river above Manchac, the Spanish could not be expected to prevent hostilities there. For the part of the river below Manchac, however, Gálvez agreed that no violence was permissible by either the British or the Americans. And to prove his sincerity he pointed out that, even before receiving Fergusson's demands, he had begun to put this policy into effect. "There are already various subjects of His British Majesty, who by virtue of the Spanish protection have recovered their captured effects and the liberty of their persons, but at the same time there are others for whom that protection is helpless, though they were seized on the Mississippi," because they were upstream where Spanish control was not absolute.[51]

---

[50] Fergusson to Gálvez, March 15, 1778, A. G. I., Cuba, 191.
[51] Gálvez to Fergusson, March 18, 1778, certified copy, *ibid.*, 1232.

Having found Gálvez ready to agree that the lower Mississippi was was not a proper place for English-American hostilities (the Pensacola prize court to the contrary notwithstanding), Fergusson received Gálvez' word that Willing would be required to surrender the English effects seized there as well as such other property as had come under Spanish protection prior to its capture. With this much accomplished Fergusson was less concerned about the propriety or impropriety of Gálvez' harboring Willing and his men. That question might be referred to the European courts. He addressed a proclamation "to all His Britannic Majesty's Loyal Subjects in the Province of Louisiana & Town of New Orleans," announcing Gálvez' promise to restore all property the Rebels had seized between Manchac and Balize. Nevertheless, since the Rebels were receiving Spanish protection and had a guardhouse in New Orleans, he urged all loyal Britishers to leave Louisiana and put themselves under his protection. But he concluded by saying, "Should you reject this offer, and blindly confide in the professions of the Enemies of your Country, you must take upon yourselves the consequences." Then, about April 10, having taken precautions to make sure there were no slaves aboard the "Sylph" who really belonged to the Americans, he sailed for Pensacola.[52]

Gálvez' decision that much of the captured property ought to be returned obviously affected the American party. Correspondence with Willing about its restoration began, therefore, about the time of the arrival of the "Sylph." The American commander was not inclined to submit without argument. With respect to a few minor items, such as a single slave belonging to George Ross, he acceded to Gálvez' order promptly and without contest, but whenever a major item was involved, he protested at length. Some of his arguments in justification of his acts seem to have validity. He upheld, for example, the capture of Campbell's vessel, the "Neptune," which was "laden with articles absolutely necessary for the Enemies of the States." She was made prize nine leagues below New Orleans on her way to the West Indies. Not the least alarm was occasioned to any Spanish subject. She was

---

[52] Fergusson, proclamation, March 23, 1778, *ibid.*, 112; Fergusson to Gálvez, April 3, 1778, *ibid.*, 191; "Diario general . . ." *ibid.*, 2351.

afloat on the Mississippi, the navigation whereof was equally free to English and Spanish, and consequently, Willing contended, she was not in a Spanish port or under Spanish protection. He cited the judgment of the court of vice admiralty at Pensacola in the case of the American vessels taken in the Mississippi, that "Captures so made came under the Denomination, as that of prizes made on the High Seas," and claimed the "Neptune," therefore, as a "Lawfull Prize." As a compromise he suggested that the vessel and cargo be sold and the proceeds sequestered in Gálvez' treasury until Congress and the court of Spain could reach a decision.[53]

Willing laid claim to Stephen Shakespear's bateau in similar fashion. It had been captured first in British territory, then was "Stolen off in the night by Mr. Shakespear contrary to his Faith pledged," and recaptured afloat in the Mississippi, "tho' fastened to a Log of Wood near the [Spanish] Shore." Shakespear told a different story, though he admitted he had not yet received formal protection from a Spanish official at the time of the capture, and Gálvez decided in his favor.[54]

As to Rapicaut's boats, they were taken above Spanish Aux Arcs (Ozarks), one on the river, the other "Boarded the Instant she touched the land on the Spanish Side of the Mississippi." They were engaged in illicit trade with Fort Vincennes, "supplyed the Enemies of the States of America," and had "neither Passport, Permission nor Protection," Willing presumed to hope, from any officer of the court of Spain. He argued that the seizure of Rapicaut's boats, therefore, was "consonant, to the Universal Custom of all Civilized Nations."[55]

Gálvez reiterated his order for the surrender of Campbell's, Shakespear's, and Rapicaut's boats and cargoes, appending a lengthy justification of his stand. Still unconvinced, Willing replied:

> The prizes in Question are now in your Power and under your Authority; But I apprehend I cannot be answerable to My Masters the Honorable Congress for the Restitution of these Prizes if your Excellency does not think proper to give me a positive Order in writing for so doing.[56]

[53] Willing to Gálvez, March 18, 1778, *ibid.*, 191.
[54] *Ibid.;* Shakespear to Gálvez, March 12, 1778, *ibid.*
[55] Willing to Gálvez, March 24, 1778, *ibid.*, 2370; John Mucklemurry, affidavit at New Orleans, March 18, 1778, *ibid.*, 191.
[56] Willing to Gálvez, April 5, 1778, A. G. I., Cuba, 2370.

Gálvez was inflexible. These captures must be returned, and he added that he would give the same reply if the whole United States navy were on hand.[57]

Other captures disapproved by the Spanish governor were foregone by the Americans, and on May 1 Gálvez could summarize to Governor Chester his decisions in favor of the English as follows:

> You will see that I have not only reclaimed and turned over to her masters the brig the *Neptune,* seized on the Spanish bank, but also your negroes, likewise those of Livingston and Bay, the property of Priest, that of Shakespear, the negroes of Poussette and Marshall, the property of Rapicaut, that of William Eason and Archibald Crawford, and finally the schooner and negroes belonging to Mr. Ross.... You understand that I cannot be responsible for what has been seized between Natchez and Manchac.[58]

The relief which Gálvez felt over Fergusson's departure was only temporary. Early in April the "Hound," under Captain Joseph Nunn, arrived before New Orleans and was joined soon by another frigate. Gálvez had taken steps to improve the defenses of New Orleans. A battery of eight cannon had been set up and the "Rebecca," the American prize ship, was before the town armed and ready to assist in its defense. Nevertheless, we must conclude that, when Gálvez wrote to his uncle, "I hope to find myself able to resist any insult which these English war vessels may intend to offer," he was not so much reporting progress in strengthening New Orleans as whistling in the dark.[59]

Although maintaining a bold front toward both the English and the Americans, Gálvez realized his predicament. On May 5 he represented to the Continental Congress that he was in a "critical situation with his neighbors in consequence of the protection and favors shown by him to Captain Willing and his Party."[60] The insinuations of Willing, the presence of the English frigates, the attitude of Captain Nunn, and the inadequacy of his own military defenses caused him

---

[57] Gálvez to Willing, April 6, 1778, copy, *ibid.,* 191.

[58] Willing to Gálvez, March 31, 1778, *ibid.;* Gálvez to Chester, May 1, 1778, draft, *ibid.*

[59] Gálvez to José de Gálvez, April 12, 1778. A. G. I., Sto. Dom., 2596; "Diario general...," A. G. I., Cuba, 2351.

[60] Burnett, *op. cit.,* III, 494 *n.*

concern. Rumor had it that an English vessel of thirty-two guns was about to enter the Mississippi and that two others were expected.

These frigates can have no other objective than this town [Gálvez reflected], because they do not need to come up or do anything at Manchac, Natchez, or the other English establishments, for there is no one at these places. He who commands these frigates is said to be a brutal man, capable of committing any atrocity without disturbing himself about the consequences. His intention apparently is to ask me to give up the prizes of the Americans and their persons, especially the commander and officers of the party, and if I do not comply to open fire on the city and destroy it.

This letter continued with a statement of his intention to utilize 'all his forces, if necessary, to protect the Americans and their legitimate prizes. But it emphasized the inadequacy of the forces at his command, requested reënforcements "con prontitud," and stressed the fact that New Orleans was not only open to attack, but also "the only frontier which Spain has with the English." New Orleans would be more secure, Gálvez suggested, if war were declared, because then the English ships could be stopped at Balize.[61]

The presence in and around New Orleans of so many armed foreigners contributed to Gálvez' uneasiness; on April 14 he supplemented his plea for more troops by requiring that every English subject in New Orleans should take an oath of neutrality or depart from the province. Captain Nunn protested strenuously, and eight or ten of the English chose to depart rather than take the oath, but the majority complied.

I have read with astonishment your ordinance of this day's date [Nunn wrote], requiring from His Britannic Majesty's Subjects, an oath comprehending allegiance and neutrality, as well as a parole of honor to the Spanish Crown. I cannot conceive what could induce your Excellency to take such measures with the Subjects of a Prince in amity with His Catholic Majesty. If you have permitted British Merchants to carry on commerce in your Province you certainly ought to protect them, and if you have given Asylum to such of his Britannic Majesty's Loyal Subjects, as have been driven from their habitations by the Enemies of their King and

---

[61] Gálvez to Navarro, April 14, 1778, A. G. I., Cuba, 1232; Gálvez to Navarro, April 21, 1778, *ibid*.

Country, you have only acted conformable to the Law of Nations, and what every civilized People would think themselves bound to do, on such occasion. . . .[62]

On the seventeenth a similar oath was administered to the Americans, who accepted it unanimously.[63] Gálvez may have achieved greater security through these oaths, though there is some doubt as to their efficacy, but he certainly incurred the displeasure and distrust of the English authorities in West Florida because of them. Nunn's protest was echoed by others from McGillivray, the commander at Natchez, and from Governor Chester.[64]

On the lakes behind New Orleans another complication arose. The English vessel "West Florida" had been there for some time and had received permission to pass and repass the Spanish fort at the bayou of St. John without being stopped. But on April 21 the officer at the fort, having received new instructions from the governor, stopped the boat and forbade Captain Burdon to proceed. Angered by this interference, Burdon served notice that during the observance of this policy, "I will not suffer a Boat to proceed across those Lakes or anywhere I may be a Cruizeing." In less than a week he had seized two boats on Lake Pontchartrain, and though Gálvez wrote to Captain Nunn for explanation and restitution, he was put off with the excuse that Burdon was not under the orders of Nunn. Here was an actual disadvantage for Spanish Louisiana incurred because of Gálvez' protection of the Americans.[65]

Without Gálvez' stalwart protection the Americans at New Orleans would have been face to face with disaster. Oliver Pollock explained the situation succinctly to Congress,

giving the greatest applause to Govr. Galvez for his noble Spirit & behaviour on this Occasion, for, tho' he had no Batteries erected, or even Men to defend the place against the Two Sloops of War, and at the same time a Small Sloop with a Hundred Men in the Lakes all coming against him

---

[62] Nunn to Gálvez, April 16, 1778, *ibid.*, 191; "Diario general . . . ," *ibid.*, 2351.
[63] *Ibid.*
[64] McGillivray to Gálvez, no date, *ibid.*, 2370; Chester to Gálvez, May 28, 1778, *ibid.*, 191.
[65] Burdon to Gálvez, April 21, 1778, *ibid.*; Gálvez to Nunn, April 29, 1778, copy, *ibid.*; Nunn to Gálvez, May 1, 1778, *ibid.*

with Demands & Threats, yet in this Situation he laughed at their Haughtiness and despised their attempts, and in short they returned as they came.[66]

Pollock was not only the only one to recognize the value of Gálvez' protection of the Americans. Congress expressed appreciation "for his spirited and disinterested conduct toward these states." Governor Chester's tribute came in the form of an upbraiding for "every possible Countenance & Encouragement given to the Rebels in Louisiana." Some years later Gálvez was to reminisce without exaggeration that Willing and his men "owed their existence to our protection."[67]

That Gálvez was not subjected to any armed attacks by the English as a consequence of his protection of Willing's party was due in part to the bold front that he assumed in answering the English demands. The English were reluctant to embroil their nation in a war with Spain. Gálvez held the whip hand, of course, in his authority over the prizes and captured goods, and he had earned some English gratitude by his opening of Louisiana to the refugees and by his restoration of some of the plunder. He improved the defenses of his colony, though by itself this military array would have been very frail protection. After the chief danger was passed, 3 vessels, 12 officers, and 212 men arrived from Havana, making Louisiana fairly safe against reprisals.[68] Delavillebeuvre reported that a contemplated English and Indian descent upon New Orleans was averted by the inconstancy of the Indian allies, and George Rogers Clark's conquest of the Illinois country frustrated another plan for vengeance upon Gálvez.[69] These later factors eventually contributed to Louisiana's security, but in the spring of 1778 Gálvez' boldness was probably the chief factor in forestalling British retribution.

Meanwhile, Willing's expedition had achieved one effect that was the exact opposite of the intention of its planners. Instead of facilitat-

---

[66] Pollock to Congress, May 7, 1778, extract, A. G. I., Cuba, 2370.

[67] United States, *Journals of the Continental Congress*, I, 91; Chester to Gálvez, May 28, 1778, A. G. I., Cuba, 191; Gálvez to Gardoqui, April 28, 1785, A. G. I., Sto. Dom., 1243.

[68] Gálvez to José de Gálvez, June 9, 1778, *ibid.*, 2596.

[69] Delavillebeuvre to Gálvez, July 6, 1778, certified copy, *ibid.*; Gálvez to Navarro, September 2, 1778, A. G. I., Cuba, 1232.

ing the sending of supplies upstream to the Revolutionists, it called forth British reënforcement of West Florida and the establishment of a virtual blockade of the river. American control of the river front was challenged as early as March when a force of fifty soldiers was sent to Manchac. They surprised the small garrison before dawn on March 19, and, surrounding the building in which Willing's men were sleeping, fired two or three rounds, killing two men and one woman and wounding eight or ten, and took fourteen prisoner. When he learned of this capture, Willing sent another detachment to Manchac, which had the good fortune to recover the post without any opposition, because the Loyalists believed that a superior force was coming against them and took to the woods.[70]

During April Pollock and Willing were more concerned about control of the Natchez district and sent some men under Lieutenant Harrison to see that the oath of neutrality was observed. Learning that these men were to go north, Colonel Anthony Hutchins broke his parole in New Orleans and hastened to his home where he "excited the inhabitants of Natchez to take up arms, by declaring on OATH to the people, that this detachment was coming up with a determination of robbing the inhabitants of their property without exception." Thus alarmed, the settlers took arms and stationed themselves at White Cliffs, prepared to resist any further American plundering. Harrison was warned of the danger by John Tally, a league below this ambush, and he sent Tally ahead with word that no hostilities were intended. Presuming that this pacific message had carried conviction, Harrison came up and across the river toward the Natchez settlers. There was a brief parley. Then Harrison discovered that he had entered a trap. He called out to all "friends to the United States" to stand apart; the reply came for all "friends to the Natchez" to fall below the gunwales of the American boat. A shot was fired—according to the settlers, by Harrison's order; according to the Americans, by those on shore. Then the firing became general. But the Americans, outnumbered and far more exposed than the settlers on shore, got the worst of it. Five were

---

[70] Gálvez to José de Gálvez, March 24, 1778, *ibid.*, 223; "Diario general...," *ibid.*, 2351.

killed; the rest quickly surrendered.⁷¹ The Americans may have fired first, since Harrison did not know how large a concealed force was arrayed against him, but there would have been less folly in the settlers' beginning the action.

Inasmuch as Gálvez had been instrumental in persuading Pollock to allow Hutchins the liberty of the town on his parole of honor, he took Hutchins' breach of the parole as a personal affront. Writing to Captain Nunn, he protested against this ingratitude and inquired what Nunn thought of such conduct. Nunn replied that he was not fully informed of the circumstances which induced Hutchins to act as he had, but that he had been "cruelly plundered by the Enemies of his Country" very recently, and that his action against Harrison was self-protective, "to prevent the people who had already distressed him, from compleating his ruin." Nunn insisted that Hutchins appreciated the assistance he had received in Spanish Louisiana, and some months later Hutchins confessed such an obligation, along with much more besides.⁷²

In May Willing was frustrated in another effort to renew his control along the Florida bank. He blamed his failure to get possession of Manchac this time on the unexpected appearance of the enemy in the Lakes, and on the discontent of his own men because Pollock had not completed the settlement of their accounts. Further grounds for Floridian apprehension of Willing appear in the latter's hope, expressed on this occasion, that "a party may yet get up time enough to open the Levy, drown the Country, Felle some Trees in the *Brice*[?] and by Burning and destroying the Buildings and other materials, put a stop to their Operations until such time as sickness or ye arrival of a Reinforcement might effectually prevent their fixing themselves solidly."⁷³ Willing was not able to carry out this desire, and instead we find Governor Chester encouraging the settlers to cast off all pretense of attachment to the Revolution. He sent garrisons to Manchac and Natchez and exhorted the refugees to come back under the British flag or be

---

⁷¹ "Deposition of James Truly, November 6, 1797," *in* Ellicott, *Journal*, 130–132; "Journal of Captain Phelps," *in* Claiborne, *op. cit.*, 121.

⁷² Nunn to Gálvez, April 23, 1778, A. G. I., Cuba, 191; Hutchins to Gálvez, August 10, 1778, *ibid.*, 192.

⁷³ Willing to Gálvez, May 24, 1778, *ibid.*, 2370.

guilty of "Criminal neglect of that duty which is due from you as faithful subjects, to the Best of Kings."[74]

Willing wrote of the loss of the English bank as "an unlucky circumstance to me and to the States." And though he tried to console himself with the thought that, at least, it had given him an opportunity to distinguish his friends from his enemies, the Americans suffered disadvantages.[75] The settlers, soon in coöperation with the troops sent from Pensacola, set up an effective blockade on the river, interrupting Pollock's shipments of supplies to Fort Pitt, intercepting some messengers on their way from the United States, and eventually becoming so suspicious of Gálvez' pro-American proclivities that they prevented the dispatch of goods even under the Spanish flag.[76]

Having aroused the West Floridians, Willing was unable to leave New Orleans by the Mississippi route. All his avenues of departure were endangered by these opponents whom he had victimized. And by tarrying on and on in New Orleans, he wore out his welcome with both Gálvez and Pollock. The Spanish governor's displeasure was incurred quite early when Willing issued a proclamation at New Orleans to his paroled prisoners. Gálvez considered it a disregard of Spanish sovereignty and called Willing to task for taking advantage of the hospitality and favors which had been extended to him. Feeling the governor's ire and realizing that he stood in need of further protection from him, Willing promptly explained that his offense had been unintentional, that he had thought this the least objectionable means of communicating with his paroled captives, and he apologized profusely for any offense he might have committed.[77] On at least one other occasion, as we have just seen, Gálvez displayed irritation toward Willing.

Indirectly, even more than directly, Willing's presence at New Orleans came to be a matter of annoyance to the Spanish governor.

---

[74] Chester to "all his Brittannick Majesty's loyal Subjects in Louisiana," May 28, 1778, *ibid.*, 191.

[75] Willing to Clark, September 1, 1778, *in* James, *George Rogers Clark Papers, 1771–1781*, 67–68.

[76] Pollock to Congress, May 7, 1778, extract, A. G. I., Cuba, 2370; Barker to McGillivray, September 12, 1778, B. L., La. Coll.

[77] Gálvez to Willing, March 27, 1778, copy *in* A. G. I., Cuba, 191; Willing to Gálvez, April 1, 1778, A. G. I., Cuba, 2370.

He and Willing got along with only a moderate amount of friction. There is reason to believe, too, that the discomfiture of the West Floridians, through Willing's expedition, was a source of satisfaction to Gálvez. But the more Willing's stay was prolonged, the more uncomfortable Gálvez' position became. He was exposed, thus, to embarrassing demands from English naval officers in the Mississippi, to unpleasant protests from the authorities at Pensacola, and to real worry about the security of Louisiana should these protests be translated into action, not to mention his fear that English complaints would result in a severe rebuke for him from the court of Spain. Proofs of Gálvez' readiness that Willing should leave are seen not only in his expressions but also in his willingness to grant loans and special permissions to expedite the departure of the American party.[78]

The friction between Gálvez and Willing, however, was as nothing compared to that which developed between Pollock and the American leader. At first Pollock had coöperated most heartily with Willing. To his influence the Americans were indebted for the warm welcome they had received in New Orleans. He had managed the sales of the plunder and had planned and assisted in some of the most important strokes against the English. But Pollock soon found that young Willing was difficult to do business with, that he had scant judgment about the probable consequences of the things he did, that he was content to dissipate in New Orleans when he should have been making genuine efforts to return to the States. This procrastination about going back north was especially aggravating. By the end of May the rift was so great that Willing felt it necessary to address Pollock in writing "to prevent any Verbal altercation." A paragraph of Willing's letter is included here because it describes the dispute and the condition of the American party, and because its style reveals the spirit of the writer. After quoting his own instructions from Congress and condemning Pollock for his administration of the finances of the expedition, Willing wrote:

---

[78] For example, the permit to fit out the "Rebecca" for the purpose, and an advance from the Spanish treasury, on Pollock's credit, of 15,948 pesos, in addition to the 24,023 pesos previously lent.—José de Gálvez to Gálvez, September 24, 1778 and February 10, 1779, A. G. I., Cuba, 174.

But it is my Business at present to Insist upon a total change of Proceedure—
My Men and Officers are discontented, myself displeased and the Governor himself highly disatisfied with your Conduct and what is of the most serious consequence My Men are deserting and the American *Bank* as it is termed is become proverbiallly rediculous. In a word the Service suffers and our Enemys rejoice—This therefore is to *insist* that You forthwith make out all your accounts so that the one half belonging to me and the Men be instantly divided and that you have the Ballance that is due on that Score ready to pay into my Hands on Monday or Tuesday next; Free of other charge or Commission than those of the Vendue Master.... I have kept a Copy of this to lay befor The Congress and Governour if needfull.[79]

Answering this "very Extraordinary and unexpected Letter," Pollock suggested that had Willing taken a moment for reflection he would not have signed it. He promised a speedy accounting but laid the delay to Willing's failure to place a valuation on the captured "Rebecca." Willing had voluntarily put the prize goods in his hands and in so doing had occasioned him "no small Expence." Expressing full confidence in a vindication from Congress should Willing lay his "unsupportable Grievances" before it, and explaining the governor's displeasure as due to Willing's military maneuvers rather than to his own conduct, Pollock concluded his letter by warning Willing "to be more cautious whom you trust as some how or other the Enemy is acquainted with all your Proceedings."[80]

As Willing's stay stretched out into months, Pollock grew increasingly anxious to be rid of him—to end the expense of maintaining him and his party, to minimize English antagonism and suspicion of commerce up the Mississippi, to put an end to the contention with Willing. Pollock's reports to the Continental Congress, together with his continued efforts to expedite Willing's departure, indicate the measure of his annoyance. From his letter of July 6:

The Small Party you sent here under the Command of Captn. James Willing without any order or subordinations has only thrown the whole river into Confusion and created a Number of Enemies and a heavy Expence.[81]

---
[79] Willing to Pollock, May 30, 1778, A. G. I., Cuba, 2370.
[80] Pollock to Willing, May 31, 1778, *ibid*.
[81] Pollock to Congress, July 6, 1778, extract, *ibid*.

Again on August 11:

> What his next Pretence for tarrying here will be God knows, but as there is a clear Passage for him and his Party to go up, part by Land and Part by Water through the Spanish Territories by way of the Appelousa & Nachetosh and join Col. Clark I am determined to stop all Supplies in order to get him away.[82]

Wishing for Willing's departure was easier than bringing it about. There was not only Willing's changeableness to overcome but a very definite English hazard as well. Nevertheless Pollock with Gálvez' assistance set himself to accomplish it. The Mississippi route was first attempted.

> Capt. Willing and his Party of Men I believe will set out from here in a few Days for Manchac where they are going to entrench themselves till you send down a proper force to assist them in making their Way back, which I hope will be soon.[83]

Pollock made this optimistic report on May 20, but, as was indicated above, "the sudden and unexpected appearance of the Enemy in the Lakes," the garrison which Chester had promised for Manchac, frustrated this plan of moving Willing out of New Orleans and toward the north. The new British garrisons, the aroused settlers at Natchez, and the Indians newly inflamed by British agents closed the Mississippi route.[84]

Pollock's next recourse was the sea route. On June 16, after unsuccessful efforts to hire a French or Spanish boat, he asked Gálvez' permission to fit out the "Morris" (the "Rebecca" rechristened) to carry Willing and his men home. Two days later he thanked Gálvez for granting the permission. There was some delay, however, in preparing the "Morris," and further postponement by Willing, who, in his reluctance to sail, urged that he ought to await the arrival of the despatches that O'Hara had left at the Arkansas.[85] Meanwhile Willing was asking the governor for permission to go north through Spanish territory and under Spanish protection, thus to escape the fury of

---

[82] Pollock to Congress, August 11, 1778, L. C., Papers of the Continental Congress, L.
[83] Pollock to the Commerce Committee, May 20, 1778, *ibid.*
[84] Willing to Gálvez, May 24, 1778, A. G. I., Cuba, 2370.
[85] Pollock to Gálvez, June 16 and 18, 1778, *ibid.;* Pollock to Congress, August 11, 1778, L. C., Papers of the Continental Congress, L.

the Natchez settlers. Gálvez refused because he suspected that this was merely a pretext to cloak new ravages of the English establishments. A partial concession was made, however, and on July 14 the governor issued a letter to the Spanish commanders along the Mississippi to allow Willing and twenty-five Americans to pass. But with the settlers so angry, the journey up the river was too hazardous a venture and no advantage was taken of this opportunity.[86]

A month later Robert George requested permission to lead the men, "lately commanded by Willing," north through Spanish territory. Gálvez replied that he would grant such permission if the American officers would swear "to follow the route directly, and not to offend or bother during the journey any English subjects, neither their possessions nor their persons, but on the contrary to treat them with the same consideration as if they were Spanish subjects." The American officers immediately furnished the required oath of honor, and Gálvez issued a formal safe-conduct for the party by way of Opelousas, Natchitoches, and the Arkansas. The court of Spain eventually gave its approval, but in the meantime the Americans were on their way.[87]

Their progress can be traced in part by certain drafts on Pollock by George, "Commandt. of the troops Imbarqued from Fort Pitt with Capn. James Willing out of the States of Virginia." At the Arkansas on January 8, 1779, there was one for $800, another on January 21 for "$708 dollars 1 ryal," and from the Spanish Aux Arcs (Ozarks), on February 4, $700 and $1000, and on February 25, $200. We can understand Pollock's report that "a very considerable expense was incurr'd ... by the Publick Agent, who had however this consolation that nothing but his unwearied efforts to surmount a variety of obstacles could possibly have enabled them to return in safety."[88] These drafts,

---

[86] Gálvez to George, August 18, 1778, draft, A. G. I., Cuba, 2370; Gálvez a todos los Comandantes de la Costa del Rio Misisipi hta. la Punta Cortada, July 14, 1778, certified copy, *ibid.*, 2351.

[87] George to Gálvez, August 14, 1778, A. G. I., Cuba, 2370; Gálvez to George, August 18 and 19, 1778, drafts, *ibid.*; George and Harrison to Gálvez, August 19, 1778, *ibid.*; José de Gálvez to Gálvez, February 10, 1779, *ibid.*, 174.

[88] Copies of these drafts, with Pollock's certificate of the reason for their non-acceptance, are in A. G. I., Cuba, 122-1; Pollock to the president of Congress, September 18, 1782, L. C., Papers of the Continental Congress, L.

it is true, reached Pollock after he had exhausted his personal fortune and credit in the service of the patriot cause, and consequently he was unable to pay them, but it was only because of Pollock's letter of credit that George was enabled to get supplies for his men on this journey back to the States.

Willing himself finally got away from New Orleans, going by sloop for Philadelphia. Pollock reported to the Commerce Committee that an additional expense of 919 pesos and 1 real had been incurred in the final settlement with Willing but implied that it was worth it to be rid of him. "I take the Liberty," he added, "of forwarding a Box of the best Havanna Segars which I wish safe."[89]

It has been said that Willing went to the Tensaw settlements above Mobile where he agitated in vain for the rebel cause, and that he was taken prisoner and would have been hanged at Mobile in expiation for his atrocities and for circulating the Declaration of Independence. He escaped this dire punishment, according to the report, only because of Washington's prompt notification that he would hang a British officer if Willing were executed.[90] Having found no direct evidence to support this story, I regard it as improbable.

But Willing's journey home was an unfortunate one; neither he nor the "Havanna Segars" arrived safe. The sloop was captured and Willing was taken a prisoner to New York. He contrived to escape and took refuge at the house of a friend but found no shelter there, for "being a person of Consequence" he was given up to the English authorities. He was transferred to Long Island and then back to New York where he was loaded with irons for having resented an insult offered by an English officer. Congress directed the commissary general of prisoners, on January 14, 1779, to supply him "with one hundred pounds, New York currency, for his subsistence at New York." On July 5, 1779, his exchange for Nicholas Ogden was proposed, and toward the close of the year he is supposed to have been exchanged for

---

[89] Pollock to the Commerce Committee, October 8, 1778, *ibid*.
[90] Hamilton, *Colonial Mobile*, 311; Mason, *Chapters from Illinois History*, 288; Pickett, *History of Alabama*, 348.

Colonel Henry Hamilton.[91] At any rate, he was back at New Orleans in 1783, making affidavit that one of the negroes seized at the time of his expedition apparently had belonged to a citizen of the United States, who was "Intitled to the Value of Said Negroe."[92]

Besides condemning Willing for his cruelty, writers have generally come to two conclusions about his expedition, to both of which I subscribe. In the first place, they recognize that, in addition to temporarily crippling the English naval forces on the Mississippi, Willing interrupted the flow of supplies, particularly of lumber, from Natchez to Pensacola and Jamaica. In the second place, they point out that because of the expedition West Florida was lost to the patriots, or at least that Loyalist feeling in the district was strengthened. George Rogers Clark voiced this in picturesque language.

The Intelligance from New Orleans is bad. I dont doubt you have before this been made Acquainted with it. I am now Convinced of what I have long suspected the bad Conduct of an American Officer in that Quarter. when plunder is the prevailing Passion of any Body of Troops wheather Great or Small, their Cuntrey can Expect but little service from them. Which I am sorry to find was too Much the Case with the party I allude to. Floriday on the Mississippi Might have been good subjects to the States if proper Measures had been taken and probably saved the Expence of a Campain. I should be happy hereaftor to find that I am Mistaken on this head.[93]

Certain other consequences of the expedition have not been so widely recognized. One concerned the strengthening of the defenses of British West Florida. In part, this had already been accomplished through the accentuation of Loyalist feeling. Now it took more concrete form. A new commander was sent to Pensacola and instructed "to erect a fort on the Mississippi, at or near where Fort Bute stood, to command entrance to the Ibberville, with a garrison of 300; also to

---

[91] "Z" to Washington, December 19, 1778, L. C., Washington Papers, XCIV; Thwaites and Kellogg, *op. cit.*, 192 n.; Randolph, *Memoirs, Correspondence, and Miscellanies from the Papers of Thomas Jefferson*, I, 169; United States, *Journals of the Continental Congress*, XII, 65; Paullin, *Out-Letters of the Continental Marine Committee and Board of Admiralty*, II, 93; Monette, *History of the Discovery and Settlement of the Valley of the Mississippi*, I, 435 n.

[92] Willing, affidavit at New Orleans, March 5, 1783, A. G. I, Cuba, 191.

[93] Clark to Leyba, November 6, 1778, A. G. I., Cuba, 1.

provide 2 or more gallies to protect the navigation of the river and to prevent any craft of the rebels descending to New Orleans."[94] This reënforcement of West Florida, especially as it added to the resistance that Gálvez had ultimately to face in the conquest of the district for Spain in 1779, was one of the most important results.

Another point not generally remarked, concerned the effect upon Pollock's usefulness to the Revolutionary cause. By the end of 1778 bankruptcy practically prevented Pollock from continuing his service of supply. The real difficulty, of course, was that neither Virginia nor the Continental Congress had sent remittances to cover the first purchases and to make others possible. But the wiping out of Pollock's personal fortune and the depletion of his personal credit were hastened by Willing's coming. Figures enough have been cited, in connection with advances to Willing, loans which Gálvez granted on Pollock's credit for the fitting out of the "Morris," the drafts of George and Harrison, etc., to indicate the financial drain on Pollock. Furthermore, the aroused ire of West Florida would have endangered the delivery of supplies had Pollock's credit still been good. No wonder Pollock grew bitter toward Willing! Yet Pollock saw the benefits which the United States might secure as a result of the expedition. On July 6, 1778, he urged Congress to follow up Willing's work with an expedition against Pensacola, and two years later he expressed the hope that Congress would not abandon the claims to the Mississippi which Willing had established.[95]

Nevertheless, our conclusion must be that Willing, while a resolute and compelling leader, was lacking in restraint and in humanity, that his raid did more harm than good, that such results as were beneficial to the United States are more to be credited to Pollock than to Willing, and that neither American leader could have accomplished much for the Revolutionary cause without the fortunate partisanship of Governor Gálvez.

---

[94] Clinton, October 27, 1778, *in* Historical Manuscripts Commission, *op. cit.*, I, 323.
[95] Pollock to Congress, July 6, 1778, extract, A. G. I., Cuba, 2370; Pollock to the Commerce Committee, January 21, 1778, L. C., Papers of the Continental Congress, L.

CHAPTER VIII

PREPARATIONS FOR WAR

GÁLVEZ SAW in the American Revolution more than an opportunity to discommode the English by giving direct assistance to their foes. When he succeeded Unzaga in 1777, the Revolution was in full progress, and though Spain was not yet a party to the struggle, her colonial empire, and particularly Louisiana, was in too great proximity to the scene of conflict for her to be unconcerned about its outcome or its conduct. She ordered her colonial officers, therefore, to gather all possible information about the war and to perfect the defense of Louisiana. Unzaga had viewed the task despondently; Gálvez took it up with verve.

He recognized the strife in the adjacent English colonies as a double danger. Each side in the conflict might take action prejudicial to Spanish control over Louisiana. The American Revolutionary leaders sought to dispel Spanish anxiety about any menace from their quarter, as for example when Patrick Henry insisted that there was no likelihood of American aggressions on Spanish territory, since the Americans already had "more land than can be settled for many ages to come."[1] And Spain seems to have taken the American peril rather lightly. Gibson as instructed had inquired in 1776

1st Wou'd the acquisition of the Town & Harbour of Pensacola be a desirable Object to His Catholic Majesty—
2d Wou'd his Catholic Majesty receive possession of the Same from the Americans—[2]

Declining to answer these queries, Unzaga forwarded them to the minister of the Indies, who replied on August 15, 1777, Gálvez acknowledging receipt of this royal order on December 30. It read:

---
[1] Henry to Gálvez, January 14, 1778, A. G. I., Cuba, 2370.
[2] Gibson [to Unzaga], inclosed with Unzaga to José de Gálvez, September 30, 1776, No. 184, A. G. I., Sto. Dom., 2596.

If the colonists take the English establishments along the river [Pensacola presumably included] and wish to deliver them to his majesty you will receive them as in deposit, provided that it will not cause violent proceedings on the part of the English.[3]

The fact that this suggestion originated with the Americans invalidates Gayarré's deduction that they would certainly have disdained "to avail themselves of the officious proposition of the king of Spain."[4] The favorable reply, coupled with the positive order to incite the Americans to the conquest of the British posts near Louisiana,[5] indicates rather that Spain had no reluctance about acquiring American neighbors and no fear of their encroachment.

Similarly, Gálvez displayed in the correspondence with George Morgan a willingness to see the Americans acquire Pensacola.[6] Yet Spanish statesmen did see in American expeditions into West Florida an indirect menace to Spanish Louisiana.[7] Such an expedition, though regarded as harmless in itself, might rouse the English to steps dangerous to Spanish Louisiana. The real danger was the English power. The American forces were apprehended only because they might incite the English. In the aftermath of Willing's expedition these forebodings were fulfilled.[8]

In other ways Louisiana was exposed to English anger. Gálvez skated on thin ice in his relations with the English, giving them several grounds for objection: he seized some of their boats engaged in smuggling, he gave the Americans covert but notorious assistance through Oliver Pollock, he sheltered and protected Willing and his expedition.[9] Gálvez, of course, might have tempered these several shocks to English dignity and prestige, but he chose rather to extend real aid to the Americans, protecting Louisiana, meanwhile, not by striving to placate his English neighbors but by rebuilding and rejuvenating the defenses of the colony.

---

[3] Quoted in Gálvez to José de Gálvez, December 30, 1777, reservada, No. 103, *ibid.*
[4] Gayarré, *op. cit.*, III, 111–112.
[5] Royal order to the governor of Louisiana, February 20, 1777, reservada, draft, A. G. I., Sto. Dom., 1598.
[6] See above, Chapter VI.
[7] Expressed, for example, in Gálvez to José de Gálvez, June 2, 1777, *in* Serrano y Sanz, *op. cit.*, 313.
[8] See above, Chapter VII.   [9] See above, Chapters V, VI, and VII.

He found the colony unprepared to resist attack. The stockades of New Orleans and the post at Bayou St. Jean were in bad repair, and the latter could not be rebuilt for lack of wood. It would be utterly useless in time of war and could be forced without artillery. "It is very sad," Gálvez wrote about New Orleans, "to see what immense cost there has been to the king without putting this place in a state of defense." The colony's vast extent, furthermore, made it impossible to cover it with the troops and local militia.[10] But though he agreed with Unzaga's estimate of the existing defenses of Louisiana, Gálvez sought to improve them instead of giving himself over to despair.

He began by building toward control of the Mississippi. Three launches were constructed, each mounting an eighteen- or twenty-four-pounder. These gunboats had the advantage over any war craft that might enter the river, since, on account of the shallowness of the passes, only small vessels, bearing nothing larger than twelve-pounders, could enter. And being propelled by either oars or sails, Gálvez' gunboats would have a second great advantage over other war craft on the winding Mississippi; they could select the range desired and without risk to themselves blow any adversary out of the river.[11]

The successive statements of the forces in Louisiana reveal that Gálvez made some progress in increasing the number of men under arms. Of regular soldiers there were 437 on June 1, 1778, including 25 sent as an escort to Mexico. Seven months later the number of regulars had mounted to 500 plus 10 artillerymen, and by July, 1779, with the addition of 153 from the Canary Islands and 106 from Mexico, there were almost half again as many regularly enrolled soldiers.[12] At least 300 of these "regulars," however, were raw recruits, untrained and untested, and the security that they imparted to the colony was more apparent than real.[13]

The militia companies likewise increased their enrollment. At New Orleans there were 136 militiamen enrolled in 1777 and 302 in 1778.[14]

---

[10] Gálvez to José de Gálvez, March 21, 1777, No. 32, A. G. I., Sto. Dom., 2656.
[11] *Idem* to *idem*, June 2, 1777, in Serrano y Sanz, *op. cit.*, 313–314.
[12] Gálvez, Estados de fuerzas, June 1, 1778, A. G I., Sto. Dom., 2596, and January 1, 1779, *ibid.*, 2662; Gálvez to José de Gálvez, July 7, 1779, No. 304, *ibid.*
[13] *Idem* to *idem*, July 3, 1779, No. 303, *ibid.*, 2656.
[14] Census of New Orleans, 1778, copy, A. G. I., Cuba, 191.

Approximately the same story could be told for other parts of the province. At Gálveztown there came to be two companies. One, of 62 men, was made up of Canary Islanders. The other, of 33, was Anglo-American. Its roll includes these names: Nicholson, Grey, Escot, Oaks, Dukenson, Devez, Parker, Beckley, Moris, Richard, Foster, Mackey, Myers, Runnells, Obryan, Fitz Patrick.[15] On January 1, 1779, there were seventeen militia companies, numbering in all 1478 men;[16] at least one company was added in the next six months, the 62 Canary Islanders of Gálveztown.

Fifteen hundred militiamen form an impressive array. Their military effectiveness was reduced, however, by their being scattered over the colony from Balize to Illinois and to Natchitoches in much the same fashion as were the regulars. Comprising virtually the entire (free) man power of the colony, they could not be mobilized for duty far from their respective homes and were not in any sense a standing army at Gálvez' disposal. Of their utility the governor wrote,

> As to the militiamen, although I am confident of their good faith, you realize that we cannot count much on them because war is not their real business and they will not undertake it eagerly; and in addition, in face of danger they will always feel consideration for their families, and this will magnify dangers for them.[17]

The rehabilitation of Louisiana's defenses was stimulated from time to time by rumors and reports of English reënforcements for West Florida. A strengthening of Pensacola was reported in the summer of 1777.[18] After Willing's expedition the English posts along the Mississippi were enlarged and improved. The commander at the Spanish post opposite Manchac reported on December 31, 1778, "that the Governor of Pensacola has received orders to construct a chain of forts and batteries all along the bank of the Mississippi." Manchac and Baton Rouge were to receive reënforcements of three hundred men, according to a communication from the governor of Pensacola. And

---

[15] Collell to Gálvez, June 27, 1779, *ibid.*, 2351.
[16] Gálvez, Estado de fuerza, January 1, 1779, A. G. I., Sto. Dom., 2662.
[17] Gálvez to José de Gálvez, July 3, 1779, No. 303, A. G. I., Sto. Dom., 2656.
[18] *Idem* to *idem*, June 2, 1777, *in* Serrano y Sanz, *op. cit.*, 313.

from the same source he was informed that "eleven thousand Russian volunteers must have landed in America, already"; and that "an alliance had been confirmed between Spain and England."[19]

The foregoing report rather exaggerated the formidableness of the British West Florida posts, though not to the degree that it overestimates the prospect of Russian and Spanish aid for England. Lieutenant Colonel Dickson reported to his superior, on March 12, 1779, that Fort Manchac was flooded, provisions were hard to get, and losses by desertion serious; that the Spaniards could cut off communications at will; that the construction of the new fort would be an arduous task, for which he would have to depend on Spanish labor.[20] But German soldiers of the Waldeck regiment were sent to Manchac, and Gálvez estimated that "the number of troops the English have in that post would exceed a thousand men."[21]

Notwithstanding Gálvez' apparent partiality toward the Revolutionists and in spite of the mutual anxiety aroused by military preparations in the Spanish and English colonies fronting on the Mississippi, there was much good neighborliness between Spaniard and Englishman. Hearing of a shortage of flour in Pensacola which reduced the greater part of the people to a diet of fish, Gálvez sent one hundred and fifty barrels of the four hundred he possessed to relieve the distress. At the same time he disclaimed any other intention than that of "succoring them in their necessity as a good neighbor and as a fellow man."[22]

We have already seen how Spanish Louisiana was thrown open as a sanctuary for the English when Willing's men were on the rampage. In similar fashion Spanish subjects in the Pointe Coupée district were offered a haven in English territory when they were victims of a flood. They were invited to come over to Manchac with their household goods, and to stay as long as they liked, and were promised full freedom to return to their homes with no difficulties interposed.[23]

---

[19] Raymundo DuBreuil to Gálvez, December 31, 1778, A. G. I., Sto Dom., 2547.
[20] Dickson to Campbell, March 12, 1779, *in* Historical Manuscripts Commission, *op. cit.,* I, 397.
[21] Gálvez to José de Gálvez, July 3, 1779, No. 303, A. G. I., Sto. Dom., 2656.
[22] Gálvez to Chester, August 23, 1777, certified copy, A. G. I., Sto. Dom., 2596.
[23] Dickson to Grand Pré, April 11, 1779, A. G. I., Cuba, 191.

In slightly different vein Colonel Campbell expressed his reliance on Gálvez to extend every aid to the "Adventure," sent by the Mississippi with supplies for Manchac, and requested further that she be permitted to return "with a Cargo of Rice, Pease, or other Species of Provisions, that can be conveniently spared from Your Province of Louisiana."[24] Another example of friendly contact was Dickson's request for permission to purchase one hundred head of cattle at Opelousas. "I would take it as a great and national favor," he wrote. Gálvez conferred the favor.[25] Courtesy and neighborliness were not discarded because of national jealousies.

Soon after the outbreak of hostilities in the American Revolution, Spain had ordered her colonial officials at Havana and New Orleans to gather information about the struggle and to use secret agents as an intelligence service. Of several such agents the one who brought back information of greatest use to Gálvez and to Spanish power on the Gulf was Jacinto Panis.

In outward appearance his mission was an attempt to secure guaranties of Spanish Louisiana's rights as a neutral in the war between England and the revolting colonies. Governor Gálvez explained to Spain's minister of the Indies:

> The repeated insults committed on the Mississippi River by the English, and on the lakes situated behind this city by a king's corsair, have obliged me to send Captain Jacinto Panis, adjutant major of this plaza, to Pensacola with a letter to the governor complaining of these things and asking a prompt remedy.[26]

But the mission had an ulterior design perhaps more important than its ostensible one. Gálvez' letter continued:

> This expedition had not only the motive of the above requests, but also that of finding out if it is true that a reënforcement of troops and two frigates has arrived at that city (as I have been informed), their intentions, their actual force, and the news of what has occurred relative to the war

---

[24] Campbell to Gálvez, July 22, 1779, *ibid.*, 192.
[25] Dickson to Gálvez, July 24, 1779, *ibid.*, 2358; draft of reply, July 27, 1779, *ibid.*
[26] Gálvez to José de Gálvez, March 11, 1778, reservada, No. 129, A. G. I., Sto. Dom., 2596.

between Great Britain and North America. I am persuaded that the commission is sufficient to prevent any suspicion of this motive.[27]

Panis, in effect, went to Mobile and Pensacola as a spy; and about a year later, when Spain entered the war against England, his plan for an attack on Pensacola became the basis for Gálvez' campaign.

Quite apart from its function in espionage, the expedition would seem to have been justified by the extraordinary activities of the English and the resultant inconvenience to Spanish Louisiana. Gálvez' letter to Governor Chester of British West Florida stresses the chief complaint.

Not a boat has come down from Illinois, and not a trapper's boat, without being fired upon at the Bluffs of Margot and Prudhomme [Chickasaw Bluffs], which have been garrisoned by a detachment of troops of your nation and of Chickesay Indians. Such offenses, which I cannot believe are approved or suggested by your prudent orders, are too irregular from any subordinate, nor can they be justified by whatever excuses you may give to color them. If the idea in stationing a detachment in this region is to extend the limits of your jurisdiction, and to acquire necessary information, it would seem to me that it would be more reasonable to send to the post someone who would indicate this with politeness and soldierly urbanity, without disturbing the prevailing peace before at least offering every assistance and hospitality, which should be necessary in imitation of that which I have always accorded to British subjects in this province.[28]

Panis was instructed to transmit this letter to Chester and to press the demand for greater politeness at Chickasaw Bluffs, taking care "neither to be so acrid as to exasperate, nor so lukewarm as to imply timidity." He was instructed to bolster the complaint by suggesting that it might become necessary to deny entrance into Louisiana to every foreigner without distinction of nation. On three other issues negotiations were to be conducted: protesting against the presence of English traders among the Indians west of the Mississippi; protesting the activities of an English corsair on Lake Pontchartrain and Lake Borgne; and proposing an agreement for the extradition of runaway slaves.[29]

---

[27] *Ibid.*   [28] Gálvez to Chester, February 20, 1778, draft, copy, A. G. I., Cuba, 2351.
[29] Gálvez to Panis, February 20, 1778, *ibid.*

Armed with a "box of white sugar and a cask of wine" as a present for Governor Chester, Panis left New Orleans on February 22, 1778, and reached Mobile on March 2, proceeding a few days later to Pensacola. Apparently the English had no inkling of Panis' secret instructions, but he did encounter some difficulties on another score.

In a letter to Gálvez, he said:

> On the night of March 2 I reached Mobile, where the following morning there arrived a messenger from Natchez with tidings of Willing's depredations. This news and the dread that he would ascend with his followers to surprise this settlement and its inhabitants frightened everybody. I was able to console them by saying that doubtless terror had exaggerated the story, and that I was persuaded you would not permit Willing or anyone to commit acts of authority or hostility in the domain of his Majesty.[80]

The effects of Willing's raid upon the Panis mission are indicated even more clearly by a letter from a Pensacola merchant to another English merchant at New Orleans:

> The Major has staid (I believe) a little longer among us than he expected, occasioned from the Confusion which the late rascally transaction of Mr. Willing has made in this province.... When the news of Mr. Willing's plundering Expedition arrived here, it was supposed, from various circumstances, that his Scout boat had arrived at New Orleans before Major Panis's departure from thence, this was, as imprudently as impolitely, told to the Major which made him very uneasy, however he soon perceived that the Civility and attention of his Friends here was not lessened on that account and of course removed his anxiety. Tho', by the by, he certainly must have known the matter before he left.[81]

But in spite of this lack of perfect confidence in him, the ambassador from New Orleans found it possible to make headway with his negotiations. In a series of letters to Chester he took up *seriatim* the Spanish grievances.[82] In one letter dated April 7, Chester replied to all four:

> The first representation You make in Your letter of the 13th of last Month, is that the English Commissaries with Indians posted near the Clifts of Prud'homme & Margot, have with violence obliged the Batteaus

---

[80] Fragment of a letter, without signature, date, or address, but evidently from Panis at Pensacola to Gálvez, *ibid.*

[81] Stephenson to Patrick Morgan, April 7, 1778, *ibid.*, 112.

[82] Panis to Chester, March 13, 16, 22, and 24, 1778, drafts, *ibid.*, 2351.

which come down from the Illinois, or any other part of Your Colony; either to cross the River Mississippi, or fire at them, if they refuse to stop. To this Complaint, I answer that the Clifts of Prud'homme & Margot, altho' under the Sovereignty of the King my Master, are notwithstanding far beyond the jurisdiction of this Province, the limits whereof do not extend farther up the River Mississippi than the mouth of the River Yassous.[33]

Having sidestepped responsibility for the violence at Chickasaw Bluffs, Governor Chester was zealous in trying to alleviate the unpleasantness. He suggested to Colonel Stuart, British Indian Commissioner for the Southern District, that no offense be given the Spaniards. Stuart had stationed some men at the mouth of Wolf River to learn about the designs of the Rebels; from them he had no report, but he now sent warnings to them not to molest the Spaniards. After reporting this, Chester went on to mention the rebellion which made necessary such actions, and to hope

that His Excellency [Gálvez] will not too Scrupulously Scrutinize Actions, which proceed from prudence and necessity at this juncture, but on the contrary, direct his Subjects in coming down the Mississippi, to communicate any useful information they may receive of the Rebels' proceedings to those parties whom Colonel Stuart has stationed on that River.[34]

Concerning the English traders west of the Mississippi, Chester's reply was equally specious or in equally good faith, as one chooses to interpret his letter. These traders, he said, are

most of them a Sett of Banditti, & Outlaws, who have fled from Justice, out of some of the Northern Colonies, and live in a Savage Manner.

Consequently, restraining them was a difficult task. As a token of his sincerity he enclosed a copy of the proclamation that he had issued a few years earlier prohibiting unlicensed trading, and promised anew to make every effort to enforce this regulation. He complained, however, that in the preceding summer Choctaws had received presents at New Orleans and Tonicas at Pointe Coupée.[35]

Chester asserted that the corsair on the lakes was likewise beyond his authority. Formal complaint should be lodged with the naval chief

---

[33] Chester to Panis, April 7, 1778, *ibid*.   [34] *Ibid*.   [35] *Ibid*.

at Jamaica. He had conferred, however, with Lieutenant Burdon, the commander of the corsair, and had received his promise not to interfere with Spanish fishermen and others on the lakes.

To the fourth proposition Chester answered:

> I consent, that it Shall be Established and agreed between the Governments of Louisiana & West Florida, That all such Negroes, as belong to the Subjects of each Province, & Such as have been or may be Stolen & carried to, or take refuge in the Colony of Louisiana or West Florida shall be restored upon requisition to their respective owners.

The expenses of apprehension, he agreed, were to be charged to the owners. Gálvez had proposed a further condition, "that Corporal Punishment shall not be inflicted upon Such Slaves, as are Capital Offenders," having in mind the protection of property rights in such slaves. But Chester objected, saying:

> It may operate as an inducement on those, who are determined to abscond, previously to commit Murder, or Some other Capital offence, which from instances, they may observe, will not only prevent their being delivered up to their Masters, as other less offending runaways are, but also Screen them from all kinds of Corporal Punishment.[86]

The negotiations ended thus with very little actually gained for Spanish Louisiana except the agreement about the return of runaway slaves. This agreement, however, was more than a temporary achievement. More than a year after Spain's entrance into the war against England, a West Florida citizen wrote to Gálvez:

> Governor Chester ... assures your Excellency he will inviolably adhere to the agreement relative to Runaway Negroes entered into between you reciprocally, when Major Panis was at Pensacola, and doubts not of your doing the same, as if Harmony & peace subsisted between our respective Nations, instead of Hostilities.[87]

Governor Chester seems not to have suspected that Panis' visit had any other purpose. After acknowledging "the box of White Sugar, and the Cask of Wine,... both of which have been accepted with a thousand thanks," he continued his letter to Gálvez with a compliment for Panis.

---

[86] *Ibid.*   [87] E. R. Wegg to Gálvez, June 14, 1780, A. G. I., Cuba, 193.

PREPARATIONS FOR WAR   145

> I have had the honor of receiving Your Excellys Letter dated the 20th of February last, commissioning Major Panis to treat personally with me upon different points which you say concern the Interests of Our two Colonies, and I am to return you many thanks for having sent an officer to me upon this Occasion of Major Panis' Rank & Credit, who I have Endeavored to receive with the distinction he is entitled to, not only from respect to your Excellency's introduction, but also from his own personal merit—and I wish he had given me an opportunity of rendering him any services.[38]

Nor was Chester aware of Gálvez' duplicity. He wrote to Panis:

> I cannot entertain the least doubt of the Sincerity of the last assurances which I have received from him, but I flatter myself, that His Excellency will continue the Same friendly disposition whenever occasions offer.[39]

In New Orleans, meanwhile, Panis' absence was being felt. Gálvez wrote to him on April 18 that, since the second adjutant was also absent, his speedy return would be appreciated. A postscript implied that his wife also would appreciate it.[40] But by this time Panis was almost home. A day earlier he had written a letter from Balize telling of his departure from Pensacola on the ninth in a boat which Chester had permitted to sail on condition that Panis would secure for it a guaranty against insult by the Americans on the Mississippi.[41] On the twenty-second Gálvez sent a safe-conduct for the boat to proceed "as though Spanish."[42]

On July 5 Panis presented the report of his mission. Quite significantly there is no mention in it of the negotiations with Chester but merely an account of his journey to Pensacola, the flurry caused by Willing's raid, and a description of the fortifications of the two towns. In this report he wrote:

> I arrived at Mobile the night of March 2. At about the same time came the news that the Americans were descending the Mississippi, taking possession of all the lands and plantations belonging to English royalists. Imagining that the hostilities of the Americans would extend to this region, the commandant and principal citizens were filled with consterna-

---
[38] Chester to Gálvez, April 7, 1778, *ibid.*, 191.
[39] Chester to Panis, April 7, 1778, A. G. I., Cuba, 2351.
[40] Gálvez to Panis, April 18, 1778, *ibid.*
[41] Panis to Gálvez, April 17, 1778, *ibid.*   [42] Gálvez to Panis, April 22, 1778, *ibid.*

tion, and sent an express to Pensacola, carrying the news and asking support for their defense in case of attack. It is evident, if the governor of Pensacola does not send assistance, that these people are exposed to great danger. The fortifications, as you know, are in very bad condition; they consist of a regular square, built of brick, and flanked with breastworks, trench, and glacis, as before, situated very near the barracks and at the shore of the bay for defense by sea, as on land by Indians. Its walls are going to ruin. Almost all the artillery is dismounted, and the trenches in some places are choked up. The barracks are in equally bad repair; in the front and side sections are housed the small garrison of forty-five soldiers, commanded by a captain, lieutenant, and sergeant; the other side, the northeast, is uninhabitable, for nothing but its walls remain, the rest having been consumed by a fire.[43]

Nor were the authorities at Mobile completely at ease about the loyalty of the inhabitants of the district.

On the sixth, when I left for Pensacola [Panis continued], the authorities called together all the people with their arms in order to enumerate them and to renew their oath of fidelity, because of lack of confidence in some, the majority being French creoles.[44]

The description of Pensacola is longer and more replete with technical details. Although the fortifications were more pretentious than those at Mobile, a similar state of decay and ill repair prevailed. The American Revolution, and particularly the recent raid of Willing, however, were spurring the English to strengthen Pensacola. Panis continued:

With the repeated bulletins which they received daily concerning the progress of the Americans, and the captures being made at Manchac, they began energetically to restore the trenches and breastworks, making gun-carriages and fittings to mount the extra mortars and cannon, and putting everything in good condition for defense. They have added an outer breastwork eight toises from the fort toward the northwest, running in the streets from this point toward the southwest, and have erected another battery near the seashore.

At the foot of the fortification and at intervals of a foot and a half they have opened three rows of funnel-shaped pits, such as are called wolf traps, with sharpened stakes in the bottom; and they are continuing to fortify the place as their skill and the sandy soil permit.[45]

---

[43] Panis to Gálvez, July 5, 1778, A. G. I., Cuba, 112.   [44] *Ibid.*   [45] *Ibid.*

PREPARATIONS FOR WAR　　　　　　　　　　147

It would be anticipating the story to notice the use that was eventually made of the information Panis secured. When Spain entered the war against England, about a year after Panis returned from West Florida, Gálvez received a royal order to the effect that the major objective of Spain, so far as America was concerned, was to be the conquest of Pensacola, Mobile, and the British posts along the Mississippi.[46] "In compliance with the king's royal wishes," Gálvez replied to this communication,

> I send you the attached plan formed at my order by the adjutant major of this plaza, Don Jacinto Panis, a reliable man and an officer of long service, to whom I turned because he was at Pensacola last year with the object of appraising me of the state of its defense.[47]

Panis' plan, dated August 16, 1779, was in part a repetition of the description of Pensacola that he had submitted to Gálvez on July 5 of the preceding year. On the basis of this information, however, he had outlined a plan of attack. He recommended a pretentious expedition to include six ships of the line, and as many frigates, such *balandras* and other armed boats as could be spared, and a landing force of seven thousand men.[48] "Without disapproving the project of Panis, who as an eyewitness ought to know whereof he speaks," Gálvez wrote, in submitting the plan,

> it seems to me that a pair of ships of the line to escort and to remain cruising during the attack, six frigates, a bomb-ketch if there is one, and other small armed boats, in addition to those necessary for transports, will suffice for the naval forces.... As to land forces, four thousand men whom you shall send ... and a thousand men, and no more, whom I can take from here ... will be enough to effect the capture with ease.[49]

Not only did Gálvez endorse the Panis plan in principle, but later when he was directing the actual operations against Pensacola, he followed it in such details as the sending of one division of his army by way of the Perdido River and the landing of a detachment on Santa

---
[46] Diego Joseph Navarro to Gálvez, July 18, 1779, A. G. I., Sto. Dom., 2543.
[47] Gálvez to Navarro, August 17, 1779, No. 201, reservada, A. G. I., Cuba, 2351.
[48] Panis to Gálvez, August 16, 1779, *ibid.*, 112.
[49] Gálvez to Navarro, August 17, 1779, No. 201, reservada, *ibid.*, 2351.

Rosa Island as a preliminary to the investment of Pensacola itself.[50] The importance attached to the secret aspect of the Panis mission to Pensacola in 1778 is sufficiently attested by these utilizations of the information thereby acquired. Gálvez did indeed scrupulously observe the outward forms of neutrality, but at the same time he not only revitalized the defenses of Louisiana, but also, by bringing more men under arms and by spying on his British neighbors, prepared for offensive warfare.

[50] Panis to Gálvez, August 16, 1779, A. G. I., Cuba, 112; "Diary of the Operations of the Expedition against the Place of Pensacola," *Louisiana Historical Quarterly*, I (1917), 44-84.

CHAPTER IX

THE STRUGGLE FOR THE MISSISSIPPI

IN THE SUMMER of 1779 the shackles of neutrality were broken, and Gálvez found himself at liberty to combat the English openly. Instead of the furtive methods of indirection—opposing the English through covert assistance to the Americans—direct action was now possible; in place of intrigue and dissimulating diplomacy, he could use military force.

On May 18 the Spanish court sent notifications to her colonial officials that war was to be declared against England, though the declaration was not formally made until June 21.[1] Not until July 17 did the news reach Havana,[2] and, although Navarro immediately forwarded the order "to direct all our efforts...to drive the British forces out of Pensacola, Mobile, and the other posts they occupy on the Mississippi,"[3] it did not come to Gálvez' hands during July. Harbingers of war had preceded the actual notice. Gálvez was aware that relations were strained between the Spanish and English courts. His suspicions were aroused, too, by the reënforcement of Manchac with four hundred Waldeck soldiers. The English represented that the purpose of these soldiers was to protect them against an expected American invasion, but Gálvez believed that the massing of troops "could have no other object than that of mobilizing their forces on the river so that they would be more ready to attack us at the first news of a rupture."[4] Intercepted letters addressed to William Horn at Natchez confirmed Gálvez' fears. Elias Durnford told Horn to hold himself "ready for

---
[1] José de Gálvez to the governor of Louisiana, May 18, 1779, No. 124, A. G. I., Cuba, 569.
[2] Navarro to José de Gálvez, July 28, 1779, No. 550, A. G. I., Sto Dom., 2082.
[3] Navarro to Gálvez, July 18, 1779, *ibid.*, 2543.
[4] Gálvez to José de Gálvez, July 3, 1779, reservada, No. 303, *ibid.*, 2656.

an expedition against New Orleans in which it is possible that we shall be engaged shortly," while William Johnstone rejoiced thus over preparations for an attack on the "Dons of New Orleans": "Thank God that we are all firm and relishing the opportunity to strike a blow against the Dons."[5] The attack, Gálvez understood, was to be twofold; 1500 men to descend the Mississippi from Canada and gathering force at Natchez, Baton Rouge, and Manchac, and an equally large expedition to come by sea from Pensacola.[6]

Anticipating the declaration of war, which would mean an attack upon his province, Gálvez redoubled his military preparations. On July 13 he convoked a *junta de guerra* or council of war, and laid before it the critical situation of Louisiana. He estimated that there were eight hundred British regulars at the Mississippi posts, besides Indian allies, hunters, and additional troops expected from Pensacola. He spread on the table a map of the lower Mississippi Valley, pointing out how New Orleans might be attacked at a "multitude of points"—by land from Manchac, by Lakes Maurepas and Pontchartrain, by the estuary of Figouyir, by that of the Germans, or by any of those leading to Lake Borgne. He took up next the Spanish forces in Louisiana: six hundred men, four hundred and fifty of them recruits "as well drilled as the time since their arrival has permitted," the other one hundred and fifty reduced in effectiveness by "the infirmities which rage at this season" and by the necessity of scattering some at the various outlying posts. Expressing the utmost confidence in the patriotism and zeal of the assembled officers to serve the king, Gálvez asked them to draw up a plan of defense.

Every officer but one urged that protection of New Orleans was the chief consideration. Forces should be concentrated there, the Hospital de Caridad and the water front fortified, the militia drilled, the fort at Bayou St. Jean strengthened, and aid requested from Havana. Cap-

---

[5] Durnford to Horn, and Johnstone to Horn, copies, *ibid.*, 2082.

[6] Gálvez to Navarro, October 16, 1779, reservada, No. 227, A. G. I., Cuba, 2351; "Suplemento á la Gazeta de Madrid," January 14, 1780, a semiofficial account of Gálvez' Lower Mississippi campaign, translated in condensed form in Gayarré, *op. cit.*, III, 122–133, and in full by Jac Nachbin, *Louisiana Historical Quarterly*, XV (1932), 468–481; *Report on Canadian Archives, 1885*, 233, 276, 302; *Wisconsin Historical Collections*, XI (1889), 144–147.

tain Manuel de Nava recommended that the commanders of the outlying posts should be ordered "in case of attack, to surrender on the best terms obtainable." Only Lieutenant Colonel Estevan Miró had a positive suggestion. He would construct four redoubts below Manchac to command the river. Then, if war came, Manchac could be taken quickly. In case of an attack on New Orleans the troops stationed at the redoubts could come down the Mississippi or the Iberville quickly. He had confidence that 100 white infantrymen, 100 blacks, and 50 white cavalrymen could be raised in the colony.[7]

Gálvez wasted no time arguing with this council of military advisers, since characterized as "old fogies,"[8] yet he secretly[9] cherished the idea of a more audacious program. Notwithstanding the obvious disparity of forces, he believed that Louisiana would be best defended by an attack on the British posts along the Mississippi. The strategy he had in mind resembled that which Clark had employed in his attack on Hamilton at Vincennes—a swift blow at the nearest enemy stronghold, delivered before the superior but scattered forces of the enemy could be gathered for an irresistible offensive.

Nominally acceding to the advice of his cautious counselors, Gálvez carried on secretly with his original plans. Under pretext of preparing for the "defense" of New Orleans, he made ready for the projected expedition. Juan Antonio Gayarré, as commissary of war, was taken into his confidence and put in charge of the preparations.[10] When Gálvez received notice of the declaration of war, he made no public announcement but kept it also secret. Supplies were collected. Several boats were commandeered and added to the little fleet of gunboats. On these the supplies and munitions and artillery were loaded. By the middle of August Gayarré had things near enough in readiness to

---

[7] Junta de guerra, July 13, 1779, A. G. I., Cuba, 112. The officers comprising the junta were: Colonel Manuel Gonzalez, Lieutenant Colonels Estevan Miró and Pedro Piernas, Captains Martin Mozun, Francisco Cruzat, Alexander Coussot, Manuel de Nava, Hilario de Estenoy, Juan Delavillebeuvre, Joaquin de Blanca, Pedro Josef Favrot, with Captain Jacinto Panis acting as secretary.

[8] Claiborne, *op. cit.*, 125.

[9] Gayarré states that he submitted his plan to the cabildo (*sic*, i.e., the junta), *op. cit.*, III, 121, but Panis' report as secretary does not mention it, Junta de guerra, July 13, 1779, A. G. I., Cuba, 112, nor does the "Suplemento á la Gazeta de Madrid," *in* Nachbin, *op. cit.*, 470–471.

[10] Gayarré, *op. cit.*, III, 122.

justify Gálvez in setting August 23 as the date for his departure. He planned to make a public appeal for support three days earlier.[11] On the eighteenth, however, his plans suffered violent interruption. A hurricane struck New Orleans and in the short space of three hours sank all the vessels that had been collected on the river, demolished a number of houses in the town, ruined crops, and laid waste the fields. It left the colony prostrate and exhausted, unable to coöperate in the governor's bold scheme. Gálvez might well have been discouraged by this catastrophe, but on the contrary he seems to have been spurred to greater exertions. Instead of worrying about the damage done by the hurricane, he hastened to reorganize the defenses of New Orleans before the English (whose establishments had not been damaged by the storm) could take the field against him.[12] He was still convinced that his surest defense was to invade English territory and dispose of part of their forces before they united to crush him. He persevered in this opinion, notwithstanding the disapproval of the junta and the discouragement of the hurricane, and by a dramatic appeal he won the support of the colonists.

With the notice of Spain's entrance into the war had come Gálvez' appointment as governor of Louisiana; up to that time he had been acting governor.[13] But he had kept the promotion secret, reserving the announcement for a more propitious occasion. Now he called the inhabitants together and spoke as pathetically as possible about the unhappy situation of the colony. He dwelt on the unfortunate circumstances under which he had to inform them that England had declared war on Spain "in consequence of the recognition of the independence of America." He said that he expected a British attack on New Orleans.[14] Then he mentioned his appointment as governor.

> I cannot avail myself of my commission [he said] without previously swearing before the *Cabildo,* that I shall defend the province; but, although I am disposed to shed the last drop of my blood for Louisiana and for my

---

[11] "Relación de la Campaña que hizo Don Bernardo de Gálvez, contra los Ingleses, en la Luisiana," *in* Serrano y Sanz, *op. cit.,* 344.

[12] Serrano y Sanz, *loc. cit.; Gazeta de Madrid,* December 28, 1779, p. 946; Gayarré, *op. cit.,* III, 123.

[13] The royal cédula is translated in French, *op. cit.,* V, 243-245.

[14] Serrano y Sanz, *op. cit.,* 345.

king, I cannot take an oath which I may be exposed to violate, because I do not know whether you will help me in resisting the ambitious designs of the English. What do you say? Shall I take the oath of governor? Shall I swear to defend Louisiana?[15]

The answer came in thunderous applause, which Gayarré has made articulate in the rather free translation:

"Fear not taking your oath of office," cried the crowd, as if with one voice, "for the defence of Louisiana, and for the service of the king, we tender you our lives, and we would say our fortunes, if we had any remaining.[16]

Encouraged by this demonstration of loyalty, Gálvez accepted the appointment and took the appropriate oath.

Preparations for the "defense" of Louisiana were continued, and to allay suspicion Gálvez announced that he was going to concentrate his troops at the points where the first English attacks seemed likely to occur. Boats from other parts of the province which had escaped the hurricane were assembled at New Orleans. Four vessels of the original fleet were raised from the bed of the river and loaded with munitions. The remaining ten cannon were put on board also. The governor planned to send this flotilla up the river under Julian Alvarez while he led the land expedition in person. Within a week after the storm the arrangements were complete. Pedro Piernas and Martin Navarro were placed in military and civil control of New Orleans, and Manuel Gonzales, Estevan Miró, and Jacinto Panis were named ranking officers under Gálvez.[17]

On the afternoon of August 27 the little army set out. It was composed of 170 veteran soldiers, 330 recruits recently arrived from Mexico and the Canary Islands, 20 carabiniers, 60 militiamen and habitants, 80 free blacks and mulattoes, and 7 American volunteers. Among the latter was Oliver Pollock, agent of Virginia and of the Continental Congress, who acted as aide-de-camp to Gálvez throughout the campaign. The force totaled 667 men "of all sorts, nationalities and colors, but without a single engineer, and with the artillery officer very sick. They had to march through thick woods and over difficult

---

[15] Gayarré, *op. cit.*, III, 124; Serrano y Sanz, *op. cit.*, 345–346.
[16] Gayarré, *op. cit.*, III, 124.   [17] Serrano y Sanz, *op. cit.*, 346–347.

trails, without tents and other supplies usually considered indispensable, but they marched on as though to a happy adventure."[18] Governor Gálvez preceded them to the German and Acadian coasts, where he collected the militia companies and enlisted as many men as possible. Through his efforts 600 men of every class and color and 160 Indians joined the expedition, raising his command to 1427 combatants. But in consequence of the rapid marching and of sickness, this number was reduced by more than one-third when they reached Manchac, their first objective. The difficult journey of thirty-five leagues was accomplished in eleven days.[19]

Meanwhile Gálvez had endeavored to conceal from the English of West Florida that Spain and England were at war. His letter to Campbell on August 23 returned compliment for compliment, carried the assurance that his "high consideration" for Campbell "would never be diminished," and discussed the proper spheres of Spanish and English influence over the Indians as though the Mississippi were still a peace-time frontier.[20] So that the alarm would not be carried to West Florida, Gálvez arrested without explanation a British Indian agent and his companions who had come on business to Bayou St. Jean. "Surely," wrote the agent, "there must be some grand mistake," and he intimated that he would rest easier if he knew how long he was to be detained and why.[21] The English commander at Manchac began on August 31 to suspect that Gálvez had hostile intentions, but because of difficulty in getting a Spanish letter translated he was not entirely sure even on September 2.[22] Gálvez' followers likewise were ignorant of their real objective. Only when they had come in sight of Fort Manchac on September 6, did Gálvez announce to them that Spain had declared war and that he was ordered to attack the posts on the Mississippi. Joyfully receiving the news, his men seemed anxious to come to grips with the English.

---

[18] *Ibid.*, 347; *Gazeta de Madrid,* December 29, 1779, p. 946.

[19] Serrano y Sanz, *op. cit.*, 347–348.

[20] Gálvez to Campbell, August 23, 1779, copy, A. G. I., Cuba, 182.

[21] Bethune to Gálvez, August 27, 1779, *ibid.*, 191; Bethune to Piernas, August 29, 1779, *ibid.*

[22] Dickson to Gálvez, August 30, 1779, A. G. I., Cuba, 2358; Dickson to Gálvez, August 31, 1779, *ibid.*, 192; Connor and Wilson to Gálvez, September 2, 1779, *ibid.*

In the face of Gálvez' advance, the main body of the English had fallen back to a new fortification at Baton Rouge. About a month earlier Lieutenant Colonel Dickson had concluded that Manchac could not be defended against an expected American expedition and had ordered his chief engineer to begin construction of a redoubt on Watts and Flowers' plantation at Baton Rogue. Immediately upon learning that the Spaniards were moving against him, Dickson and his fellow-officers had agreed to make their defense at Baton Rouge.[23] A few men were left at Fort Manchac, however, and Gálvez had first to capture it. On the night of the sixth he stationed his regulars north of it to prevent rumored relief from Baton Rouge, and at dawn the militia carried the fort by assault. Gilbert Antonio de St. Maxent, brother-in-law of Unzaga, was the first to enter. One officer and five soldiers escaped "in the imperfect light of breaking day," one soldier was killed, and two officers and eighteen soldiers were made prisoners.[24] As Gayarré remarked, "This certainly was no great exploit."[25] But it was a good initiation for the militia. It was their battle. They behaved well in the face of danger and they were greatly heartened by their victory.

Gálvez tarried at Manchac for a few days to allow his sick to recover, and then set out for Baton Rouge, taking five prisoners on the way. Although the fort at Baton Rouge had been thrown up in six weeks, it was much more formidable than the one at Manchac. It was surrounded by a ditch eighteen feet wide and nine deep. Inside the ditch was an earthen wall, and outside it a circle of palisades in the form of *chevaux de frise*. The armament consisted of thirteen cannon (three more than Gálvez possessed), and four hundred regulars and one hundred and fifty settlers and armed negroes made up its garrison. Manifestly, the tactics of the Manchac battle could not be repeated

---

[23] Dickson and Graham, statements of reasons for removing to Baton Rouge, September 22, 1779, *Louisiana Historical Quarterly*, XII (1929), 263–264.

[24] Serrano y Sanz, *op. cit.*, 348; Gálvez to ——, September 10, 1779, A. G. I., Cuba, 2358; Gálvez to Piernas, September 18, 1779, B. L., La. Coll.; Gálvez to Navarro, October 16, 1779, reservada, No. 227, A. G. I., Cuba, 2351; Juan Antonio Gayarré (inventory of supplies captured at Manchac), September 7, 1779, A. G. I., Sto. Dom., 2572; Dickson reported two lieutenants, three sergeants, and nineteen rank and file, *Louisiana Historical Quarterly*, XII (1929), 265.

[25] Gayarré, *op. cit.*, III, 127.

here. An assault would be too costly unless a breach in the fortifications were first effected by the artillery, and the advantage of a surprise attack like the one at Manchac was not possible here.[26]

In a letter written at the time of the brief siege that followed, Gálvez tells how he took stock of the situation.[27] The British had eighteen cannon, Gálvez only ten, though of larger caliber; their veteran troops numbered more than four hundred, his only three hundred and eighty-four; he had four hundred "peasants, Indians, and negroes, without discipline or subordination"; they also were supported by people of this sort; he had only fourteen artillerymen, and considered his force obviously not superior to the English. Yet he had been fortunate, having intercepted assistance sent from Pensacola, cut them off from Natchez, and captured Manchac, "the key to their establishments." Consequently, if he could hold on where he was, they would have to surrender within two months. But since his men were beset by sickness and poorly provided on account of the hurricane, he resolved to attack "before his small force melted away."[28] Mindful, however, that many of his men were heads of families "and that a costly victory would fill the whole Province with grief and mourning," he resisted the clamor for an assault and decided to open a trench and bring his artillery into action.[29]

The first problem, therefore, was to get his artillery in position. Gálvez' success in this maneuver was the tactical climax of his lower Mississippi campaign. The feat was accomplished in this way. A small grove of trees reaching out toward the fort appeared to be the most advantageous position from which to attack. To this wood, on the night of September 20, Gálvez sent a detachment of white militiamen, colored troops, and Indians. Some of them chopped down trees, others threw up earthworks, others fired on the fort as if protecting the laborers, but the chief function of the whole group was to make as much commotion as possible and thereby to attract the entire attention of the English. While the English, without wounding a single

---

[26] Gálvez to José de Gálvez, October 16, 1779, A. G. I., Cuba, 2351; Serrano y Sanz, *op. cit.*, 348–349.

[27] Gálvez to Navarro, September 18, 1779, No. 208, A. G. I., Cuba, 1232.

[28] *Ibid.*   [29] "Suplemento á la Gazeta de Madrid," *in* Nachbin, *op. cit.*, 474–475.

person, wearied themselves in an all-night bombardment of this grove, the Spaniards were installing their cannon unmolested and unobserved in a garden on the opposite side of the fort and within musket shot of it. In the morning the English discovered their mistake and directed a heavy fire against the Spanish batteries. It was too late; the Spanish guns and gunners were well sheltered.[30]

Early that morning the Spanish batteries opened fire with good effect; notwithstanding the spirit with which the besieged served their cannon, their fort was so much damaged by the middle of the afternoon that they were compelled to submit. At half-past three two officers came out to propose a truce. Gálvez insisted that Dickson surrender at discretion and that Fort Panmure at Natchez, with its garrison of eighty grenadiers, be included. Dickson perforce assented.[31] Twenty-four hours were allowed the English in which to bury their dead, after which they marched out of the fort, delivered up their arms, surrendered their flags, and became prisoners of war. The three hundred and seventy-five surviving regulars were detained as prisoners, but the enlisted settlers and negroes were set free "because of the generous heart of our commander, and because of the impossibility of guarding them."[32]

Captain Juan Delavillebeuvre was sent north with fifty men to receive the surrender of Fort Panmure at Natchez. He was accompanied by Captain Barber, who bore a letter from Dickson instructing the English officer there to surrender the fort[33] and a letter from Pollock addressed to the inhabitants of the district. Just after the capture of Manchac, Pollock had urged upon the people of Natchez that "all the Subjects and well-wishers of the American Cause are in duty bound to give every assistance to his most Catholic Majesty's Arms"; he had reminded them of Gálvez' past favors to them, promised them pro-

---

[30] Gálvez to José de Gálvez, October 16, 1779, A. G. I., Cuba, 2351; Serrano y Sanz, *op. cit.*, 349.

[31] Articles of capitulation at Baton Rouge, the original in French, signed by Gálvez and Dickson, September 21, 1779, A. G. I., Cuba, 197; copies, *ibid.*, 83 and 2351; *Louisiana Historical Quarterly*, XII (1929), 258–262. Dickson to Gálvez, September 21, 1779, A. G. I., Cuba, 197; Gayarré [inventory of supplies captured at Baton Rouge], September 22, 1779, A. G. I., Sto. Dom., 2572.

[32] Serrano y Sanz, *op. cit.*, 351.

[33] Dickson to Forster, September 21, 1779, copy, A. G. I., Cuba, 2351.

tection against the savages through an expedition which had "gone to take Pensacola,"[34] and guaranteed certain favors from Gálvez, including full enjoyment of their religion, purchase of their tobacco crop, and freedom to remove to the United States whenever they desired.[35] His letter from Baton Rouge held out further inducements:

> I have the happiness to inform you that his most Catholick Majesty the King of Spain has declared the Independency of the United States of America, as also War against our tyrannical enemy Great Britain, in consequence whereof I take this first occasion of congratulating you, knowing that your favorable sentiments towards the glorious Cause of Liberty will now have an opportunity of being distinguished, and securing the enjoyment of the good protection of his Most Catholic Majesty's Arms.
>
> Coll. Dickson has capitulated with Governor Galvez, and surrendered his Garrison prisoners of war, he has obliged himself to withdraw the British Forces from your Quarter, and deliver up the Fort to the Spanish Officer who goes for that purpose.
>
> The Spirit of Liberty, the protection which every American has received on this River from his Excellency Govr. Galvez, his generous behaviour towards all the Inhabitants, with the advantages which must now spring from an uninterrupted commerce with New Orleans, where you will meet with a good market for all your produce, and the necessary supplies for your Families, will I hope be sufficient inducements to you to render all the Services in your power to his Catholick Majesty's Arms. There is a sufficient Force gone to reduce Pensacola by which you will be totally secured against the Insults of the Savages. For further particulars I refer you to my good Friend Captn. Barber the bearer hereof.
>
> By my latest Accounts from the Northward I have reason to hope that the time is not very distant when our inveterate Foes will be entirely excluded from the Continent.[36]

These letters from Pollock and Dickson were apparently the first intimations to the people at Natchez that war had been declared. Captain Forster, of course, was bound by the capitulation at Baton Rouge to surrender the fort and its garrison, the ceremony taking place on October 5.[37] Convinced by Pollock's arguments or by the inexorable

---

[34] Here he anticipated by two years.

[35] Pollock to the inhabitants of the Natchez district, September 8, 1779, copy, A. G. I., Cuba, 192.

[36] Pollock to the inhabitants of the Natchez district, September 23, 1779, copy, *ibid.*

[37] 1 captain, 2 lieutenants, 3 sergeants, 2 drummers, 54 rank and file, and 13 women and children. Return of the garrison, signed by Edw. Byrne, October 6, 1779, *ibid.*

logic of their situation, the settlers submitted peacefully to Delavillebeuvre's control. A few days later they heard from the commander at Pensacola that they were at war with Spain, but they had to reply that they were *hors de combat* and could not engage in the proposed "surprise" attack on New Orleans.[38]

With forces drawn from Pointe Coupée, Carlos Grand Pré had already seized the British posts on Thompson's Creek and the Amite. As a reward for this service, and in recognition of his good work in cutting communications between Baton Rouge and Natchez, Gálvez placed him in command of the district, and, leaving small garrisons of regular troops at the various captured forts, returned to his capital.[39]

Under the command of William Pickles, meanwhile, an American privateer known as the corvette of the "Morris" (formerly the "Rebecca") had set out upon Lake Pontchartrain. Overtaking the English "West Florida," which for two years had dominated the lakes, Pickles demanded her surrender. The English captain refused. Both sides opened fire. The Americans boarded the "West Florida," killed four, including Captain Paine, and took the rest prisoners. Pickles succinctly reported his only loss: "Brown Traitor to our Cause swimd ashore." His victory was the more impressive because the "West Florida" carried two six-pounders, two four-pounders, and one nine-and-a-half, and had a crew of twenty-eight or thirty men, though some were impressed Americans, whereas the American sloop mounted only four two-and-a-half-pounders and one one-and-a-half. "It is unbelievable that he should have captured it," according to a Spanish report, on account of the disparity in the size of the ships, their armaments, etc."[40]

---

[38] Campbell to Forster, September 9, 1779, *ibid.;* Stuart to Forster, October 1, 1779, *ibid.;* Wm. Hiorn, J. Blommart, Alex McIntosh, Sam Wells, Wm. Courtney, John Ellis, Franc. Farrell, Patrick Foley to Stuart, October 12, 1779, copy, *ibid.*

[39] Gálvez to José de Gálvez, October 16, 1779, A. G. I., Cuba, 2351; Serrano y Sanz, *op. cit.,* 350–351. Return of prisoners taken at Thompson's Creek (13) and the Amite (12), *Louisiana Historical Quarterly,* XII (1929), 265.

[40] Pickles to Piernas, September 12, 1779, A. G. I., Cuba, 192; Pierre Rousseau (Pickles' mate), Relacion du Combat de la Goëletta Taindre de la Frigate Maurice Captne Guillaume Pickles Americaine, Contre le Bateau le Ouest floride de Pancacol Capitaine Painne, September 12, 1781 (*sic*), copy, A. G. I., Cuba, 2358; Serrano y Sanz, *op. cit.,* 352.

Four days after his exploit against the "West Florida," Pickles wrote a letter to the commanding officer at New Orleans in which is revealed a high standard of conduct along with most corrupt English.

I am informed that theare is asmall Vesel afitting out in ye Corrutor of acrusor. I am told she is a privit proporty if so she is only fitting out to go ovor ye lakes to plundor ye inhabitanes, if so I could Abeen adoing of that, but its my opinion its not right I am sarten we have anumbor of frends theare, & they hav been obliged to stay thear own acct. of theare Familes & what littel proporty they had, & now we to go & take it away from them it indoubtedly will Mak them ower Inemes, in my Opinien its Ower business to make all ye frends we can, in the rume of making of Inimes, if I had amind to plundored them i cout adun that sum time ago but my mining is to secure ye lakes, & take Care if Enemy dont slip out of ower hands, if ower frends was to be destressed I can soon do that.

I may cum across this vessel in ye night & may do hir som mischeaf dont blame me for it For I trust to none, for what trifel can be got From them is no obgect at this time, & I am shure in my own opinien that so smal a vesel, as I understand she is cant be own any other desire only plundering of ye inhabitanes.[41]

On the very day that Gálvez was bombarding Baton Rouge, Pickles landed on the northern shore of Lake Pontchartrain, took possession for the United States, and received an oath of allegiance from the settlers between Bayou La Combe and the Tauchipaho River. "We do hereby acknowledge ourselves," they affirmed, "to be natives as well as true and faithful subjects to the United Independent States of North America."[42] On September 26 Pickles ferried one hundred and twenty-two Indians across the lake to New Orleans, and the following day took a prize on the Mobile coast with thirteen negroes aboard valued at $2660.[43] Gálvez approved Pickles' actions, and when Pollock inquired if keeping the "West Florida" cruising in the lakes was "useful for the Common Cause" or whether she should be sent home in place of the "Morris," which had been lost, Gálvez urged that she be retained.[44]

---

[41] Pickles to Piernas, September 14, 1779, A. G. I., Cuba, 192.
[42] Claiborne, *op. cit.*, 122 n.
[43] Pickles, Presa hecha por el Corsario la Corbetta de la Fragta. la Moreis, October 8, 1779, A. G. I., Cuba, 701 E.
[44] Pollock to Gálvez, October 15, 1779, *ibid.*, 192.

At Gálveztown the Spaniards seized three galleys and a brig which were returning to Pensacola after having taken supplies and munitions to Manchac. Another boatload of supplies was seized on the river, and three more were captured on the lakes.[45]

The most spectacular victory was that of Vizente Rillieux, the commander of a Spanish ship in this locality. Having sighted an English transport on its way to Manchac, Rillieux landed his crew and artillery at the pass between the lakes, felling a few trees for their concealment. When the English ship was directly under his guns, he blazed away at it, and raised such a bedlam of bloodcurdling yells that the English, persuaded that they were beset by four or five hundred men, with one accord sought refuge below deck. Rillieux and his men straightway jumped on board and made them prisoners. "What was their surprise to find themselves, numbering fifty-six soldiers of the Waldeck regiment and ten or twelve sailors, apprehended by fourteen creoles, the entire command of Rillieux!"[46]

In less than a month Gálvez and his cohorts had achieved signal success. Three forts had been captured, one by assault, one by bombardment and capitulation, the other by cession. Five hundred and fifty regular soldiers had been taken prisoners, without counting the sailors on the eight boats seized, or the more than five hundred settlers and negroes taken with arms in their hands at Manchac, Baton Rouge, and elsewhere.[47] More important than the prisoners taken was the territory acquired. Four hundred and thirty leagues of the best land along the Mississippi, richer and more fertile than that on the opposite bank, with better establishments, and better peopled with nations that supported the fur trade, had been subjugated for Spain.[48]

Nevertheless, victory had its embarrassments. Even after the captured negroes and militiamen had been released, Gálvez had more than five hundred prisoners at New Orleans, and only fifty regular

---

[45] Collell to Gálvez, September 3, 7, 10, 1779, *ibid.*, 2351. Collell reports a total of eighty-two prisoners at Gálveztown.

[46] "The captain of the troops is named Christoval Alverti, and the lieutenant who was killed federico Noltid. All Germans."—Collell to Gálvez, September 7, 1779, *ibid.;* Serrano y Sanz, *op. cit.*, 352.

[47] *Louisiana Historical Quarterly*, XII (1929), 264–265; Gálvez to José de Gálvez, October 16, 1779, A. G. I., Cuba, 2351.

[48] Serrano y Sanz, *op. cit.*, 352

soldiers to guard them. But the English did not violate the parole which gave them freedom within the limits of the town. The Indian allies, likewise, created no disturbances. By the time the eighty additional prisoners arrived from Natchez, Gálvez' position had been made secure by a reënforcement from Havana. From the entrenchments before Baton Rouge, Gálvez had written to thank the captain general for sending these seven hundred men of the Second Battalion of Spain. They were too late to help him in the eventuality of defeat, but they would protect New Orleans against an attack from Pensacola. He was especially grateful to Navarro because the reënforcement was unsolicited, a justification of his perfect confidence that help would be forthcoming from Havana when necessary.[49]

The English prisoners were kept at New Orleans for several months. Some of the officers received paroles to go to Pensacola or to England, the only stipulation being that they should not serve against Spain or her allies until duly exchanged.[50] In the summer of 1780 the rest of the prisoners were sent to Vera Cruz and forwarded thence to Havana.[51] Dickson gave Gálvez credit because the prisoners, both officers and soldiers, were "treated with the greatest generosity and attention, not only by the officers, but even the Spanish soldiers seem to take pleasure in being kind and civil to the prisoners in general."[52]

Gálvez did not miscalculate the effect of his campaign. In addition to the tangible profit of prisoners and territory won, it served as a potent defense against British attack. Witness this statement of a Pensacola Britisher:

Immediately under a knowledge of a Spanish War we all thought that we must take Orleans; and preparations for an expedition were immediately commenced, but to our utter disappointment, just as we were ready to embark, an account was received that Don Galwas had obliged all our troops on the Mississippi to capitulate.[53]

---

[49] Gálvez to Navarro, September 18, 1779, No. 208, A. G. I., Cuba, 1232.
[50] E.g., paroles to Jas. Wilson, May 20, 1780, Alex. Dickson, July 4, 1780, August Alberti, July 5, 1780, A. G. I., Cuba, 193; Bern. Lintot, July 13, 1780, *ibid*., 2370.
[51] Mayorga to José de Gálvez, October 4, 1780, A. G. I., Ind. Gen., 146-2-7.
[52] Dickson to Campbell, October 20, 1779, *Louisiana Historical Quarterly*, XII (1929), 258.
[53] Gordon to Thompson & Campbell, November 18, 1779, Historical Manuscripts Commission, *op. cit*., II, 63.

From Dickson, too, Gálvez got confirmation of the English plan for a double attack on New Orleans from Canada and Pensacola. Since Navarro had criticized his audacious plan of taking the offensive, Gálvez seems to have taken keen delight in pointing out to him the happy result of his prompt action. After describing the English plans for a descent on New Orleans, he concluded his letter:

> I believe that you will not disapprove my resolution to attack them first, taking advantage of their ignorance of the declaration of war; for if this opportunity had been allowed to pass, and they had had time to put their plans into execution, there is no doubt that there would have been a very different outcome for our arms in this province. This is all that I can say to you in reply to your confidential letter of September 22 last.[54]

Credit for the successful campaign must be divided. The militia, particularly the Acadians, who had not forgotten the persecutions they had suffered at the hands of the English, behaved splendidly. The "black and gray" companies, usually employed as skirmishers and scouts, displayed as much valor as the whites. The Indian allies, thanks to the influence of Santiago Tarascon and Joseph Sorelle, of Opelousas, refrained from the cruelties generally expected of them.[55] Commendation should also be accorded to the Americans under Pickles and the French creoles under Rillieux. More than any other one person, however, Gálvez should be recognized; not for the brilliance of his military maneuvers, though he demonstrated his capability as a general; but rather for his vision in planning the campaign, for his disregard of timid advisors, for his courage in the face of a disconcerting disaster, and, most of all, for the enthusiasm with which he inspired the creoles to whole-hearted participation in the expedition.

Consequences of the campaign extended even farther than has been indicated. Not only was Campbell's attack thwarted at its source and the lower Mississippi Valley secured for Spain, but also the Canadian attack, though not prevented entirely, was given a serious setback,

---

[54] Gálvez to Navarro, October 16, 1779, reservada, No. 227, A. G. I., Cuba, 2351; Navarro to Gálvez, September 22, 1779, reservada, A. G. I., Sto. Dom., 2543.

[55] "Suplemento á la Gazeta de Madrid," January 14, 1780, quoted in Gayarré, *op. cit.*, III, 131–132 *n*.

and English influence in the upper Mississippi Valley was greatly diminished. That this was in part a consequence of Gálvez' first campaign has not been generally recognized.

In fulfillment of the English general plan, which called for an expedition down the Mississippi from Canada in conjunction with an attack from Pensacola,[56] Sinclair gathered a force of Indians and traders at Michilimackinac. There were Sioux warriors under Wabasha, a chief "of very singular & uncommon abilities"; there were Menominee, Puant, Sauk, Fox, and Ottawa braves. Captain Hesse commanded, assisted by Chief Machiquawish of the Ottawa and Chief Wabasha. In all there were perhaps nine hundred and fifty men in the expedition.[57] They expected to capture St. Louis easily. "The reduction of Pencour [St. Louis], by surprise," Sinclair wrote, "from the easy admission, of Indians at that place, and from assault from those without, having for its defense, as reported, only 20 men & 20 brass Cannon, will be less difficult than holding it afterwards."[58] The Spanish commandant shared this opinion of the weakness of St. Louis. "Sixteen men, including the drummer," he had reported to Gálvez, "are all the troops I have; of the militia, it is true, there are forty able to bear arms, but at this time they are all trading on the Misury."[59]

Nevertheless, when the English and Indians made their attack on May 26, 1780, St. Louis did not fall. Many reasons have been adduced for the failure of the assault, no one of which is a complete explanation. Sinclair blamed the treachery "of Mr. Calve and the Sacks & Renards (for whom he is paid by the crown as Interpreter). His partner in commerce a Monsr. Ducharme," Sinclair continued, "has kept pace with him."[60] There can be no doubt that this lack of unanimity contributed to the failure of the attack. The Winnebagos and Sioux

---

[56] Germain to Haldimand, June 17, 1779, *Report on Canadian Archives, 1885*, 276.

[57] Sinclair to Haldimand, May 29, 1780, *Wisconsin Historical Collections*, XI, 151; Sinclair to Brehm, February 25, 1780; *ibid.*, 145. The estimates do not agree, however. The Spanish report was three hundred whites and nine hundred Indians, *ibid.*, XVIII, 407, 416. One estimate was as high as fifteen hundred, James, *George Rogers Clark Papers, 1771–1781*, p. cxxviii, *n.* 3.

[58] Sinclair to Haldimand, February 15, 1780, *Wisconsin Historical Collections*, XI, 148.

[59] Leyba to Gálvez, February 5, 1779, A. G. I., Cuba, 1.

[60] Sinclair to Bolton, June 4, 1780, *Wisconsin Historical Collections*, XI, 156.

"would have stormed the Spanish lines if the Sacks and Outagomies under their treacherous leader Monsr. Calve had not fallen back so early, as to give them but too well grounded suspicions that they were between two Fires."[61]

Another factor was the lack of secrecy. Leyba received information on May 9 that a force of three hundred English and nine hundred Indians was only eighty leagues distant from St. Louis.[62] He at once instituted frantic measures for defense. The Ste. Geneviève militia under Cartabona was summoned to St. Louis. Entrenchments were thrown up around the town and a tower was erected upon which five cannon were mounted. By the time of the attack Leyba had mustered twenty-five regulars and two hundred and eighty-nine villagers.[63] On May 23 he received a second warning to the effect that the English were within twenty leagues of St. Louis. Even so, the attack was more or less unexpected. A number of farmers with their slaves were busy in the fields adjoining the town when the onslaught was made. Most of these unfortunates were murdered or carried away as prisoners. But thanks to repeated warnings, Leyba had gathered enough fighting men to put up a stiff and successful resistance.[64]

There is something to be said also for the valor of the defenders and the backwardness of the Canadians. Leyba's report unblushingly mentioned "this bold opposition on our part." And Sinclair remarked that "the Traders who would not assist in extending their Commerce cannot complain of its being circumscribed."[65]

In the opinion of Professor James, the most potent cause for the precipitate retreat was the opportune appearance of George Rogers Clark across the river at Cahokia.[66] Clark modestly admitted in 1793 that he and his men had saved St. Louis and the rest of Louisiana for the Spaniards. He may have been correct. Yet in Sinclair's elaborate at-

---

[61] Sinclair to Haldimand, July 8, 1780, *ibid*.
[62] Leyba to Gálvez, June 8, 1780, A. G. I., Cuba, 193.
[63] James, "The Significance of the Attack on St. Louis, 1780," *Proceedings of the Mississippi Valley Historical Association*, II, 208–209.
[64] Leyba to Gálvez, June 8, 1780. A. G. I., Cuba, 193.
[65] *Ibid.;* Sinclair to Haldimand, July 8, 1780, *Wisconsin Historical Collections, loc. cit.*
[66] James, "The Significance of the Attack on St. Louis, 1780," *op. cit.*, 210.

tempts to palliate the failure of the foray there is no mention of Clark as an obstacle to its success.[67]

Sinclair's apology contains one significant suggestion. In his list of handicaps he mentions the fact that the expedition was "unsupported ... by any other against New Orleans," and goes on to refer to "the advances made by the Enemy on the Mississippi."[68] I would not go quite so far as one writer, who says, "It was the sudden knowledge of Gálvez's success in driving the British utterly out of the Mississippi Valley that had made the horde of savages post back so suddenly and inexplicably."[69] But in view of the fact that Gálvez' success was known to the Canadians, and because his conquests had frustrated the British general plan, it seems that they must be counted as a contributory cause for the British retreat. Gálvez' conquests on the lower Mississippi were significant for the entire Mississippi Valley—not alone for the immediate vicinity of Baton Rouge and Natchez.

Retaliation for the St. Louis attack was effected by two expeditions. The first went to Rock River. Leyba and Clark had exchanged letters relative to this project prior to the English and Indian raid on St. Louis. Leyba had agreed to supply one hundred well equipped men, with boats, arms, artillery, and provisions. Stimulated to action by the English invasion, they put their plans into immediate operation. Under Colonel Montgomery a force of three hundred or three hundred and fifty men was sent against the Sauk and Fox Indians. They went by boat up the Illinois as far as Peoria and then marched overland to Rock River. The Indians had fled, and, after burning the villages, Montgomery returned. Impressed perhaps by this punishment, the Fox Indians became more friendly to the Spanish in the fall of 1780.[70]

The second measure of retaliation was less directly an outgrowth of the St. Louis attack. Early in 1781 Cruzat, who had succeeded Leyba

---

[67] Clark to Genet, February 5, 1793, quoted *ibid.*, 212-213; Sinclair to Haldimand, July 8, 1780, *op. cit.*, XI, 155-157.

[68] *Ibid.*, 156.

[69] Phelps, *Louisiana*, 147.

[70] Cruzat to Gálvez, November 14, 1780, B. L., La. Coll.; Meese, "Rock River in the Revolution," *Transactions of the Illinois State Historical Society*, XIV (1921), 97-103.

at St. Louis, sent a small band of Spaniards and Indians against the English post at St. Joseph on Lake Michigan. On the morning of February 12 these men took the post by surprise, made the small English garrison prisoners, divided the plunder among the local Indians and those of the expedition, burned the remaining supplies, and, after going through the form of taking possession for Spain, departed that same morning.[71]

Concerning the reasons for this expedition, several historians have indulged in somewhat acrid controversy.[72] Mason believed it an attempt to extend Spanish claims to territory east of the Mississippi. Alvord labeled it a design of certain Cahokia Frenchmen to get revenge for English and Indian depredations and to pillage the stores of the fort. Teggart stressed the fact that formal possession was taken for Spain, agreeing thus far with Mason, but maintaining also that the attack was devised by Cruzat in order to destroy supplies with which the British intended to outfit another expedition against St. Louis.

A document in the Louisiana Collection of the Bancroft Library, brought to light by Dr. Kinnaird, helps to clear up the difficulty. It is Cruzat's report to Gálvez concerning the despatch of the expedition under Captain Eugene Pourré.[73] "The urging of the Indians Heturno and Naguiquen," he wrote, "to persuade me to make an expedition against the English at Fort St. Joseph ... forces me to send a detachment of sixty men.... It was absolutely necessary to take these measures as I shall explain to you." The first reason was that refusal might have caused the two chiefs to abandon the Spanish side in favor of the English; the second, that the capture of St. Joseph would intimidate the Indians whom the English hoped to send against St. Louis in the spring; the third, that the stirring up of hostilities toward the pro-English Indians was sound and approved strategy.[74]

---

[71] Cruzat to Miró, August 6, 1781, B. L., La. Coll.

[72] Mason, "The Spanish March across Illinois in 1781," *Magazine of American History*, XV (1886), 457–469; Alvord, "The Conquest of St. Joseph, Michigan by the Spaniards, 1781," *Missouri Historical Review*, II (1908), 195–210; Teggart, "The Capture of St. Joseph, Michigan, by the Spaniards in 1781," *ibid.*, V (1911), 214–228. For an excellent discussion of the controversy and of the problem see Kinnaird, "The Spanish Expedition against Fort St. Joseph in 1781, a New Interpretation," *Mississippi Valley Historical Review*, XIX (1932), 173–191.

[73] Cruzat to Gálvez, January 10, 1781, B. L., La. Coll.   [74] *Ibid.*

Perhaps it is not too unkind to say that none of these attempts to discover the exact reason or reasons for the expedition is completely successful. Motives are hard to detect and harder still to isolate. There is no direct evidence, for example, that a desire to establish Spain's claim to the region around St. Joseph prompted the despatch of the expedition. Mason and Teggart, influenced by Pourré's action at the post and by Spain's subsequent use of the incident as the basis for such a claim, apparently project this into the past and make a motive of it. Absence of direct evidence, nevertheless, does not absolutely rule out this desire as a possible purpose. Even such a statement as Cruzat's letter is something short of perfect evidence. He may have withheld advisedly or by oversight some argument that impelled his action; there may have been influences of which he was not conscious.

Of the several reasons for the attack on St. Joseph, the first and most important was the importunity of the Indian chiefs, Heturno and Naguiquen, and Cruzat's desire to retain their friendship. There was an opportunity to turn this to good account by an attack on St. Joseph, which would serve the double purpose of warding off a second attack on St. Louis, which the English seemed to be planning, and of producing a wholesome effect on the nonfriendly tribes near Lake Michigan.[75] Heturno and Naguiquen, however, had been stirred up by the very occurrence which Alvord names as the outrage which caused the French at Cahokia to become the real fathers of the expedition.[76] The two chiefs prefaced their suggestion of the war party by an account of the massacre of a party of seventeen Frenchmen from Cahokia who had had the misfortune to encounter a band of Canadians under Dequente.[77] Evidence is lacking, however, to decide whether Heturno's wrath was spontaneous or had been roused by the Cahokians. Finally, there is the bare possibility that the expedition was designed to furnish the basis for a Spanish claim to the region.

[75] *Ibid.*

[76] Alvord, *op. cit.*, 210.

[77] "Llego el veinte y seis del mes pasado el Gefe el Heturno atraharme la Noticia de la Destrucion (por un partido de canadianos del Estrecho mandados por un tal Dequente) de un Destacamento de diez y siete franseses que havian salido ay serca de tres meses del Pueblo de Kaó para ir a aupararse dle Fuerte de Sn. Jph."—Cruzat to Gálvez, January 10, 1781, B. L., La. Coll.

Much more important than the abstruse question of motives were the effects of the expedition. The English dismissed it casually. "The attack on St. Joseph," Sinclair wrote, "was nothing more than an outrage committed by a band of marauders and of little consequence."[78] Cruzat's estimate of the results was more discerning: "Not only are we pleased over the happy outcome of this expedition, the destruction of the store of food and goods that the enemy had in St. Joseph, but also over the intimidation of the tribes hostile to us in those districts, since this affair forced them to remain neutral." If the Cahokians had desired revenge and plunder, they were in large part disappointed. Pourré took special precautions for the protection of the captured Englishmen. The portable plunder was divided between the local Indians and those of the expedition, and the rest of the supplies was destroyed.[79]

In the negotiations for peace with England, Spain made the foray the basis for claims to territory east of the Mississippi. After the capture of the fort, on the morning of February 12, the Spaniards had tarried long enough for Pourré to read a proclamation in which he said,

> I annex and incorporate with the domains of his Very Catholic Majesty, the King of Spain, my master, from now on and forever, this post of St. Joseph and its dependencies, with the river of the same name, and that of Islinois, which flows into the Missicipy River.[80]

But this proclamation obviously constituted a weaker claim to sovereignty than the capture and continued occupation of the territory farther south. And although this claim is the most advertised result of the expedition, it was of far less importance than the effects upon the Indian situation and the additional security won for St. Louis.

The military activities with which this chapter has dealt were primarily measures of Spanish defense. The exigencies of affairs led Gálvez and Cruzat into aggressive action, but the conquest of the Baton Rouge-Natchez region and the temporary occupation of St. Joseph

---

[78] Sinclair to Powell, June 5, 1781, *Wisconsin Historical Collections*, XI, 163.
[79] Cruzat to Miró, August 6, 1781, B. L., La. Coll.
[80] Pourré, proclamation, February 12, 1781, B. L., La. Coll.

were, so to speak, by-products of the defense of New Orleans and St. Louis. Gálvez' lower Mississippi campaign and Pourré's St. Joseph expedition are linked to each other by more than a structural similarity. Both were factors in the struggle between England and Spain for control of the Mississippi, and for dominant influence over the Indian tribes of the entire valley. In 1781, after the St. Joseph expedition, it appeared that the duel had been settled in favor of Spain. English rule had been demolished all along the Mississippi. Spain was dominant along the entire western bank and on the eastern bank below the Ohio. Above the Ohio the Spaniards and the Americans exercised an informal sort of joint control.

Chapter X

THE CAPTURE OF MOBILE

GÁLVEZ' CAPTURE of the English forts on the lower Mississippi spread consternation in the other English establishments in the Floridas. Major General Campbell refused at first to believe the report, considering it a Spanish ruse to draw him out of Pensacola.[1] When a second messenger corroborated the news, he determined to launch a counter-attack, but since transports were available for only two hundred and fifty men, he had to content himself with strengthening the defenses of Pensacola.[2] As far away as St. Augustine there was serious apprehension. On hearing of Dickson's surrender, the St. Augustine commander appealed to Clinton for more troops. "Should we receive a similar visit from the Havanna," he wrote, "I shall do what ought to be done; but I have not the gift to perform miracles."[3]

The Spaniards likewise regarded the lower Mississippi expedition as but the prelude to more ambitious campaigns. Mobile and Pensacola were the next objectives. With the official notice of the rupture between Spain and England, Gálvez had received instructions "to drive the British forces out of Pensacola, Mobile, and the other posts they occupy on the Mississippi."[4] A subsequent royal order defined the Spanish objective more exactly:

> The king has determined that the principal object of his forces in America during the war against the English shall be to expel them from the Gulf of Mexico and the banks of the Mississippi where their establishments are so prejudicial to our commerce and also to the security of our more valuable possessions.[5]

---

[1] Hamilton, *Colonial Mobile*, 252.
[2] Historical Manuscripts Commission, *op. cit.*, II, 32; Hamilton, *op. cit.*, 252.
[3] Lieutenant Colonel Füser to General Clinton, December 12, 1779, *in* Historical Manuscripts Commission, *op. cit.*, II, 71.
[4] Navarro to Gálvez, July 18, 1779, A. G. I., Sto. Dom., 2543.
[5] José de Gálvez to the governor of Havana, August 29, 1779, certified copy, A. G. I., Cuba, 2358.

This order specified also that command over the expedition should be entrusted to Bernardo de Gálvez. The king chose Gálvez in preference to officers of greater experience, because he had formed a plan for the campaign, he knew the country, he had communicated with the enemy, he had coöperated with the Georgians, he had gained the friendship of the Choctaws and other Indians, and had won the approbation of the American Congress.[6]

Before setting out for Manchac and Baton Rouge, Gálvez had begun to plan the conquest of Pensacola and Mobile. He called on Panis, who had described the defenses of these places,[7] to prepare a plan for their seizure, and forwarded this with amendments to his superior officer, the captain general at Havana. Panis' plan called for a formidable naval force and a landing party of seven thousand men. Gálvez thought fewer ships of the line would suffice, and not more than four thousand men from Havana.[8] But further modifications of the plan were necessary almost at once. Gálvez had written on August 17; on the eighteenth the hurricane struck New Orleans. On the nineteenth, therefore, he wrote again to Navarro that an additional thousand men from Havana would be required. Succeeding letters elaborate the plan.[9]

Not tarrying for a reply from Havana, Gálvez launched his lower Mississippi expedition. This campaign was an integral part of his preparations for the more important Gulf Coast campaign. In the first place, it was a tactical necessity to remove the danger of an attack on New Orleans before drawing away troops for use elsewhere. Then, too, the victory at Baton Rouge guaranteed confidence in Gálvez, both on the part of the colonists and on the part of higher Spanish officials. Doubly strengthened, therefore, by the favorable outcome of his first expedition against the English, Gálvez was able, in the fall of 1779, to push forward his military preparations much more rapidly than had been possible the preceding summer. With Gayarré again acting in

---

[6] *Ibid.*

[7] Panis to Gálvez, July 5, 1778, *ibid.*, 112.

[8] *Idem* to *idem*, August 16, 1779, *ibid.;* Gálvez to Navarro, August 17, 1779, reservada, No. 20, *ibid.*, 2351.

[9] Gálvez to Navarro, August 19, 21, 23, 25, 1779, reservada, Nos. 202–205, *ibid.*, 1232.

the capacity of commissary of war, Gálvez spent the remaining months of 1779 in collecting the sinews of war. The captured English ships were refitted as transports, and the captured military supplies became the nucleus of the equipage for 1780. Louisiana furnished some of the things that were necessary, and powder and shot were sent from Havana.[10]

The militia and light artillery, the launches and the handful of regulars, with which Gálvez had succeeded in his first campaign, were inadequate for the reduction of fortifications such as those at Mobile and Pensacola. Help from Havana was imperative. Yet it was not immediately forthcoming.

Navarro did not see how so many men could be spared from Havana. First, he would delay any action until news arrived of the outcome of the Manchac expedition.[11] Secondly, he offered a substitute plan for the seizure of West Florida, which would emphasize a naval onslaught on Pensacola. Navarro and Huet, whose plan this really was, believed that Pensacola would capitulate after a naval bombardment without troops having to be landed, and that Mobile and the other posts would automatically share the same fate. But Gálvez reminded the captain general that there were thirty-six- and forty-two-pounders in front of Pensacola and at the harbor entrance, before which the Spanish frigates would be sacrificed. It would be necessary, therefore, to land troops. He renewed his recommendation that the campaign should begin with an attack on Mobile, because it was a source of supplies for Pensacola and a strategic point for Indian control.[12]

The captain general attempted a second rebuttal of Gálvez' plan. Huet outlined an approach entirely by land beginning at Mobile and going on to Fort Barrancas Coloradas at the Pensacola harbor entrance. Seven batteries being thus overcome by a flank attack, Huet expected that the Spaniards would be sure of the acquisition of Pensacola without bloodshed.[13] At the same time the captain general

---

[10] Gayarré to José de Gálvez, May 31, 1780, A. G. I., Sto. Dom., 2572.
[11] Navarro to Gálvez, September 22, 1779, *ibid.*, 2543.
[12] Gálvez to Navarro, October 16, 1779, reservada, No. 228, A. G. I., Cuba, 2351.
[13] Huet to Gálvez, November 20, 1779, A. G. I., Cuba, I.

stated that seven thousand men could not be spared from Havana because of the many prisoners that had to be guarded there, but it seemed to him that with half that number Gálvez could undertake his project with full confidence.[14]

Refused the necessary reënforcements from Havana, Gálvez decided to concentrate first on the capture of Mobile. He communicated this decision to Navarro, pointing out that this conquest would protect Louisiana and the previous gains along the Mississippi as well as make easier a subsequent attack on Pensacola. A marginal note on Navarro's report to the court indicates that the king received this news "con mucho disgusto" and ordered more reënforcements sent and a more vigorous campaign.[15]

As a last effort to extract more assistance from Havana, Gálvez sent Colonel Estevan Miró as his personal representative to ask the captain general "for 2000 men, to be sent to Mobile and Pensacola by the middle of February at the latest." If this number could not be spared, fifteen hundred or even thirteen hundred would be acceptable "if no other recourse remained."[16] Miró reached Havana on January 24, 1780. After prolonged argument he induced the authorities there, although they were loath to reduce their own garrison, to send five hundred and sixty-seven men of the Regiment of Navarra to coöperate with Gálvez. In four transports this detachment sailed from Cuba on February 10, and though buffeted by a strong northwest wind of almost hurricane proportions that made headway impossible for several days, it reached Mobile Bay toward the end of the month.[17]

On January 2, 1780, Gálvez gave final instructions to the officials who were to remain in Louisiana and set the tenth as the time for mobilization of his expeditionary force. On the eleventh he reviewed his men as they embarked at New Orleans: 43 men of the Regiment of Principe of the Second Battalion of Spain, 50 of the fixed regiment

---

[14] Navas to Gálvez, November 20, 1779, *ibid*.

[15] Navarro to José de Gálvez, January 2, 1780, reservada, No. 99, A. G. I., Sto. Dom., 2082.

[16] Gálvez to Miró, December 31, 1779, *ibid*., 2543.

[17] Diario de Estevan Miró, January 24-March 7, 1780, *ibid*.; Gálvez to Navarro, January 1, 1780, A. G. I., Cuba, 2351.

of Havana, 141 of the fixed regiment of Louisiana, 14 artillerymen, 26 carabiniers, 323 white militiamen, 107 free blacks and mulattoes, 24 slaves, and 26 Anglo-American auxiliaries—altogether, 754 men. His fleet consisted of one merchantman frigate, four settees, one packet boat, two brigs, the frigate of war "Volante," the galliot "Valenzuela," the brig "Gálvez," privately armed as a corsair, and the king's brig "Kaulican."[18]

After a leisurely descent of the river, the ships arrived at its mouth on the eighteenth. Riaño was sent to sound the southwest pass, and returned two days later to report no more water there than at the east pass. Some of the vessels had to be lightened. They waited for good weather until the twenty-eighth when all the vessels save the "Kaulican" sailed out upon the Gulf. The wind failed before this brig could come out, and it was delayed until February 4. The entire fleet was becalmed until the sixth when a strong southwest wind carried them twenty leagues on their way. The weather report for that night mentions wind, rain, thunder, lightning, and hail, and a whirlwind at half-past ten, yet in the morning the commander sighted his whole convoy from the "Gálvez." On the second morning, however, only four vessels were in sight, and one of these was shipping water. On the third morning the coast near the Perdido was recognized and the ships were turned west toward Mobile. That evening they sighted others of the fleet off Mobile but were becalmed before they could reach them.

That same night an English vessel was descried just inside Mobile Bay. Reconnoitering in an armed launch, Riaño captured five men and the second officer of this vessel as they were leaving it in a skiff. These prisoners described the ship as a merchant frigate from Pensacola, mounting sixteen guns but with a crew of only twenty men. Riaño returned to seize it, but after his galliot had run aground three times, he gave up the effort.

On the tenth a strong southwest wind and a heavy sea determined Gálvez to enter the bay. The "Volante" led, followed by the "Gálvez."

---

[18] The account which follows is based on the "Diario... de la Expedición contra Panzacola y Mobila," January 2-March 18, 1780, A. G. I., Cuba, 2351.

On the treacherous bar these two vessels and four others went hard aground. By strenuous efforts the "Gálvez" was floated free at one o'clock that night, but only after twelve hours on the bar, as a result of which she was "well maltreated" and taking nine inches of water an hour. But the "Volante" and two of the other ships could not be budged.

The eleventh was so stormy that the stranded vessels could not be aided. On the twelfth, however, part of the troops were landed from the sloops that had entered without mishap, and under St. Maxent's direction soldiers and sailors were taken off the ships on the bar. The two smaller craft were worked clear, and hope was renewed for the "Volante." On the thirteenth the other vessels of the convoy appeared, except the "Kaulican." Since these vessels had lost their anchors, they were ordered to attempt to enter the bay. Two of them accomplished the feat safely, but the hospital ship grounded. Then followed more work taking off men and trying to save the stranded vessels. On February 17 the "Volante" and the English ship were abandoned to their fate.

The accepted story has been that in the improvised camp on Mobile Point, Gálvez, forsaken by his customary confidence, was on the verge of abandoning his impedimenta and retreating by land to New Orleans.[19] The outlook was discouraging. Taking stock of the situation, Gálvez found that he had some eight hundred men but that the shipwrecks had entailed loss of supplies and artillery as well as hardships and danger. Nevertheless, his attitude was cheerful. He prepared to attack rather than to retreat. He reported excellent morale among his men and even that they were making ladders out of the wreckage with which to scale the walls of Fort Charlotte.[20]

Using guns from the "Volante," Gálvez established a battery on the point to command the entrance to the bay, and reëmbarked the rest of his men to move up the bay toward Mobile. Just as they were about to start, a small ship came in from Havana with news that reënforce-

---

[19] Gayarré, *op. cit.*, III, 135–136; Hamilton, *op. cit.*, 253.

[20] "Diario... de la Expedición contra... Mobila," A. G. I., Cuba, 2351. Incidentally, there is so little dry land between Mobile Point and New Orleans that a retreat by land was almost out of the question.

ments were on the way, and on the twentieth five ships appeared. Two days later two of these ships, having lost their anchors, essayed to enter the bay, and with no respect for precedent crossed the bar safely.

February 24 and 25 were given up to the move from Mobile Point to Dog River, three leagues from Mobile, where M. Orbane Demouy's house became Gálvez' headquarters. A prisoner and an English deserter revealed that the English had been encouraged by a report that seven hundred men were lost in the shipwrecks. On the next two days more men were landed, and while the "Valenzuela" fired her twenty-four-pounder at the fort, a place to land the artillery was sought. On the twenty-eighth they crossed Dog River and moved to a new camp just two thousand varas from the fort. But not until the twenty-ninth did they face the enemy's fire. On that day the English greeted a scouting party of four companies with cannon balls and grapeshot and sent a few balls through the "Valenzuela's" rigging.

On March 1 Gálvez began a most chivalrous correspondence with Captain Elias Durnford, the commander of Fort Charlotte. Bouligny was sent in to demand surrender to Gálvez' somewhat exaggerated but still preponderant force. Durnford replied that since he had the advantage of position honor forbade his surrendering without resistance.[21] To his superior at Pensacola Durnford reported a very pleasant conversation with his old acquaintance Bouligny. They continued friends though national enemies, dined together, and drank "a cheerful Glass" to the healths of their sovereigns and friends. Bouligny admitted that the shipwrecks had involved great hardships and danger, but denied any loss of life. He represented that there were twenty-five hundred men in the Spanish force. Trusty Indians, however, assured Durnford that negroes and mulattoes formed a large part of this force, and he believed their number to be "greatly magnified." And though Bouligny said that the "Valenzuela" had been "just hit," Durnford was sure she had been "well mauled."[22]

---

[21] Copies of these two letters and of subsequent correspondence are inclosed in the "Diario" cited in the preceding note.

[22] Durnford to Campbell, March 2, 1780, *Publications of the Louisiana Historical Society*, I, No. 2, p. 33.

This letter gives further light on the state of defense in the fort.

> As soon as Colonel Bolyny left me I drew up my Garrison in the square, read to them Don Gálvez' summons, and then told them that if any man among them was afraid to stand by me, that I should open the gate and he should freely pass. This had the desired effect, and not a man moved. I then read to them my answer to the summons, in which they all joined in three cheers and then went to our necessary work like good men.[23]

A few days later Durnford presented to his adversary a dozen bottles of wine, a dozen chickens, a dozen loaves of fresh bread, and a mutton, and sent other provisions which he asked should be turned over to Sergeant Gun's wife and child and to Charles Stuart, prisoners in the Spanish camp. Responding with a case of Bordeaux wine and one of Spanish, a box of citrons and oranges, a box of tea biscuits and corn cakes, and a box of Havana cigars, Gálvez assured the English commander that all the prisoners were being well taken care of.

Apologizing profusely for introducing a harsh note into their dulcet discourse, Gálvez felt impelled, nevertheless, to offer "a small reproach." He regretted that military necessity had dictated to Durnford the reduction to ashes of a charming section of Mobile. "Fortresses," he pointed out, "are constructed solely to defend towns, but you are commencing to destroy the town in favor of a fortress incapable of defense." For the sake of the poor citizens of Mobile, Gálvez was willing, if Durnford would stay his incendiarism, to promise not to establish batteries behind any house.[24]

Replying, the English commander extolled Gálvez' humanity and generous character. He denied having harbored doubts that any prisoners were receiving less than the best possible treatment, and he thanked Gálvez for releasing two men of the town on their word of honor. Then, in more spirited language, but still with graciousness, he endeavored to exculpate himself for burning down houses around the fort. He was not to blame for the unfortunate location of the fort, and he agreed with Gálvez in criticizing its proximity to the town. But to make the sturdiest defense of Fort Charlotte was his primary

---

[23] *Ibid.*
[24] Durnford to Gálvez, March 6 (*sic*, 5), 1780; Gálvez to Durnford, March 5, 1780, copies, "Diario ... de la Expedición contra ... Mobila," A. G. I., Cuba, 2351.

THE CAPTURE OF MOBILE   179

responsibility and justified any house burning he had ordered. Very few houses had been destroyed at his command, and he was as provoked as Gálvez over the pointless destruction of the last several days. In the name of the townspeople he appreciated Gálvez' generosity in offering to attack from the other side so that the remaining houses might be spared, and he expressed the opinion that there was sufficient expanse of terrain there for the Spanish approach.[25]

But Durnford had mistaken a conditional for an absolute promise, and Gálvez hastened to draw attention to the mood. He had written "I would promise" instead of "I do promise." His intention had been that his agreement not to erect batteries sheltered by the houses should be balanced by an agreement on Durnford's part not to open new embrasures on the vulnerable side and not to mass men or artillery there. But endeavoring to avoid all semblance of faithlessness, Gálvez asked if Durnford considered him bound by his unintended promise, implying that he would live up to it, if this were demanded.[26]

In his answer the English officer was as punctiliously honorable. He was effusively grateful to Gálvez for his most generous and charitable interest in the welfare of the townspeople, but would not think of holding him to his "promise." Nevertheless, the conditions proposed to the English were impossible of acceptance. Since it was his duty to defend and resist as long as he could reasonably do so, he could not promise not to use his men and batteries to the best advantage. Thus the matter ended.[27]

Between letters preparations went forward for an attack on Fort Charlotte. The soldiers showed great good will in the work of unloading supplies and moving them to the new camp. On March 4, for example, two eighteen-pounders were moved more than half a league in half an hour. On the seventh a corporal and two men were injured in cutting down a tree, the corporal and one other so seriously that they died the next day.

An intercepted letter that same day revealed that the enemy expected to be rescued by a large force from Pensacola. The captain of

---
[25] Durnford to Gálvez, March 6, 1780, copy, *ibid*.
[26] Gálvez to Durnford, March 6, 1780, copy, *ibid*.
[27] Durnford to Gálvez, and Gálvez to Durnford, March 7, 1780, copies, *ibid*.

the frigate riding at anchor outside the bay was warned to be on the lookout, and land parties were sent out to investigate. As early as February 12 Campbell had learned of the Spaniards' arrival at Mobile, but he was dilatory in taking the steps necessary for its relief.[28] He sent a promise of help to Durnford, which that officer welcomed as a great encouragement. "Your great good news hath just arrived. I thank you, dear Sir, for the consolation it affords me."[29] Durnford's defensive measures were designed merely to retain Fort Charlotte until this succor arrived, and conversely Gálvez aimed at a rapid reduction of the fort before it could be relieved.

By the ninth the work of preparing fagots, large fascines, and other materials for the attack was completed. At nightfall, after Gálvez had made a short speech to raise their spirits, two hundred armed men and three hundred laborers left the camp to open a trench. They worked so zealously that by ten o'clock they were sheltered and had set up a shoulder of fagots to hide the battery from the enemy. Before dawn these men were relieved by one hundred and fifty to stand guard and one hundred and fifty to work on the erection of the battery. Throughout the night it was their good fortune to be undetected by the enemy, but in the morning the trench and battery could no longer be concealed from the English, who directed toward them a lively fire with cannon, both ball and grape, and with carbines and muskets. By eleven o'clock the Spaniards had suffered six killed and five wounded; accordingly Gálvez called off work until night when it could be done with less risk. The night was stormy, however, and little more was accomplished until the next day.

Two scouting parties returned on the eleventh, reporting that they had seen two English camps in the Tensaw region, one with twenty tents, the other with many fires, and they estimated the force at four hundred or six hundred men. Hearing this, Gálvez took additional precautions against being surprised. He attempted also to divert the enemy's attention from the trench and battery by having the launches

---

[28] Historical Manuscripts Commission, *op. cit.*, II, 89.

[29] Durnford to Campbell, March 2, 1780, *Publications of the Louisiana Historical Society*, I, No. 2, pp. 33-34.

and small craft feign a movement in front of the wharf, but the fire on the Spanish works was not slackened.

By ten o'clock in the morning of the twelfth the Spanish battery of eight eighteen-pounders and one twenty-four-pounder was completed. A lively fire commenced, the English responding in kind. The Spanish fire was more effective, doing real damage to the parapets and embrasures of the fort, but whenever an English cannon was dismounted, another was brought in its place. During the day the Spaniards lost one dead and three wounded.

At sundown the English ran up a white flag and sent out an officer to propose a cessation of hostilities and of work on the fortifications for the night so that terms of surrender might be arranged. Gálvez agreed on condition that Durnford promise not to make unnecessary delays in the hope of receiving a reënforcement, and that the sailors and the habitants who had assisted in the defense should not be sent out of the fort.

Durnford proposed first that the garrison of the fort should be allowed to evacuate it and to proceed by the Perdido River trail or by sea to Pensacola, but Gálvez branded these terms as "inadmissible."[30] With a reminder that only the truce had stayed the Spanish troops from occupying the fosse and the commanding corners of the barricade and that the breach was already large enough to permit their entrance, though with some difficulty, Gálvez gave his opponent four hours in which to come to terms.

The English captain thereupon submitted other terms of capitulation whereby the fort would be surrendered with the garrison prisoners but accorded all the honors of war and with certain guaranties of protection for the townspeople. Gálvez accepted the major tenets of these proposals, the only serious qualification being with respect to the citizens under arms in the fort. They should be considered prisoners of war, he insisted, and not released as the Baton Rouge settlers had been, and should he attack Pensacola, the same policy would prevail. But if Pensacola should not be attacked, he would liberate them within

---

[30] Article 1, "Artículos de Capitulación propuestos por Dn. Elias Durnford Esqr.," A. G. I., Cuba, 2351.

eight months on condition only that they swear not to bear arms again during the war.[31]

Since Indian allies reported that General Campbell was in the Tensaw district with eleven hundred men, two field pieces, a howitzer, and Creek allies, Durnford's capitulation was the more welcome. Extra sentinels were put out that night, and the whole army slept on its arms to be ready for any contingency. Then at ten the following morning, March 14, the Spaniards took possession of the fort. As Durnford described the scene:

> It is my misfortune to inform you that this morning my small but brave garrison marched down the breach, and surrendered themselves prisoners of war to General Bernardo de Galvez' superior arms. I write for your information, and request you will do me the favor to inform Mrs. Durnford that I am in good health, and that she ought to be under no uneasiness at my fate. When it is in my power to send you the capitulation and state preceding it for a few days, will do it; in the meantime I assure you, sir, that no man in the garrison hath stained the lustre of the British arms.[32]

The prisoners were: 1 captain, 2 lieutenants, 2 ensigns, 15 sergeants, and 78 soldiers of the Sixtieth Regiment; 1 sergeant, 15 artillerymen, 1 corporal, 2 soldiers, and an armorer of the Maryland Corps; 2 surgeons, 60 sailors, 54 habitants, and 51 negroes.[33]

While his troops stood at arms after the ceremony, Gálvez thanked them in the name of the king for the firmness they had displayed in all the misfortunes they had suffered and for the zeal, valor, and courage with which they had carried on to attain the victory. For their reward he offered them, again in the king's name, a third part of the value of the goods found in the fort.

The following days were occupied in repairing Fort Charlotte, mounting additional guns, and strengthening its defense. Gayarré made an inventory of the captured property. Four vessels arrived from

---

[31] Articles 2-11, *ibid*.

[32] Durnford to Campbell, March 14, 1780, *Publications of the Louisiana Historical Society*, I, No. 2, p. 32.

[33] "Diario... de la Expedición contra... Mobila," A. G. I., Cuba, 2351. A slightly different rendition a few days later gave 13 officers, 113 soldiers, 56 sailors, 70 hunters and habitants, 55 armed negroes—total, 307. Gálvez, Relación de... Prisioneros de Guerra en el sitio de la Mobila," March 20, 1780, *ibid*.

New Orleans with thirty militiamen who had been left behind for lack of transports and twenty-six Americans and twenty-seven other militiamen who had started on the "Kaulican" along with the main force. Irked by the delays in sailing from the river, these Americans entered strong protests that they had not enlisted to serve the king on the sea and complained so vehemently that the captain of the "Kaulican" sent them back to New Orleans. Coming later by the lakes, they arrived too late even for the capitulation ceremony.[34]

On the fifteenth a scouting party confirmed the report that Campbell with eleven hundred regulars, Indians, and field artillery was advancing to Durnford's relief. Two days later scouts brought in a captain and sixteen dragoons made prisoner ten leagues from Mobile, and word that Campbell, having heard of the fall of Fort Charlotte, was retreating toward Pensacola.

On the seventeenth, eighty English civilians took an oath of fidelity to the Spanish king, and on the twenty-second Chastane *l'aîné*, Antoine Marbone, and seventy-six others whose names are mostly French, took a similar oath.[35]

The following letter from Gálvez to his uncle, the minister of the Indies, serves not only as a summary of the Mobile campaign but also as a commentary upon it, especially in relation to the larger aspect of Gálvez' military plans for gaining control of both Floridas. It was written just one week after the capitulation.

I have the satisfaction of relating to you how on the twelfth instant, four days after the opening of the trench, the fort of Mobile with three hundred men of the garrison who have remained prisoners of war, thirty-five cannon, and eight mounted mortars, has surrendered to the forces of the king. This capture has cost us some loss and much more time than was expected, because, in addition to its being a fort presenting plenty of resistance, for four months the enemy had done nothing but fortify it, giving its parapets seven feet more thickness than they had in the time of the French. The resistance they made was vigorous, and although this alone would not fail

---

[34] "Diario ... de la Expedición contra ... Mobila," *ibid.*; Piernas to Gálvez, February 29, 1780, A. G. I., Cuba, 4 (was formerly in 2); James Robinson, Pollock and Gálvez, conditions of enlistment of fifteen Americans, November 20, 1779, *ibid.*, 192.

[35] [Oath of allegiance], March 17, 1780, *ibid.*, 200; Chastane *l'aîné* and others, [oath of allegiance], March 22, 1780, *ibid.*, 193.

to give sufficient merit to the capture made by troops fatigued, scantily clad, and saved from shipwreck, there is another circumstance which I believe merits your bringing it to the consideration of his majesty.

This circumstance is, that after the notice of our shipwreck reached Pensacola with the exaggeration that we had lost 700 men, General Campbell resolved to leave a small garrison there and to come to attack us by land with the greater part of his forces, with the purpose of deciding here the fate of the province. He put it into practice and came with 1100 men within nine leagues of our camp. His vanguard was in sight before we had finished opening the trenches; because, having lost most of the launches in the shipwreck, we consequently had to use those that remained to carry supplies for our subsistence and had transported munitions too slowly.

You can understand our situation, on the verge of having our food give out, with very little munitions (for the greater part was lost in the shipwreck), with 1100 men in sight from whose muskets their general had removed the flints in order to attack us with cold steel, with 300 in the fort, who with those of General Campbell totaled 1400, a number equal to ours, and with the country on their side, and the protection of a fort.

The whole disagreeable prospect did not take away from our officers and troops the least part of their confidence and hope of victory. On the contrary, believing that new efforts were necessary, they persevered in their labors, opened the trench, established the battery, attacked and conquered the fort in view of the vanguard of the enemy and of General Campbell, who contented himself with observing us. For eight days he was a witness of the valor and courage of our troops, with which, having changed his mind, he broke camp to return to Pensacola with his army, from whose rear guard one of our parties took prisoner a captain and twenty men.

I cannot give expression to the sentiments with which all the individuals of my small army saw the retreat of General Campbell without coming to grips with us, nor could we reflect without sadness that if the expedition from Havana had arrived to join with us we could have succeeded over the English the same as at Saratoga. And so that you may know whether this belief is well or ill founded, I would have you know that General Campbell set out with only enough bread for eight days and the meat which was to be found in the houses, counting on arriving at the fort before it was taken; that the road by which they are returning is seven leagues longer than the one we would have taken to cut off the retreat and block the crossing of the Perdido River, indispensable for their return to Pensacola.

I know that you will read with the same feeling with which I write the notice of what has marred an occasion which otherwise would have given us Pensacola, which would have been glorious for the nation, but at the

THE CAPTURE OF MOBILE   185

same time I have the pleasure of assuring you that all the officers and troops desire nothing more than to continue proving to his majesty the resolution which they have of sacrificing themselves in his service, leaving for the next occasion, for lack of time in this, the list of those who must be recommended to his royal compassion.[36]

The effect of the victory was more than local. The commandant of Fort Panmure at Natchez reported, on April 25, that an Englishman had arrived from the Choctaw nation with the news of the fall of Mobile. According to his report the Choctaws were turning against the English as a result of this defeat; nor could the latter be sure of protection in the Chickasaw nation. "The benevolence of our governor toward the English militiamen captured at Mobile, which the Englishman who has come from the Choctaws has made known here," the commandant continued, "seems to have satisfied the people of this vicinity ... who accord our Governor the praise he deserves."[37]

In appraising Gálvez' management of the Mobile campaign, it is obvious that one cannot use the simple numerical yardstick. The Spanish force outnumbered the garrison of Fort Charlotte times over, yet the result was not a foregone conclusion. The campaign was first a contest in diplomacy, the problem being to get men from Havana; secondly, it was a battle with the elements, a near hurricane on the Gulf and the treacherous bar at the entrance to Mobile Bay; finally, it was a race with General Campbell, won because Gálvez recovered quickly after the shipwrecks and pushed on to the attack, while Campbell dallied and was balked by the Tensaw. Incidentally, of course, the campaign involved the overwhelming of Fort Charlotte. Yet the fact that this seems an incidental part of the campaign should not rob Gálvez of the credit due him for the highly efficient investment of the fort. The assault was admirably planned; his men's spirits were kept up despite discouragements; the trench and battery were placed most effectively, and with a minimum of hazard to his men, and the artillery fire battered the fort into submission promptly but without much loss of life on either side. Gálvez and his opponent

[36] Gálvez to José de Gálvez, March 20, 1780, certified copy, A. G. I., Cuba, 2351.
[37] Delavillebeuvre to ——, April 25, 1780, B. L., La. Coll.

deserve recognition, too, for waging war in chivalrous fashion, as national enemies but courteous gentlemen, with tender regard for noncombatants.

Manifestations of royal appreciation of Gálvez' good work at Mobile were soon forthcoming. Navarro was criticized for his undue caution about reënforcing and coöperating with Gálvez. Thanks to his backwardness the English still held Pensacola. "The experience of all the centuries," the king's minister asserted, "has demonstrated that in war he who is more active and who fixes his attention less on the perils inseparable from war will ordinarily have the victory."[38] To Gálvez, the minister rejoiced over the fall of Mobile, which he described as "important not only for its situation on the Gulf of Mexico but also for being in a fashion the outpost of the plaza of Pensacola." After relating how the king had publicly eulogized Gálvez' prudence, ability, and military talent, the minister continued:

> Of a truth the capture of an important town, well fortified and defended with vigor, is an act worthy of praise; but how much more praise is due this exploit, accomplished with a meager force, just rescued from two shipwrecks, scantily supplied and oppressed by fatigue, and more so since the attack was conducted under the eyes of a superior force. . . .[39]

Finally, in reward for the capture of Mobile, Gálvez was made field marshal in command of Spanish operations in America, and he received the augmented title, "Governor of Louisiana and Mobile."[40]

---

[38] José de Gálvez to Navarro, April 24, 1780, A. G. I., Sto. Dom., 2082.

[39] José de Gálvez to Gálvez, June 22, 1780, A. G. I., Cuba, 175.

[40] *Idem* to *idem*, February 12, 1781, *ibid*.

CHAPTER XI

PREPARATIONS FOR THE SIEGE OF PENSACOLA

BEFORE THE INK HAD DRIED on the capitulation of Mobile, Gálvez turned to plans for the conquest of Pensacola, the real objective of his Gulf Coast campaigns. An immediate attack would take advantage of the disorder incident to Campbell's fruitless journey to the Tensaw. Furthermore, it was advisable to invest Pensacola before reënforcements arrived, and news of the fall of Mobile was certain to suggest such strengthening. Gálvez had detailed information about the forces at Pensacola; 1302 regular soldiers, 600 hunters and habitants, 300 sailors, and 300 armed negroes made a total of 2500, without counting the Indian allies which were admittedly numerous.[1] His own effective force in the capture of Mobile had been not much larger than the regular garrison of Pensacola, but he still had hopes that more troops would be sent to him from Havana. On February 15, 2065 men actually embarked, but when the captain general learned that Pensacola was being reënforced from Jamaica, he gave up all hopes for immediate success there and ordered the men to disembark.[2] These men would have arrived in time for use against Campbell at the Tensaw or the Perdido. Perhaps the minister of the Indies was too opti-

---

[1] The itemized statement:

The general and 4 aides-de-camp	5
Artillery	62
Of the 16th Regiment	135
Of the 60th Regiment	200
Of the Waldeck Regiment	351
Of the Pennsylvania Regiment	242
Of the Maryland Regiment	300
Of the 57th Regiment	7
	1,302

Gálvez to Navarro, March 20, 1780, No. 254, A. G. I., Cuba, 1232.

[2] Navarro [statement of troops embarked], February 16, 1780, A. G. I., Sto. Dom., 2082; Navarro to José de Gálvez, February 26, 1780, reservada, No. 106, *ibid*.

mistic when he asserted that had they been sent Pensacola would have fallen, but certainly it was this hesitancy on the part of the captain general that incurred for him the court's censure.[3]

Again on March 7 an expedition was organized at Havana. It sailed for Pensacola but returned on May 21 "without having accomplished anything because it had not appeared possible to the commander of the squadron for the vessels of war to come near enough to silence the forts which defend the said port."[4]

Gálvez' board of strategy urged upon him first an approach to Pensacola by a supposed inland passage. "The project you have indicated," Gálvez replied to the proponent of the scheme, "to attack Pensacola by a branch of the Perdido is impracticable. Would to God it were as you have been informed and as Don Miguel de Goycochea has explained to me, but unfortunately there is a vast difference between the description and the reality."[5] Instead, Gálvez recommended an approach by sea. He had been informed that the English had withdrawn the troops and cannon from Barrancas Coloradas, the fort at the entrance to Pensacola Bay, thereby reducing the defense of the harbor entrance to two frigates, one of thirty-six guns, the other much smaller. In this relaxation of defense Gálvez saw an opportunity to gain entrance to the harbor. He was resolved to attack Pensacola notwithstanding the large force available for its defense.[6]

The officers of the Spanish ships may have been impressed by the ardor of the youthful governor, but they were not moved by it. In response to his asking whether or not his sea forces were sufficient for an attack, they replied in the negative. Gálvez argued with them in vain. He listed the ships in their fleet: the "Caiman" with twenty-two eight-pounders, the "San Pio" with eighteen six-pounders, the "San Perigrino" with fourteen and the "Carmen" with twelve four-pounders, the "San Juan Bautista" with eight twenty-four- and four-pounders, the "Valenzuela" with one twenty-four-pounder, the "Gálvez-

---

[3] José de Gálvez to Navarro, April 24, 1780, *ibid.*

[4] Saavedra to José de Gálvez, February 16, 1781, No. 3, A. G. I., Ind. Gen., 1578.

[5] Bonet to Gálvez, March 15, 1780, No. 14, A. G. I., Sto. Dom., 2543; Gálvez to Bonet, March 22, 1780, No. 16, *ibid.*

[6] *Ibid.*

town" with twenty four-pounders, and the "Wet-Florida" ("West Florida"); and asked if these were not a match for the English frigates. Goicochea assured him they were not.[7]

Additional reënforcements, particularly a couple of frigates, had been requested from Havana. Gálvez perforce awaited their coming. The enforced inactivity gave him opportunity to make a humanitarian appeal to Campbell.

> The Indians who support the side of the English [he wrote] believe that they do them a service by pillaging and destroying all the habitants of the other nation. Those who have embraced the cause of Spain imagine that for the sake of reprisal they can commit the same hostilities against the English habitants.... In this war, which we wage by obligation and not by hate, I hope that you will be inclined to join me in a reciprocal convention to shelter us from the horrible censure of inhumanity.[8]

The suggestion of Indian neutrality, it will be observed, was unimpeachable in its high moral tone. To the Spaniards it was also recommended by its expediency. Virtually all the Indians in the region were under English influence, and their neutrality would be a distinct boon to the Spanish cause. Nevertheless, it would seem that Gálvez' suggestion was not governed solely by ulterior designs. The remarkable restraint exercised over his Indian allies in the lower Mississippi campaign seems to me proof of his genuine aversion to unnecessary savage atrocities.

Campbell apparently was not disposed to sacrifice security for idealism. If he replied directly to Gálvez' suggestion, the letter has not been located, but it is certain that he continued to use Indian auxiliaries. They formed an important division in the defense of Pensacola. On July 18, 1780, Alexander Cameron praised the services of the English Indian allies, writing that he would "venture to say that the possession of this place [Pensacola] is owing entirely to the great number of Indians who repaired here to assist and who waited near a month for the Spaniards." Perhaps this is fulsome praise. His further observations, however, to the effect that the Indians had been abundantly

---

[7] Goicochea to Gálvez, April 6, 1780, No. 24, *ibid.*; Gálvez to Goicochea, April 6, 1780, No. 25, *ibid.*; Goicochea to Gálvez, April 7, No. 26, *ibid.*

[8] Gálvez to Campbell, April 9, 1780, No. 27, copy, *ibid.*

worth the six thousand pounds sterling they had cost since March, 1780, and that it was a wise investment to continue to keep them opposed to the Spaniards, do not exaggerate.[9]

On April 13 Gálvez received discouraging news. He was informed that eleven vessels had entered Pensacola harbor, two of them naval vessels, the others privateers or armed merchantmen.[10] The news traveled rapidly. On April 26 Lieutenant Alexander Fraser was writing from Yassou (Yazoo):

> I have the pleasure to acquaint you that Wm. Swanson McMain with 5 ships more with goods likewise 5 frigates and 2 of the gunships are arrived at Pensacola likewise Gl. Clintone expected daily from Savanna with troops from whence he sett of a long time agoe, we had at Pensacola before the arrival of these shipping 1500 troops with 1500 Indians so that if Governor Galvez does go there I hope he will meet with a warm reception we understand that he sailed for their about 7 days ago but it is supposed he will go back to Orleans and not attempt Pensacola at all. All this news came up to the Tombegbe river by Joel Walker who came to see his unkle Captn. Walker who was wounded at Mobille. I hope you will make yourself easier in your situation as I hope everything will turn out for the better.[11]

On May 13 Campbell reported that contrary to expectations he was still unattacked. He accounted for this delay

> by the fact that the enemy's fleet finding that Don Gálvez was not here stood to the westward and was, it is supposed, deceived by the appearance of two sloops of war with merchant and transport vessels from Jamaica all of which it is said were taken for frigates and sloops of war.[12]

While Gálvez was suffering these discouragements at Mobile, the English at Pensacola were commiserating themselves as the victims of exposure and neglect. Campbell's letters betray the low morale of his troops. "The Regiment of Waldeck," he wrote, "think themselves particularly aggrieved in being detached to so disagreeable a part of the world, with dear provisions, and harassed in erecting works and with-

---

[9] Historical Manuscripts Commission, *op. cit.*, II, 159–160.
[10] Gálvez to Goicochea, April 13, 1780, No. 31, A. G. I., Sto. Dom., 2543.
[11] Alexander Fraser to ———, April 26, 1780, B. L., La. Coll.
[12] Campbell to Clinton, May 13, 1780, *in* Historical Manuscripts Commission, *op. cit.*, II, 121–122.

out bat and forage money."[13] A private communication to Clinton goes into greater detail:

> By my public despatches of this date to your Excellency, you will plainly perceive the disagreeable situation we are in here at present. The monthly returns of the forces are transmitted you by this opportunity. I sincerely hope I shall prevail with your Excellency to order such a reinforcement as you may judge proper for our relief as soon as possible,—at the same time give me leave to assure you, that every exertion in my power shall be used in defending our works on Gage Hill, to the last extremity, against any force that Don Galvez can bring to attack us.—It only grieves me that I have not sufficient strength to act offensively. I therefore earnestly beg and entreat your Excellency will be pleased to reinforce me with such troops as shall enable me to retaliate, which will afford me real pleasure & satisfaction, and more than probable may be the means of gaining honour & glory to His Majesty's arms in this quarter of the continent. Otherwise permit me to solicit your Excellency for permission to join the army, rather than remain here, with such troops as compose my pitifull command, without the least chance of serving with credit to myself or with honour and advantage to my royal master,—pestered with innumerable difficultys, and a multiplicity of perplexing business—you may therfore conceive my present situation, which I humbly submit to your serious consideration.[14]

But the plans for an immediate attack on Pensacola had been abandoned. A council of war advised on May 4, because of the nonappearance of the assistance desired from the general of marine, and because of inability to transport the expedition by sea, that the attack was impracticable.[15] "Seeing my fondest hopes blasted in spite of the good disposition of my soldiers," Gálvez replied, "I am filled with sadness to have to leave incomplete a task which the king had seen fit to entrust to me."[16] But however much he might regret it, Gálvez realized that postponement of the adventure was necessary. A garrison was therefore left at Mobile under Ezpeleta, and the greater part of the forces returned to Havana and New Orleans. By July the British were breathing easier, having learned that the Spanish attack was definitely

---

[13] *Loc. cit.*
[14] Campbell to Clinton, May 18, 1780, *op. cit.*, II, 124.
[15] Ezpeleta, Giron, Navas, Romero, and Miró, May 4, 1780, Nos. 37 and 38, A. G. I., Sto. Dom., 2543.
[16] Gálvez to Bonet, May 4, 1780, No. 39, *ibid.*

postponed until the fall of the year. Campbell expressed the hope that by that time "a reinforcement will be sent to effect a recovery of the territories lost, and to add Louisiana to British dominions."[17]

Having failed by correspondence to budge the captain general from his policy of complacent conservatism, Gálvez decided to go to Havana and urge personally the formation of an expedition to finish the conquest of West Florida. He arrived on August 2 and spent the next few weeks in conference with the military authorities of the captaincy general. By and large, Gálvez had his way in these and subsequent juntas de guerra, a success which historians have ascribed to his powerful family connections and particularly to the fact that he was deferred to as the nephew of José de Gálvez.[18] Doubtless his name carried weight, but his two previous campaigns had brought him prestige in his own right. Moreover, he had been placed in charge of operations in America, and the program he advocated was in full harmony with the king's outline of war aims.

On August 11 a junta de guerra determined that 3800 men should sail under Gálvez' command with provisions for three months. At a subsequent meeting the junta decided to provision the ships for six months and to ask for two thousand men from Mexico and Campeche and as many as could be spared from Puerto Rico and Santo Domingo.[19] Almost four thousand men are indicated on August 29 for the four divisions of the expedition.[20] Even the report of six or eight English ships in the Gulf failed to intimidate the junta, and on September 4 it recommended that the fleet proceed to Vera Cruz, convoying the expedition from there to Pensacola.[21] The captain general assured the court that "with respect to the expedition against Pensacola not a moment would be lost in providing Field Marshal Don Ber-

---

[17] Campbell to Clinton, July 22, 1780, *in* Historical Manuscripts Commission, *op. cit.*, II, 162.

[18] Gayarré, *op. cit.*, III, 137; Rousseau, *Règne de Charles III d'Espagne*, II, 156 ff.

[19] Diego Joseph Navarro, Victorio de Navia, Juan Bautista Bonet, Guillermo Waughan, and Gálvez composed the junta. Junta de guerra, August 26, 1780, copy, A. G. I., Sto. Dom., 2082; Urriza to José de Gálvez, August 27, 1780, reservada, No. 42, *ibid.*

[20] Giron, Estado que manifesta el número de Oficiales y Tropa que se compone la Expedición encargada al mando del Mariscal de Campo Dn. Bernardo de Gálvez, August 29, 1780, A. G. I., Cuba, 134 A.

[21] Junta de guerra, September 4, 1780, A. G. I., Sto. Dom., 2082.

nardo de Gálvez whatever he asks and whatever he believes can assist him to the most rapid and happy conquest."[22]

The elaborate preparations for this expedition lasted until early in October. Rainy weather delayed its departure for a few days, but on the sixteenth the fleet set sail. The English underestimated the force slightly, "six King's ships and 51 transports ... to be joined by transports with provisions from La Vera Cruz and Campeachy," yet they regarded it as a formidable array.[23] As a matter of fact it consisted of seven warships, five frigates, one packet boat, one brig, one armed lugger, and forty-nine transports carrying a landing force of 164 officers and 3829 men.[24] Concluding a report on the assistance he had lent the project, the captain general observed:

> There is needed now, as we hope, only a happy outcome in order for his majesty to have the glory of seeing under his sovereign dominion so important a post; to which end for some days past the diocesan bishop has had rogations in the churches of this city, and they will continue, as we have agreed.[25]

It is not for us to say that these prayers were unavailing. But for the third time in as many years Nature intervened to disrupt Gálvez' preparations for an attack on the English. A hurricane, which raged from October 18 to 23, struck the fleet soon after its departure from Havana, crippling many of the vessels and scattering the fleet hopelessly. "The warships which tried to stand by the cape were unmasted, the transports were driven, some to New Orleans, others to Mobile, and most of them to Campeche."[26] After fruitless efforts to reunite his fleet, Gálvez returned to Havana, a month and a day after he had set out, "with the sorrow of not knowing the whereabouts of his convoy." One vessel seems to have been lost, at least it had not been heard of by the following February.[27]

---

[22] Navarro to José de Gálvez, September 6, 1780, No. 843, *ibid*.
[23] Historical Manuscripts Commission, *op. cit.*, II, 233.
[24] Navarro to José de Gálvez, October 17, 1780, No. 893, A. G. I., Sto. Dom., 2083; Navarro [statement of troops under Gálvez], January 17, 1781, *ibid*.
[25] Navarro to José de Gálvez, October 17, 1780, No. 893, *ibid*.
[26] Saavedra to José de Gálvez, February 16, 1781, No. 3, A. G. I., Ind. Gen., 1578.
[27] "Diary of the Operations of the Expedition against the Place of Pensacola, Conducted by the Arms of H. Catholic M., under the Orders of the Field Marshal Don Bernardo de Gálvez," *Louisiana Historical Quarterly*, I, No. 1 (1917), 46; Navarro [statement of troops under Gálvez], January 17, 1781, A. G. I., Sto. Dom., 2083.

The English at Pensacola, for the time being safe from invasion, were not at once aware of their salvation. "We are still uninvaded," Campbell reported on October 31, "some disaster must have befallen the expedition from the Havannah, but no news can be had." Invasion was still expected on November 15. It was not until January 5 of the next year that Campbell took courage to write, "This place has once more providentially escaped a formidable invasion."[28] Heartened by this unexpected deliverance, Campbell proposed to employ the large force of Indians that he had gathered for the defense of Pensacola in an attempt to recover Mobile. Mobile's exposure had worried Gálvez. In spite of the confusion resulting from the hurricane, he was able to send Joseph Rada with a small reënforcement for Ezpeleta early in December. With two ships of war, two supply ships, four transports, and five hundred soldiers, Rada enjoyed a favorable passage.

But notwithstanding that after a few days navigation he arrived safely at the entrance of Mobile [Bay], he determined not to enter the bay on account of having found (so he assured) some variation in the channel, and he made sail directly for Balize on the Mississippi, at whose entrance he left the convoy and returned to Havana.[29]

Another attempt to strengthen Mobile was determined upon, but it could not be put into effect before the English made their attack.

Early in January Campbell sent Colonel von Hanxleden with 60 men of his Waldeck Regiment, 100 men of the Sixtieth Regiment, 11 militia cavalrymen, 200 or 250 men of the Pennsylvania and Maryland Loyalists, and about 300 Indian allies. Von Hanxleden was directed to seize first a Spanish outpost known as the Village of Mobile on the east shore of the bay, delaying the attack until Sunday morning, January 7, so that Captain Deans with the frigate "Mentor" could be on hand in the bay to prevent the crossing over of assistance from Mobile.[30] The assault was made at daybreak. Taken somewhat by surprise, the Spaniards suffered some losses, but in the hand to hand

---

[28] Historical Manuscripts Commission, *op. cit.*, II, 201, 209, 233.
[29] Urriza to José de Gálvez, February 13, 1781, reservada, No. 54, A. G. I., Sto. Dom., 2083; "Diary ... of the Expedition against ... Pensacola ...," *op. cit.*, 45.
[30] Campbell to Von Hanxleden, January 4, 1781, A. G. I., Cuba, 2359.

fighting inflicted severer punishment on the attacking force. To quote an enthusiastic account:

> One hundred and fifty men, commanded by Ramon del Castro, Lieutenant of the Principe Regiment, repelled gloriously a corps of three hundred English veterans and three hundred Indians which attacked them during a tempestuous night, having left dead in the very fort, into which they had begun to penetrate, the Waldeck colonel who led the attack and who was the best officer of Pensacola, a sergeant major, an adjutant, a captain of grenadiers, and sixteen men.[31]

After Colonel von Hanxleden and Lieutenants Sterlin and Gordon were killed, and Captain Baumback and another officer were wounded, the command fell to Captain Key of the provincial troops, "who judged best to order a retreat." Mobile was saved, but at the expense of fourteen killed and twenty-three wounded.[32]

The attack on the Village of Mobile and the gallant defense of its small garrison helped Gálvez to get another West Florida expedition. Ezpeleta had wasted no time about asking for help. He sent a negro messenger to New Orleans at six o'clock on the morning of the seventh, as soon as he learned that two English frigates flying Spanish flags had appeared on the bay.[33] This advice, together with later news of the attack, made it obvious that additional support was necessary in order to conserve the gains of Gálvez' previous campaigns in West Florida.

Gálvez' spirits, if dampened at all by the hurricane, had recovered very rapidly, and in November of 1780 he was urging upon the junta at Havana the rehabilitation of his scattered expedition. His argument before the junta[34] deserves extended notice.

---

[31] Saavedra to José de Gálvez, February 16, 1781, No. 3, A. G. I., Ind. Gen., 1578.

[32] Ezpeleta to Gálvez, January 22, 1781, A. G. I., Cuba, 2359. Spanish accounts of the battle are: Piernas to Navarro, January 16, 17, and 18, 1781, Nos. 297-299, A. G. I., Cuba, 1233; Ezpeleta to Gálvez, January 20, 1781, *ibid.*, 2359. From the other side: Historical Manuscripts Commission, *op. cit.*, II, 233-234; Von Eelking, *Die deutschen Hülfstruppen im nordamerikanischen Befreiungskriege*, 147-149. See also Hamilton, *op. cit.*, 256-257.

[33] Piernas to Navarro, January 12, 1781, No. 296, A. G. I., Cuba, 1233.

[34] Gálvez [opinion and vote in junta de guerra], November 30, 1780, A. G. I., Sto. Dom., 2083.

Notwithstanding an intercepted letter in which Campbell asserted that Pensacola had been put in condition for defense against five thousand Spaniards, and another in which he disclaimed fear of any force that might attack,[35] Gálvez asked for only three thousand suitably supplied soldiers from Havana and expressed confidence that the attack would succeed unless the enemy received new succor. He explained that his earlier insistence on a larger force was an extra precaution, justified by the greater number of men then available and by the king's great zeal for this conquest.

Taking up the difficulties in the way of sending this force, he referred first to provisions. "Either we have them or not. If we have them, it is the same to eat them here or elsewhere." He could not see that shortage of foodstuffs had necessitated recourse to any provender not suitable for use on shipboard. The troops had not substituted, for example, cassava for bread.

As for the troops needed, he cited the statements of the captain general and commandant general. He pointed out that the king had ordered the conquest of Pensacola with forces from Havana when there were only four or five thousand men in its garrison. Now that the garrison had been augmented to six or seven thousand, refusal to furnish an army was unreasonable. In earlier statements of the Marquis de la Torre and the present captain general, well drilled militia to the number of several thousand had been listed as available to help defend Havana. "Unless it is to be suspected that these statements of troops were imaginary, these corps must exist, for since then there has not been action of war to destroy them, or reform to disperse them." Furthermore, since France had offered two thousand men and the Spanish court had accepted the offer, Gálvez concluded that "no one could imagine that forces and means to attack Pensacola were lacking in Havana."

He insisted that Havana was not in danger of attack. The fleet that had brought troops to the English islands had left; the soldiers at Jamaica were beset by sickness; and although the English possessed superior naval force, they could not invest Havana successfully with-

---

[35] June 17, and October 14, 1780.

PREPARATIONS FOR THE SIEGE OF PENSACOLA   197

out corresponding land forces. Denying that the advantage lay with the enemy, he insisted that the English had suffered more serious damages from the hurricane than had the Spaniards. They were damaged on land as well as sea, part of Jamaica being desolated and destroyed. The Spaniards had suffered, to be sure, but he considered the hurricane a disturbance, not a rout.

With an appeal for a less timorous expression of loyalty to the king, Gálvez closed his argument:

> The English, departing for Charlestown, encountered weather which scattered their squadron and drove some of the convoy as far as the very coasts of England. This is more or less what happened to us. But the English were not dismayed; they found themselves, reunited, and attacked with happy result as you know. Are we not capable of so much? Has that military virtue that was characteristic of our nation deserted us and passed to the enemy? Have we so little constancy and tenacity in the continuation of an enterprise that a single tropical storm suffices to halt us? Such will be the idea formed of us, and that a single blow has vanquished us, unless it was not thought an object of greater consequence. If this is so, I retract whatever I have said, for, occupied with the advantages of the nation, I have sacrificed my personal affairs as is my obligation. I am the first who would desist from my importunity and would see with satisfaction and without envy the glories of another, but I fear that advising a lesser program for economy and parsimony will also be useless. Let us reflect a long time on what is to be decided. The king decreed that the theater of war should be in America, and perhaps our compatriots in Europe, with less hope of attaining, have succeeded in conquering while we tranquilly waste time that might be employed more gloriously. At any moment peace can surprise us, and if this should happen, all the other branches of the service will rejoice in the happy hour. But we military men, whom the king, after maintaining during peace, found useless during war—with what grace can we continue to wear a sword covered with rust, which was not drawn when the occasion demanded! Protesting again that if all or any part of my application is contrary to the purpose of later orders to desist further (as I have already said), I ask that I be blamed only for an earnest desire to fulfill the first orders while I did not know the later.[36]

Unanimously the junta decided that a new expedition against Pensacola should be undertaken, but in spite of Gálvez' plea for prompt

---
[36] Gálvez [opinion and vote in junta de guerra], November 30, 1780, A. G. I., Sto. Dom., 2083.

action, the opinion was that collecting supplies would be a task requiring some time, that winter was a poor season for the enterprise, and that the middle of March would be soon enough to consider setting a date for the departure.[87]

By using the English attack on Mobile as an argument for the reenforcement of Louisiana and Mobile, Gálvez persuaded the Havana authorities to act more promptly, though they acted on a smaller scale. They agreed to provide him 1315 men to strengthen Spanish defenses on the mainland, and authorized him, if opportunity offered and if sufficient forces could be drawn from New Orleans and Mobile, to attempt to capture Pensacola.[88]

On the understanding that large vessels could not enter Pensacola Bay, naval officers had recommended that the transports be convoyed merely by the frigate "Santa Clara" of thirty-six guns, the "Chambequin" of twenty, and the packet boat "San Pio" of eighteen. But upon learning that three English frigates of forty guns had sailed from Jamaica to cruise off Cape San Antonio, the junta de guerra reflected "that it would be a great misfortune if, because a warship was not accompanying so important an expedition, it should be exposed to disaster a third time through casual encounter with two of these said frigates." The council therefore assigned to the fleet the warship "San Ramon" of seventy-four cannon and the frigate "Santa Cecilia" of thirty-six, in addition to the vessels already designated. Furthermore, to avoid the friction and ineffectiveness that usually results from divided control, Gálvez was given full authority over the naval as well as the land forces of the expedition.[89]

Gálvez boarded the "San Ramon" on February 13 in spite of the fact that he was not completely recovered from a severe hemorrhage. The next afternoon the troops embarked. "The officers as well as the soldiers went most contentedly and felt almost certain of the outcome under a chief of whom they as well as the enemy held a high opinion."[40] For a fortnight the wind was contrary, but on the twenty-

---

[87] Junta de guerra, November 30, 1780, *ibid*.
[88] "Diary ... of the Expedition against ... Pensacola ... , *op. cit.*, 46–47.
[89] Saavedra to José de Gálvez, February 16, 1781, No. 3, A. G. I., Ind. Gen., 1578.
[40] *Ibid*.

seventh it began to veer, and the next day the fleet set sail. The vessels formed in three lines with the "Santa Cecilia" at the head, the "Santa Clara" at the rear, the "San Ramon" on the windward side, and the "Chambequin" and "San Pio" keeping the transports together and in good order. The offshore breeze died just after the fleet cleared the harbor, and a fresh southwest wind sprang up, carrying the whole fleet out of sight of land within three hours and giving promise of a favorable passage.[41]

[41] Saavedra to José de Gálvez, March 5, 1781, No. 7, *ibid*.

Chapter XII

"YO SOLO"

SOME OF THE MEMBERS of the junta at Havana may have thought that this expedition which sailed on February 28 was primarily for the defense of the Spanish possessions on the mainland; but Gálvez intended to use it for a siege of Pensacola.[1] His emphasis upon the need for additional forces for defense was obviously for the persuasion of the cautious councillors and not a reliable index of his intentions. As early as February 1 he had ordered Piernas at New Orleans to mobilize the forces there, including the fraction of the October expedition that had found refuge in Louisiana and the five hundred men whom Rada had failed to deliver at Mobile. Just before leaving Havana, be sent instructions for these forces to proceed to Pensacola, and on March 1 he ordered Ezpeleta to march from Mobile by way of the Perdido with as many men as possible.[2]

The voyage was uneventful, except that on March 3 a fleet of ten vessels was sighted to windward. The Spaniards gave chase, but, reluctant to scatter their convoy and handicapped by failing wind, they were unable to overtake these vessels. Later they discovered that they were English ships from Pensacola, but at the time they consoled themselves with the thought that it was the provision fleet from Vera Cruz.[3]

Sighting Santa Rosa Island on March 9, Gálvez gave final orders concerning the landing party that was to gain possession of the Eng-

---

[1] Several diaries of the siege of Pensacola have been printed: "Diary ... of the Expedition against ... Pensacola," *Louisiana Historical Quarterly*, I, No. 1 (1917), pp. 44–84; "Diario de Panzacola," *Archivo del General Miranda*, I, 141–147; "Diario de lo ocurrido en la escuadra," *ibid.*, 150–179; "A Journal of the seige [*sic*] of Pensacola West Florida 1781," *ibid.*, 179–191. The Library of Congress has a less abbreviated MS copy of this last diary that reveals the author: Robert Farmar, "Journal of the Seige of Pensacola."

[2] "Diary ... of the Expedition against ... Pensacola," *op. cit.*, 47–48.

[3] "Diario de Panzacola," *op. cit.*, 141–142; "Diary ... of the Expedition against ... Pensacola," *op. cit.*, 48.

lish battery at the western tip of the island. That night, with Gálvez at their head, grenadiers and light infantry landed "with some misgivings, but without the least opposition." Still under cover of darkness they marched along the beach to Sigüenza Point, where they found, not the stronghold they had expected, but an abandoned breastwork and three dismounted cannon. Soon after daybreak nine men[4] came over from the English frigate "Port Royal" to tend cattle on the island. They were taken prisoners, whereupon the English frigates discovered the presence of the Spaniards and began a lively but harmless bombardment assisted by the fort at Barrancas Coloradas (Red Cliffs). Gálvez therefore landed a pair of twenty-four-pounders and some lighter guns, as well as one hundred and fifty campaign tents, and erected a battery which forced the "Mentor" and "Port Royal" to withdraw out of range.[5]

On the afternoon of the eleventh the Spanish fleet weighed anchor to enter the bay. Gálvez went out to board the "San Ramon" "in order to be in this operation and pass through the risk," but Captain José Calbo de Irazabal insisted that he return to the island. With the flagship in the van the fleet approached the harbor entrance, but, much to the chagrin of the anxious spectators on Sigüenza Point, the "San Ramon" grounded on the first bar. She was worked free almost immediately, but came about and followed by the squadron returned to her former anchorage.[6]

The failure of the ships to force an entrance left the landing party in a precarious position. Should a storm arise the supporting fleet would have to sail out to sea to avoid being dashed ashore, and Gálvez and his men would be left without supplies or provisions, stranded on a barren island. In such a predicament they would be virtually at the mercy of the English. During the next few days, therefore, Gálvez' efforts were concentrated on two tasks. The first was to land supplies so that the army would be more or less secure on Santa Rosa Island. Some progress at this was made on the thirteenth and fourteenth, but

[4] Two boats and seven men, according to the "Diary . . . of the Expedition against . . . Pensacola," *op. cit.*, 49.
[5] Farmar, *op. cit.*; "Diario de Panzacola," *op. cit.*, 141–142; "Diary . . . of the Expedition against . . . Pensacola," *op. cit.*, 48–49.
[6] *Ibid.*, 49.

on the fifteenth the surf got so rough that landing was almost impossible.[7] The second task was to get the fleet into port. Calbo tried to lighten the "San Ramon" by throwing overboard more than two thousand hundredweight of ballast, not to mention firewood, but still his vessel drew nineteen feet. On the twelfth Gálvez came out to urge Calbo to send the frigates and transports in ahead of the "San Ramon" so that if the warship went aground again the fleet's entrance would not be blocked. Calbo did not take kindly to this suggestion. He exhibited, in fact, reluctance to attempt the entrance again, in ignorance of the channel, without pilots, and exposed to fire from Fort Barrancas Coloradas.[8]

Although Gálvez had been named commander in chief of this expedition with authority over the naval as well as military forces, yet Calbo was still responsible for the fleet's safety and could refuse to risk the entrance. Calbo's inquiry before leaving Havana concerning the exact extent of his subordination to the youthful general may be indicative of jealousy and distrust, but there can be no question that he had honest doubts of the possibility of the fleet's getting in safely. The loss of the "Volante" and the grounding of several other vessels at Mobile had not won Gálvez the reputation of being an expert authority on entering ports. Then, too, Calbo demonstrated the utmost willingness to coöperate in other matters. For example, when Ezpeleta asked that launches be sent to the Perdido to ferry his nine hundred men across, Calbo anticipated Galvez' desires and sent not only launches but also the "San Pio" to escort them and "to provide Sr. Espeleta a few cannons and provisions if he should need them."[9]

Realizing that the success of the whole expedition hinged upon the entrance of the fleet, Gálvez forsook argument for action. There were a few Louisiana boats over which he had complete command, two armed launches, Riaño's sloop "Valenzuela," and the brig "Gálveztown." With these he decided to force the harbor on the eighteenth "in the conviction that this last resort would stimulate the others to

---

[7] *Ibid.*, 49–51.
[8] "Diario de Panzacola," *op. cit.*, 142–143; Calbo's letter to Gálvez is quoted in Gayarré, *op. cit.*, III, 138–139.
[9] "Diary ... of the Expedition against ... Pensacola," *op. cit.*, 47, 51.

follow." Preliminary to this brave action he allowed an indulgence in melodrama to triumph over his discretion. He sent an officer to the "San Ramon" to deliver in the presence of the crew a message

> that a thirty-two-pound ball received in the camp, which he brought and presented, was one of those fired by the fort at the entrance, but that whoever had honor and valor would follow him [Gálvez], for he was going in advance with the *Gálveztown* to remove fear.[10]

Infuriated by this insolent message, Calbo retorted, likewise in the hearing of the entire crew, that Gálvez was "an audacious and unmannerly upstart, a traitor to his king and country." He promised to give the king a report of this insult to himself and to the entire naval corps, and he hoped to have the satisfaction of hanging Gálvez at the yardarm.[11]

Without tarrying to placate Calbo, Gálvez boarded the "Gálveztown." He ran up a broad pennant, signifying a rear admiral's presence on board, and ordered a salute of fifteen guns so that the army, the fleet, and the enemy would have no doubt who was aboard. Stationing himself on the quarter-deck, he ordered all sails set. The tiny squadron came on bravely, crossed the bar, and entered the channel. Fort Barrancas belched forth a heavy fire, particularly toward the "Gálveztown," but though twenty-seven or twenty-eight balls of heavy caliber fell around the brig, none scored an effective hit. Amidst "the extraordinary applause of the army, who with continuous cheers demonstrated to the General its delight and loyalty to him," the four ships entered the harbor and anchored under the shelter of the Spanish battery on Sigüenza Point. As a *feu de joie* the "Gálveztown" saluted Fort Barrancas with fifteen guns loaded only with powder.[12]

After witnessing the spectacular entry of Gálvez' vessels, the ship captains insistently urged upon Calbo that the whole fleet follow his example. But Calbo, still smarting under the insult, was adamant in his refusal and issued a very positive command that no ship should move until expressly ordered to do so by him. That night, however,

---

[10] "Diario de Panzacola," *op. cit.*, 143.

[11] *Ibid.*, 143–144.

[12] "Diary ... of the Expedition against ... Pensacola," *op. cit.*, 52; Saavedra to José de Gálvez, April 7, 1781, No. 12, A. G. I., Ind. Gen., 1578.

after a messenger from Gálvez had brought a careful description of the channel, and after the other naval officers had renewed their supplications, Calbo agreed that the fleet should sail in on the morrow. The next afternoon the entire fleet except the "San Ramon" attempted the entry. During the hour that these vessels required for passing the fort, they were the targets of one hundred and forty cannon shots which did slight damage to some of the ships but injured no one. Throughout the entire maneuver Gálvez, in his gig, took up a position in the center of danger in order to encourage and assist the convoy.[13]

Having got the fleet safely inside the bay, Calbo announced that his work was done. As soon as the launch returned from the Perdido, he would return in the "San Ramon" to Havana. Apparently he still felt the sting of Gálvez' challenge, for he attempted to minimize the exploit of entering the bay by observing that his first attempt to force the port had been solely to determine whether it was as easy as it had been described.[14] At Havana the people, uninformed about Calbo's secret instructions, regarded his return as ignominious, especially since he gave as the reason that he could not enter Pensacola Bay.[15]

In after-dinner conversation on March 22 the army-navy feud broke out afresh. Gálvez insinuated that all the naval officers had shared Calbo's timidity about forcing the port; they demanded that he retract this reflection on the naval service, whereupon he took offense and asked if they meant to insult him. Alderete then tried to pour oil on the troubled waters, but when he questioned Gálvez' use of a rear admiral's pennant, he provoked a worse quarrel. Shouting that the naval forces were not necessary for anything and that they could all go to Havana whenever they wished, Gálvez turned his back on the naval officers. The next day, however, he sought reconciliation with them and invited himself to dinner on Alderete's frigate. Meeting Gálvez halfway, Alderete ordered his subordinates to "maintain perpetual silence on the recent affairs." The king seems not to have taken notice of the quarrels, and the semi-official diary does not mention them, but one of the naval officers did confide them to his diary.[16]

---

[13] "Diario de Panzacola," *op. cit.*, 144.   [14] *Ibid.*
[15] "Diario de lo ocurrido en la escuadra," *ibid.*, 151.
[16] *Ibid.*, 145–147; "Diary . . . of the Expedition against . . . Pensacola," *op. cit.*, 52.

While waiting for the forces from Mobile and New Orleans, Gálvez corresponded with his adversary concerning the rules of battle that should be observed.[17] Gálvez' first letter, modeled after one sent by Lord Albemarle to the Spanish commander at Havana in 1762, was a terse threat of dire punishment if public or private buildings in Pensacola were burned or other property destroyed. Campbell dismissed the threats as artifices of war but was willing to negotiate for the security of the town of Pensacola. He proposed that both sides should spare the buildings of the town and that noncombatants should be safeguarded. Through Campbell's emissary, the paroled Dickson, Gálvez gave verbal assurance that the suggestions would be approved, but on account of illness he postponed making a formal answer until the next day. In the night, however, the British commander at Fort Barrancas thought it advisable to burn several houses near his fort. This action so incensed Gálvez that he wrote Campbell the following letter:

Most Excellent Sir, My dear sir: At the time we are reciprocally making one another the same propositions, for both of us aimed at the conservation of the goods and property of the individuals of Pensacola, at the same time, I say, the insult of burning the houses facing my camp on the other side of the bay is committed before my very eyes. This fact tells of the bad faith with which you work and write, as also the conduct observed with the people from Mobile, a great many of whom have been victims of the horrible cruelties protected by your Excellency; all proves that your expressions are not sincere, that humanity is a phrase that although you repeat it on paper, your heart does not know, that your intentions are to gain time to complete the destruction of Western Florida; and I, who am indignant at my own credulity and the noble manner in which it is pretended to halucinate me, must not [hear], nor do I wish to hear, other propositions than those of surrender, assuring your Excellency, that as it will not be my fault, I shall see Pensacola burn with the same indifference, as I shall see its cruel incendiaries perish upon its ashes. God keep your Excellency many years.[18]

A week later Gálvez' righteous indignation welled up again. Commissioner Stephenson had been sent by Chester and Campbell to re-

---

[17] Copies of this correspondence form part of the "Diary... of the Expedition against ... Pensacola," *op. cit.*, 53–58.

[18] *Ibid.*, 56–57.

new negotiations for the protection of the town. In the midst of his interview with Gálvez three Spanish sailors who had managed to escape from prison in Pensacola arrived in camp. They reported mistreatment at the hands of the English. Gálvez was so greatly enraged upon hearing this that he dismissed Stephenson and refused to listen to any proposal.[19]

Meanwhile, seven paroled officers who had been made prisoners in Gálvez' previous campaigns came out to surrender to him "Agreeable to their Promise given and Faith pledged." These were Lieutenant Colonel Dickson, Captain Alberti, Captain Miller, Lieutenant Bard, Quartermaster Lowe, Dr. Grant, and William Whissel, Armorer of the Ordinance. They were accompanied by their families and slaves and three servants of Dickson and Alberti.[20]

Within a week after the forcing of the channel, the detachments from Mobile and New Orleans arrived. On the twenty-second Ezpeleta and his men appeared on the inner shore of the harbor. Gálvez immediately crossed with five hundred men from the island so that the soldiers could rest after their march from Mobile. That afternoon the "San Pio" and four launches returned from the Perdido and entered the harbor unscathed by the fire of the English fort. The following afternoon the squadron from New Orleans arrived, the English blazing away at them without accomplishing much beyond the tattering of a few sails. These additions more than doubled Gálvez' forces. From Mobile came 905 men, from New Orleans 1348, making a total of 3553 in his command.[21]

Actual operations against Pensacola could now begin. On the twenty-fourth the troops were ferried across from Santa Rosa Island to the mainland behind Barrancas. The new camp was a more convenient base for the attack on Fort George, but it was more exposed than the camp on the island, as the Spaniards were not long in discovering. Indians attacked some stragglers on the twenty-fifth, and

---

[19] *Ibid.*, 59.

[20] Campbell [permit to leave Pensacola and proceed to the Spanish camp], March 23, 1781, A. G. I., Cuba, 188–3.

[21] Saavedra to José de Gálvez, April 7, 1781, No. 12, A. G. I., Ind. Gen., 1578; Martin Navarro [statement of troops sent from New Orleans], February 28, 1781, A. G. I., Cuba, 83; "Diary . . . of the Expedition against . . . Pensacola," *op. cit.*, 56, 58.

the experience was repeated, with some variation, from day to day and night to night. The Indian onslaughts were not on a very large scale nor long sustained, but they forced the Spaniards to be constantly on guard and somewhat hindered preparations for the investment of the fort.[22]

Most of the Southeastern tribes contributed auxiliaries for the defense of Pensacola. Choctaws, Creeks, Seminoles, and even Chickasaws came to coöperate. These parties of warriors were led by white men or half-breeds, several of whom later associated themselves with the Spaniards and helped to keep Spanish influence dominant among the Indians in the Old Southwest during the post-Revolutionary period. Alexander McGillivray, Benjamin James, and Alexander Frazer were of this category. But James Colbert, Colbert's half-breed son, and Alexander Cameron remained more consistent in their opposition to Spain.[23]

The Indians caused most of the Spanish casualties during March and April. They accounted for six men from one of the launches sent to assist Ezpeleta across the Perdido. Farmar's "Journal" mentions at least a score of times when parties of Indians went out as skirmishers, drove in the enemy's pickets, or executed flank attacks. In the "Journal" also are statements such as the following, which give some measure of the Indians' effectiveness:

> The Indians report that they killed and wounded a number of the enemy but could not get their hair....
> The Indians brought in with them a scalp....
> The Indians came about 2 o'c and brought a great number of scalps, firelocks, and bayonets....
> the Indians brought in a prisoner which they took close to the enemy work. it was with great difficulty thay gave him up....
> They returned in a short time with ten scalps....[24]

To the Indians, perhaps, should be charged the mishap of March 26 when two parties of Spanish soldiers, going by different routes to the same destination, mistook each other for the enemy and engaged in a lively skirmish in which several were killed and wounded.[25]

---
[22] *Ibid., passim;* Farmar, *op. cit.*   [23] *Ibid.*   [24] *Ibid.*
[25] "Diary...of the Expedition against...Pensacola," *op. cit.*, 59.

Most of April passed with little outward change. The Spaniards were familiarizing themselves with the approaches to the English fortifications but avoiding a pitched battle for the time being. When their observers approached too near the English lines, they were usually fired upon, and once or twice the English came out in sorties to drive back overbold Spaniards. Gálvez suffered a wound on one such occasion. Yet on the whole it was a period of marked inactivity. Though the hostile armies were encamped almost within shot of each other, neither showed much insistence upon real fighting.[26]

On April 19 a fleet was sighted off the coast, "which caused a great deal of preoccupation as it was deemed likely to be the help the enemy expected." But apprehension turned to joy when an officer reported that it was a Spanish fleet of more than twenty sail.[27] Fearing that several English frigates which had appeared off Cuba were proceeding to Pensacola to interfere with the siege, the officials at Havana had resolved to reënforce Gálvez. They sent a strong naval force under Chief of Squadron Josef Solano and sixteen hundred soldiers under Field Marshal Juan Manuel de Cagigal. Sailing with this Spanish force were four French frigates with 725 soldiers aboard.[28]

Solano, in contrast to Calbo, displayed great readiness to work with Gálvez for the capture of Pensacola. He authorized Cagigal to offer gunners and others of the ship crews to the number of 1350 as well as the two groups of soldiers. Gálvez acquiesced "in order that they also might share in the glory of this conquest." Heavy seas on the twenty-first prevented any landing of troops, but boats and launches went out to the ships. On the two following days approximately 3675 men were brought in to the Spanish camp, increasing Gálvez' force to more than 7000. Fort Barrancas again provided a generous but harmless cannonade.[29]

---

[26] *Ibid.*, 61–71; Mathews, "Journal of the Siege and Fall of Pensacola," *in* Claiborne, *op. cit.*, 126 *n.*

[27] "Diary . . . of the Expedition against . . . Pensacola," *op. cit.*, 66.

[28] "Diario de lo ocurrido," *op. cit.*, 150–152.

[29] Cagigal to Gálvez, April 18, 1871, *Archivo del General Miranda*, I, 147–148; "Diary . . . of the Expedition against . . . Pensacola," *op. cit.*, 66–67; "Diario de lo ocurrido," *op. cit.*, 157–161.

Gálvez' problem at Pensacola was somewhat like the one he had faced at Baton Rouge. Fort George was too strong to be taken by assault except at the expense of terrific carnage. The sensible solution was to subject it first to a strenuous bombardment. But siege batteries could not be erected safely in the open, nor was it possible to construct them in one night under cover of a diversion such as that employed at Baton Rouge. Some other stratagem had to be devised. After more than a month of scouting and scheming, a plan was perfected.

On the last three nights of April hundreds of men were detailed to dig a covered trench or tunnel from the Spanish lines to a small hill, where a battery was to be constructed which would command the part of the English fortifications known as the crescent or advanced redoubt. On the night of May 1 these men succeeded in installing a battery of six twenty-four-pounders at this point. The engineers continued the trench to Pine Hill and started to erect a stronger battery there. But the English had tasted the fire of the first battery and found it not to their liking. When they observed the activity on Pine Hill, they opened a vigorous cannonade, and under cover of the barrage their infantry charged the redoubt. The assault succeeded. The Spaniards had to fall back to the other redoubt, the enemy pursuing with fixed bayonets. By the time Gálvez was able to push more troops to the point of attack, the English had retired, "leaving the trench on fire, four field pieces spiked and besides carrying away the Captain and Lieutenant of the Hibernians and the officers of the same grade from the Mallorca Regiment, for these being seriously wounded were unable to retire." Of the Spanish rank and file eighteen were killed and sixteen wounded.[30]

The material damage, however, was soon repaired. Both batteries bombarded the crescent vigorously. An assault on the crescent was planned for the early morning of the seventh, but because an enforced detour deprived it of the element of surprise, Ezpeleta called it off. The artillery fire continued brisk. Early in the morning of the eighth came the turning point. A shot from one of the howitzers struck the

---

[30] "Diary . . . of the Expedition against . . . Pensacola," *op. cit.*, 72–73; "Diario de lo ocurrido," *op. cit.*, 161–171.

powder magazine of the crescent. There was a terrific explosion. The crescent was ruined. At least 85 men were killed; the Spanish estimate was 105.[31] As a last echo of the friction between Gálvez and the naval officers, there is to be noted a lack of coöperation at this crucial moment. Cagigal urged Alderete to move up his frigate and bombard Fort George, but there was no disposition to comply.[32]

The army was able to prevail, however, without assistance. Under Giron and Ezpeleta light troops advanced to the smoking ruins of the crescent. They brought forward howitzers and cannon from the trench and battery and opened a heavy fire on the center redoubt, wounding Lieutenant Ward and thirty men, some of whom died of their wounds.[33] So exposed was Fort George to this fire and so open to the assault which the Spaniards were organizing that Campbell was compelled to run up a white flag at three o'clock in the afternoon of May eighth.

> In order to prevent a further Effusion of Blood [he wrote to Gálvez], I propose to your Excellency a Cessation of Hostilities untill to morrow at noon, in which Time Articles of Capitulation shall be considered of & prepared, provided your Excellency is disposed to accede to Terms honourable to the Troops under my Command, and such as may afford Safety, Security and Protection to the Inhabitants.[34]

Gálvez agreed to the truce and hostages were exchanged. The first offer of terms of surrender was not entirely satisfactory. Campbell and Chester then proposed other conditions of capitulation which they described as "nearly the same granted by the British last War, to your nation at the Havannah." Urging their acceptance, Campbell wrote:

> I trust they will not be objected to:—Should they however be refused contrary to my Expectations, I still do not consider my Case desperate, nor my Situation past Hope; And am determined once more to abide the Chance of War, rather than comply with the Terms you have been pleased to offer.[35]

---

[31] "Diary ... of the Expedition against ... Pensacola," *op. cit.*, 73-75; "Diario de lo ocurrido," *op. cit.*, 171-174; Farmar, *op. cit.*

[32] Cagigal to Alderete, May 8, 1781, *Archivo del General Miranda*, I, 148.

[33] Farmar, *op. cit.*

[34] Campbell to Gálvez, May 8, 1781, A. G. I., Cuba, 198.

[35] *Idem* to *idem*, May 8, 1781, *ibid.*, 194.

And the next day he reminded Gálvez, "we are in Possession of Works that would cost blood and require Time to reduce."[36] The differences, however, were not so serious as might be inferred. They were ironed out satisfactorily in a conference that lasted until one o'clock on the night of the ninth (i.e., one A.M. on the tenth)[37]

The English surrendered the entire province of West Florida, the fort at Barrancas Coloradas included. Gálvez promised to accord his adversaries the honors of war, to protect noncombatants and unarmed laborers, to restore slaves, etc. Prisoners when exchanged were to be carried to any desired port except Jamaica or St. Augustine. In conclusion, there was this article illustrative of the negotiators' nobility of spirit:

> The full and entire Execution of the present Capitulation shall be observed bona Fide, and where doubts shall arise not provided for in the preceeding Articles it shall be understood to be the Intention of the contracting Parties that they be determined in the manner most conformable to Humanity and Liberality of Sentiment.[38]

Formal surrender of the fort took place on the afternoon of May 10, and Fort Barrancas was taken over the following day. Preparations were ordered at once for sending the Spanish troops back to Havana.

> The total number of prisoners [the official report reads] reaches the sum of 1113 men, who, added to the 105 blown up in the crescent, 56 deserters that had presented themselves during the siege, and 300 who whilst the capitulation was being drawn up retired to Georgia, shows that the garrison was composed of about 1600 men, without counting the many negroes that helped in its defense, the dead they had before, and the multitude of Indians that inundated the woods and country.[39]

Another measure of the victory is in the inventory of military supplies captured. Obviously, Fort George did not surrender for lack of military equipment. The statistics are significant, though not the most

---

[36] *Idem* to *idem*, May 9, 1781, *ibid*.

[37] "Diary ... of the Expedition against ... Pensacola," *op. cit.*, 74–75; Farmar, *op. cit.*

[38] Articles of capitulation, May 9, 1781, A. G. I., Cuba, 188–3; *Louisiana Historical Quarterly*, I, No. 1 (1917), pp. 75–83.

[39] "Diary ... of the Expedition against ... Pensacola," *op. cit.*, 75; Gálvez to José de Gálvez, May 26, 1781, *Gazeta de Madrid*, August 7, 1781.

exciting reading. They mention 4 mortars, 143 cannon, 6 howitzers, 40 swivel guns, 2142 guns, 8000 flints, 298 barrels of powder, bombs, bullets, balls, cartridges, grenades, bayonets, etc.[40] This victory was Gálvez' greatest military success, and his most costly. The itemized list of casualties indicates 74 killed and 198 wounded. Analysis of this list gives a fairly accurate index of the intensity of the fighting. From March 25 through March 30, while the Spaniards were moving camp from the island to the mainland, there were rather heavy losses, mostly incurred in Indian attacks. The month of April saw a great diminution of activity, the casualties being less than the total for the preceding five days. Active work on the trench brought more losses late in the month. Then came the English assault of May 4, with the highest loss of life of any one day in the campaign, a three-day artillery duel, and the final advance of May 8 during which more men fell than in the entire month of April.[41]

The prisoners remained in camp on the east side of town until June 1 when most of them sailed on Spanish transports for Havana. After a ten-day stop to take on water and provisions they continued their voyage to New York, arriving there on July 12.[42] Gálvez left soon after the prisoners, giving final instructions on June 4 to Arturo O'Neill, who was to be the new commander at Pensacola.[43] His instructions related mostly to military defense, but since the town's principal merchants had expressed concern that the "Courts of Judicature" should continue to operate,[44] he ordered O'Neill to promulgate the Code O'Reilly, which had been the basic law of Louisiana since November 25, 1769.

Fort Barrancas' obvious ineffectiveness called for some remedy. A Spanish naval officer, diagnosing the difficulty, had found that the battery was too far from the channel (700 fathoms or 1533 yards), and at so great an elevation that accurate marksmanship was almost

---

[40] "Statement of the Arms and Munitions of War," *Louisiana Historical Quarterly*, vol. I, No. 1 (1917), p. 84.

[41] Ezpeleta, statement of the dead and wounded, *ibid.*, 83–84.

[42] Farmar, *op. cit.*

[43] Gálvez to O'Neill, June 4, 1781, A. G. I., Cuba, 2359.

[44] Chester to Gálvez, May 21, 1781, *ibid.*, 194.

impossible. According to this same authority a second battery on Sigüenza Point would have prevented Spanish access to the bay.[45] Gálvez ordered O'Neill to submit plans for approval before placing a post and garrison on the island, but there was to be no delay about refashioning Fort Barrancas. On the beach in front of the old fort O'Neill was to erect a raised battery, installing the five thirty-two-pounders from Fort Barrancas. Gálvez admonished him not to postpone relocating these cannon, for the English very probably might try to recapture Pensacola. Similarly, Fort George must be better prepared at once to withstand an attack from the northwest. Finally, observing that the Indians had been the best defense which the English had for Pensacola, Gálvez ordered O'Neill to secure their friendship and alliance. He was to do so, not by soliciting peace with the tribes, but by making advances of friendship and trade.[46]

Military and political preferment had accrued to Gálvez after his two previous campaigns, but the capture of Pensacola was particularly gratifying to the king. The king appreciated the valuable territory won, but more especially "the expulsion of the English from the entire Gulf of Mexico, where they have so prejudiced my vassals and my royal interests in times both of peace and of war."[47] As the first mark of appreciation the king, in one of those super-sentences which the Spaniards toss off with such clarity, ordered Pensacola Bay rechristened.

Bearing in mind that the great Bay of Pensacola was named from its first discovery in the reign of Señor Don Philip II *Bahía de Santa María,* and that retaining this most worthy name there was added *de Galve* in memory of the count of this name who was viceroy of Mexico when Pensacola was occupied and settled by his order at the end of the last century; bearing these things in mind, his majesty has seen fit to resolve that henceforth and forever it shall be named *Bahía de Sta. María de Gálvez,* to the honor and glory of the Holy Virgin, and in memory also of the conqueror who has recovered it for the crown of Spain; that the Fort at the Cliff called of old *Sto. Tomé* shall receive the name *San Carlos* which will indicate

---

[45] "Diario de lo ocurrido," *op. cit.,* 160, 177.
[46] Gálvez to O'Neill, June 4, 1781, *ibid.,* 2351.
[47] Royal cédula, José de Gálvez to Gálvez, November 12, 1781, certified copy, *ibid.,* 2359; also printed in 1782 at Santa Fé de Bogotá under the title *Real Cédula de S.M.* . . .

when it was founded by Don Carlos II and that its recovery was effected in the happy reign of his majesty [Carlos III]; and that *Fort George,* constructed by the English, where they ran up the flag asking capitulation and where they surrendered the garrison as prisoners of war, shall be called *San Miguel,* since it surrendered on the day of the appearance of this Holy Archangel, General of the God of armies...."[48]

More substantial tokens of the king's appreciation followed. He promoted Gálvez to the rank of lieutenant general, conferred on him the commission of governor of West Florida as well as Louisiana, at the same time making him independent of New Spain, set his salary at ten thousand pesos annually during the war, and made him a count. Finally, "to perpetuate for posterity," reads the royal order, "the memory of the heroic action in which you alone forced the entrance of the bay, you may place as the crest on your coat of arms the brig *Gálveztown* with the motto 'Yo Solo'."[49]

---

[48] Royal cédula, José de Gálvez to the governor *ad interim* of Pensacola, August 9, 1781, A. G. I., Cuba, 2359. I have italicized the names.

[49] Royal cédula, José de Gálvez to Gálvez, November 12, 1781, certified copy, *ibid.*

CHAPTER XIII

THE NATCHEZ REBELLION

THE SIEGE OF PENSACOLA had a strange repercussion in the Natchez district. The settlers of this locality, when they first came under Spanish authority in the fall of 1779, had been apprehensive that Spanish rule would be a blight to their prosperity and happiness. Experience, however, soon set them at ease. Gálvez treated them leniently and considerately, and they found real advantage in trade with Louisiana and in the availability of New Orleans as a trading port.[1]

Nevertheless, subversive influences impinged upon these people. English control persisted over the neighboring Indians, and when the officers at Pensacola ordered the agents resident among the tribes "to form a company of as many whites as possible as well as Indians" to go first to the relief of Mobile and then to the aid of Pensacola, the suggestion was carried to Natchez, producing, however, no favorable response from the settlers.[2]

Soon after Gálvez arrived off Pensacola Bay to begin the actual attack upon Fort George, Campbell appealed more directly for the support of the Natchez settlers. Stretching the truth, though perhaps without exaggerating his optimism, he sent them word that an English fleet was in the Gulf, that it would move against New Orleans, and he appealed to them to assist in the restoration of English control over Natchez. That this uprising might have the appearance of a regular military action, he sent a number of captain's commissions, such as the following, which were to be distributed among the leading settlers where they would do the most good.[3]

---

[1] Their change of heart is described in Anthony Hutchins to [Miró], July 10, 1785, A. G. I., Cuba, 198.

[2] Orders from Charles Stuart and General Campbell, quoted in Delavillebeuvre to Gálvez, December 12, 1779, *ibid.*, 107; Farmar, *op. cit.*

[3] Declaration of Jacob Winfree, July 25, 1781, A. G. I., Cuba, 114.

Being informed that the Inhabitants of the Natchez who preserve a Spirit of Loyalty to their Rightful Sovereign and retain an Attachment to the happy free and glorious Constitution of Great Britain are sorely etc., etc. etc. greivously and Tyrannically used by the Despotism of Spain, and Reposing especial Confidence and Trust in your courage, Influence and Abilities to deliver them from such Slavish Oppression, I do therefore by Virtue of the Authority and command to me entrusted by my Sovereign, hereby constitute and appoint you a Captain or Leader of such Volunteer Inhabitants as you can procure to serve under your Command who prefer the British Government to Tyrannick despotism and Rule and are willing to risk their Lives for the attainment thereof and you and all those who shall put themselves under your command are directed and required to act in arms against the Spaniards and against all and every His Majesty's Enemies According to the Rules and Practice of War. And for so doing this shall be to you and them sufficient Warrant and Authority.[4]

This move by Campbell is open to criticism for its disregard of the Baton Rouge capitulation, not to mention the oath the settlers had taken "to be faithful subjects of the [Spanish] king as long as they lived in his territory; neither doing nor permitting to be done anything against his royal person, possessions, or officers."[5] Yet it was perfectly natural that Campbell should want to foment a disturbance which would create a diversion handicapping Gálvez' attack on Pensacola.

Anthony Hutchins asserts that Campbell was not the prime mover in this scheme, that he was persuaded to endorse it by John and Philip Alston and John Turner, who in turn had been stirred up by Colonel Montgomery of the Americans. These men, according to Hutchins, fostered the rebellion in hopes that they would be able to swing the district under American control. Their emissary duped Campbell, convincing him that their intentions were patriotically English. The seal of Campbell's approval, made apparent to the Natchez settlers in the commissions and in an order on the Choctaw traders for ammunition, convinced even the most reluctant that they were in duty bound to support the rebellion. Without this hallmark of respecta-

---

[4] Campbell, Captain's Commission to Blommart, March 17, 1781, A. G. I., Cuba, 173 c. Winfree's is identical, *ibid.*, 114.

[5] Oath of fidelity administered by Delavillebeuvre and signed by thirty-one settlers, October 20, 1779, A. G. I., Cuba, 107.

bility it is doubtful that the more substantial citizens would have followed leaders like Christopher Marr, the man who brought the commissions from Pensacola. Hutchins depicts him thus:

> a noted vagabond of bad character & abandoned principles, well known in most of the Provinces & the States on the Continent for the many capital crimes he had (for a series of years) committed, and for the jails he had broken to make his escape; this respectable Embassader ...[6]

In his antagonism toward the Alstons *et al.*, Hutchins may exaggerate, but obviously revolutionary sentiment in the district was carefully nursed along. Marr first confided his success to the Alstons and Turner; then the English aspect of the scheme was revealed to a few more settlers; but those, such as Hutchins, whose approval was most doubtful, were informed only at the eleventh hour. To them were presented the bald alternatives of supporting the rebellion or losing their lives and property. Thanks to this skillful and unscrupulous management by the original instigators, the rebellion received virtually unanimous support from the settlers, and one of the most reputable of them, John Blommart, was induced to assume leadership.[7]

On April 22 with a force of two hundred men—settlers and Indians—Blommart began his attack on Fort Panmure. In spite of their endeavors at secrecy, the rebels found Delavillebeuvre prepared to meet them. He had been warned by "Mr. Mac Yntosh Alexandre" that a movement against the fort was contemplated, and the garrison had slept on its arms. He had sent to Pointe Coupée for help also, but doubted that the messenger got through. Warning the settlers of the consequences of their actions, Delavillebeuvre urged them to disperse. Their answer, however, was to begin firing on the fort. Their fire did some damage—Corporal Blar was wounded on the twenty-third and died a few days later—but in order to bring about the surrender of the fort the rebels had to supplement absolute military force with deception.[8] A messenger from McIntosh was intercepted, who carried a letter vouching for the verbal communication that the messenger

---

[6] Hutchins to [Miró], July 10, 1785, *ibid.*, 198.
[7] *Ibid.;* declaration of Jacob Winfree, July 25, 1781, A. G. I., Cuba, 114.
[8] Journal of Juan Delavillebeuvre, April 21–May 4, 1781, A. G. I., Cuba, 194; [certificate of enlistment under Blommart], April, 1781, *ibid.*

would bring. Another carrier was substituted, given the note, and sent in to say that the fort was undermined and that Delavillebeuvre had better surrender. The ruse succeeded. Delavillebeuvre was convinced and agreed to terms of capitulation.[9]

Soon after the fort surrendered, the English party began to break into factions. The fate of the prisoners became an issue. One proposal was to send them to Pensacola, but Hutchins persuaded Blommart that the self-nominated guard for this journey intended to act as executioners as soon as they got away from Blommart's control. Blommart was persuaded to send Delavillebeuvre and his seventy-six men down to Baton Rouge under reliable guard. They made the journey unmolested. Another issue was the question of raising the American flag instead of the English. Blommart was sufficiently warned and nipped this plan in the bud. The Alston-Turner faction hoped to plunder and divide the stores of supplies at Natchez. They went so far as to break into Delavillebeuvre's baggage, but Blommart administered the captured fort with care. He appointed a commissary, had careful records kept, and only permitted the issuance of such supplies and ammunition as were actually needed. Blommart found an effective check on the more bloodthirsty and avaricious of his followers when he recognized the civil authority of Anthony Hutchins, who had been chief magistrate at Natchez during the old English régime. Most of the settlers approved this step since it seemed to be perfectly regular and in accord with English practice. Its chief consequence was that the more tempestuous holders of Campbell's commissions were shorn of power.[10]

The rebels' confusion was completed when news arrived that Pensacola had fallen to Gálvez. Since the Natchez Loyalists had counted upon English success there and upon a naval attack upon New Orleans, this news paralyzed the rebellion. Some of the settlers fled from the district; others advocated a division of the goods in the fort pre-

---

[9] Journal of Juan Delavillebeuvre, April 21–May 4, 1781, *ibid*. According to Claiborne, *op. cit.*, 127–128, the deception was carried out through a handwriting expert who placed the ominous message over McIntosh's signature.

[10] Daybook of the clerk of the garrison and works, April 23–June 1, 1781, A. G. I., Cuba, 194; receipt book of Blommart's commissaries, Williams and Ferguson, May 14–June 14, 1781, *ibid.;* Hutchins to [Miró], July 10, 1785, *ibid.*, 198.

liminary to dispersal of the group; Blommart and a majority of the settlers elected to protect the fort until it could be turned back to the Spaniards and to remain in the district, confident that the Spanish authorities would deal with them as participants in a regular military maneuver rather than in a rebellion.[11]

As soon as Gálvez heard of the Natchez uprising, he reproached his prisoner, Campbell, for having instigated such an irregular and improper opposition to Spanish authority. Campbell, notwithstanding the commissions he had issued, denied responsibility.

Further Sir the very existence of such an event I have only from your Excellency's Information, and you yourself lately allowed, that you was ignorant of the particulars. Perhaps (if it has a Being) it may be by orders from Canada; or the Ambition of some restless and aspiring Rebel Americans may have been the cause thereof.[12]

This conjecture of American causation has added interest in view of Hutchins' assertion that a pro-American faction had hoodwinked Campbell.

A few days later, having been informed of the terms of capitulation of Delavillebeuvre to Blommart with mention therein of the commission from Pensacola, Campbell wrote more frankly to Gálvez. He admitted that the Natchez uprising had been undertaken by virtue of his orders and authority, and he proposed to set matters right by ordering the resurrender of Fort Panmure, "provided that a general Amnesty and Indemnity shall be granted for all past acts whatsoever and that every Inhabitant or others in the District of Natchez shall in every Respect be given the same Footing as those of the District of Pensacola."[13] Proposing two "Further Additional Articles" for the Pensacola capitulation, he embodied the foregoing suggestions with a statement of the extent of Spanish West Florida, which might have been worth having in Spain's later diplomacy anent the boundary.

That the District of the Natchez and all and every part, Portion and Division of the Province of West Florida According to its most extensive Limits when entirely under the British Government shall be understood to be comprehended and included in this Capitulation.[14]

---

[11] *Ibid.;* Panis' examination of Williams, July 2, 1781, A. G. I., Cuba, 173 c.
[12] Campbell to Gálvez, May 29, 1781, A. G. I., Cuba, 2359.
[13] *Idem* to *idem*, June 3, 1781, *ibid.*   [14] *Ibid.*

But Gálvez refused to agree to Campbell's proposals on the ground that the Natchez uprising was in the nature of a civil war, a rebellion against Spanish authority, for the settlement of which the proposed treaty negotiations were inappropriate. A series of reports from Piernas persuaded him that he would have to go to Natchez in person, at the head of an army of seven hundred men. His mind was made up on June 4, and he left soon after this for New Orleans, setting aside plans to go to Havana.[15]

Gálvez' disapproval of Campbell's connection with the rebellion found further expression in the detention of Major James Campbell as a hostage, long after the rest of the Pensacola prisoners had been sent to New York. Replying to Gálvez' charge that Blommart's commission from General John Campbell contained reference to complaints of Spanish misrule at Natchez, the hostage replied that there had been such complaints, though not from Blommart. He asserted also that the Natchez people had been instructed to rise in arms after Gálvez had met defeat at Pensacola and that in their impatience they did not wait.[16] In the wording of Campbell's commissions, however, there is no indication of a time qualification.[17]

Before Gálvez arrived at New Orleans, the provincial authorities had sent a small force to recover Fort Panmure. Command of this expedition gravitated to a militia captain, Estevan Robert de la Morandiere. He started from Atakapas with forty militiamen to report to Grand Pré for service against the Natchez rebels. Grand Pré sent him on to Roche á Davion, where other militiamen joined his party. After a few days Grand Pré ordered him on to Natchez.[18]

Morandiere's journal suggests that his northward trip began in timorous and hesitant fashion, but took on courage and ended in the utmost confidence. Hearing on June 2 that Blommart had prepared four bateaux for a raid on Pointe Coupée, he posted sentries in the

---

[15] Gálvez to Navarro, June 4, 1781, A. G. I., Cuba, 1233; Gálvez to José de Gálvez, July 19, 1781, No. 462, A. G. I., Sto. Dom., 2083.

[16] James Campbell to Ezpeleta, December 18, 1781, A. G. I., Cuba, 194.

[17] See Campbell's commissions to Blommart and Winfree, March 17, 1781, *ibid.*, 173 c and 114.

[18] Miró to Navarro, May 25, 1781, No. 4, *ibid.*, 1304; journal of Morandiere, *ibid.*, 2359.

woods and on the river and sent scouts ahead. The next day George Rapalje and William Courtney appeared as deputies of the "habitants who were still loyal." Morandiere interviewed them and sent them on to Grand Pré. On the twelfth St. Germain and Charbonaux were captured. Later on he came to the conclusion that these men had been sent by Blommart to disaffect the Indians and turn them against the Spanish force.[19]

The next emissaries encountered were "Colonel Otchin [Hutchins] & Docteur flavelle [Farrell]." They bore a letter from Blommart supplementing his earlier proposal of "Terms of Accomodation" that he had addressed to the governor. In brief, he had suggested a return to the *status quo ante "rebellum"*; the complete fort would be restored to Spain, and the Natchez people would regain all the rights and privileges provided for by the capitulation of Baton Rouge.[20] This proposal, made on June 2, was almost a duplicate of Campbell's of June 3, except that Campbell would have brought Natchez under the comprehension of the Pensacola capitulation.

Morandiere sent Hutchins and Farrell back with a promise of personal protection, which he made conditional on Grand Pré's approval. Incidentally, he represented that Grand Pré was on the way with artillery and a considerable reënforcement. But as for treating with Blommart, he told them that

an officer of his majesty, although in the militia, could never treat with one who was not only a rebel but even a traitor, who had voluntarily taken an oath of fidelity to the king but had felt free to return to the service of his former sovereign.[21]

The next day, June 14, he sent a circular through the Natchez district, notifying the habitants that if they returned to their homes the troops and Indians would be ordered not to molest them. For the sake of security he advised them to fly a Spanish flag in front of their houses.

---

[19] *Ibid.;* Blommart to McIntosh, Rapalje, and Courtney, June 3, 1781, A. G. I., Cuba, 194.

[20] Blommart to His Excellency the Governor or the Commdr. in Chief of his most Catholic Majesty's Forces in Louisiana etc., June 2, 1781, *ibid.*, 114; journal of Morandiere, *ibid.*, 2359.

[21] *Ibid.*

On the eighteenth one band of Indians deserted, and he was left with only 43 Indians, 40 militiamen from Atakapas, 26 from Pointe Coupée, and 40 Canadians under Alain's command. To his diary he confided a fervent wish that Grand Pré would hurry, but finding the inhabitants disposed to favor the Spaniards, he resolved to continue.[22]

With Blommart and an armed force looking on, Morandiere landed at Natchez on June 22. Blommart announced that he came not to attack but to treat for the rendition of the fort. Morandiere replied that he could not and must not treat with a rebel and a traitor. He added that an officer of his Catholic majesty would merit death if he condescended to such negotiations. Blommart's only recourse was to evacuate the fort, surrender his person of his own volition, and throw himself upon the mercy of Governor Gálvez.[23]

Blommart countered with a proposal of conditions of surrender. He proposed that, pending orders from Pensacola, the terms of the Baton Rouge capitulation should apply, a white flag should fly over the fort, and the person of John Blommart should be free. The garrison should be allowed to go home, except four hostages to be chosen by lot. The formalities of surrender would be observed at ten o'clock on the morning of the twenty-third.[24]

But Morandiere found it unnecessary to enter into a formal agreement. Forty of his men occupied Fort Panmure unopposed, later the guard was doubled, and at sunrise on June 23 Morandiere entered the fort. He sent twenty of his militiamen and eighty of the settlers in pursuit of fugitive rebels, and at ten o'clock (the hour Blommart had proposed for the surrender of the fort) he sent Blommart and three others, Eason, Williams, and Benjamin, under guard to Grand Pré.[25]

Although he deserves a compliment for the efficiency of his actions, Morandiere is open to criticism for the precipitate shipment south of Blommart and his three associates. Blommart may have deserved such treatment, but it was a tactical blunder, for it alarmed several of the other leaders in the revolt and sent them scurrying into the woods

---

[22] *Ibid.* [23] *Ibid.*

[24] Blommart, proposed terms of surrender to Morandiere, June 23, 1781, A. G. I., Cuba, 2359.

[25] Journal of Morandiere, *ibid.*

where their apprehension was difficult.[26] Hutchins criticized Morandiere later for an indiscriminate acceptance of incriminating testimony from many of the most guilty participants in the rebellion. What hurt especially was that to Hutchins was assigned a leading rôle—and indeed, through his issuance of warrants for goods commandeered while the siege was on and by his acting as civil magistrate after the capture of Fort Panmure, he had been prominent. Asserting that Morandiere's mind had been poisoned against him, Hutchins deemed it prudent to absent himself from his home and even from the district.[27] Yet it is easy to see how Morandiere found it difficult to determine the truth. A tangle of conflicting testimony confronted him, and the settlers vied with one another in laying the blame on someone else. If Hutchins was dealt with unjustly, Morandiere was not entirely to blame.

News of the fall of Pensacola had struck terror to the hearts of many of the Natchez settlers. Realizing that their rebellion could now be easily crushed by the Spaniards, and recalling perhaps the fate of Lafrénière and the other French insurgents in 1768 and 1769, a substantial number fled from the district. About eighty took refuge with the Chickasaws and thirty with the Choctaws. Another small group[28] took to the wilderness with such provisions as they could snatch and headed for the English posts in Georgia and the Carolinas. Pickett, Gayarré, and Claiborne called on their best rhetoric to bring out the pathos of this tragic trek. "Fearful of pursuit, fearful of ambush, dogged by famine, tortured by thirst, exposed to every vicissitude of weather, weakened by disease, more than decimated by death, the women and children dying day by day"—Claiborne conservatively estimates that these poor unfortunates suffered as if in purgatory.[29]

The saddest thing about this hegira is that it was unnecessary. Spanish retribution turned out to be unexpectedly mild. Amnesty was granted to the ordinary participants in the uprising. Some two hun-

---

[26] Hutchins to Miró, July 1, 1781, A. G. I., Cuba, 114.
[27] Hutchins to [Miró], July 10, 1785, *ibid.*, 198.
[28] Estimated at "a dozen," presumably a dozen families, Panis' examination of Williams, July 2, 1781, *ibid.*, 173 c.
[29] Claiborne, *op. cit.*, 128–132; Gayarré, *op. cit.*, III, 149–151.

dred and forty settlers took a new oath of fidelity to Spain soon after Morandiere recovered Fort Panmure, and the fugitives who had fled to the Indian villages began to come back.[30] At the very time that the flight began, Gálvez was expressing himself thus at New Orleans:

> The conduct of the people of Natchez has been infamous, a reflection on all good Englishmen, and a scandal to other nations. Nevertheless, we who know the insignificant effects of the rebellion realize that punishment need not be made severer than to establish respect for the law, and ought not to extend to any innocent habitants.[31]

To be sure, the heads of the revolt were sought out, particularly those who had held commissions. Blommart, Eason, Williams, and Benjamin had been sent to New Orleans on the day the fort was recovered. Captains Marr, Fulsom, Turner, and the two Alstons were pursued, and an offer of £100 sterling was made for their apprehension. Some of these men were never captured, but most of them were brought to trial.[32]

Because other duties called him away to Havana, Gálvez turned the trial of the Natchez leaders over to Jacinto Panis, whose knowledge of English made it more appropriate that he should conduct the trials. Gálvez recommended also that he should avail himself of the advice of Manuel Andres Lopes de Armesto.[33] Panis began his examination of these first prisoners on July 2. Eason's replies shed little new light on the affair. Williams, as Blommart's commissary, though not a holder of one of Campbell's commissions, had a better knowledge of what had gone on at Natchez. He had not participated in the attack and had not seen any of the commissions. He said that Blommart had observed scrupulously the terms of Delavillebeuvre's capitulation, but that Kit Marr and Turner had broken into the Spanish captain's baggage. He said that Blommart had no thought of attacking other Spanish posts.[34] Panis probably interrogated Benjamin, but a record of this examination has not been found.

---

[30] Journal of Morandiere, A. G. I., Cuba, 2359; Hutchins to Miró, July 1, 1781, *ibid.*, 114.
[31] Gálvez to ———, June 16, 1781, draft, *ibid.*
[32] Hutchins to [Miró], July 10, 1785, A. G. I., Cuba, 198.
[33] Gálvez to Panis, June 30, 1781, *ibid.*, 173 c.
[34] Panis' examinations of Eason and Williams, July 2, 1781, *ibid.*

The most thorough questioning was naturally that of Blommart. Panis put to him fifty-six queries. The answers revealed that he was a native of Geneva and a Protestant, that he had been commissioned captain by Campbell, receiving the commission on April 20, just two days before the attack was launched. He freely admitted that he was in the district when it was surrendered with Baton Rouge, and that he had taken an oath of fidelity to the king of Spain. Denying that he had any grievance against Spain, he asserted that he joined in the uprising only because he felt that Campbell's orders compelled him to do so. He insisted that he had lived up to the terms of Delavillebeuvre's capitulation and denied ordering the seizure of any boats on the river.[35]

Panis took the case under advisement until the next day, July 6, when he ordered Blommart's property confiscated and the four men detained. Zenon Trudeau, apparently acting in the capacity of attorney for the defense, pleaded with Panis for leniency, chiefly because of the peaceful submission to Morandiere.[36] The extenuating circumstances in Blommart's favor were best set forth by Hutchins in a letter which arrived after Panis had announced his decision.

I beg leave to trouble you with a word in favor of Capt Blommart that let the beginning of his conduct be what it will which I can't Judge of but by information, yet I can truly say that during the time the Fort was in his possession after the Flag was sent that great merit was due to him as he exerted himself to the utmost of his power to preserve from violation the Fort and Military Stores for the use of His Most Catholic Majesty against the will of those who set out with him in the unhappy enterprize, and with certain assistance and other exertions therein thwarted and broke through their intentions machinations and designs. This I only say in his favor in the way of mitigation being tied down both by Honor and principle to plead the cause of one who tho' almost unpardonable on the one hand yet on the other has sacrificed all favor friendship Interest liberty and expectation of every kind to effect at last certain worthy and Honorable purposes enjoin'd of him.[37]

---

[35] Panis' examination of Blommart, July 5, 1781, *ibid*.

[36] Panis, sentence of Blommart, July 6, 1781, *ibid*.; Trudeau to [Panis], July 7, 1781, *ibid*.

[37] Hutchins to Miró, July 1, 1781, A. G. I., Cuba, 114; Williams' receipt book, May 14–June 14, 1781, corroborates, *ibid*, 194.

Jacob Winfree was the next one apprehended. In his declaration on July 25 he asserted that he had accepted a commission as the only apparent means of protecting his property against the pro-British Indians who were said to be moving toward Natchez. He took credit also for doing all in his power after news came of Pensacola's fall to prevent Eason and some others from destroying the fort.[38] When cross-examined on September 4 and 5, Winfree endeavored to shift responsibility to Blommart, the real captain. Concerning his oath of fidelity in 1779 he maintained that he had thought it binding for eight months only.[39] Winfree was in error on this point; the oath that Delavillebeuvre administered had no time limitation.[40] The confusion probably arose from the fact that the Mobile settlers were to become eligible for an oath of neutrality eight months after the capitulation of Fort Charlotte.[41] With Winfree, Joseph Holmes was also interrogated.[42]

Scattered sporadically through the next several months there are bits of evidence about further punishment for the Natchez uprising. Four sons of John Alston and fourteen slaves arrived at New Orleans on September 25.[43] Grand Pré reported the confiscation of all property of the promoters of the rebellion, and sent down John Smith and Parker Caridine on November 1. He asked what to do about an offer from the chief of Achafalé to surrender four of Delavillebeuvre's soldiers who had joined Blommart's rebels. The offer of surrender was on condition that these men be promised their lives. He reported also that he had despatched a party of English settlers to the Chickasaw villages north of Natchez to seize John Alston and Turner.[44] Turner escaped, but Alston and one son and ten slaves were captured. Grand Pré confiscated the slaves, released the son, and sent Alston under guard to New Orleans.[45] On May 6, 1782, Grand Pré rendered an

---

[38] Declaration of Jacob Winfree, July 25, 1781, *ibid.*, 114.
[39] Cross-examination of Winfree, September 4 and 5, 1781, *ibid.*, 1376.
[40] Oath administered by Delavillebeuvre, October 20, 1779, *ibid.*, 107.
[41] Article 3, "Artículos de Capitulación . . . ," A. G. I., Cuba, 2351.
[42] Examination of Joseph Holmes, September 5, 1781, *ibid.*, 1376.
[43] Piernas to Gálvez, September 26, 1781, *ibid.*
[44] Grand Pré to Piernas, November 1, 1781, Nos. 192 and 193, A. G. I., Cuba, 114.
[45] *Idem* to *idem*, November 20, 1781, No. 198, *ibid.*

account of the proceeds from public sale of the property of twenty-one rebel leaders, some of them in prison at New Orleans, most of them fugitives from the district. After the expenses of judge, sheriffs, interpreters, etc. were paid, a balance of 3121 pesos, 4 reales, 17 sueldos remained.[46]

Several of the insurgents, however, found havens of refuge among the Indians. For example, John Holston wrote to his parents:

> ... we got all safely to the Chickasaws & are living all together with Thomas Holmes & wife. my greatest unesiness at present is on account of the great Distance thats Between us, but I still flatter myself that we shall see the day before long that we shall have an opportunity of getting together again. I'd advise you to stay there & Content yourselves as well as you can for I expect an alteration Shortly.[47]

The leaders of the Natchez insurrection did not lack for intercessors. The governor of Jamaica sent Gálvez a letter typical of the more polite pleas.

> Permit me to trouble Your Excellency in regard to two Captains, two Lieutenants, one Store Keeper, one Serjeant, and several privates taken at Natchez Fort....
> I am informed that the harsh treatment which Captain Blommart, the head of the party, had met with; so unusual under Your Excellency's command, has arisen from the neutrality which he had infringed; a circumstance I have reason to believe, originated from intemperate zeal and indiscretion in him, & his perfect ignorance of the customary Laws of Nations.
> From such persuasions I am led to solicit Your Excellency's forgiveness to those unfortunate men.[48]

The respectful requests of Hutchins and of John and James Campbell have already been noticed.

Other champions of the Natchez leaders utilized threats. Ferqr. Bethune, English deputy superintendent of Indian affairs for the Mississippi district, wrote from the Chickasaw nation demanding clemency and threatening retaliation.

---

[46] Resultar des ventes publique des Biens des rebeldes fugitives et autres dans les prisons de la Nelle. Orleans, May 6, 1782, A. G. I., Cuba, 193.

[47] John Holston to Stephen Holston & Judah his wife, May 15, 1782, *ibid.*, 194; see Houck, *op. cit.*, I, 220–221.

[48] Archibald Campbell to Gálvez, November 29, 1781, B. L., La. Coll.

In short Sir the Fate of your Power depends on the treatment of the Natchez Inhabitants; Lenity & Compassion shown them will stop a Torrent ready to pour out and deluge the Banks of the Mississippi with blood.[49]

Later, Alston and Turner were reported organizing a party of Chickasaw, Choctaw, and Yazoo Indians to make reprisals on the Spaniards at Natchez.[50] These threats were only words, however, and it was not until April of the next year that the real champion of the Natchez insurrectionists arose in the person of James Colbert. Described by Adair as "Capt. J. C-l-b-rt, who has lived among the Chikkasah from his childhood, and speaks their language even with more propriety than the English,"[51] Colbert was now a man of about sixty years, but still of good health and strong constitution. He had lived among the Indians for forty years and had a rich lodging among the Chickasaws, one hundred and fifty negro slaves, and several sons by Chickasaw women.[52] During the siege of Pensacola he had rendered assiduous assistance to the English, along with some of his sons and a band of Chickasaw braves.[53]

A combination of influences roused Colbert to try to force the release of Blommart and the other Natchez prisoners by reprisals upon Spaniards passing through the Chickasaw country. The British agent Bethune, who had threatened retaliation soon after Morandiere recovered Fort Panmure, was located conveniently to exert persuasion.[54] The Spaniards were never convinced that Colbert was properly accredited to wage war, but he referred to himself as "sent by his superiors," and insisted that he was duly commissioned.[55] Besides this official encouragement there was the pressure of the numerous English refugees in the Chickasaw country, fugitives from Natchez as well as

---

[49] Ferqr. Bethune to the Commandant at Natchez, July 19, 1781, A. G. I., Cuba, 114.
[50] Grand Pré to Piernas, November 1, 1781, No. 192, *ibid.*
[51] Adair, *The History of the American Indians,* 370.
[52] Declaración de Silvestre L'Abbadie á Franco. Cruzat, July 5, 1782, B. L., La. Coll.
[53] Farmar, *op. cit.*
[54] [Declaration of Madame Cruzat], May 30, 1782, certified copy, A. G. I., Sto. Dom., 2656; copy, translated in Houck, *op. cit.,* I, 221–231.
[55] Colbert to Miró, October 6, 1782, B. L., La. Coll.; Colbert to [DuBreuil], April 17, 1783, copies, A. G. I., Cuba, 2360 and 107.

from Georgia, the Carolinas, and farther north. Many of these men were personal friends of Colbert. One of them set him an example.

On April 25 fourteen Natchez fugitives led by John Turner seized Pourré's boat on its way to Illinois. Pourré and his crew were disarmed, their weapons were placed in a canoe in the custody of four men, and Turner and nine men took charge of the captured boat and the prisoners. Four hours later Pourré and his men rose against their captors, pitched them into the river, and with only the oars as weapons killed six Englishmen and two negroes. Turner and one negro, also thrown into the water, had the good fortune to reach the canoe. Pourré turned back to Natchez, but went north again shortly in company with two other launches, while Grand Pré sent out two bands of Indians to capture or kill these pirates, "since humanity and clemency do not engender in them the slightest emotion."[56]

Colbert followed Turner's example on May 2 and with better success. He captured a boat commanded by Silvestre L'Abbadie and carrying a valuable cargo, including 4500 pesos that were being sent north to meet government expenses in Spanish Illinois. Also on board was a more important prize—Madame Cruzat, the wife of the Spanish commander at St. Louis, and her four sons.[57]

The full story of this capture and the experiences of the prisoners is too long to present here. Both L'Abbadie and Madame Cruzat put much of the blame for their capture on Joseph Meson [Mason], who assured them, as they approached Chickasaw Bluffs, that everything was tranquil on the river. Consequently, they were not alarmed to see a boat moored to the west bank opposite the mouth of the Margot River. Hailed from this boat by Thomas Prince, who said that he had letters for Madame Cruzat, they crossed over, threw a line ashore, and allowed their boat to be tied up. As L'Abbadie was about to step ashore to receive the letters, forty Englishmen jumped out of the woods, leveled muskets and carbines at the Spanish boat, and their leader

---

[56] Miró to Cagigal, May 4, 1782, No. 16, A. G. I., Cuba, 1304; Miró to Gálvez, copy, translated in Houck, *op. cit.*, I, 213.

[57] There are two chief sources for information about this capture and the subsequent developments: Declaración de Silvestre L'Abbadie á Franco. Cruzat, July 5, 1782, B. L., La. Coll.; and [declaration of Madame Cruzat], May 30, 1782, certified copy, A. G. I., Sto. Dom., 2656, copy, translated in Houck, *op. cit.*, I, 221–231.

shouted in clear and intelligible French, "Surrender yourselves, you are our prisoners, and if you move or shake your heads, we will fire on all of you and kill you." L'Abbadie attempted to parley but received very short answers. They were English; their arms constituted their flag; and powder and ball would serve as their orders. Surrender was inevitable.[58]

Colbert immediately assured Madame Cruzat that she and her sons would be well treated. Then they all crossed the river and went up the Margot about a quarter of a league where the captured boatmen were put in a log jail. The next day, because of an alarm that an American boat was approaching, Colbert hurriedly moved his prisoners about four leagues up the Margot. Here a new jail was built. Here also the captors had the pleasure of dividing up the booty. They began with about six thousand pesos, the king's and the captives'. Then the tableware and slaves were auctioned off, the guns, clothes, etc., distributed. The real celebration, however, was reserved for a few days later when some two hundred Chickasaws had arrived and the distribution of powder and brandy took place. The Indians accepted some of the booty and took charge of some prisoners, but though Colbert's son William was their head war chief, yet it seemed that the Indians were tolerating these actions against the Spaniards rather than participating in them. Madame Cruzat was especially appreciative of the protection that William Colbert gave her.[59]

Several other less valuable boats were captured, the most important of which was Lafont's with a cargo of maize and meal from St. Louis, nine of its crew becoming prisoners while the tenth joined Colbert's forces.

Both Madame Cruzat and L'Abbadie stress the insurbordination that was rife among their captors. The white men in this district, numbering more than three hundred, were refugees from Georgia, the Carolinas, and the Cumberland region as well as from Natchez. They were restless spirits, many of them deserving the characterization of vagabonds and ruffians. They acknowledged Colbert's leadership only

---

[58] Declaración de Silbestre L'Abbadie, *op. cit.*

[59] *Ibid.;* [declaration of Madame Cruzat], *op. cit.*

in a limited degree, and accorded him even this partial obedience chiefly because of the influence he enjoyed over the Chickasaws in whose lands they were being tolerated. Colbert was somewhat responsible for the air of uncertainty that prevailed among his followers, for he was himself undecided about just how to accomplish the exchange of these prisoners for Blommart and the rest.

Although hazy as to the methods he should follow, Colbert was not at all reticent about his plans. He talked very freely to his prisoners, boasting of his intelligence service which informed him in advance of all movements of boats along the Mississippi, and showing L'Abbadie a letter in English from some informant in New Orleans. He said also that, if he had not taken L'Abbadie's boat, he would have seized the Arkansas fort. Admitting that the fort at Natchez would be difficult to take, he told of plans to blockade it. He counted on support from the inhabitants who were not content under Spanish rule, and threatened fire and sword for any settlers who would not support him. Even if Fort Panmure did not fall, Colbert said that his party would retire "content with having done all the damage possible."[60] He also mentioned a "Mr. Aricson (who is a colonel escaped from Naeché)," whose name Madame Cruzat gave as Anthony Hutchins. He had gone to Georgia to get two regiments, so Colbert affirmed, and his return, expected momentarily, would be the signal for attacks on the Arkansas post, Ste. Geneviève in Illinois, Natchez, and even the capital itself.

L'Abbadie spoke of Colbert as a Hispanophobe.

This man is one of the greatest enemies of our nation. He has such an irritation against it that notwithstanding the continued suplications of myself and Madame Cruzat he would not liberate Joseph Crespo, a soldier of this detachment, saying in a tone insolent, ironical, and contemptuous, that this one was a native Spaniard, and that therefore he wished to retain him, for he had a high regard for those of this nation, and that he wished that all the other prisoners were of the same nationality.[61]

To Madame Cruzat, too, he expressed great regret that he had captured her instead of her husband, for whom he had a special aversion.[62]

---

[60] Declaración de Silbestre L'Abbadie, *op. cit.*   [61] *Ibid.*   [62] *Ibid.*

Colbert might have revealed more details of his plans if Alexander McGillivray had not interrupted and advised him to hold his tongue. "You are speaking very openly," he said, "and are making our projects known to a man, who, if he is given his liberty today or tomorrow, will not forget to make public our intentions, which in no wise would be favorable to us for their execution."[63]

In the course of the next decade Alexander McGillivray became the foremost chief of the Creeks and the dominant authority among the Southeastern Indians.[64] During the Natchez rebellion his position was not so exalted, but he demonstrated more sagacity and incisiveness of mind than Colbert or any of the other rebel leaders. With his arrival on May 15 a better defined program of action was launched. He had come from Savannah by way of the Chickasaw towns, and, according to L'Abbadie, brought orders "which seemed to emanate from Monr. Tranble who is in the said Chickasaw nation."

On the day of his arrival he drew up a "Parole of Honour," whereby L'Abbadie and nine other prisoners were permitted to go to New Orleans. It reads as follows:

We the Subscribers, prisoners of War to his Britannick Majesty, taken by Capt. James Colburt,[65] do hereby engage upon our Word & Honor (comprehending therein, all that is good & sacred in men) that we will remain, and consider ourselves as prisoners of War, to return to any of the British Dominions if called upon, unless Exchanged for the men under mentioned, it is hereby understood that we not only Bind ourselves, but the Spanish Nation, whose Subjects we are

John Blommart	Jacob Winfree	Wm. Eason
John Alston	John Turner[66]	Parker Caridine
Joseph Holmes	John Green	John Smith[67]

---

[63] *Ibid.*

[64] See my "Alexander McGillivray and the Creek Crisis, 1783-1784," in *New Spain and the Anglo-American West*, I, 263-288; Whitaker, "Alexander McGillivray, 1783-1793," *North Carolina Historical Review*, V (1928), 181-203, 289-309.

[65] McGillivray thus spelled and signed Colbert's name.

[66] Turner, though not a Spanish prisoner, was "under indictment" and his arrest was sought.

[67] A parole of honour, May 15, 1782, copy not signed by L'Abbadie *et al.*, A. G. I., Cuba, 2359; see Houck, *op. cit.*, I, 220.

The signatories repurchased L'Abbadie's boat for 400 pesos, Madame Cruzat giving her note for the sum, which was to be paid "to Mr. Blommart when he comes off for the Chickasaws," and L'Abbadie bought back one of his slaves for 250 pesos. On May 22 they started south; L'Abbadie and nine[68] other prisoners, accompanied by Madame Cruzat, her four sons, and a negress of hers. L'Abbadie bore a letter to the governor of Louisiana, explaining the exchange that was proposed, stressing the humanity and consideration that Colbert had shown to his prisoners, and protesting against "a matter that is prevalent in West Florida, particularly at Mobill, that is offering Great rewards to Indians for the Heads of particular Men in the Indian Country."[69]

On their way downstream they met three boats commanded by Luis Villars, Francisco Vallé, and Eugenio Pourré. Madame Cruzat broke her promise to Colbert and warned these men of the danger at Chickasaw Bluffs. In view of his April experience Pourré must have felt special appreciation for this warning. They all went down to Arkansas; from there L'Abbadie sent Madame Cruzat and his boat on to New Orleans, while he journeyed with the others to St. Louis. Madame Cruzat arrived on May 30 and immediately gave to the authorities a long account of what had transpired.[70] L'Abbadie reached St. Louis on June 29 and made a similar declaration to Francisco Cruzat.[71] From New Orleans and St. Louis measures were instituted to suppress this outgrowth of the Natchez rebellion.

After careful consideration Miró concluded that an expedition against Colbert would be impracticable. In the first place, the territory was so remote and so extensive that it would be very difficult to run down these latest insurgents. Establishment of a fort at Chickasaw Bluffs would not solve the problem, because they could attack anywhere along more than three hundred leagues of the river. In the second place, a Spanish attack would probably force them to take

---

[68] Eleven, according to the Declaración de Silbestre L'Abbadie, *op. cit.*

[69] Colburt [*sic*] (though penned and signed by McGillivray), to [the governor of Louisiana], May 15, 1782, A. G. I., Cuba, 2359; Spanish translation, retranslated in Houck, *op. cit.*, I, 219.

[70] Printed in Houck, *op. cit.*, I, 221–231.

[71] Declaración de Silbestre L'Abbadie, July 5, 1782, B. L., La. Coll.

refuge with the Chickasaws, and to preserve Spain's reputation the Chickasaws as well as Colbert's men would have to be attacked. Miró reminded Gálvez of the "small gain and great loss" that resulted from two French attacks on the Chickasaws.[72] He proposed instead to go to Natchez with two hundred men to perfect its defenses.[73]

Miró went on to point out that the extensive additions to Spanish territory on the left bank of the Mississippi, the results of Gálvez' conquests, made advisable a relocation of the frontier posts. He urged two new forts between Natchez and Illinois, one to be at Barrancas á Margot (Chickasaw Bluffs). Arkansas might as well be abandoned, especially since the post had been moved ten or twelve leagues from the Mississippi to avoid the floods at the old location. The new post did not protect river traffic. The new international boundaries had made Baton Rouge and Manchac obsolete. Designed by the English to guard against Spanish Manchac, they were not as effective as Gálveztown for the protection of New Orleans.[74]

With one hundred men Miró set out on June 17 and reached Natchez on July 1. After his engineer had surveyed the defenses and reported them in very bad condition, Miró declared that a garrison of three hundred was indispensable if the district and river traffic were to be protected at all.[75] He remained at Natchez until late in October, though Piernas had to come up and substitute for him during an illness. When he left, he reported that the reënforced garrison had reassured the people of the district.[76]

Miró felt that the Natchez district had been governed with unnecessary harshness. He had already released Parker Caridine and John Smith, whom Grand Pré had sent to prison in New Orleans upon suspicion of communicating with the fugitive rebels. Three men at New Orleans certified that Caridine was blameless, that he had refused a

---

[72] In 1736 and 1740.

[73] Miró to Gálvez, June 5, 1782, copy, translated in Houck, *op. cit.*, I, 214–218; Martin Navarro to José de Gálvez, June 4, 1782, No. 120, A. G. I., Sto. Dom., 2656; Miró to Cagigal, June 5 and 15, 1782, Nos. 23 and 27, A. G. I., Cuba, 1304.

[74] Miró to Gálvez, June 5, 1782, *loc. cit.*

[75] Piernas to Gálvez, June 22, 1782, No. 36, A. G. I., Cuba, 1377; Miró to Cagigal, July 6, 1782, No. 29, *ibid.*, 1304.

[76] Bouligny to Cagigal, October 7, 1782, No. 40, *ibid.;* Miró to Cagigal, November 2, 1782, No. 44, *ibid.*

commission, and had helped Samuel Bell to escape to New Orleans.[77] From Madame Cruzat, Miró had learned of English protest against the fines Grand Pré had imposed to compensate for the seizure of a boat while Blommart held the fort. They protested that he had confiscated more than twenty times the value of this boat.[78] He also proposed to release Mrs. Judah Holston, for whose return Colbert had offered five men. Mrs. Holston was old, she was charged merely with sheltering some of the fugitives, and some return was in order for the kindnesses shown to Madame Cruzat.[79] Gálvez approved this clemency but cautioned Miró to retain most of the relatives and friends of the rebels in order that retaliation would be possible if any prisoners in the Chickasaw country were mistreated.[80]

A more perplexing problem for the acting governor was in what fashion to negotiate with Colbert. Should he accept him as a regularly commissioned British officer waging regular warfare, or treat him as a rebel chieftain outside the pale of international relations? Though he realized that, in order to avoid a possible diplomatic dispute after the war, it might be best to give Colbert the benefit of the doubt, yet he resolved to refuse to deal with him, on the ground that by placing himself at the head of a band of rebels he had become an accomplice in their crimes and had forfeited whatever international standing he might once have possessed.[81] Accordingly, Blommart and the other Natchez prisoners were not released, and the men who had signed Colbert's parole of honor were advised to consider it null and void because Colbert was merely a rebel.

While at Natchez, Miró entered into no negotiations with Colbert for the exchange of prisoners, but he did write one letter of explanation. Colbert's captures were not war prizes, he insisted, because Colbert was not commissioned by his king to wage war. Furthermore, all West Florida had been surrendered to Gálvez. Blommart and the

---

[77] Miró to Gálvez, June 5, 1782, *loc. cit.*; certificate by Jacinto Gaillard, Samuel Bell, and Geo. Rapalje, 1782, A. G. I., Cuba, 9.
[78] [Declaration of Madame Cruzat], May 30, 1782, *op. cit.*; Grand Pré [list of 290 Natchez inhabitants, many fugitives from the district, fined 34 pesos each], May 6, 1782, A. G. I., Cuba, 193.
[79] Miró to Gálvez, June 5, 1782, *loc. cit.*
[80] Gálvez to Miró, July 21, 1782, *in* Houck, *op. cit.*, I, 232–234.
[81] Miró to Gálvez, June 5, 1782, *loc. cit.*

other men from Natchez were political prisoners, not military, as Colbert seemed to think, and consequently could not be exchanged. Any negotiations concerning them must be through the governor of Jamaica.[82]

I Receivd yours of the 29th July this day [Colbert replied] Wherein you mention as follows Concerning the late Inhabitents of the Notches Which you Term as Reb[els] & Signifys in your As I harbourd them Rebles. Now Sir you Ought to be the Last Person that Should Even mention Anything Of that Nature to me When you Upheld Mr. Willing in Robing & plundering the Inhabtents On the Missisippy before war was Ever declared between the Crown of great Brittain & his Catholick majisty notwithstanding I never mein to Uphold Or harbour Rebles Of Any kind. for those People that Left the notches I do not Look Upon them as Rebles Neither do I emagine they were ever your Subjects therefore I can but Look on them as Other Inglish Subjects. you Signify in your Letter as though I had no right to go to war Without an authaurity. I would have you to know that I have as much Authority to distress my kings Enymys As you have to mantain Notches Or Any Other place in behalf of your King therefore The Prisoners I now have & any Others I may take you may depend I shall Look On As prisoners of war & Keep Them As Such till proper Exchanges are made for them I am well Satisfyed with your Humanity in Regard Of not Setting the Indians On White People. I have prevaild With my Indians to make Peace both With you & the Americans & with all the world as it is proper that no Indians Ought to interfare with what Concerns none but white [Men.] As for the White People that Left Notches I much blame them for Not Remaining in Peace till war was desided between great Brittain & Spain. Do Not think that Capn. Blommart had no Authority for what he did for he as well as many Others had from Genl. Campbell— Therefore I desire you will Return the Prisoners I wrote for & at the Same time I shall Return those I have here. If not I shall detain them As Such further Orders— I shall Send Monsr. Laffunt to his Parents as he is A youth I wish Well & having No Oppirtunity Of Education here I would Not wish to keep him. I hope you will make Some Retalliation to the Indian that takes him in— If you Shauld have Any Occation to write Any More to me, Please to write in Inglish Or Send An Interpreter with it having None here

       I am Sir Yours &c
        JAMES COLBURT
       Captn. in his Majestys Serv.[83]

---

[82] Miró to Colbert, July 29, 1782, draft, A. G. I., Cuba, 182.
[83] Colburt [sic] to Miró, October 6, 1782, B. L., La. Coll., a copy in A. G. I., Cuba, 114.

Meanwhile, Madame Cruzat's husband had been busy at St. Louis undermining the position of the English in the Chickasaw country. Hearing that an attack on L'Abbadie's boat had been plotted, he sent Diego Blanco and twenty-five men to protect it. This force was dispatched on June 2, unfortunately a full month after Colbert captured the boat. On June 5 a party of Loups reached Ste. Geneviève from the Chickasaw nation with sure news that L'Abbadie's and Lafont's boats had been seized. Cruzat therefore sent Jacobo DuBreuil to Ste. Geneviève to take suitable measures. DuBreuil dispatched Carlos Salle and eight men, who joined Blanco and his force and descended to the Margot, where they found Colbert's camp deserted. They burned the log prison and returned to Ysla del Buey (Ox Island) near the mouth of the Ohio.[84]

DuBreuil also sent some Loups, Peorias, and Kaskaskias into the Chickasaw country to recover the Spanish prisoners and to remove the menace to use of the river. These Indians returned with three soldiers of the Arkansas garrison who had been captured on the River of San Francisco on January 11, a civilian captured on the same boat, another from Lafont's boat, and a soldier taken by Colbert at Mobile on June 5, 1780. These Indians reported that six Chickasaw chiefs and a number of warriors had promised in the name of Panimatajá not to try to help the rebels and pirates, but to try to expel the bandits from their territory. Cruzat promised them reciprocal generosity.[85] Cruzat had also gathered a party of Kickapoos and Mascoutens, had told them that the Chickasaws and rebels had seized the boat with *their* presents, and incited them to avenge a theft which was really against themselves. Although this party had not returned, Cruzat attributed to it the willingness of the Chickasaws to surrender these six captives, the only ones they had. The Chickasaw chiefs asked Cruzat to dissuade the northern Indians from attacking them, and he promised to do so if the Chickasaws would agree to his conditions, which they very gladly did.[86] Here was a method, less expensive than a frontal attack, for reducing the menace of Colbert and his English "pirates."

---

[84] Cruzat to Miró, August 8, 1782, B. L., La. Coll.
[85] *Ibid.*
[86] *Ibid.*

So far as the Natchez prisoners were concerned, the Chickasaw uprising brought them harsher treatment instead of release. Blommart and his fellows had been treated leniently. From one of the most prosaic of documents—a board bill—it appears that they were allowed to live in more comfortable quarters than the *calabozo*. Edm. Connelly presented a bill amounting to 829 pesos, 2 reales, for Blommart's board and wine from June 27, 1781, to April 8, 1782, and for Eason, Williams, and Benjamin's board to August 5, 1781.[87] A more romantic document reveals the discomfort that Colbert's seizures produced for Blommart. It is the plea of his daughter on the eve of the proposed removal of the Natchez prisoners to the islands.

... in the hour of taking leave perhaps forever, of my fond, tender and affectionate Father, The unfortunate Mr. Blomart—I dare not (however much I wish it) petition for Pardon, but let me at least intercede with Your Excellency for Your Compassion in so far as to Order his Irons to be taken off. This will be an act of great pity, and give much Relief and Ease to him, and my consolation will be extreme.[88]

Unfortunately, Miró's response has not been discovered. The Spanish plans, however, changed very shortly. Removal of the prisoners from New Orleans, which had been thought advisable for their safe-keeping, was adjudged unnecessary after all, and they were held at the capital until the last of April, 1783.

When Spain, England, and France drew up preliminary articles for a treaty to conclude the war in January, 1783, the imprisonment of the Natchez leaders acquired a different complexion. The court had already approved Gálvez' leniency to these men in refraining from executing upon them the severe penalties which justice would countenance for their treason.[89] In April the arrival at Jamaica of Prince William, Duke of Lancaster, afforded Gálvez the occasion for a more striking display of generosity. The letters they exchanged are self-explanatory.

The Spanish troops stationed at this camp [Gálvez wrote] have not had the good fortune which the French had of taking arms to show your high-

---

[87] Edm. Connelly, [bill], April 6, 1782, A. G. I., Cuba, 193.
[88] Ann Blommart to Miró, November 19, 1782, *ibid.*, 191.
[89] José de Gálvez to Gálvez, November 20, 1782, No. 186, *ibid.*, 175.

ness the honor which they would accord you, or to give any proof of the high respect and consideration that is due you, a sentiment they hold eternally. But, Sir, I have in prison at New Orleans the chief of the Natchez rebellion with some of his accomplices, who, having broken their word and their oath of fealty, are condemned to death by a council of war on the basis of just and equitable laws; the execution of the sentence waits only the approval that I am empowered to give as governor of that colony.[90] These culprits are all English. Would your highness like to accept the thanks and the lives of these men, in the name of the army and of my sovereign? I believe, Sir, that this present is the most appropriate that could be offered to one prince in the name of another; I know that my extremely generous prince will approve it. If your highness would deign to be concerned for them, I have the honor to enclose an order for them to be handed over at once to whatever vessel your highness may send to Louisiana to make known your will. Great satisfaction will be ours, if by this means we shall have succeeded in doing something that pleases your highness.

I have the honor, etc.,
Bdo. de Gálvez [rubric][91]

Prince William accepted the present with ardent appreciation.

I want words to convey to your Excellency the just Sense I entertain of the delicate manner in which you was pleased to transmit me your very polite letter, and of your generous conduct towards those unhappy objects, Whose punishment you have thought proper to remit on my account: A present of all others, the most acceptable to me, and truly characteristic of such a Brave and Gallant Nation as the Spanish, and which I consider as an additional proof of that generosity of Sentiment which your Excellency has in so many instances displayed in the course of the late war.

Admiral Rowley wil dispatch a Vessel to Louisiana to fetch these prisoners, who I trust will ever remember with gratitude your clemency. I have sent to the King my Father a Copy of your letter, who I am sure, will feel your Excellencys attention to me.

I desire my compliments to Madame de Galvez together with the assurance that your Excellencys attention will ever be remembered by

William Henry[92]

---

[90] This may have been true, but I have found no record that the case was prosecuted this far.

[91] Gálvez to "Serenissimo Principe Guillermo, Duque de Lancaster," April 6, 1783, certified copy, A. G. I., Ind. Gen., 1578.

[92] [Prince] William Henry to Gálvez, April 13, 1783, *ibid*.

Gálvez had already dispatched an order to New Orleans that the Natchez prisoners should be released "on the single condition that under no excuse shall they return to the territory of that colony."[93] On April 28 the six prisoners signed a parole not to leave New Orleans until authorized by the governor, and Miró granted them full liberty of the town.[94] Shortly thereafter an English ship arrived to carry them to Jamaica, and the incident was closed except for the Spanish court's approval of their release and the manner of their release.[95]

In the Chickasaw country, however, to which news came tardily of the peace negotiations and of Blommart's release, Colbert made one last outburst. At the head of one hundred whites and forty Indians he advanced on Fort Carlos III of Arkansas, and captured Lieutenant Luis Villars, ten soldiers, and four of the principal inhabitants of the Arkansas village. The other six escaped to the fort. Colbert summoned the fort to surrender, but DuBreuil resisted. He had only four Arkansas Indians and forty soldiers, but the fort was strongly built and of hard wood. Colbert kept the fort besieged from April 17 to April 24. Then, receiving warning that Spaniards and Indians were coming to the rescue, he withdrew, releasing all his prisoners except four soldiers, the son of one villager, and three slaves.[96]

Undismayed by the faithlessness of L'Abbadie and the others whom he had released on parole eleven months earlier, Colbert allowed Villars to go to New Orleans on his word of honor. Villars obligated himself as a prisoner of war to have released in exchange for his own freedom "Blommart, Jacob Winfret, Jean Olsen [Alston], William Eton [Eason], and William Williams." If these men were not at New Orleans, he promised to find out where they were and inform Colbert.

---

[93] Gálvez to the acting governor of Louisiana, April 5, 1783, No. 88, copies, A. G. I., Cuba, 1377, and Ind. Gen., 1578.

[94] Parole signed by J. Blommart, Jacob Winfree, Will Eason, John Alston, W. L. Williams, Saml. Benjamin, April 28, 1783, A. G. I., Cuba, 196.

[95] José de Gálvez to Gálvez, June 24, 1783, *ibid.*

[96] DuBreuil to Miró, May 5, 1783, copy, *ibid.*, 2360; Colbert to DuBreuil, April 17, 1783, copies, *ibid.*, 2360 and 107. The declaration of one of Colbert's prisoners released just before this episode reveals the more important men of Colbert's following: Simon Burney, Ziblan Mathews, James Clonketin, Juan Hosten, Ricardo Hall, Betnigo Swallen, Patricio Rogers, Joel Starn, James Mchim, William Windrigth, and Patricio Maar. Declaración de Henoc Wales, April 9, 1783, *ibid.*, 196.

If he failed to secure their release, he promised to surrender to Colbert by August 1 or to pay a ransom of two thousand piastres.[97]

Of course, when Villars reached New Orleans, the Natchez prisoners had been released to Prince William, and thus he was saved the predicament of surrendering again to Colbert, ransoming himself with two thousand piastres, or breaking his parole as the others had done. Miró wrote to Colbert berating him for his latest violence and charging that it was undertaken after peace had been agreed upon and that it was not legitimate by the laws of war. He called upon Colbert to surrender all remaining prisoners immediately.[98]

Colbert replied on August 3, employing an amanuensis whose French was barbarous. Reminding Miró that three months and twelve days had elapsed before news of the peace reached him, he insisted that he had released his prisoners as soon as he learned of the truce. He had called on the Chickasaws to liberate any they held; their reply was that they had sent several the preceding summer by the Kaduké [Cadoucas] and Loups on condition that Cruzat would deliver to them some of their people held prisoners by the Kickapoos. Loving their own people as much as Miró loved his fellow-Spaniards, they were surprised and dejected that Cruzat did not live up to his agreement. Colbert expressed gratification over Blommart's release and departure for Jamaica, and he announced that since he was about to start for St. Augustine to render account to his superior, further negotiations would be postponed until his return.[99]

This letter, however, marks the end. Colbert went to St. Augustine, and "concerning demands that was made on him by the Governor of New Orleans for damages he did on the Mississippi he got full powers to Clear up that Complaint." But three days after he left McGillivray's house on the return journey, "his horse threw him down and Killd him before his Servant could assist him."[100]

---

[97] Villars [parole], April 24, 1783, copy, A. G. I., Cuba, 2360.

[98] Miró's letter is referred to in Colbert to Miró, August 3, 1783, A. G. I., Cuba, 196, and in DuBreuil to Colbert, July 25, 1783, *ibid.*, 107.

[99] Colbert to Miró, August 3, 1783, A. G. I., Cuba, 196.

[100] McGillivray to O'Neill, January 7, 1784, *ibid.*, 197.

The verdict of history probably will be that Blommart, Colbert, and their followers engaged in quixotic schemes. Though one holds that a miss is as bad as a mile, in fairness one must note that Blommart's venture might have had a different outcome had it not been for the explosion of the powder magazine at Pensacola on May 8, and that if Colbert had held his prisoners instead of trusting them with paroles he probably would have compelled the release of Blommart. Certainly the Louisiana authorities did not dismiss the menace lightly. Gálvez and Miró regarded the successive rebellions as serious problems. Gálvez paid Blommart the compliment of making a special trip to New Orleans, which delayed his arrival at Havana at least two months. He submitted to this delay in spite of the fact that the call to the islands was for a very important commission, namely, the organization of an attack upon Jamaica and the Bahamas.[101] Miró responded personally the next summer when Colbert's uprising threatened Natchez, and he spent four months there getting this insurrection under control. Such official cognizance proves that the Natchez-Chickasaw rebellions deserve notice as a major menace to Spanish control on the left bank of the Mississippi.

In comparison to O'Reilly's punishment of the insurrectionists a dozen years earlier when six lives were exacted for a bloodless revolt against Spain's vaguely asserted authority, Gálvez displayed great leniency. The Natchez rebellion was against fully constituted authority, for Spain had controlled the district a year and a half, had garrisoned the fort, and exacted an oath of fidelity from the inhabitants. The Natchez rebellion, furthermore, was no mere flourish; the Spanish flag was fired upon, a Spanish fort captured, and Spanish blood shed. Yet Gálvez took pains to reassure the populace, moderated the punishment of the leaders, and within two years released even them.

---

[101] Gálvez to José de Gálvez, August 17, 1781, No. 1, A. G. I., Ind. Gen., 1578; see below, Chapter XIV.

CHAPTER XIV

THE CLOSE OF GÁLVEZ' CAREER

IMMEDIATELY AFTER THE CAPTURE of Pensacola, Gálvez was ordered to the islands to undertake the conquest of Jamaica.[1] The Natchez rebellion called him to New Orleans and prevented his departure for a few months, and there was further vexatious delay in a forty-day passage to Havana, but by the end of August, 1781, the new task had been taken up.[2]

Jamaica was much more of a stronghold than Pensacola had been. The English had controlled the island for a century and a quarter, had fortified Port Royal, and counted it their most important and staunchest naval base in the entire Caribbean and Gulf district. For its reduction Gálvez obviously would need a much larger landing force than the one employed at Pensacola, and also a supporting fleet adequate to overcome the English ships stationed there. Any attack on Jamaica, furthermore, would not be a surprise, since after the fall of Pensacola the English were only in doubt whether the Spaniards would next attack St. Augustine, the Bahamas, or Jamaica.

Gálvez began his preparations much as he had for his Gulf Coast campaigns. He first gathered as reliable information as possible about the defensive arrangements of his opponents. He sent Francisco de Miranda, soon to be the precursor of Spanish American independence, as a spy. Nominally, Miranda was to arrange for an exchange of prisoners, and he did conclude these negotiations successfully, some 22 officers and 850 men being returned to Cuba through his instrumentality.[3] But in pursuance of secret orders Miranda also reported on the

---

[1] José de Gálvez to the governor of Havana, October 18, 1780, copy, A. G. I., Cuba, 1290.

[2] Gálvez to José de Gálvez, August 17, 1781, No. 1, A. G. I., Ind. Gen., 1578; Cagigal to José de Gálvez, August 17, 1781, No. 62, A. G. I., Sto. Dom., 2083.

[3] Convention for the exchange of prisoners, November 18, 1781, A. G. I., Cuba, 1330.

martial forces of Jamaica: the regulars, militia, negroes, cavalry, beasts of burden, the inhabitants. He described the maritime forces, the ships on hand, those expected, their guns, etc. In addition, he submitted maps of Jamaica, of Port Antonio, and of the bays of Kingston and Port Royal.[4]

This is not the place to follow in full detail the story of Gálvez' preparations for the Jamaica campaign.[5] The story would prove about as interesting as the usual description of military preparations, bereft, however, of the glamor that we read back into the preliminaries to successful adventures. For the attack on Jamaica never materialized. A large force was mobilized at Guarico on the island of Española, and ships, munitions, and supplies were gathered, but a series of difficulties arose to make the plans miscarry. The Natchez rebellion was the first delaying circumstance. Then the revolt of the *comuneros* in New Granada called away seven ships and a regiment of soldiers.[6] Another postponement was necessary because the French who were to coöperate were tardy in completing their preparations at Martinique.[7] Rodney's victory over De Grasse brought the whole project to a standstill because it gave England naval supremacy in the Caribbean and made Gálvez' and the French armies ineffectual. Perhaps with exaggeration Rodney wrote, "Had not Providence ordained that His Majesty's arms should be successful against the French Fleet, and an opportunity given of Bringing them to battle, Jamaica must have been lost."[8] Prospects of success revived after Spain abandoned the siege of Gibraltar, but before the sea forces thus released could reach the West Indies, peace had interposed a final obstacle in the way of the conquest of Jamaica.

Though balked in this major undertaking, Gálvez found a lesser project feasible. In January of 1782 he communicated to Cagigal the

---

[4] Cagigal, Extracto de los servicios que ha hecho en su viage á la ysla de Jamayca el Teniente Coronel dn. Franco. de Miranda, January 6, 1782, A. G. I., Sto. Dom., 1234; Cagigal to José de Gálvez, January 22, 1782, reservada, No. 22, *ibid.*

[5] See especially Gálvez' letters to José de Gálvez, 1781–1783, A. G. I., Ind. Gen., 1578 and 1579.

[6] *Idem* to *idem*, December 31, 1781, reservada, No. 9, A. G. I., Ind. Gen., 1578.

[7] *Idem* to *idem*, December 31, 1781, reservada, No. 10, *ibid.*

[8] Rodney to Archibald Campbell, Historical Manuscripts Commission, *op. cit.*, II, 525; Gálvez to José de Gálvez, June 30, 1782, A. G. I., Ind. Gen., 1578.

royal order to abate the privateer nuisance centering at New Providence in the Bahamas and appointed him to lead the expedition.[9] Cagigal's army was mobilized almost at once, but the naval authorities offered one excuse after another for dilatoriness in providing ships to convoy the transports. Finally, in desperation it would seem, Cagigal accepted the offer of Captain Alexander Gillon, of the American privateer "South Carolina," to safeguard the fleet on its way to the Bahamas.[10]

Sailing from Havana on April 22, Cagigal arrived off New Providence on May 6. At 6 p.m. he called on Governor Maxwell to surrender, giving him just twelve hours in which to contemplate alternatives. At 7:40 Maxwell agreed that terms of surrender should be arranged, though he asserted, "This is surely the hardest service that I have ever undertaken as a soldier," and at 5 the following morning he sent a representative with proposed articles of capitulation. Cagigal pondered these in conection with his instructions, and then sent his aide-de-camp, Francisco de Miranda, to arrange the final provisions. They were signed on May 8, Maxwell surrendering his entire force and turning over to the Spaniards all the Bahama Islands that were occupied by the English. Cagigal reported that his only loss was one schooner captured by a Charlestown privateer and that the prize was greater than expected because reënforcements and additional supplies had arrived from Charlestown just before the Spanish force appeared.[11]

By the terms of surrender the English troops were permitted to go anywhere except to Jamaica. American criticism of the terms of some of Gálvez' earlier paroles was avoided by the requirement that these soldiers were not to serve against any of England's enemies until exchanged.[12] A statement of the population of the Bahamas indicates

[9] Gálvez to Cagigal, January 20, 1782, A. G. I., Sto. Dom., 2085.

[10] Cagigal to José de Gálvez, March 14, 1782, reservada, No. 27, *ibid.*, 1234; Gillon to Cagigal, January 16–April 5, 1782, Nos. 7–13, A. G. I., Cuba, 1318.

[11] Cagigal to Maxwell, May 6, 1782; Maxwell to Cagigal, May 6 and 7, 1782; Cagigal to Maxwell, May 7, 1782; Maxwell and Cagigal, articles of capitulation, May 8, 1782; Cagigal to Juan Dabán, May 18, 1782; Cagigal to Gálvez, May 20, 1782: certified copies, A. G. I., Sto. Dom., 2085.

[12] Articles of capitulation, May 8, 1782, *ibid.*

more than three thousand persons, the majority at New Providence.[13] The garrison comprised 274 regulars and 338 militiamen, while the inventory of martial supplies indicates 199 cannon, 868 muskets, 41 hundredweight of powder, besides balls and shells.[14] The most important gain, however, was the capture of 12 privateers and 65 merchant vessels. During the war these privateers had made prizes of 14 Spanish, 24 French, 1 Dutch, and 137 American vessels.[15]

In an earlier communication Cagigal had commented on the unwisdom of dividing authority between a military and a naval officer.[16] Soon after the surrender of Providence his fears were realized. A difference of opinion arose with the American captain. Gillon expressed a desire to pursue some British vessels reported in the Florida channel; Cagigal urged that he stay to protect the Spanish transports.[17] Gillon left in a huff, and Cagigal had to beseech Spanish naval protection from Havana. A junta deliberated and ordered that two frigates should be despatched at once, and fortunately they arrived before any accident had befallen Cagigal's transports or garrison at New Providence.[18]

The authorities in Spain, however, raised the embarrassing question, Why had Gálvez and Cagigal disregarded the royal orders not to coöperate with the Americans "both because of the bad example to our colonies and because of the impropriety of our king aiding a revolt"? Besides reflecting on the honor of the Spanish navy, the use of an American escort had made a dispute possible over control and possession of the Bahamas, and Gillon's desertion had jeopardized Cagigal's entire force as well as his conquests.[19] In answer Gálvez and Cagigal pleaded the saving to the royal treasury through utilizing

---

[13] Estado que manifeste ... el numero de Avitantes, May 8, 1782, *ibid*.

[14] Estado que manifeste las fuerzas ... , May 8, 1782, *ibid*.

[15] *Idem*.

[16] Cagigal to José de Gálvez, March 14, 1782, reservada, No. 27, A. G. I., Sto. Dom., 1234.

[17] Gillon to Cagigal, May 8, 1782, translation, A. H. N., Consejo, 20,170–4; Cagigal to Gillon, May 9, 1782, copy, *ibid*.

[18] Cagigal to Dabán, May 18, 1782, certified copy, A. G. I., Sto. Dom., 2085; Dabán to José de Gálvez, May 27, 1782, copy, A. H. N., Consejo, 20,170–4.

[19] El Marqués de Gonzz. de Castejon to José de Gálvez, October 15, 1782, A. G. I., Sto. Dom., 2085; José de Gálvez to Gálvez, November 10, 1782, copy, *ibid*.; José de Gálvez to González de Castejon, Novembr 28, 1782, draft, *ibid*.

the American ships. They maintained that the Spanish islands had been left more secure since none of the protecting fleet had been drawn away with the expedition. They denied that the expedition had become semi-American, insisting that it was "Español, y muy Español."[20] They hesitated, apparently, to stress the procrastination and reluctance to coöperate on the part of the Spanish naval authorities, but these were obviously factors in the acceptance of Gillon's offer. The situation seems, in part at least, an echo of the naval-military feud at Pensacola.

Gálvez and his advisors contemplated other military actions in the closing months of the war, favoring especially a sudden descent upon St. Augustine or possibly upon Halifax,[21] but the armistice early in 1783 prevented these forays as well as the more ambitious Jamaica campaign. For Gálvez and for the Spanish operations in America the climax had come at Pensacola; the rest was merely dénouement.

Gálvez' conquests went far to determine the provisions of the peace treaties. England recognized her loss of the Gulf Coast and ceded East Florida as well as West Florida to Spain. Spain's recovery of the Floridas was to have manifold consequences, of which mention only is here possible. For example, the cession of the trans-Appalachian region to the United States was due more to England's loss of the Gulf Coast than to the prowess of American arms in the West. Another consequence was renewed Spanish interest in the affairs of the Southeastern Indians and strenuous efforts during the next two decades to enlist the support of these powerful tribes. The Spanish dispute with the United States over the Florida boundary was in reality an attempt to reap the full rewards of Gálvez' victories. Even the question of closing the Mississippi could arise only because Spain, through having the Floridas, controlled the other convenient outlets for the American West.[22]

The most obvious Spanish gain was the removal of the English menace along the Mississippi and Florida frontiers. This gain was

---

[20] Gálvez to José de Gálvez, June 7, 1783, No. 264, A. G. I., Sto. Dom., 2085; Cagigal to Gálvez, May 30, 1783, certified copy, *ibid*.

[21] José de Gálvez to Gálvez, November 16, 1781, reservada, No. 12, A. G. I., Cuba, 175.

[22] See Whitaker, *The Spanish-American Frontier, passim*.

fully appreciated. Ulloa had recognized the danger almost on the day of his arrival; it had determined O'Reilly's measures of defense; it had sent shivers up and down Unzaga's back in 1770 and 1776. To dispose of it had been the motive of Gálvez' campaigns, and, in fact, Spain's major American objective during the war. Now the Anglo-Spanish frontier had practically disappeared, except an insignificant segment in the far north. There, in the upper Missouri Valley and near the source of the Mississippi, English encroachments on the fur trade were feared and felt, but the danger was remote compared to the previous dread of English aggressions against New Orleans and the very vitals of Spanish America.

The prevailing tendency, nevertheless, is to commiserate Spain on the change that had taken place—to say that in exchanging English rivalry for competition with the United States she had jumped from the frying pan into the fire.[23] Quite possibly this view is correct. It seems to have been a tactical blunder on Spain's part to help create the new nation whose manifest destiny demanded growth at the expense of her neighbors. This conclusion, however, is much more evident after the experience of a century and a half than it was at the conclusion of the war with England. However correct it may be as a statement of what has actually happened, there is room to question its inevitability in 1783. To the men of that period, who shared the common lot of mankind in not being markedly endowed with powers of prescience, such a conclusion seemed unwarranted rather than inevitable. The issue turns upon whether or not the United States was created in full stature in 1776. A few utterances of the period have the ring of prophecy in pointing out the United States' magnificent potentialities for vigorous nationalism and expansion and dominance in the western hemisphere,[24] but the more generally accepted view was that they formed an infant nation in all senses of the adjective.[25] Accordingly Gálvez was praised not only for his conquests of territory but also for

---

[23] Whitaker, *op. cit.*, 3-4.

[24] Rippy has collected a few such statements under the heading, "Inklings of Manifest Destiny," in his *Latin America in World Politics*, 13-14.

[25] Fiske, *The Critical Period in American History, passim;* McMaster, *A History of the People of the United States,* I, *passim.*

his important service in securing for Spanish Louisiana an American instead of an English frontier.

This is not to say that there was no concern about the proximity of the Americans. As early as 1780 Intendant Navarro expressed this sentiment:

> The location of the Americans at the entrance of the Belle Rivière [the Ohio], or, to speak better, on the shores of the Mississippi, gives us a motive to reflect very seriously on this particular. Although the English posts no longer exist, we must count upon new enemies[26] who are regarding our situation and happiness with too great jealousy. The intensity with which they are working to form a city and establish posts, and their immediate neighborhood to our posts of the Illinois may be harmful to us some day, unless we shelter ourselves in time by promoting a numerous population in this province in order to observe and even to restrain their intentions.[27]

But Spain seems not to have worried so much about the dangerousness of the Americans per se, as about the pernicious example of revolt that they had set for the Spanish American colonies. This latter concern was the real reason for her refusal to enter into an alliance with the United States.[28]

Gálvez' military campaigns had accomplished another purpose, that of completing the establishment of Spanish control over Louisiana. The first rumors of transfer to Spain had called forth a burst of protest in the colony. Ulloa's maladroitness augmented this dissatisfaction until it culminated in the insurrection of 1768. O'Reilly quashed the insurgency with promptitude and vigor, earning for himself a degree of opprobrium among the creoles that was to be magnified by a later

---

[26] This statement was made in 1780, when the United States and Spain were both at war with England! Serrano y Sanz suggests 1782 as the date of the letter (*Documentos Históricos de la Florida y la Luisiana*, 361–379), and Robertson gives 1785 (*Louisiana under the Rule of Spain, France, and the United States*, I, 241–274). Internal criticism of the document would indicate the fall of 1780 or the spring of 1781 as the proper date. There is reference to Clark's campaign of 1779 (Robertson, *op. cit.*, I, 247), to the hurricane of August, 1780 (*ibid.*, 254), and to the "newly conquered district of Natchez" (*ibid.*, 256). But Navarro also mentions "the prospect of capturing Pensacola" (*ibid.*, 253). A certified copy of the document in the Bancroft Library bears the date, September 24, 1780.

[27] Robertson, *op. cit.*, I, 247.

[28] Grimaldi to Arranda, quoted in Doniol, *Histoire de la Participation de la France à l'Etablissement des Etats-Unis d'Amérique*, II, 192; Winsor, *Narrative and Critical History of America*, VII, 54.

generation. But when he left the colony, he had not a few friends there and Spain had many loyal supporters. Unzaga's mild benevolence soothed the wounded feelings and furthered reconciliation. Finally, in the war with England, when the colonists were drawn toward Spain by the mutual animosity toward England, Gálvez' compelling personality, his youth, his warmth, his valor, not to mention his Louisiana wife, drew the creoles into ardent support of Spain. O'Reilly had imposed Spanish rule. Gálvez, by more subtle means, acquired dominion over the hearts of the Louisianians.

At the end of the war Louisiana found herself the beneficiary of a relaxation in trade regulation. Though sometimes named as another consequence of Gálvez' campaigns,[29] this concession seems rather to have come about through his recommendations. He convinced the court that Louisiana's existence as well as her prosperity depended upon a trade that Spain was totally unable to provide. England or the United States could furnish it, but to grant to either of these nations privileges in Louisiana would nullify the gains of the war. Instead, Spain should turn to her Catholic and absolutist ally, France, and countenance commerce between Louisiana and her former mother country.[30] The sagacity of Gálvez' counsel is not materially impugned by its strong savor of nepotism. Its inspiration may have come through the desire of his father-in-law for permission to import French goods for the Indian trade in Louisiana and West Florida, but it was sound statesmanship nevertheless.[31]

Acting upon Gálvez' advice Spain announced that for a decade Louisiana and West Florida would be permitted to trade with France and under certain conditions with the French West Indies. There were a few minor qualifications, such as a 6 per cent duty on imports and exports and a 2 per cent duty on exports to other Spanish colonies,

---

[29] Gayarré, *op. cit.*, III, 154–155.

[30] Summary of a report by Governor Bernardo de Gálvez at New Orleans on October 24, 1778..., *in* Whitaker, *Documents Relating to the Commercial Policy of Spain in the Floridas*..., 11–21; summary of a representation by Gilbert Antoine de St. Maxent..., October 4, 1781, *ibid.*, 22–29.

[31] Whitaker, *op. cit.*, p. xxviii.

but the privilege of direct trade with a foreign nation was absolutely unprecedented in Spanish colonial practice.[32]

Immediately after the cessation of hostilities Gálvez returned to Spain. In the correspondence incident to his departure are some indications of the cordial relationship existing between him and the people under his jurisdiction. He took this opportunity to thank the Louisianians for urging the king to honor him with the title of Viscount of Gálveztown. Of the "gold fleur-de-lis on field of blue" that the king had approved for his coat of arms he was especially proud. "It will always be," he wrote them, "an incontestable proof of your love for me and a public testimony of my good conduct toward you."[33]

Another letter expresses the regard of the conquered English of West Florida.

> With the greatest Deference And Greatest Pleasure I take the liberty of Congratulating Your Excellency on Your Safe Arrival in Europe, with Madam Galvez and your fair Daughters; This is a tribute due by all who know you but more particularly by me & my family, who were happily distinguished with such Extraordinary Marks of Your Grace Countenance (& permit me to Say friendshipe) as we shall never forget, while we Exist....
>
> It has been my wish to have the Historicale Powers of Quintus Curtius, by whom Alexander the Great is Celebrated for his polite & Generous Treatment of the Queen, & Daughters of Darius, when they became Captives; His Greatness of Soule then shone forth withe uncommon Splendor, this was a Counterbalance to the Murder of Clytius; but as the Actions of all men are Judged by the Motives whence they Originate, the World may say (tho improperly) that Alexander's Behaviour to these Ladies was because they were Royale & Ranked with himself & from Pirsons in so Exalted a State, he Promised himself a greater Share of Glory than could be Expected from those of a Lower Rank.
>
> But this, Sir, Even this, Cannot be Said of *You,* when my wife & Daughters became Your Captives, they were as well treated as the Queen & Daughters of Darius were by Alexander. Nothing was wanting to make them forget theire Cares, & Misfortunes by the fate of War; in Order to Sooth their Tender Minds, You Brought along with you the Powerfull

---

[32] The cédula is printed in Spanish and in translation in Whitaker, *op. cit.*, 30-39; see also Antúnez y Acevido, *Memorias Históricas sobre la Legislación y Gobierno del Comercio de los Españoles con sus Colonias en las Indias Occidentales*, 37.

[33] Gálvez to the Louisianians, July 15, 1783, copy, A. G. I., Cuba, 196.

Assistance of Musick, tho' the Daily honour of Your Presence & Conversation was sufficient harmony.

In my own humble Impartiale Opinion You doe Merit more praise on this occasion than Alexander & in the General Opinion of all People here, Your humane disenterested treatment of all the British Subjects was truely noble & Reflects more glory & honour upon Spaniards (& indeed mankind) than if you had Conquered all America. . . .

I Doe humbly Request that Your Excellency will be pleased to Interest Yourself in Getting my Lands & Possessions Restored to me.[34]

Such fulsome praise obviously must be discounted. The concluding sentence suggests the appropriate rate.

Of the royal appreciation we have more tangible evidence. New honors, new titles, promotions, additional salaries, requests for advice and counsel—these were the tokens of the king's confidence. Gálvez was in Spain from September, 1783, until October, 1784. During these months Spain was formulating the policies that were to prevail on her new Mississippi and Florida frontiers. The questions of recognition of the United States, of the Florida boundary, of the use of the Mississippi, of American immigration into Spanish territory, of relations with the Southeastern Indians—these were some of the problems arising. Through his experience Gálvez was well fitted to give advice on these questions, and he was called upon frequently.[35]

Late in 1784 Gálvez returned to America, coming to Havana as captain general of Cuba and retaining also the governorship of Louisiana and the Floridas. He was at Havana only a short while,[36] long enough, however, to be of some assistance to Oliver Pollock. But upon the death of his father, Matías de Gálvez, he was sent to Mexico City to succeed him as Viceroy of New Spain. His full title had now come to be: Conde de Gálvez, Viscount of Gálveztown, Knight Pensioner of the Royal and Distinguished Order of Carlos III, Commander of Bolaños in the Order of Calatrava, Lieutenant General of the Royal Armies, Inspector General of all the Troops in America, Captain General of the Province of Louisiana and of the two Floridas, Viceroy,

---

[34] Arthur Neile to Gálvez, October 6, 1783, A. G. I., Cuba, 1377.

[35] For example, his letter to José de Gálvez relative to the Indian trade of the Floridas, December 20, 1783, printed in Whitaker, *op. cit.*, 38–41.

[36] From February 4 until the last of April, 1785.

Governor, and Captain General of the Kingdom of New Spain, President of its Royal Audiencia, Superintendent General of the Royal Estate and the Division of Tobacco, Judge Conservator of the latter, President of its Junta, and Subdelegate General of the Revenue of the Mails in this Kingdom.

Together with his wife and their three children[37] he arrived at Vera Cruz on May 21, 1785. He spent several days there, making a thorough inspection of the garrison, customhouse, squadrons of launches, and the fortress San Juan de Ulloa.[38] The viceregal party was received at Mexico City on January 17, "with the greatest pomp and jubilee," and that same day Gálvez took the oath of office. According to the report of the *audiencia,*

> There was extraordinary and general delight among all the people and very complete approval on the part of all the ministers of this tribunal that God and the king had sent to these provinces for their best fortune and mutual happiness a chief so highly accredited in all the virtues, military, political, and personal....[39]

In Mexico as in Louisiana Gálvez attained remarkable popularity. His reputation for mild and enlightened government had preceded him. The memory of some ran back fifteen years to his dashing campaigns against the Apaches on the Nueva Vizcaya frontier, while all were mindful of his brilliance during the war just ended. His personality and the charm of Doña Felícitas, his wife, made popular acclaim almost inevitable.

Some of his actions added to the incipient popularity. Frost, crop failures, famine, and pestilence beset the Valley of Mexico during his rule, and to relieve the suffering Gálvez contributed the remainder of his father's estate augmented by 100,000 pesos which he borrowed for the purpose. Hearing one day that the public granary was empty, he rushed into the streets bareheaded and without an escort and hurried to the *alhóndiga* to arrange for the morrow's dole of maize to the desti-

---

[37] Miguel and Matilda, and their half-sister by their mother's former marriage, Adelaide d'Estrehan.

[38] Miguel de Corral to José de Gálvez, June 2, 1785, A. G. I., Mexico, 1512.

[39] The audiencia of Mexico to José de Gálvez, June 28, 1785, No. 197, *ibid*.

tute. In gratitude the populace escorted him back to his palace with an ardent ovation.[40]

On another occasion he chanced to meet three criminals on their way to the scaffold, and acceding to the importunities of the rabble he stayed the execution of the sentence and sent the prisoners instead to confinement at hard labor in Acapulco.[41] The king rather grudgingly approved this suspension of the sentence, but ordered the viceroy "to abstain from going out in public on the days and hours of executing sentences of capital punishment, and the deciding judge to notify him of the day and hour of execution."[42]

Gálvez' critics protested that this spontaneous act of executive clemency was a studied bid for popularity with the Mexicans. They remarked that in his conversations the viceroy frequently seemed to hint at the idea of Mexican independence and of a monarchy for which he would be the logical choice. They pointed out that he had discarded the reserve carefully maintained by the previous viceroys and associated freely with many of the creoles. They saw ulterior motives in his enrolling his son Miguel as an honorary private of grenadiers in the Corunna regiment, and in his invitation to the *ayuntamiento* of Mexico City to stand as sponsor of an expected child, who, if a girl, was to be named after the city's patron saint Guadalupe. They looked askance at the rebuilding of the viceroy's palace at Chapultepec suspiciously along the lines of a fortress. Bustamante, Alaman, and Gayarré repeat the charges of treason and give them a qualified endorsement, while Lacunza hints that the court, on the basis of such suspicion, had Gálvez poisoned.[43]

Others, including Humboldt, Bancroft, and Whitaker, find no basis for the accusations.[44] I find no evidence that the court gave credence

---

[40] Bustamante, "Suplemento," in Cavo, *Los Tres Siglos de Mexico*, III, 58.

[41] Gómez, "Diario," *Documentos para la Historia de Mexico*, ser. 2, III, 236; Bustamante, *op. cit.*, 62–65.

[42] Royal order to Gálvez, August 5, 1786, draft, A. G. I., Mexico, 1513.

[43] Bustamante, *op. cit.*, III, 65; Alaman, *Disertaciones sobre la Historia de la República Mejicana*, III, Appendix, 74–76; Gayarré, *op. cit.*, III, 165–166; Lacunza, *Discursos Históricos*, 528; Rivera, *Los Gobernantes de Mexico*, I, 457.

[44] Humboldt, *Essai Politique sur le Royaume de la Nouvelle Espagna*, I, 203; Bancroft, *History of Mexico*, III, 397–398; Whitaker, "Bernardo de Gálvez," *Dictionary of American Biography*, VII, 119–120.

to the charges or took them seriously. Indeed, with his uncle minister of the Indies and with the palpable evidences of royal favor that he had already received, it is hard to imagine Gálvez wishing to exchange the sure advantages of loyalty for the uncertainties of a revolutionary endeavor. Furthermore, at the end of his first year as viceroy the audiencia reported most favorably upon his rule and urged that he be continued in office.

The General Conde de Gálvez has the most glorious record of his conquests, exploits, and generous, gallant spirit in the many royal orders... with which your majesty has seen fit to perpetuate his great name and to augment the splendor of his very noble and ancient family. He has also received magnificent recognition from all Europe and from many of its princes, who have attested and honored his virtues and heroic actions.

Now New Spain would praise him and sing of a perfect viceroy, a most upright judge, and a father whose consolation has been received during calamities. The wisdom of his benevolent rule has resulted in effective arrangements for the total subjugation of the hostile Indians... in the Provincias Internas. At the same time he has been of the greatest importance to the state by his zeal for justice and for all that is conducive to the public welfare and happiness, by his humanity, and by an agreeableness and natural affability that enchants everyone and commands public confidence.

The royal audiencia concludes by petitioning your majesty that this North America may continue to flourish under his rulership, because such an auspicious beginning as marked the first year of his rule deserves him the viceroyalty for many years.

May God guard the important life of your majesty the many years that would serve the interests of church and state.[45]

And the king replied that he was "well satisfied with the prudent, proper, and active conduct of Conde de Gálvez, the present viceroy of that kingdom, and that he would continue him in that employ for the satisfaction and consolation of his subjects in New Spain, as long as he was not urgently needed for some other destination or charge."[46]

Popular esteem and royal approbation were not the only favors attending Gálvez' viceregal administration. To him was granted

---

[45] The audiencia of Mexico to the king, May 22, 1786, A. G. I., Mexico, 1513.
[46] The king to the audiencia of Mexico, August 18, 1786, draft, *ibid*.

wider jurisdiction than to any of his predecessors. Cuba, the Floridas, and Louisiana, though not parts of the viceroyalty of New Spain, were left under his authority. His power was likewise extended over the rest of the northern borderlands, which for some years had been administered separately by the commandant of the Provincias Internas. Gálvez therefore really ruled all Spanish North America. Pressure of viceregal problems and difficulties in communicating with these outlying provinces reduced his actual participation in their administration and left much responsibility with the local officials, yet his control was far more than a mere formality. The king's willingness to concentrate in Gálvez' hands such exceptional powers reflects not only his confidence but also his appreciation of the viceroy's wide experience in North America and the West Indies.

In the first year of his administration Gálvez made a promising beginning. His chief activity was in relieving the distress occasioned by crop failures and a fever epidemic, but he was also able to bring about improvements in frontier defense, the completion of the cathedral, the rebuilding of the viceregal palace at Chapultepec, and the establishment of a botanical garden. His term as viceroy so auspiciously begun, a favorite of the king, the idol of all classes at Mexico City, with power and prestige unrivaled by any other colonial official, he apparently was on the threshold of even greater success.

But death suddenly intervened. Early in the fall of 1786 after the epidemic of fever had apparently run its course, he was stricken as one of its last victims. Everything possible was done to bring about his recovery. There were rogations in the cathedral and the churches, while daily prayers for the beloved ruler were offered in almost every household. His medical advisers recommended a change of air, and so he was moved in a litter to Tacubaya on October 31. But all efforts were unavailing. He was so weak on November 8 that he surrendered the government to a regent.[47] The same day he made his will. On the sixteenth the sacrament of extreme unction was administered, and

---

[47] Gálvez to Francisco Fernández Córdova, November 8, 1786, certified copy, A. G. I., Mexico, 1512.

two weeks later, at a quarter past four on the morning of November 30, he died.[48]

His untimely death—he was only thirty-eight—was received with general and genuine lamentations. The audiencia confessed itself "overwhelmed by grief and confusion in the unexpected great loss of its just, prudent, magnanimous, and beloved viceroy president,"[49] while the archbishop wrote, "All the kingdom of New Spain is filled with mourning and tears and overwhelmed by the deepest sadness because of the unlooked for death of its most beloved viceroy."[50]

Church and state and people united to make his funeral a tribute to his memory. The religious had a special regard for Gálvez because he had brought about the completion of the cathedral, a task suspended for more than a century though repeatedly ordered finished. The archbishop directed the service, and the cathedral chapter spared no effort or expense to make the funeral "most decorous and magnificent,... a public testimony of the singular love and respect that the foremost church of America professed toward his excellency Señor Don Bernardo." At the request of the cabildo his remains were deposited temporarily in the cathedral's "most distinguished sepulchre," and a year later were transferred to the San Fernando church where they were placed beside his father's.[51]

No more touching proof of Gálvez' place in the affections of his subjects could have been given than the honors lavished upon the daughter born on the eighth day after the funeral. The archbishop christened, baptized, and confirmed the infant a week later, with "la nobilísima ciudad de México" as one of the sponsors. In accordance with her father's wish she was christened María de Guadalupe, Bernarda, Felipa de Jesus, Isabel, Juana Nepomucena, Felícitas, y Fernanda. The interest shown by all the people and the prodigality of the

---

[48] *Gazeta de Mexico, 1786-1787*, II, 251-252; Bancroft, *op. cit.*, III, 398.

[49] The audiencia of Mexico to José de Gálvez, December 1, 1786, A. G. I., Mexico, 1512.

[50] The archbishop of Mexico, November 30, 1786, *ibid.*, 1513.

[51] Franco. Martz. Cavezon and Juan Antonio de Yermo to José de Gálvez, December 2, 1786, *ibid.*, 1512.

presents made this "the grandest performance of its kind hitherto witnessed in Mexico."[52]

Thus the meteoric career of Bernardo de Gálvez came to its close. The king provided liberal pensions for the widow, the three daughters, and the only son, Miguel. Miguel, however, died before reaching manhood, and so the "Yo Solo" on Gálvez' escutcheon proved sadly prophetic as well as commemorative.

---

[52] From the city, mother and babe received pearl necklaces valued at eleven thousand and four thousand pesos; from both the archbishop and the godfather a gold plate, knife, fork, and spoon. The vicereine gave the godmother dress material to the value of one thousand pesos, the godfather rich material for two dresses, the archbishop a pectoral of diamonds and a gold box studded with emeralds, and Francisco Crespo (who represented the city) a diamond-garnished, gold-headed cane. Gómez, "Diario," *op. cit.*, 252–253, 261; Bancroft, *op. cit.*, III, 399–400.

BIBLIOGRAPHY

MANUSCRIPT SOURCES

THE MANUSCRIPT MATERIALS upon which this monograph is based were found for the most part in the Archivo General de Indias at Seville. Other repositories yielded many important documents, especially the Bancroft Library at Berkeley, the Library of Congress at Washington, the Archivo Histórico Nacional at Madrid, and the Henry E. Huntington Library at San Marino, California.

Letters written by and addressed to Spanish officials in the mother country and in the colonies constitute the greater part of this material, but a fair fraction was sent or received by English, French, or Americans. Enumeration of the items would run into tens of thousands; hence a complete list is out of the question. Instead, there follows an approximately chronological list of the larger items and of the more significant series of correspondence. Archival location is indicated by the same abbreviations as those used in the footnotes.

Ulloa-Grimaldi correspondence, A. G. I., Cuba, 174, Sto. Dom., 1215, 2542.

Ulloa-Bucareli correspondence, A. G. I., Cuba, 1054, 1055.

Ulloa's correspondence with Louisiana local officials, A. G. I., Cuba, 82, 109, 187 A, 188-1, 2357.

[Account of the Louisiana insurrection], 1768, A. G. I., Sto. Dom., 2543.

Manifeste des Habitans, negociants, et Colons de la Province de la Louisianne au sujet de la Revolution que est arrive le 29 8bre 1768, A. G. I., Cuba, 1054.

Nota de Personas de que se componia la familia con que se transporta á España dn. Antonio de Ulloa, December 14, 1768, A. G. I., Sto. Dom., 2542.

Joseph Melchor de Acosta, Relacion diaria, veridica, y circunstanciada de todas los acaecimientos havidos en la Colonia de la Luisiana, y Ciudad del Nuevo Orleans, desde 1º de Noviembre de 1768 que salió de ella su governador y Capitán Gñral. dn. Antonio de Ulloa hasta 20 de Abril de 1769 que salió la Fragata de mi mando nombrada el Volante, May 22, 1769, A. G. I., Sto. Dom., 1221.

Joseph Melchor de Acosta, Yndividuos que merecen el Rl. Desagrado, May 22, 1769, A. G. I., Cuba, 1054.

O'Reilly-Grimaldi correspondence, A. G. I., Cuba, 174, 2357, Sto. Dom., 1221, 2543; A. H. N., Consejo, 20,854.

O'Reilly-Arriaga correspondence, A. G. I., Cuba, 1055, Sto. Dom., 1221, 1223, 2543.

O'Reilly-Bucareli correspondence, A. G. I., Mexico, 1242, Cuba, 174, 1054, 1055.

O'Reilly-Munian correspondence, A. G. I., Mexico, 1242, Sto. Dom., 1220, 2543, 2656.

Bucareli-Arriaga correspondence, A. G. I., Sto. Dom., 1220, 1221, Ind. Gen., 1630.

O'Reilly's correspondence with Louisiana local officials, A. G. I., Cuba, 110, 134 A, 181–1, 1054, 1055, 2357, 2370.

Testimonio sacado por el Escrivano Francisco Xavier Rodríguez su fecha . . . de la sentencia dada y pronunciada por mi en 24 de Octubre de 1769 contra las Cavezas commovedores y principales complices de la conspiracion acaecida en esta Colonia el dia 29 de Octubre de 1768, A. G. I., Cuba, 81.

Francisco Xavier Rodríguez, De los meritos de la causa seguida en la Nueva Orleans . . . , October 29, 1769, A. G. I., Sto. Dom., 2543.

Aubry-Bucareli correspondence, A. G. I., Cuba, 1054, 1055.

O'Reilly-Unzaga correspondence, A. G. I., Cuba, 179, 181, 204, 2357.

Unzaga-Torre correspondence, A. G. I., Cuba, 1145, Sto. Dom., 1211.

Unzaga's correspondence with Arriaga and José de Gálvez, A. G. I., Sto. Dom., 2547, 2582, 2596, 2656.

Unzaga's correspondence with Louisiana local officials, A. G. I., Cuba, 81, 82, 110, 111, 112, 188, 189, 193, 585, 626, 630, 2357, 2358; B. L., La. Coll.

Unzaga's correspondence with English and Americans, A. G. I., Cuba, 112, 189, 573, 1336, 1355, 2357, 2370, Sto. Dom., 2596.

Israel Putnam, Journal of an exploring expedition to the Natchez—in the year 1773, L. C., copy made in 1845 from the original in the hands of Lemuel Grosvenor of Pomfret, Conn.

Testimonio del proceso contra Jph. Nach & Co., 1774, A. G. I., Sto. Dom., 2582.

Cuellar-José de Gálvez correspondence, A. G. I., Guad., 416; H. L., Gálvez Papers.

Fayni's correspondence with Croix, José de Gálvez, and Arriaga, A. G. I., Guad., 512.

Croix-Arriaga correspondence, A. G. I., Mexico, 1167, Guad., 416, 512.

Gálvez-Croix correspondence, A. G. I., Guad., 512.

Relacion que en Extracto ha remitido el Capn. Ynfanteria dn. Bernardo de Gálvez de los sucesos conseguidos pr. la Expedicion que bajo su comando se dispuso y salió desde la Villa de Chihuahua contra los Yndios Apaches, November 23, 1770, A. G. I., Guad., 416.

Extracto de los Diarios con que en Carta de 10 de Mayo ultimo ha informado al Virrey de Nueva España el Capitán Dn. Bernardo de Gálvez las ocurrencias y accion de la segunda Campaña que acababa de hacer contra los Barbaros Apaches, February 26, 1771, A. G. I., Guad., 512.

Gálvez-José de Gálvez correspondence, A. G. I., Cuba, 174, 175, 223 C, 569, 1375, 2351, 2359, Ind. Gen., 1578, 1579, Sto. Dom., 1218, 1243, 1595, 1598, 2083, 2084, 2543, 2574, 2596, 2656, 2661, 2662, Mexico, 1417, 1513; A. H. N., Estado, 3885; H. L., Gálvez Papers.

BIBLIOGRAPHY

Gálvez' correspondence with Louisiana local officials, A. G. I., Cuba, 1, 107, 112, 114, 173 C, 1376, 2351, 2358, 2360, Sto. Dom., 2547, 2661; B. L., La. Coll.

Gálvez' proclamations, A. G. I., Cuba, 1232, Sto. Dom., 2596; B. L., La. Coll.

Gálvez-Diego Joseph Navarro correspondence, A. G. I., Cuba, 1146, 1232, 1233, 2351, Sto. Dom., 2082, 2083, 2543.

Gálvez' correspondence with the English and Americans, A. G. I., Cuba, 9, 112, 114, 173 C, 182, 188, 191, 192, 193, 194, 196, 1232, 2351, 2358, 2359, 2370, Ind. Gen., 1578, Sto. Dom., 1598, 2596, 2656, 2661; B. L., La. Coll.

Gálvez-Willing-Pollock correspondence, A. G. I., Cuba, 88, 112, 122–1, 184, 191, 192, 193, 274, 569, 1232, 1233, 1354, 1374, 1377, 1393, 1469, 2351, 2370, Sto. Dom., 2553, 2596; L. C., Pollock Papers, and Papers of the Continental Congress.

Expedientes del Gobernador de la Luisiana sobre el comiso de once embarcaciones que hacian el comercio ilicito en el Rio Misisipi de aquella Provincia (1777–1788), A. G. I., Sto. Dom., 2652.

Leyba-Clark correspondence, A. G. I., Cuba, 1.

Diario general de todas las ocurrencias, y noticias que con motivo de la vajada de los Americanos por el Rio Misisipy han sobrevenido en la Provincia de la Luissiana ..., 1778, A. G. I., Cuba, 2351.

Junta de Guerra, New Orleans, July 13, 1779, A. G. I., Cuba, 112.

James Willing, oath administered to the settlers at Natchez, 1778, A. G. I., Cuba, 2351.

Articles of capitulation at Baton Rouge, September 21, 1779, A. G. I., Cuba, 197.

Diario que yo Dn. Bernardo de Gálvez Brigadier de los reales Extos. Governador de la Provincia de la Luisiana, y encargdo. por S. M. de la Expedicion contra Panzacola y Mobila forma de los acaecimientos qe. ocurren en ella, January 2–March 3, 1780, A. G. I., Cuba, 2351.

Diario de Estevan Miró, January 24–March 7, 1780, A. G. I., Sto. Dom., 2543.

Continuacion del Diario de la Expedicion de la Mobila formado por el Brigadier Dn. Bernardo de Gálvez Gobernador de la Prova de la Luisiana y Comte. Gral de dha. Expedicion, March 4–18, 1780, A. G. I., Cuba, 2351.

Articulos de la Capitulacion propuestos por Dn. Elias Durnford ... acordados por el Sor. Dn. Bernardo de Gálvez ..., March 13, 1780, A. G. I., Cuba, 2351.

Gálvez, Relacion de ... Prisioneros de Guerra en el sitio de la Mobila, March 20, 1780, A. G. I., Cuba, 2351.

Noticias dadas por Roberto Holmes Vecino y hacendado de Panzacola apresado á tres leguas de la Movila el dia 5 del preste. mes, 1781, A. G. I., Cuba, 2359.

Junta de Guerra, Havana, August 26, 1780, A. G. I., Sto. Dom., 2082.

Junta de Guerra, Havana, November 30, 1782, A. G. I., Sto. Dom., 2083.

Saavedra-José de Gálvez correspondence, A. G. I., Ind. Gen., 1578.

Robert Farmar, Journal of the Seige of Pensacola from the time the enemy's fleet first appeared to the 10th of May the day we surrendered to the arms of Spain, L. C.

Journal of Juan Delavillebeuvre, April 21–May 4, 1781, A. G. I., Cuba, 194.

Daybook of the Clerk of the Garrison & Works, Natchez, April 23–June 1, 1781, A. G. I., Cuba, 194.

Articles of capitulation, Pensacola, May 9, 1781, A. G. I., Cuba, 188–3.

Convention for the exchange of prisoners ... signed by John Dalling, Peter Parker, Francisco de Miranda, John Clements, Samuel Hodgson, November 18, 1781, A. G. I., Cuba, 1330.

Juan Manuel Cagigal, Extracto de los servicios que ha hecho en su viage á la ysla de Jamayca el Teniente Coronel dn. Franco. de Miranda, January 6, 1782, A. G. I., Sto. Dom., 1234.

Cagigal-José de Gálvez correspondence, A. G. I., Sto. Dom., 1206, 1218, 1234, 2085.

Cagigal-Miró correspondence, A. G. I., Cuba, 1304.

Gálvez-Cagigal correspondence, A. G. I., Sto. Dom., 2085.

Resultar des ventes publique des Biens des rebeldes fugitives et autres dans les prisons de la Nelle. Orleans, May 6, 1782, A. G. I., Cuba, 193.

Articles of capitulation, New Providence, May 8, 1782, A. G. I., Sto. Dom., 2085.

Estevan Robert de la Morandiere [Journal of the expedition against Natchez, May 25–July 13, 1781], A. G. I., Cuba, 2359.

Capitulation of John Blommart to Estevan de la Morandiere, June 28, 1781, A. G. I., Cuba, 173 C.

Declaracion de Señora Cruzat, May 30, 1782, A. G. I., Sto. Dom., 2656.

Declaracion de Silbestre L'Abbadie á Franco. Cruzat, July 5, 1782, B. L., La. Coll.

Colbert's correspondence with Gálvez and Miró, A. G. I., Cuba, 114, 2359; B. L., La. Coll.

Miró-Cruzat correspondence, B. L., La. Coll.

Audiencia de Mexico, correspondence with the king, A. G. I., Mexico, 1512, 1513.

PRINTED SOURCE MATERIALS

ADAIR, JAMES. *The History of the American Indian*. London, 1775.

ALVORD, CLARENCE WALWORTH, ed. *Cahokia Records, 1778–1790*. Springfield, 1907.

———. *Kaskaskia Records, 1778–1790*. Springfield, 1909.

ALVORD, CHARLES WALWORTH, and CARTER, CLARENCE EDWIN, eds. *The Critical Period, 1763–1765*. Springfield, 1915.

———. *The New Régime, 1765–1767*. Springfield, 1916.

BEER, WILLIAM, ed. "The Capture of Fort Charlotte," *Publications of the Louisiana Historical Society*, I (1895), No. 3, pp. 31–34.

BJORK, DAVID KNUTH, ed. "Alexander O'Reilly and the Spanish Occupation of Louisiana, 1769–1770," in *New Spain and the Anglo-American West* (Los Angeles, 1932), I, 165–182.

———. "Documents Regarding Indian Affairs in the Lower Mississippi Valley, 1771–1772," *Mississippi Valley Historical Review*, XIII (1926), 398–410.

——. "Documents Relating to Alexandro O'Reilly," *Louisiana Historical Quarterly*, VII (1924), 20–39.

——. "Documents Relating to the Establishment of Schools in Louisiana, 1771," *Mississippi Valley Historical Review*, XI (1925), 561–569.

BOLTON, HERBERT EUGENE, ed. *Athanase de Mézières and the Louisiana-Texas Frontier, 1768–1780.* 2 vols. Cleveland, 1914.

BURNETT, EDMUND CODY, ed. *Letters of Members of the Continental Congress.* 5 vols. Washington, D. C., 1921–1931.

CANADA. *Report on Canadian Archives, 1883–1905*, Douglas Brymner, ed. 24 vols. Ottawa, 1884–1906.

CANTILLO, ALEJANDRO DEL, ed. *Tratados, Convenios y Declaraciones de Paz y Comercio que han hecho con las Potencias Estranjeras los Monarcos Españoles de la Casa de Borbon.* Madrid, 1843.

CARTER, CLARENCE EDWIN, ed. *The Correspondence of General Thomas Gage.* New Haven, 1931.

CAUGHEY, JOHN WALTON, ed. "Alexander McGillivray and the Creek Crisis, 1783–1784," in *New Spain and the Anglo-American West* (Los Angeles, 1932), I, 263–288.

CHALMERS, GEORGE, ed. *A Collection of Treaties between Great Britain and Other Powers.* 2 vols. London, 1790.

"A Contemporary English View on the Trade and Prospects of New Orleans at the Close of the French Domination; an Extract from Jacob Blackwell, Observations on West Florida, (c. 1776)," *Louisiana Historical Quarterly*, VI (1923), 221–222.

CROIX, CHARLES FRANÇOIS, ed. *Correspondence du Marquis du Croix.* Nantes, 1891.

CRUZAT, HELOISE H., PORTEOUS, LAURA L., and JAMESON, J. FRANKLIN, translators. "Trial of Mary Glass for Murder, 1780," *Louisiana Historical Quarterly*, VI (1923), 589–654.

CUNNINGHAM, CHARLES H., ed. "Financial Reports Relating to Louisiana," *Mississippi Valley Historical Review*, VI (1919), 381–397.

DART, HENRY P., ed. "Fire Protection in New Orleans in Unzaga's Time," *Louisiana Historical Quarterly*, IV (1921), 201–204.

——. "A Louisiana Indigo Plantation on Bayou Teche, 1773," *ibid.*, IX (1926), 565–589.

——. "The Oath of Allegiance to Spain," *ibid.*, IV (1921), 215.

DEVRON, GUSTAVUS, ed. "Two Original and Newly Found Documents on the Departure, Shipwreck and Death of Mr. Aubry," *Publications of the Louisiana Historical Society*, II (1895), No. 1.

"Diary of the Operations of the Expedition against the Place of Pensacola, Conducted by the Arms of H. Catholic M., under the Orders of the Field Marshall Don Bernardo de Gálvez," *Louisiana Historical Quarterly*, I (1917), No. 1, pp. 44–84.

Documentos para la Historia de Mexico. 20 vols. 4 series. Mexico, 1853–1857.

"Documents Relating to the Attack upon St. Louis in 1780," in *Collections of the Missouri Historical Society*, II, 41–54.

FRENCH, BENJAMIN FRANKLIN, ed. *Historical Collections of Louisiana.* 5 vols. New York, 1846-1853.

———. *Historical Collections of Louisiana and Florida.* New York, 1869.

Gazeta de Madrid. 1768, 1774-1779, 1781-1786.

GREAT BRITAIN, HISTORICAL MANUSCRIPTS COMMISSION. *Report on American Manuscripts in the Royal Institution of Great Britain.* 4 vols. Dublin, 1904-1909.

HOUCK, LOUIS, ed. *The Spanish Régime in Missouri.* 2 vols. Chicago, 1909.

"Index to the Spanish Judicial Records," *Louisiana Historical Quarterly,* VI- (1923-).

JAMES, JAMES ALTON, ed. *George Rogers Clark Papers, 1771-1781.* Springfield, Ill., 1912.

———. *George Rogers Clark Papers, 1781-1783.* Springfield, Ill., 1926.

KINNAIRD, LAWRENCE, ed. "American Penetration into Spanish Louisiana," in *New Spain and the Anglo-American West* (Los Angeles, 1932), I, 211-237.

LEWIS, ANNA, ed. "Fort Panmure, 1779, as Related by Juan Delavillebeuvre to Barnardo [*sic*] de Galvez," *Mississippi Valley Historical Review,* XVIII (1932), 541-548.

MALLOY, WILLIAM, ed. *Treaties, Conventions, International Acts, Protocols, and Agreements between the United States of America and Other Powers, 1776-1923.* 3 vols. Washington, D. C., 1910-1923.

MARGRY, PIERRE, ed. *Découverture et établissements des Français dans l'ouest et dans le sud de l'Amerique Septentrionale, 1614-1754.* 6 vols. Paris, 1879-1888.

MIRÓ, ESTEVAN. "Representation upon the Limits of Louisiana Made to his Excellency the Duke of Alcudia," *Publications of the Louisiana Historical Society,* IX, 80-85.

NACHBIN, JAC, ed. "Spain's Report of the War with the British in Louisiana," *Louisiana Historical Quarterly,* XV (1932), 468-481.

NASATIR, A. P., ed. "St. Louis during the British Attack of 1780," in *New Spain and the Anglo-American West* (Los Angeles, 1932), I, 239-261.

"New Orleans and Bayou St. John in 1766; Extract from the Journal of Captain Harry Gordon," *Louisiana Historical Quarterly,* VI (1923), 19-20.

New Spain and the Anglo-American West, Historical Contributions Presented to Herbert Eugene Bolton. 2 vols. Los Angeles, 1932.

"Papers from the Canadian Archives, 1778-1783," *Collections of the Wisconsin State Historical Society,* XI (1889), 97-212.

PAULLIN, CHARLES OSCAR, ed. *Out-Letters of the Continental Marine Committee and Board of Admiralty, August, 1776-September, 1780.* 2 vols. New York, 1914.

PITTMAN, PHILIP. *The Present State of the European Settlements on the Mississippi.* London, 1770; Hodder, Frank Heywood, ed., Cleveland, 1906.

POLLOCK, OLIVER. "Deposition, June 8, 1808," *in* Wilkinson, *Memoirs of My Own Times,* II, Appendix I. 3 vols. Philadelphia, 1816.

PORTEOUS, LAURA L., ed. "Contract to Build a Ship in New Orleans, 1769," *Louisiana Historical Quarterly,* IX (1926), 593-597.

———. "Index to the Spanish Judicial Records," *Louisiana Historical Quarterly,* VI- (1923-).

BIBLIOGRAPHY

———. "A Suit for Debt in the Governor's Court, New Orleans, 1770," *Louisiana Historical Quarterly*, VIII (1925), 240–247.

———. "Torture in Spanish Criminal Procedure in Louisiana, 1771," *ibid.*, 5–22.

———. "Trial of Pablo Rocheblave before Governor Unzaga, 1771," *ibid.*, 372–381.

PRICE, EDITH DART, and CRUZAT, HELOISE H., eds. "Inventory of the Estate of Sieur Jean Baptiste Prevost, 1769," *Louisiana Historical Quarterly*, IX (1926), 411–498.

RANDOLPH, THOMAS JEFFERSON, ed. *Memoir, Correspondence, and Miscellanies from the Papers of Thomas Jefferson*. 4 vols. Charlottesville, Va., 1829.

The Remembrancer: or Impartial Repository of Public Events. 17 vols. London, 1775–1784.

Real Cédula de S. M. en que se erigen por ahora las provincias de la Luysiana, Panzacola, Movíla, y demás que poseián los Yngleses con el nombre de Florida Occidental, en Govierno, y Capitanía General independiente: y nombra por su primer governador, y capitan general al teniente general de los reales exercitos Don Bernardo de Galvez. Santa Fé de Bogota, 1782.

ROBERTSON, JAMES ALEXANDER, ed. *Louisiana under the Rule of Spain, France and the United States*. 2 vols. Cleveland, 1911.

———. "A Projected Settlement of English Speaking Catholics from Maryland in Spanish Louisiana, 1767, 1768," *American Historical Review*, XVI (1912), 319–327.

———. "Spanish Correspondence Concerning the American Revolution," *Hispanic American Historical Review*, I (1918), 299–316.

SERRANO Y SANZ, MANUEL, ed. *Documentos Históricos de la Florida y la Luisiana, Siglos XVI al XVIII*. Madrid, 1912.

———. *España y los Indios Cherokis y Chactas en la Segunda Mitad del Siglo XVIII*. Sevilla, 1916.

SPARKS, JARED, ed. *The Diplomatic Correspondence of the American Revolution*. 12 vols. Boston, 1825–1830.

STEVENS, BENJAMIN FRANKLIN, ed. *Facsimiles of Manuscripts in European Archives Relating to America, 1773–1783*. 25 vols. London, 1889–1895.

THWAITES, REUBEN GOLD, ed. *Jesuit Relations and Allied Documents*. 73 vols. Cleveland, 1912.

THWAITES, REUBEN GOLD, and KELLOGG, LOUISE PHELPS, eds. *Frontier Defense on the Upper Ohio, 1778–1779*. Madison, 1912.

———. *The Revolution on the Upper Ohio, 1775–1777*. Madison, 1908.

TURNER, FREDERICK JACKSON, ed. "Correspondence of the French Ministers to the United States, 1791–1797," *Annual Report of the American Historical Association*, 1903, II.

ULLOA, ANTONIO DE. *Noticias Americanas de los Territorios, Climas, y Producciones con Relación de las Petrifacciones de Cuerpos Marinos de las Antiquitades*. Madrid, 1772.

ULLOA, ANTONIO DE, and JORGE Y SANTACILLA, JUAN. *Observaciones astronomicas y phisicas hechas de orden de S. Mag. en los reynos del Perú*. Madrid, 1748.

———. *Relacion historica del viage a la America Meridional hecho de orden de S. Mag.* ... Madrid, 1748.

UNITED STATES OF AMERICA. *American State Papers.* 38 vols. Washington, D. C., 1832–1861.

———. *Journals of the Continental Congress, 1774–1783.* 25 vols. Washington, D. C., 1904–1922.

WHARTON, FRANCIS, ed. *A Digest of International Law of the United States.* 3 vols. Washington, D. C., 1887.

———. *The Revolutionary Diplomatic Correspondence of the United States.* 6 vols. Washington, D. C., 1889.

WHITAKER, ARTHUR PRESTON, ed. *Documents Relating to the Commercial Policy of Spain in the Floridas, with Incidental Reference to Louisiana.* Deland, Fla., 1931.

WILKINSON, JAMES M. *Memoirs of My Own Times.* 3 vols. Philadelphia, 1816.

WISCONSIN HISTORICAL COLLECTIONS. See "Papers from the Canadian Archives, 1778–1783."

PRINCIPAL SECONDARY MATERIALS

ABBEY, KATHRYN. "Efforts of Spain to Maintain Sources of Information in the British Colonies before 1779," *Mississippi Valley Historical Review*, XV (1928), 56–68.

ADDISON, JOSEPH. *Charles the Third of Spain.* Oxford, 1900.

AITON, ARTHUR S. "The Diplomacy of the Louisiana Cession," *American Historical Review*, XXXVI (1931), 701–720.

ALVORD, CLARENCE WALWORTH. "The Conquest of St. Joseph, Michigan, by the Spaniards, 1781," *Missouri Historical Review*, II (1908), 195–210.

———. *The Illinois Country, 1673–1818.* Springfield, 1920.

———. "Virginia and the West: an Interpretation," *Mississippi Valley Historical Review*, III (1916), 19–38.

ANTÚNEZ Y ACEVEDO, RAFAEL. *Memorias Históricas sobre la Legislación y Gobierno del Comercio de los Españoles con sus Colonias en las Indias Occidentales.* Madrid, 1797.

ARTHUR, S. C., and KERNION, G. C. H. de. *Old Families of Louisiana.* New Orleans, 1931.

AUSTIN, MATTIE ALICE. "The Municipal Government of San Fernando de Béxar, 1730–1800," *Texas State Historical Quarterly*, VIII (1904), 277–352.

BALDWIN, CHARLES C. "Francis Vigo and General George Rogers Clark," *Magazine of Western History*, I (1884), 230–235.

BANCROFT, HUBERT HOWE. *History of Mexico.* 6 vols. San Francisco, 1883–1888.

BARBÉ MARBOIS, FRANÇOIS. *The History of Louisiana.* Philadelphia, 1830.

BECATTINI, FRANCISCO. *Vida de Carlos III de Borbon, rey católico de España y de las Indias.* 2 vols. Madrid, 1790.

BELEÑA, EUSEBIO BENTURA. *Recopilación Sumaria de Todos los Autos Acordados.* 2 vols. Mexico, 1787.

BERRY, JANE M. "The Indian Policy of Spain in the Southwest, 1783–1795," *Mississippi Valley Historical Review*, III (1917), 462–477.

BISPHAM, CLARENCE WYATT. "Contest for Ecclesiastical Supremacy in the Valley of the Mississippi, 1763–1803," *Louisiana Historical Quarterly*, I (1917), 154–189.

———. "New Orleans, a Treasure House for Historians," *Louisiana Historical Quarterly*, II (1919), 237–247.

BJORK, DAVID KNUTH. *The Establishment of Spanish Rule in the Province of Louisiana, 1762–1770*. MS, Ph.D. thesis, University of California, Berkeley, 1923.

BODLEY, TEMPLE. *George Rogers Clark, His Life and Public Services*. New York, 1926.

BOIMARE, A. L. "Notes Bibliographiques et raisonnés sur les principaux ouvrages publiés sur la Florida et l'ancienne Louisiane, depuis leur découverte jusqu'à l'époque actuelle," *Louisiana Historical Quarterly*, I (1917), No. 2, pp. 9–78.

BOLTON, HERBERT EUGENE. "Defensive Spanish Expansion and the Significance of the Borderlands," in *The Trans-Mississippi West* (Boulder, Colorado, 1930), 1–42.

———. *Guide to Materials for the History of the United States in the Principal Archives of Mexico*. Washington, D. C., 1913.

———. "Spanish Abandonment and Re-occupation of East Texas, 1773–1779," *Texas State Historical Quarterly*, IX (1905), 67–137.

———. *The Spanish Borderlands*. New Haven, 1921.

———. *Texas in the Middle Eighteenth Century*. Berkeley, 1915.

BOLTON, HERBERT EUGENE, and MARSHALL, THOMAS MAITLAND. *The Colonization of North America, 1492–1783*. New York, 1920.

BOYD, CARL EVANS. "The County of Illinois," *American Historical Review*, IV (1898), 623–635.

BREVARD, CAROLINE M. *A History of Florida from the Treaty of 1763 to Our Own Times*. 2 vols. Deland, 1924.

BROWN, VERA LEE. "Anglo-Spanish Relations in America," *Hispanic American Historical Review*, V (1922), 325–483.

———. "Contraband Trade: a Factor in the Decline of Spain's Empire in America," *ibid.*, VIII (1928), 178–189.

BRY, H. "The Louisiana Ouachita Region," *De Bow's Review*, III (1847), 225–230, 324–325.

CARTER, CLARENCE E. "The Beginnings of British West Florida," *Mississippi Valley Historical Review*, IV (1918), 314–341.

———. "British Policy towards the American Indians in the South, 1763–1783," *English Historical Review*, XXXIII, 37.

———. *Great Britain and the Illinois Country, 1763–1774*. Washington, D. C., 1910.

CAUGHEY, JOHN WALTON. "Bernardo de Gálvez and the English Smugglers on the Mississippi, 1777," *Hispanic American Historical Review*, XII (1932), 46–58.

———. "The Natchez Rebellion of 1781 and Its Aftermath," *Louisiana Historical Quarterly*, XVI (1933), 57–83.

———. "The Panis Mission to Pensacola, 1778," *Hispanic American Historical Review*, X (1930), 480–489.

———. "Willing's Expedition down the Mississippi, 1778," *Louisiana Historical Quarterly*, XV (1932), 5–36.

CHADWICK, FRENCH ENSOR. *The Relations of the United States and Spain*. New York. 1909.

CHAMBERS, HENRY EDWARD. *History of Louisiana: Wilderness, Colony, Province, Territory, State, People*. 3 vols. Chicago, 1925.

———. *Mississippi Valley Beginnings*. New York, 1922.

———. *West Florida and Its Relation to the Historical Cartography of the United States*. Baltimore, 1898.

CHAPMAN, CHARLES E. *A History of California: The Spanish Period*. New York, 1921.

———. *Catalogue of Materials in the Archivo General de Indias for the History of the Pacific Coast and the American Southwest*. Berkeley, 1919.

CHURCHILL, C. ROBERT. *The Forces of Gálvez*. MS in Howard Memorial Library, New Orleans. New Orleans, 1925.

CLAIBORNE, J. F. H. *Mississippi as a Province, Territory and State*. Jackson, Miss., 1880.

COLLETT, OSCAR W. "The Relations of Lieutenant-Governor de Leyba and George Rogers Clark and the American Authorities, and the Alleged Offer of Military Aid by Clark previous to the Attack on St. Louis in 1780," *Magazine of Western History*, I (1885), 271–277.

CONROTTE, MANUEL. *La Intervención de España en la Independencia de los Estados Unidos de la América del Norte*. Madrid, 1920.

COX, ISAAC JOSLIN. "The Louisiana-Texas Frontier," *Texas State Historical Quarterly*, X (1906), 1–75.

———. "The New Invasion of Goths and Vandals," *Proceedings of the Mississippi Valley Historical Association*, VIII (1915), 176–200.

———. "The Significance of the Louisiana Frontier," *ibid.*, III (1911), 198–213.

DAENELL, ERNST. *Die Spanier in Nordamerika von 1513–1824*. Berlin, 1911.

DANVILLA Y COLLADO, MANUEL. *Reinado de Carlos III*. 6 vols. Madrid, 1890–1896.

DART, HENRY PLANCHÉ. "The Archives of Louisiana," *Louisiana Historical Quarterly*, II (1919), 249–267.

DEILER, J. HANNO. *The Settlement of the German Coast of Louisiana*. Philadelphia, 1909.

DIMITRY, JOHN. "A King's Gift," *Magazine of American History*, XVI (1887), 305–328.

DOUGLAS, WALTER BOND. *The Spanish Domination of Upper Louisiana*. Madison, 1914.

DOWNING, MARGARET BRENT. "Oliver Pollock, Patriot and Financier," *Illinois Catholic Historical Review*, II (1919), No. 2.

DUNBAR-NELSON, ALICE. "People of Color in Louisiana," *Journal of Negro History*, I (1916), 361–376; II (1917), 51–78.

ENGLISH, W. H. *The Conquest of the Country Northwest of the River Ohio*. 2 vols. Indianapolis, 1896.

FISKE, JOHN. *The American Revolution*. 2 vols. Boston, 1891.
FORTIER, ALCÉE. *A History of Louisiana*. 4 vols. Paris and New York, 1904.
FRANZ, ALEXANDER. *Die Kolonization des Mississippitales bis zum Ausgange der französischen Herrschaft*. Leipzig, 1906.
GAYARRÉ, CHARLES. *History of Louisiana*. 4 vols. Ed. 2; New Orleans, 1879.
GÓMEZ DEL CAMPILLO, MIGUEL. "Chronological Statement of Manuscripts and Documents to be Found in the National Historical Archives in Madrid, Spain, Relative to Louisiana during the Spanish Domination," *Publications of the Louisiana Historical Society*, IV, 121-144.
GOODSPEED, WESTON A., ed. *The Province and the States; a History of the Province of Louisiana under France and Spain*. 7 vols. Madison, 1904.
GOODYKOONTZ, COLIN BRUMMITT. *Spanish Exploration of Louisiana and the Adjacent Borders of New Spain, 1762-1800*. MS, M.L. thesis, University of California, Berkeley, 1914.
GUÉNIN, EUGÉNE. *La Louisiane*. Paris, 1904.
HALL, FERNE. *The Officials of Spanish Louisiana as Deducted from Documents in the Bancroft Library*. MS, M.A. thesis, University of California, Berkeley, 1909.
HAMILTON, PETER J. "British West Florida," *Publications of the Mississippi Historical Society*, III (1903), 399-426.
———. *Colonial Mobile, 1519-1821*. Ed. 2; Boston, 1910.
HATCHER, MATTIE AUSTIN. "The Louisiana Background of the Colonization of Texas, 1763-1803," *Southwestern Historical Quarterly*, XXIV (1921), 169-194.
HAYDEN, HORACE EDWIN. "Oliver Pollock, his Connections with the Conquest of Illinois," *Magazine of American History*, XXII (1893), 414-420.
HILL, ROSCOE R. *Descriptive Catalogue of the Documents Relating to the History of the United States in the Papeles Procedentes de Cuba, Deposited in the Archivo General de Indias at Seville*. Washington, D. C., 1916.
HODGE, FREDERICK WEBB, ed. *Handbook of American Indians North of Mexico*. 2 vols. Washington, 1907-1910.
HOUCK, LOUIS. *A History of Missouri*. 3 vols. Chicago, 1908.
"Index to the Spanish Judicial Records," *Louisiana Historical Quarterly*, VI- (1923-).
Indice de pruebas de los caballeros de la Real y distinguida Orden de Carlos III desde su institución hasta el año 1847. Madrid, 1904.
JACKSON, GEORGE B. "John Stuart, Superintendent of Indian Affairs for the Southern District, 1763-1779," *Tennessee Historical Magazine*, III (1917), 165-191.
JAMES, JAMES ALTON. "Illinois and the Revolution in the West, 1779-1780," *Transactions of the Illinois State Historical Society*, XV (1915), 63-71.
———. "Indian Diplomacy and the Opening of the Revolution in the West," *Proceedings of the State Historical Society of Wisconsin*, LVII (1909), 125-142.
———. *The Life of George Rogers Clark*. Chicago, 1928.
———. "The Significance of the Attack on St. Louis, 1780," *Proceedings of the Mississippi Valley Historical Association*, II (1910), 199-217.

———. "Some Problems of the Northwest in 1779," *Essays in American History* (New York, 1910), 57–83.

———. "Spanish Influence in the West during the American Revolution," *Mississippi Valley Historical Review*, IV (1918), 193–208.

———. "To What Extent was George Rogers Clark in Military Control of the Northwest at the Close of the American Revolution?" *American Historical Review*, XXIII (1918), 313–329.

———. "Oliver Pollock, Financier of the Revolution in the West," *Mississippi Valley Historical Review*, XVI (1929), 67–80.

JOHNSON, ROXANA G. *Spanish Activities in the Louisiana Territory.* MS, M.A. thesis, University of California, Berkeley, 1921.

JONES, O. GARFIELD. "Local Government in the Spanish Colonies as Provided by the Recopilación de Leyes de las Reynos de las Indias," *Southwestern Historical Quarterly*, XIX (1915), 65–90.

KELLOGG, LOUISE PHELPS. *Frontier Advance on the Upper Ohio, 1778–1779.* Madison, 1916.

———. *Frontier Retreat on the Upper Ohio, 1779–1781.* Madison, 1917.

KING, GRACE. *Creole Families of New Orleans.* New York, 1921.

———. *New Orleans: the Place and the People.* New York, 1907.

———. *Stories from Louisiana History.* New Orleans, 1905.

KINNAIRD, LAWRENCE. *American Penetration into Spanish Territory, 1776–1803.* MS, Ph.D. thesis, University of California, 1928.

———. "The Spanish Expedition Against Fort St. Joseph in 1781, a New Interpretation," *Mississippi Valley Historical Review*, XIX (1932), 173–191.

McCARTHY, CHARLES HALLAM. "The Attitude of Spain during the American Revolution," *Catholic Historical Review*, II (1916), 47–65.

McMURTRIE, DOUGLAS C. *Early Printing in New Orleans, 1764–1810, with a Bibliography of the Issues of the Louisiana Press.* New Orleans, 1929.

MARTIN, FRANÇOIS-XAVIER. *The History of Louisiana.* 2 vols. New Orleans, 1827–1829.

MASON, EDWARD GAY. *Chapters from Illinois History.* Chicago, 1901.

———. "The Spanish March across Illinois in 1781," *Magazine of American History*, XV (1886), 457–469.

MECHAM, J. LLOYD. "The Northern Expansion of New Spain, 1522–1822: a Selected Descriptive Bibliographical List," *Hispanic American Historical Review*, VII (1927), 233–276.

MEESE, W. A. "Rock River in the Revolution," *Transactions of the Illinois State Historical Society*, XIV (1909), 97–103.

MONETTE, JOHN W. *A History of the Discovery and Settlement of the Valley of the Mississippi.* 2 vols. New York, 1848.

———. "The Progress of Navigation and Commerce in the Waters of the Mississippi and the Great Lakes, 1700–1846," *Publications of the Mississippi Historical Society*, VII, 479–523.

NASATIR, ABRAHAM PHINEAS. *Indian Trade and Diplomacy in the Spanish Illinois, 1763–1792*. MS, Ph.D. thesis, University of California, Berkeley, 1926.

OGG, FREDERICK A. *The Opening of the Mississippi*. New York, 1904.

O'HART, JOHN. *Irish Pedigrees*. 2 vols. Ed. 5; Dublin, 1892.

PALMER, FREDERICK. *Clark of the Ohio; a Life of George Rogers Clark*. New York, 1929.

PELZER, LOUIS. "The Spanish Land Grants of Upper Louisiana," *Iowa Journal of History and Politics*, XI (1913), 3-37.

PÉREZ, LUIS MARINO. *Guide to Materials for American History in Cuban Archives*. Washington, D. C., 1907.

PHELPS, ALBERT. *Louisiana, a Record of Expansion*. Boston, 1905.

PHILLIPS, PAUL CHRISLER. "American Opinions regarding the West, 1778–1783," *Proceedings of the Mississippi Valley Historical Association*, VII (1913), 286-305.

———. *The West in the Diplomacy of the American Revolution*. Urbana, 1913.

PICKETT, ALBERT JAMES. *History of Alabama, and Incidentally of Georgia and Mississippi from the Earliest Period*. Ed. 2; Sheffield, Alabama, 1896.

PRIESTLEY, HERBERT INGRAM. *The Coming of the White Man, 1492–1848*. New York, 1929.

———. *José de Gálvez, Visitor-General of New Spain, 1765–1771*, Berkeley, 1916.

RANDALL, J. G. "George Rogers Clark's Service of Supply," *Mississippi Valley Historical Review*, VIII (1921), 250-263.

REYNOLDS, ALFRED WADE. *The Alabama-Tombigbee Basin in International Relations, 1701–1763*. MS, Ph.D. thesis, University of California, Berkeley, 1928.

RIVERA CAMBAS, MANUEL. *Los Gobernantes de Mexico*. 2 vols. Mexico, 1872–1873.

ROBERTSON, JAMES ALEXANDER. *List of Documents in Spanish Archives Relating to the History of the United States which have been Printed or of which Transcripts are Preserved in American Libraries*. Washington, D. C., 1910.

ROUSSEAU, FRANÇOIS. *Règne de Charles III d'Espagne, 1759–1788*. 2 vols. Paris, 1907.

SCRAMUZZA, V. M. "Gálveztown, a Spanish Settlement of Colonial Louisiana," *Louisiana Historical Quarterly*, XIII (1930), 553-609.

SCROGGS, WILLIAM O. "The Archives of the State of Louisiana," *Annual Report of the American Historical Association for 1912*. Washington, D. C., 1914.

SHEPHERD, WILLIAM R. "The Cession of Louisiana to Spain," *Political Science Quarterly*, XIX (1904), 439-458.

———. *Guide to the Materials for the History of the United States in Spanish Archives*. Washington, D. C., 1907.

SIEBERT, WILBUR H. "Kentucky's Struggle with Its Loyalist Proprietors," *Mississippi Valley Historical Review*, VII (1920), 113-126.

———. "The Loyalists in West Florida and the Natchez," *ibid.*, II (1916), 465-483.

SLICER, SUE STONE. *The Geography of Louisiana under Spanish Administration*. MS, M.A. thesis, University of California, Berkeley, 1908.

STODDARD, AMOS. *Sketches Historical and Descriptive of Louisiana*. Philadelphia, 1812.

SURREY, N. M. MILLER. *The Commerce of Louisiana during the French Régime, 1609–1763*. New York, 1916.

TARLETON, LIEUTENANT-COLONEL. *A History of the Campaigns of 1780 and 1781 in the Southern Provinces of North America*. Dublin, 1787.

TEGGART, FREDERICK J. "The Capture of St. Joseph, Michigan, by the Spaniards in 1781," *Missouri Historical Review*, V (1911), 214–228.

THOMAS, DAVID YANCY. "The Diplomatic Struggle for the Mississippi and the Southwestern Boundary," *Gulf States Historical Magazine*, II (1904), 343–363.

THOMPSON, J. J. "Penalties of Patriotism," *Transactions of the Illinois State Historical Society*, IX (1916–1917), 401–449.

THOMPSON, THOMAS PAYNE. *Index to a Collection of American Art and Miscellanea*. New Orleans, 1912.

THWAITES, REUBEN GOLD. *How George Rogers Clark Won the Northwest*. Chicago, 1903.

VALDES, MANUEL ANTONIO, ed. *Gazetas de México, 1784–1821*. 44 vols. Mexico, 1784–1821.

VILES, JONAS. "Population and Extent of Settlement in Missouri before 1804," *Missouri Historical Review*, V (1911), 189–213.

VILLIERS DU TERRAGE, MARC. *Les Dernières Années de la Louisiane française*. Paris, 1903.

VIOLETTE, E. M. "Early Settlements in Missouri," *Missouri Historical Review*, I (1906), 38–52.

VOGEL, CLAUDE L. *The Capuchins in French Louisiana, 1722–1766*. Washington, D. C., 1928.

VON EELKING, MAX. *Die deutschen Hülfstruppen im nordamerikanischen Befreiungskriege, 1776 bis 1783*. Hannover, 1863.

WEST, ELIZBETH HOWARD. "The Indian Policy of Bernardo de Gálvez," *Proceedings of the Mississippi Valley Historical Association*, VIII (1916), 95–101.

WHITAKER, ARTHUR PRESTON. "The Commerce of Louisiana and the Floridas at the End of the Eighteenth Century," *Hispanic American Historical Review*, VIII (1928), 190–203.

———. *The Spanish American Frontier, 1783–1795*. Boston, 1927.

WINSOR, JUSTIN. *The Mississippi Basin*. Boston, 1898.

———. *The Reader's Handbook of the American Revolution, 1761–1783*. Boston, 1899.

———. *The Westward Movement*. Boston, 1897.

WINSOR, JUSTIN, ed. *Narrative and Critical History of America*. 8 vols. New York, 1884–1889.

WINSTON, JAMES E. "The Cause and Results of the Revolution of 1768 in Louisiana," *Louisiana Historical Quarterly*, XV (1932), 181–213.

YELA UTRILLA, JUAN F. *España ante la independencia de los Estados Unidos*. Ed. 2; 2 vols. Lérida, 1925.

INDEX

Achafalé, 226
Acosta, Joseph Melchor de, 18, 24, 30
Adams, Samuel, 102, 103
Albemarle, Lord, 205
Alberti, Captain, surrender of, to Gálvez, 206
Alderete, Miguel de, attempt of, to end quarrel of Gálvez with naval officers, 204; and Gálvez' desire for reconciliation, 204; action of, in attack on Fort George, 210
Alibamons, 3
Alston, John: part played by, in Natchez rebellion, 216, 217, 218, 224, 226, 228; release of, 240
Alta California, 5
Alvarez, Julian, commander of flotilla on Mississippi River, 153
Alvord, C. W., 167, 168
Amelot, 17, 18
American Revolution, 19, 53; important assistance to, rendered by Gálvez, 85; Pollock's rôle in, 98
Andry, Luis, cartographer, 80
Apaches, 52, 62, 64, 65, 66, 68, 82, 253
Arensburg, 26
Arkansas Post, purpose of establishment of, 39
Armesto, Manuel Andrés Lopes de, 224
Arriaga, Julian de, 28
"Atlanta," British frigate, 72, 73, 75, 115
Attacapas, 68
Aubry, Philip, French governor of Louisiana, 10, 12; Ulloa's orders effective only as announced through, 13; advice of, to Ulloa at time of insurrection, 15; letters of, to France after expulsion of Ulloa, 16; became nominal head of colony, 18; expulsion of, and of French troops proposed, 19; information given by, concerning leaders of insurrection, 24; report required from, by O'Reilly, 30

Bahamas: English feared possible attack on, by Spaniards, 243; Cagigal appointed to lead expedition against privateers in, 245; surrender of, by Governor Maxwell, 245; statement of population of, 245–246
Bahía de Santa María, 213
Bahía del Espíritu Santo, 68
Balize, 12, 13, 14, 16, 17, 21, 35, 40, 41, 68, 122, 138, 145
Barber, Captain, letter from Dickson carried by, to officers of Natchez district, 157
Bard, Lieutenant, surrender of, to Gálvez, 206
Barrancas á Margot, 234
Barrancas Coloradas, fort at, 173, 188, 201, 202, 203; burning of several houses at, by British commander, 205; harmless cannonade from, 208; taken over by Spaniards, 211; ineffectiveness of defenses of, remedied, 212–213
Barry, captain of frigate "Columbus," 88
Baton Rouge, 72, 138, 150, 155, 158, 160, 166, 172, 181, 209, 216, 222, 225
Baumback, Captain, 195
Bayou La Combe, 160
Bayou Lafourche, settlement at, 79
Bayou St. Jean, 18, 123, 137, 150, 154
Bayou Teche, settlement at, 81
Becerril, Lieutenant Diego, 62
Benjamin, Samuel, 222, 224, 238
Bethune, Ferqr., English deputy superintendent of Indians, 227, 228
Bienville, Jean Baptiste le Moyne, Sieur de, 2, 3, 6, 37
Biloxi, 2
Black Code, 3, 30, 32
Blanchard, Carlos, 49
Blanco, Diego, 237
Blommart, John: induced to assume leadership of Natchez rebellion, 217; attack of, on Fort Panmure, 217, and its sur-

Blommart, John (*continued*)
render, 218; careful administration of fort by, 218; assistance given to, by Hutchins, 218; decision of, to protect fort, 219; exonerated from charges of complaint by Campbell, 220; prepared for raid on Pointe Coupée, 220; endeavor of, to turn Indians against Spaniards, 221; "Terms of Accomodation" of, 221; Morandiere's reply to, 221–222; evacuation of fort by, 222; conditions of surrender, 222; sent under guard to Grand Pré, 222; sent with others to New Orleans, 224; Williams' statement concerning acts of, 224; questioning of, by Panis, 225; commissioned a captain by Campbell, 225; confiscation of property of, 225; pleas for leniency for, received from various quarters, 225, 227, 228; Winfree's attempt to shift responsibility to, 226; and other Natchez prisoners not released, 235; treatment received by, while prisoner, 238. *See also* Colbert; Cruzat, Madame; L'Abbadie; Miró; Natchez rebellion
Blommart, Mary, 109
Boüe, 18
Bouligny, Francisco, 81, 177
Braud, Dionisio, 49
Bucareli y Ursúa, Antonio María, 13, 35, 65
Burden, captain of the "West Florida," 123; Lieutenant, 144

Cabildo, 31
Cádiz, 13, 44
Cadodacho, 38, 51
Cagigal, Juan Manuel de: field marshal, 208, 210; Gálvez' communication of royal order to, 244–245; arrival of, off New Providence, Bahama Islands, 245; surrender of Governor Maxwell to, 245; reported small loss, 245; difficulties arising from differences of opinion of, and Gillon, 246–247
Cahokia: Clark's powwows at, 94–95; contributions of people of, to Clark's expedition, 98; massacre of seventeen Frenchmen at, 168
Cainiones, 51
Calbo de Irazabal, Captain José, 201; vain attempts of, to lighten the "San Ramon," 202; Gálvez' suggestion to, not kindly received, 202; willingness of, to coöperate with Gálvez in other matters, 202; message of Gálvez to, 203; retort of, 203; agreed to allow fleet to sail on the following day, 204; return of, to Havana, 204
Cameron, Alexander: praised services of English Indian allies, 189; consistent in opposition to Spain, 207
Campbell, owner of the "Neptune," 119, 120
Campbell, John: reliance of, on Gálvez for aid, 140; Gálvez' letter to, 154; attack of, on New Orleans thwarted, 163; refusal of, to believe reports concerning Gálvez' success in Mississippi Valley, 171; had heard of Spaniards' arrival at Mobile, 180; allies reported presence of, in Tensaw district with reënforcements, 182, 183; retreat of, toward Pensacola, 183; humanitarian appeal made to, by Gálvez, 189; continued to use Indian auxiliaries, 189; letter of Lieutenant Fraser, 190; attempt made by, to recover Mobile, 194; correspondence of Gálvez with, concerning destruction of property in Pensacola, 205; compelled to run up white flag at Fort George, 210; appeal of, to settlers in Natchez district for aid, 215–216; denial of, of responsibility in Natchez rebellion, 219, and later admission thereof, 219; refusal of Gálvez to agree to proposals of, 220; Blommart commissioned a captain by, 225
Campeche, smuggling into, from Louisiana, 34
Canada, 2, 4, 150, 163, 164, 219
Canadian control of Illinois district, 3

INDEX

Canadians, 81, 82, 165, 166, 168
Capuchins: Louisiana, 45; Spanish, 45; French, 46, 51
Caridine, Parker, 226, 234
Carlos II, 214
Carlos III, xi, 4, 5, 6, 29, 61, 214
Carolinas, English traders from, 2
Cartabona, Silvio Francisco de, commander of militia at Ste. Geneviève, 165
Castillo del Morro, 26
Catalonia, wine from, 35
Champigny, 6
Chester, Governor of West Florida: protest of, to Gálvez, 92, 123; summary of decisions in favor of English sent by Gálvez to, 121; tribute paid by, to Gálvez, 124; exhorted refugees to return to protection of British flag, 126–127; Gálvez' letter to, 141; gifts carried by Panis for, 142; had no inkling of Panis' secret mission, 142, 144; series of letters from, to Panis respecting Spanish grievances, 142–143, 144; sidestepped responsibility at Chickasaw Bluffs, 143; complimented Major Panis, 144–145; request of, for safe-conduct of boat carrying Panis, 145
Chickasaw: Bluffs, 143, 229, 233, 234; chiefs, 237; country, 235, 240; nation, 185, 227; uprisings, 238, 242; villages, 226, 232
Chickasaws, 3, 207, 223, 228, 230, 231, 233, 234, 237, 241
Choctaw: Indians, 3, 40, 143, 172, 185, 207, 223, 228; traders, 216
Choiseul, Duke de, 6
Cirilo, Father, 45, 46
Claiborne, J. F. H., 223
Clark, George Rogers, 85, 110; exploits of, 93 ff.; expedition of, against Vincennes on information of François Vigo, 96 ff.; intrepid leadership of, 97; reliance of, on Pollock and Gálvez for supplies and credit, 98 ff.; Rocheblave's distrust of, 106; Willing's letter to, 106; conquest by, of Illinois country frustrated plan for vengeance upon Gálvez, 124; sentiment of, respecting Willing, 133; part played by, in defense of St. Louis, 165–166
Clinton, Henry: appeal to, for more troops by commander of St. Augustine, 171; Campbell's letter to, 190, 191
Code O'Reilly, 32, 212
Colbert, James: consistent in opposition to Spain, 207; real champion of the Natchez rebellion, 228; captured boat commanded by L'Abbadie, 229, 237; leadership of, acknowledged only in a limited degree, 230–231; L'Abbadie's estimate of, 231; association of, with McGillivray, 232; difficulties of negotiating with, 235; letter from, 236; attack on Fort Carlos III by, 240; allowed Villars to go to New Orleans in exchange for Natchez prisoners, 240, 241; correspondence of, with Miró, 241; statement of, concerning prisoners held by Cruzat, 241; gratification of, over Blommart's release, 241; departure of, for St. Augustine, 241; tragic death of, 241; probable verdict of history concerning, 242. *See also* Cruzat, Madame; L'Abbadie; Miró
Commerce Committee, Continental Congress: Willing's conferences with, 103; Pollock's report to, concerning final settlement with Willing, 132
Continental Congress: instructions of, to Willing, 102, 103; Pollock as agent for Virginia and, at New Orleans, 112; Gálvez' communication to, 121; Pollock's reports to, concerning Willing, 129–130; failure of, to send remittances for expenses incurred by Willing, 134; approbation of, won by Gálvez, 172
Contraband trade, 11, 33, 50, 70; Gálvez disrupted, of English, 71–72, 73, 76, 88
Council of the Indies: consideration of Louisiana problem by, 20; recognition of need for spiritual reënforcement by, 47; seizure of British vessels reviewed by, 76

Creeks, 182, 207
Creole Republic, 19
Creoles, French: assistance given by, of Illinois to Clark, 97–98; commendations accorded to, under Rillieux, 163
Croix, Teodoro de, 64, 82
Cruzat, Antoine: responsibility of Louisiana colony shifted to, 2; forts established by, 3; fortune lost by, in enterprise, 4
Cruzat, Francisco: attempt of, to bring settlers to Spanish Illinois, 81; Gálvez kept in touch with, respecting Indian affairs, 82; letter from, to Morgan intercepted by Willing, 106; expedition against English at St. Joseph sent by, 166–168; report of, to Gálvez, 167; capture of wife of, by Colbert, 229; L'Abbadie reported happenings in Natchez district to, 233; busy at St. Louis undermining position of English in Chickasaw country, 237; belated assistance sent by, to L'Abbadie, 237; asked by Chickasaw chiefs to dissuade northern Indians from attacking them, 237; Colbert's statement concerning prisoners held by, 241
Cruzat, Madame: captured with sons by James Colbert, 229; assured of good treatment, 230; grateful for protection of William Colbert, 230; stressed the insubordination among captors, 230; James Colbert's regret at capture of, instead of her husband, 231; gave personal note for repurchase of L'Abbadie's boat, 233; warned other boats of danger at Chickasaw Bluffs, 233; upon arrival at New Orleans gave account of what had happened, 233; told Miró of protest of English against Grand Pré's fines, 235
Cuba, freedom of commerce with, 76

D'Abbadie: report of, concerning condition of Louisiana, 3; received official notice from king of France concerning coming of Spaniards, 6

D'Aunoy, Favre, 70
Dagobert, Father, 16, 45, 46
Deans, captain of the frigate "Mentor," 194
De Mezières, Athanase, 30, 37; made commander at Natchitoches, 38; duties and responsibilities, 38; success of, 51; received permission from Unzaga to appoint traders, 52; prosperous condition of Natchitoches district, 52; Gálvez kept in touch with, respecting Indian affairs, 82; statement of, concerning instructions to Willing, 104
De Sasier, 26
Delavillebeuvre, Juan: granted provisional welcome to emigrants to Louisiana, 111; statement of, respecting reason for averted attack upon New Orleans, 124; sent to receive surrender of Fort Panmure at Natchez, 157, 159, 226; forced to agree to terms of capitulation, 217–218, 219; terms of capitulation of, scrupulously observed by Blommart, 224, 225
Dequente, commander of band of Canadians, 168
Dickson, Alexander: report of, respecting Fort Manchac, 139; Gálvez conferred permission on, to purchase cattle, 140; defense of, at Baton Rouge, 155, and surrender of the fort, 157; confirmed British plan for attack on New Orleans, 163; effect of surrender of, on commander of St. Augustine, 171; in rôle of Campbell's emissary, 205; surrender of, to Gálvez, 206
DuBreuil, Raymundo, 237, 238, 240
Ducharme, Juan María, 164
Dunbar, William, statement of, concerning instructions to Willing, 104
Durnford, Elias: letter of, to William Horn of Natchez intercepted, 149; correspondence of Gálvez with, 177; letter of, 178; Campbell's promise of help to, 180; cessation of hostilities proposed by, 181; terms of surrender submitted by, 181; scene of surrender described by, 182

Eason, William, 222, 224, 238, 240
Echevarria, Bishop, 46
Eduardo, Miguel, of Havana, 89; became an object of suspicion, 89
England, Spanish court declared war against, 149
English: contraband trade disrupted by Gálvez, 71–72, 73 ff., 88; complaint of, respecting arms and supplies furnished to Revolutionists by Gálvez, 92; resentment of, at Gálvez' pro-American activities, 93; at Vincennes, 96; chronic dislike of Louisianians for, 112; ports along Mississippi improved and enlarged by, 138; long, control of Jamaica, 243
Export commodities, 52–53
Ezpeleta, Josef de: left in command of garrison at Mobile, 191; small reënforcement sent to, 194; request for help from, 195; ordered by Gálvez to march to Pensacola, 200; launches with provisions sent to, 202; casualties caused by Indians in expedition of relief to, 206, 207; attack on crescent at Fort George called off by, 209; advance of troops under, and Giron, 210

Falkland Islands dispute, 44
Family Compact, 4, 5
Fayni, Joseph, persistent critic of Gálvez, 66, 68
Fergusson, John, commander of the "Sylph," correspondence of, with Gálvez concerning Willing's victims, 114 ff.; departure of, for Pensacola, 119
Fleurian, 18
Forster, Anthony, surrender of Fort Panure by, 158
Fort Barrancas, 173, 188, 201, 203, 205
Fort Bute, 12, 40, 133
Fort Carlos III, 240
Fort Charlotte, 176, 177, 178, 182, 185, 226

Fort George, 206, 209; explosion of powder magazine at, 210; capture of, greatest military success of Gálvez, 212; to be rechristened San Miguel, 214
Fort Panmure: included in surrender of Baton Rouge, 157, 158; effect on English of loss of, 185; Blommart's attack on, 217; surrender of, 218; force sent from New Orleans to recover, 220, 228; unopposed occupation of, 222; Hutchins' connection with, 223; Colbert's part in capture of, 231
Fort Pitt, 86, 87, 90, 94, 98, 102, 103, 127
Fort Real Católica, 40
Fort Rosalie, 3
Fort San Luis de Natchez, 40
Fort Toulouse, 3
Foucault, 10, 17
France, 4, 5, 16, 17, 30
Fraser, Alexander, letter of, to Campbell, 190; association of, with Spaniards, 207
French measures in Louisiana, 84
Frontenac, Louis de Buade de, 37

Gage, Thomas, British commander, 41, 44, 45
"Gálvez," a brig, 175, 176
Gálvez, Bernardo de, xi, 57; advantage of family connections of, 61; attractive personality of, 61; nephew and protégé of José de Gálvez, 61; previous experiences of, 61 ff.; expeditions against Apaches of Nueva Vizcaya, 62, 63, 64, 82; return to Spain of, 66; admiration of, for fortitude and skill of Apaches, 67; frontier training seen in handling of Indian problems in Louisiana, 67; perfected himself in military science in France, 67; subsequent activities of, 67; made governor of Louisiana, 67; popularity of, 68; duties of, outlined, 68 ff.; faced by problem of regulation of trade, 70; permitted French ships to load anywhere on river, 70; treatment of English merchants by, 71–72; desire of, to enforce regulation against smuggling,

Gálvez, Bernardo de (*continued*)
72; correspondence of, with Lloyd about confiscations on the Mississippi, 72–73, 74 f.; appeal of, for naval and military reënforcements, 73; permitted temporary revival of English commerce, 76; encouraged agriculture, 77; result of census taken after, became governor, 78; interest of, in Indian affairs, 82; personal relation of, with Indians, 82; statement of, respecting English, French, and Spanish treatment of Indians, 83; marriage of, to creole beauty, 84; popularity of, enhanced by this act, 84; accomplishments of, in domestic affairs of Louisiana, 84; captivating creoles the most noteworthy service of, to Spain, 84; aided American Revolution, 85 ff.; displayed partiality toward Americans, 88; vigorous pro-Americanism of, 88, 93, 127; two royal orders received by, in 1777 concerning Spanish supplies for Revolutionists, 88 ff.; response of, to Morgan concerning expedition against Pensacola, 91; guaranty of, for American trade with New Orleans, 91; Governor Chester's protest to, concerning transmission of arms, 92; Clark's reliance upon, 98 ff.; Pollock's relations with, 98; placed government funds at disposal of Pollock, 99–100; meeting of, with Pollock in Havana, 100; part played by, in Revolution while Spain was neutral, 101, 148; Pollock's tribute to, 101; complaints made to, by Willing's victims, 108; proclamation concerning Spain's perfect neutrality by, 111; appreciation of kindness of, by refugees, 112; extended freedom of New Orleans to Americans, 112; sale of plunder justified by, 113; English protests sent to, concerning welcome to Willing, 113–114; correspondence of, with Fergusson, 114 ff.; correspondence of, with Willing about restoration of captured property, 119–121; armed foreigners caused uneasiness to, 122; oath of neutrality or departure demanded by, from English in New Orleans, 122; protested by Captain Nunn, 122–123; oath of neutrality administered to Americans, 123; disadvantage for Spanish Louisiana because of protection of Americans by, 123; earned English gratitude for opening Louisiana to refugees, 124; annoyance of, at Willing's presence in New Orleans, 127–128; worry of, about real security of Louisiana, 128; fortunate partisanship of, in Revolutionary cause, 134; attitude of, toward American Revolution, 135; correspondence of, with George Morgan about Pensacola, 136; agreement of, with Unzaga respecting defenses of New Orleans, 137; defense measures taken by, 137–138; statement of, respecting militia, 138; relief given by, in flour shortage in Pensacola, 139; letter of complaint to Governor Chester by, 141; Chester's replies to, about Spanish grievances, 142 ff.; letter of, to king, 147; with shackles of neutrality broken, was able to fight English openly, 149; tardy arrival of order to drive out British forces, 149; suspicions of, aroused by reënforcement of Manchac, 149; redoubled military preparations of, 150, 151–152; conference of, with junta de guerra, 150–151; desire of, for more audacious program, 151; made no public announcement of Spain's declaration of war, 151; plans of, to invade English territory disrupted by hurricane, 152; appointment of, as governor of Louisiana, 152; departure of army under leadership of, 153; hardships of march, 153–154; Manchac was first objective of, 154; West Florida not told of Spain's entry into war, 154; arrest of British Indian agent by, 154; announced Spain's declaration of war when in sight of Fort Manchac, 155; siege and surrender of Baton Rouge, 155 ff.; terms of sur-

Gálvez, Bernardo de (*continued*) render, 157; Pickles' actions approved by, 160; decision of, respecting "West Florida," 160; signal success achieved by, and his cohorts, 161 ff.; recognition of leadership of, 163; consequences of campaign of, 163 ff.; weak condition of St. Louis reported to, by Spanish commandant, 164; success of, frustrated British general plan, 166; Cruzat's report to, 167; consternation among English because of capture of forts by, 171; instruction received by, respecting British forces, 171–172; plans made by, for conquest of Pensacola and Mobile, 172; request of, for additional men from Havana, 172; Mississippi expedition an integral part of Gulf Coast campaign of, 172; preparations for expedition against Pensacola by, 173; reënforcements from Havana refused to, 174; concentrated on capture of Mobile, 174; Miró sent to Havana by, 174; aid promised to, 174; final instructions by, to officers at New Orleans, 174; departure of troops, 174–175; plans made by, for attack on Fort Charlotte, 176; established a battery at entrance to bay, 176; headquarters of, 177; correspondence of, with Durnford, 177 ff.; additional precautions taken by, against surprise attack, 180; agreed to cessation of hostilities, 181; acceptance of Durnford's surrender by, 181; ordered Fort Charlotte repaired and strengthened, 182; Campbell's retreat toward Pensacola reported to, 183; letter of, to uncle respecting Mobile campaign, 183–185; management of Mobile campaign by, appraised, 185; chivalry of, and his opponent recognized, 185–186; royal appreciation of work of, 186; made field marshal, 186; further plans for conquest of Pensacola by, 187, 188, 189; humanitarian appeal of, to Campbell, 189; aversion of, to savage atrocities, 189; discouraging news received by, 190; arrival of, in Havana to confer with military authorities, 192; decision of junta to assist, in every possible manner, 192–193; departure of, with fleet from Havana, 193; organized another West Florida expedition, 195 ff., 197–198; success of, in persuading Havana authorities to act more promptly, 198; authorized to attempt to capture Pensacola, 198; "Yo Solo," 200 ff.; ordered Piernas to mobilize forces at New Orleans, 200; landing of, on Santa Rosa Island, 201; efforts of, concentrated on two tasks, 201–202; the forcing of the channel by, 202–203; quarrel between, and naval officers, 204, 210, 247; reconciliation sought by, 204; correspondence of, with adversary, 205; incensed at action of British commander at Fort Barrancas, 205; arrival of reënforcements for, 206, 208; readiness of Solano to coöperate with, 208; problem of, at Pensacola, 209; flag of truce run up by Campbell, 210; consideration of terms of capitulation by, 210; surrender of English, 211; Spanish troops ordered back to Havana by, 211; victory at Fort George the greatest military success of, 212; capture of Pensacola by, pleasing to king, 213; Campbell's desire to handicap, by fomenting disturbance in Natchez district, 215–216, 219; refuses to accept Campbell's proposal concerning Natchez rebellion, 220; persuaded by Piernas to go to Natchez in person, 220; Blommart advised to throw himself on mercy of, 222; absence of, in Havana, 224; trial of Natchez leaders turned over to Panis by, 224; urged by Miró to erect new forts, 234; approved Miró's plan to release Mrs. Holston, 235; letters exchanged by, with Duke of Lancaster, 238–239; order of, to release Natchez prisoners, 240, and leniency toward, 242; ordered to undertake conquest of Jamaica, 243; departure of, to

280 INDEX

Gálvez, Bernardo de (*continued*)
Havana, 243; preparations of, for Jamaica campaign, 244; effect of Rodney's victory over De Grasse on plans of, 244; communication of royal order by, to Cagigal, 244-245; Spain's criticism of, and Cagigal in disregarding royal orders, 246-247; climax for operations of, in America had come at Pensacola, 247; effect of conquests of, on provisions of peace treaties, 247 f.; praise accorded to, for securing American instead of English frontier for Spanish America, 248-249; completed establishment of Spanish control over Louisiana, 249-250; method of, in acquiring dominion over Louisianians, 250; recommendations of, for trade regulations, 250; return of, to Spain, 251; regard of conquered English for, 251-252; evidences of royal appreciation of, 252; return of, to America, 252; became viceroy of New Spain upon death of father, 252; titles of, 252-253; arrival of, with family at Vera Cruz, 253; reception at Mexico City, 253; popularity of, 253; protests of critics of, 254; favorable report of audiencia respecting rule of, 255, and king's reply, 255; wide jurisdiction granted to, 255-256; death of, 256-257; funeral, 257; birth and christening of posthumous daughter of, 257-258; pension for widow of, provided by king, 258

Gálvez, José de, 27, 62, 192; inquiries made by Gibson forwarded by Unzaga to, 135, and his reply, 136; Governor Gálvez' letter to, 140-141

Gálvez, Matías de, viceroy of New Spain, 61; death of, 252

Gálveztown: settlement of refugees, 79; militia available at, 138; war activities of Spaniards at, 161; proposed title of Viscount of, for Gálvez, 251

"Gálveztown," brig, 202; used by Gálvez to force the harbor at Pensacola, 202-203; fired upon from Fort Barrancas, 203; saluted Fort Barrancas, 203

Garden of New France, 53

Gayarré, Charles, 4, 10, 53, 68, 75, 136, 151, 153, 155, 172-173, 182, 223

George, Robert, 131

Gibault, Father, 95

Gibson, George, 56, 87, 98; arrest of, at New Orleans, 87; inquiries made by, of Unzaga, 135

Gillon, Alexander, captain of the "South Carolina," 245; differences of opinion of, with Cagigal, 246; Cagigal's force and conquest jeopardized by desertion of, 246

Giron, Gerónimo, 210

Goicochea, Don Miguel, 188, 189

Gonzales, Manuel, named ranking officer under Gálvez, 153

Grand Council of Virginia, 87

Grand Pré, Carlos, 17, 18; granted provisional welcome to emigrants to Louisiana, 111; seizure of British posts by, 159; placed in command of Natchez district by Gálvez, 159; Morandiere reported to, 220; deputies from Natchez sent to, 221; reënforcements to be brought by, 221-222; Blommart and three others sent under guard to, 222; subsequent activities of, 226-227; bands of Indians sent out by, to capture pirates, 229; English protest against fines of, 235

Grant, Dr., surrender of, to Gálvez, 206

Great Britain, Spain's entrance into war against, 77

Grimaldi, Marquis de, 13, 15, 20, 28

Guarico, Española Island, 244

Guinea, introduction of negroes from, 77, 78

Haldimand, Frederick, 44

Hamilton, Henry, 96, 106, 133; surrender of, at Vincennes, 97

Hand, Edward, commander at Fort Pitt, 103

Hanxleden, Colonel von, 194, 195

INDEX

Harrison, Richard, sent to Natchez district, 125; Hutchins' action against, 125–126
Havana, 13, 15, 16, 33, 35, 41, 44, 45, 70, 85, 89, 100, 124, 149, 150, 172, 173, 174, 185, 189, 191, 193, 196, 200, 202, 204, 211, 220, 243
Helm, Leonard, at Vincennes, 96
Henry, Patrick, 16; governor of Virginia, urges Gálvez to aid Revolutionists, 92–93; gave colonel's commission to Clark for attack on Kaskaskia, 94; statement of, respecting American aggression on Spanish territory, 135
Hesse, Emmanuel, commander of Canadian forces against St. Louis, 164
Heturno, Indian chief, 168
"Hinchenbrook," British boat captured by Willing, 108
Holston, John, 227
Horn, William, intercepted letter to, confirmed fears of Gálvez, 149–150
Hospital de Caridad, 150
"Hound," British frigate, 121
Hutchins, Anthony: made prisoner by Willing, 106, 108; broke parole and incited people of Natchez to arm, 125; confession of obligation by, 126; assertion of, respecting Campbell's part in the Natchez rebellion, 216, 219; informed of English aspect of scheme at eleventh hour, 217; effectiveness of civil authority of, 218; emissary for Blommart, 221; criticism of Morandiere by, 223; rôle of, at Fort Panmure, 223

Iberville, Pierre le Moyne, Sieur d', sent by Pontchartrain to establish settlements on lower Mississippi, 2
Iberville River: fort on, opposite Fort Bute, 12, 40, 133; settlement at confluence of, and Amite, 80; troops stationed at redoubts to come down, 151
Illinois: district, 33, 54; Spanish, 53; French, 53; lead mines of, 54; salt works of Spanish, 54; friendship of, Indians, 54; attempt to procure settlers for, 81; Clark's conquests welcomed in, 95; militia scattered from, to Balize, 138
Indian policy of New Spain, 52
Indigo, 34, 52

Jamaica: reënforcements for Pensacola sent from, 187; part of, desolated by hurricane, 197; English frigates sailed from, to cruise off Cape San Antonio, 198; exchanged prisoners not to be taken to, 211; Natchez prisoners in New Orleans released and taken to, 240; Gálvez ordered to capture, 243; attack on, never materialized, 244; English troops from Bahamas not permitted to go to, 245
James, Benjamin, association of, with Spaniards, 207
Jesuits, 45
Johnstone, George, preparations of, for an attack on "Dons of New Orleans," 150
Joliet, Louis, 1

Kaskaskia, 94, 95, 97, 105, 106
"Kaulican," the king's brig, 175, 176, 183
Kelly, Juan, 30
Kerlérec, 3, 6
Kichai Indians, 51

L'Abbadie, Silbestre: boat commanded by, captured by James Colbert, 229; seizure of, and Madame Cruzat by English, 229–230; stressed insubordination rife among captors, 230; Colbert discussed plans freely with, 231; statement of, concerning Colbert, 231; connection of, with McGillivray, 232; "Parole of Honour" signed by, 232; boat of, repurchased by signatories, 233; bought back one of his slaves, 233; departure for Louisiana, 233; letter from, to governor of Louisiana, 233; went to St. Louis, 233; gave account of what had happened to Cruzat, 233; faithlessness of, toward Colbert, 240
La Salle, Robert Cavelier, Sieur de, 1

Lafitte, Captain Paul, 110
Lafont, Jean Baptiste, 230, 237
Lafrénière, Nicolas Chauvin de, 15, 16, 19, 21, 223
Lake Borgne, possible British attack on New Orleans by way of, 150
Lake Maurepas, 150
Lancaster, Duke of: arrival of, at Jamaica, 238; correspondence between, and Gálvez, 238–239; release of Natchez prisoners to, 240, 241
Lassois, 18
Laussel, 17, 18
Law, John, 3, 4
Le Moyne family, of Canada, 2
Lee, General Charles, appeal of, to governor of Louisiana for help, 55–56, 86; sale of Spanish goods to, through New Orleans merchant, 88–89
Leyba, Fernando de, 82, 95, 165, 166
Linn, Lieutenant, 56, 86, 98
Lloyd, Thomas, captain of the "Atlanta," 72, 115, 118
Louis XIV, 2
Louis XV, 15
Louisiana: founded by Iberville, 2; cession to Spain, 4–6; restrictions on trade of, with Spain, 11; confusion the chief characteristic in, after Ulloa's departure, 18; insurrection hailed as first American Revolution, 19; aims of revolt in, 19; O'Reilly sent to, 20, and became dictator of, 21; O'Reilly's administration of, 29 ff.; drastic change in, 32; French policy continued in, by Spain, 35; threefold resistance organized to keep English out of, 40; exact number of soldiers kept in, not available, 41; Unzaga's governorship of, 43 ff.; danger of an English attack on, 44–45, 82; increase of settlements in, 54; menace of undesirable immigrants, 55; Spain's efforts to attract settlers to, 78; treatment of immigrants by, 79; new settlements, 79 ff.; Gálveztown, 79; Gálvez' accomplishments in domestic affairs of, 84; two royal orders received by governor of, 88; Leyba's report to governor of, concerning Clark's victories, 95; Hamilton's protest to officials of, against Spanish assistance to rebels, 96; integration of Clark's expedition with history of, 98; motive of, in giving aid to Revolutionists, 101; emigration to Spanish, 111; Gálvez' protection of Americans a disadvantage for, 123; English gratitude for opening of, by Gálvez to refugees, 124; reënforcements for, from Havana, 124; factors constituting security of, 124; exposed to English anger, 136; statement of forces in, 137, 150; militia, 137–138; agreement to return fugitive slaves to, 144; critical situation of, laid before the junta de guerra, 150; preparations for defense of, 151, 153; announcement of war with England to, 152–153; Gálvez appointed governor of, 152; Campbell's desire to add, to British dominions, 192; Gálvez secured an American instead of an English frontier for, 248–249, and completed establishment of Spanish control over, 249–250; inhabitants of, thanked by Gálvez for urging king to bestow honors upon him, 251
Louisiana Division of Immigration and Indian Affairs, 81
Lowe, Quartermaster, surrender of, to Gálvez, 206
Loyola, Juan Joseph de, 19
Lumber, 34, 35

Macarti, 17, 18
McGillivray, Alexander: protest of, against oath of neutrality, 123; later association of, with Spaniards, 207; association of, with James Colbert, 232; became foremost chief of the Creeks, 232; position of, during Natchez rebellion, 232; "Parole of Honour" drafted by, 232
McIntyre, Thomas, complaint against, 115–116

INDEX

Málaga, 43, 56, 81
Manchac, 11, 80, 108, 109, 114, 117, 118, 125, 138, 139, 149, 150, 151, 154, 161, 172; district, 54; British post at, 72; Fort, 154; expedition to, 173
Mandeville, Marigny de, 79
Manumission, 50
Marquette, Jacques, 1
Marquis, Pierre: drafted a frame of government on Swiss model, 20; appeal for leniency of, 21
Marr, Christopher, part played by, in Natchez rebellion, 217, 224
Martin, François-Xavier, 27
Martinique, French preparations at, 244
Mason, Edward Gay, 167, 168, 229
Maurepas Lake, a possible point for British attack, 150
Maxwell, John, governor of Bahama Islands, 245
"Memoir against the Republicans," 20
Mexico, export of tobacco to, 77
Michilimackinac, 96, 164
Milhet, Jacques, 21, 25
Milhet, Jean, 6, 25, 26
Militia: citizen organization of, 41; better-disciplined, to be organized, 69
Miller, Francis, surrender of, to Gálvez, 206
Miranda, Francisco de: sent to Jamaica as a spy, 243; success of enterprise of, 243–244; maps of fortifications submitted by, 243–244; final provisions of surrender of Bahama Islands by Governor Maxwell arranged by, 245
Miró, Estevan, 84, 86, 151; named ranking officer under Gálvez, 153; sent to Havana to ask for more men, 174; concluded expedition against Colbert not practicable, 233; urged Gálvez to erect new forts, 234; sent by Gálvez to Natchez to perfect defenses, 234; statement of, concerning government of Natchez district, 234; release of some prisoners by, 234–235; plan of, approved by Gálvez, 235; had no negotiations with Colbert while at Natchez, 235; letter to, from Colbert, 236; Natchez prisoners granted full freedom of town, by, 240; exchange of letters between, and Colbert, 241; spent four months in getting Colbert's uprising under control, 242. *See also* Colbert; Natchez rebellion
Mississippi River: maps to be made of, 68; gunpowder shipped up, for Americans, 87; chain of forts to be constructed along, by British, 138; control over, settled in favor of Spain, 170
Mississippi Valley: lower, secured for Spain, 163–164; significance of Gálvez' conquests for entire, 166
Missouri, fortifications at mouth of, 12, 41
Mobile, 2, 80, 132, 141, 146, 149, 171, 174, 175, 183, 194, 198, 201, 206, 215, 226, 237
Molino, 18
Montgomery, John: expedition of, against Sauk and Fox Indians, 166; part played by, in Natchez rebellion, 216
Morales, Juan, 99
Morandiere, Estevan Robert de la: in command of expedition to Natchez district, 220; reported to Grand Pré, 220, and ordered to Natchez by him, 220; sent deputies to Grand Pré, 221; emissaries bearing letter from Blommart to, 221; promise of, of protection made conditional on Grand Pré's approval, 221; occupation of Fort Panmure by, 222, 224, 228; treatment of Blommart by, criticized, 222; criticized by Hutchins, 223
Morgan, George: proposed expedition against Pensacola to Gálvez, 90, 103; response of Gálvez to, 91; communication from Cruzat to, intercepted by Willing, 106; correspondence of Gálvez with, about Pensacola, 136
Morgan, Patrick, 76
Morris, Robert, 102
"Morris," the "Rebecca" rechristened, 130

Nach, Joseph, 51
Naguiquen, Indian chief, 168
Narváez, Pánfilo, 1
Natchez, 2, 12, 54, 102, 106, 125, 126, 130, 150, 157, 159, 166, 215, 218, 219, 220, 228; district, 103, 125, 157, 215; oath, 107; Fort Panmure at, 157, 219; rebellion, 215 ff.; leaders, 227
Natchez rebellion, 215 ff.; part played by Campbell in, 215, 219; Blommart induced to assume leadership of, 217; attack on Fort Panmure, 217; terms of capitulation of, 218; part played by Hutchins in, 218; effect of fall of Pensacola on, 219; Campbell reproached by Gálvez for instigating, 219; Campbell's proposals to Gálvez concerning, 219–220; small force sent from New Orleans to recover Fort Panmure, 220; Blommart's emissaries bearing "Terms of Accommodation," 221; landing of Morandiere at Natchez, 222; evacuation of fort, 222; criticism of Morandiere's action, 222–223; could easily be crushed by Spaniards, 223; fleeing inhabitants of district, 223; mild Spanish retribution, 223–224; trial of leaders of, by Panis, 224 ff.; account by Grand Pré of proceeds of sale of confiscated property, 226–227; part played in, by Alston and Turner, 228 ff.; James Colbert's part in, 228 ff.; position of McGillivray during, 232; measures to suppress, instituted, 233. *See also* Blommart; Colbert; Cruzat, Madame; L'Abbadie; Miró
Natchitoches, 3, 38, 68, 131, 138; district, 33, 51, 52
Nava, Captain Manuel de, 151
Navarro, Diego Joseph, captain general at Havana: report of, concerning audacity of English merchants, 71; order of Spain's declaration of war forwarded by, to Gálvez, 149; reënforcements sent to Gálvez by, 162; Gálvez wrote to, for additional forces from Havana, 172; offered a substitute plan for seizure of West Florida, 173; informed by Gálvez of decision to concentrate on capture of Mobile, 174; criticized by Spain, 186; reënforcements sent by, and then recalled, 187; assurances of, to provide Gálvez with whatever he required sent to court, 192–193
Navarro, Martin, 71; placed in civil and military control of New Orleans, 153; sentiment of, concerning proximity of Americans, 249
Negro slaves, introduction of, for agriculture, 79
"Neptune," English brig seized by Americans, 110–111, 119, 120, 212
New Granada, revolt of comuneros in, 244
New Iberia, founded by settlers from Málaga, 81
New Orleans: founding of, 3; island of, retained by France, 4, 5; export trade of, under France, 10; trade of with England, 11; trade restrictions imposed by Spain on, 11; arrival of Spanish troops in, 13; civic pride of, hurt by Ulloa, 13, and his departure from, 17; financial support of Spain for, 19; arrival of Spanish fleet at, 22; O'Reilly's entry into, 23; political reorganization of, 31; Pollock remained in, 34; no duties charged at, 35; Indian Council convened at, 36; contract for trade goods made with Piseros of, 38; heaviest garrison of soldiers maintained at, 41; census taken, 68; marriage of Spanish officers to creoles of, 84; arrest of Gibson at, 87; opened to American privateers, 88; Morgan's request to trade freely with, 90, 91; Willing welcomed at, 102; coöperation of volunteers from, with Willing's men, 110; arrangements for Willing's arrival at, 112–113; lack of adequate defense for, 122; situation of Americans at, 123–124; annoyance occasioned by Willing's presence in, 127–128; attempts to move Willing out of, 130 ff.; stockades of, in bad repair, 137;

INDEX   285

New Orleans (*continued*)
  increased militia enrollment in, 137–138; English planned twofold expedition against, 150; protection of, chief consideration, 150; Gálvez expected British attack on, 152–153; Piernas and Navarro placed in control of, 153; statement of a Pensacola Britisher respecting, 162; Dickson's confirmation of English plan for attack on, 163; greater part of forces against Pensacola returned to, 191; Piernas ordered to mobilize forces at, 200; as a trading post for Natchez district, 215; prisoners of Natchez rebellion at, 224, 226, 227, 234, 239, 240, 241
New Spain, Indian policy of, 52
Norteños, 37, 38
"Nuestra Señora de los Remedios," 18
Nueva Vizcaya, Gálvez campaign against Apaches in, 62, 63, 82, 253
Nugent, Eduardo, 30
Nuñez Cabeza de Vaca, Alvar, 1
Nunn, Joseph, commander of the "Hound," 121; protest of, against oath of neutrality, 122–123

Oconor, Hugo, 66
Odoardo, Cecilio, 48
O'Hara, 130
O'Neill, Arturo, new commander at Pensacola, final instructions of Gálvez to, 212, 213
Opelousas, 33, 68, 131, 163
O'Reilly, Alejandro: task of establishing Spanish control in Louisiana assigned to, 20; experiences of, 20–21; personality of, 21; comparison of Ulloa and, 21; became dictator of Louisiana, 21; landing of, at New Orleans, 22–23; arrest of leaders of insurrection by, 23; trial and sentence by, 24–26; "Bloody O'Reilly," 27; criticism of, 27; king's approval of, 28; activities of, in Louisiana, 29; allowed much of the old French system to remain, 30 ff.; treatment of creoles by, 31; reform of trade regulations by, 33; attempts of, to prevent smuggling, 34; curtailment of trade with England by, 34, 70; recognized need for foreign trade, 34 ff.; promotion of trade with Havana by, 35; convened an Indian Council at New Orleans, 36–37; organization of citizens' militia by, 41; other reforms instituted by, 42; Unzaga a protégé of, 43; officially appointed Unzaga governor, 44; departure of, 44; recommendations of, respecting military equipment for Louisiana, 45; established Spanish control in Louisiana, 57; censured Bernardo de Gálvez' Apache campaigns, 66; Gálvez as captain of infantry under, 67; friendship of, with Pollock, 85, 86; quelled insurgency of 1768 in Louisiana, 249

Panimatajá, 237
Panis, Jacinto: marriage of, to creole, 84; went to Mobile and Pensacola as spy, 141, 142; planned attack on Pensacola, 141; carried Gálvez' letter of complaint to Chester, 141; conducted other negotiations, 141; letter of, to Gálvez, 142; complimented by Governor Chester, 144–145; requested to return to New Orleans by Gálvez, 145; presented report of commission, 145 ff.; named ranking officer under Gálvez, 153; instructed by Gálvez to prepare plans for seizure of Pensacola and Mobile, 172; trial of Natchez rebellion leaders turned over to, by Gálvez, 224 ff.
"Parole of Honour," 232
Pensacola: reënforcement of, reported by Unzaga, 44; intercession of commissioners from, for British merchants, 75–76; proposed expedition against, 90, 103; Fergusson's departure from New Orleans for, 119; protest from authorities at, concerning Willing's presence in New Orleans, 128; new commander sent to, 133; Pollock urged Congress to send

Pensacola (*continued*)
expedition to, 134; correspondence of Gálvez with Morgan concerning, 136; strengthening of, reported, 138; flour shortage in, relieved by Gálvez, 139; attack on, planned by Panis, 141; letter of merchant of, to one at New Orleans, 142; Panis' departure from, 145; description of, given in report, 146; Spain's desire for conquest of, and Mobile, 147; order to drive British forces out of, 149, 171–172; English expedition against New Orleans to come from, 150; declaration of war with Spain by commander of, 159; defenses of, strengthened, 171; attack on, to be made after capture of Mobile, 174; reënforcements for Fort Charlotte promised from, 179–180; retreat of Campbell and his forces toward, 183; plans for conquest of, made by Gálvez, 187; detailed forces of, 187; Gálvez determined to attack, 188; Indian auxiliaries formed important division in defense of, 189, 207; abandonment of Gálvez' attack on, 191; New Orleans forces instructed to proceed to, 200; willingness of Campbell to negotiate for security of town of, 205; beginning of Gálvez' operations against, 206; Gálvez' problem at, 209; surrender of, and entire province of West Florida, 211; Gálvez' fear that English might try to recapture, 213; rechristening of Bay of, 213; repercussion of siege of, in Natchez district, 215, 218 ff.; terror of Natchez settlers at news of fall of, 223; James Colbert gave assistance to English during siege of, 228; Gálvez ordered to Jamaica immediately after capture of, 243

Perdido River, 147, 175, 187, 207

Phelps, Albert, 53

Philadelphia: gunpowder shipped to, from New Orleans, 87; Willing's return to, 103

Pickett, Albert James, 223

Pickles, William: exploits of, on Lake Pontchartrain, 159, 160; letter of, to commanding officer at New Orleans, 160; ferried Indians across lake to New Orleans, 160; took prize on Mobile coast, 160; actions of, approved by Gálvez, 160; commendation accorded to Americans under, 163

Piernas, Pedro, 30, 33, 39, 53, 153, 200, 220

Pineda, 1

Piseros, Juan, 38

Pointe Coupée, 30, 41, 44, 139, 159, 217, 220

Pollock, Oliver: Anglo-American merchant not expelled from New Orleans, 34; encouraged Unzaga to aid Americans, 56; momentous work of, 85; friendship of, with O'Reilly, 85; Wilkinson's comment respecting connection of, with Spanish officers, 86; ardent partisan of colonies, 86; Clark's reliance upon, 98 ff.; contributions of, to success of American Revolution, 99; Gálvez placed government funds at disposal of, 99; used personal fortune and credit, 99–100, 132; arrested in Havana, 100; meeting of, with Gálvez in Havana, 100; letter of instruction to, concerning Willing, 104; letter from Willing to, 105; organized volunteers from New Orleans to aid Willing, 110; named Virginia's agent at New Orleans, 112; arrangements made by, for arrival of Willing, 112–113; was permitted to auction plunder, 113, 118; explanation of, respecting Gálvez' part in situation of Americans at New Orleans, 123–124; concern of, respecting control of Natchez district, 125; blamed by Willing for lack of success at Manchac, 126; hearty coöperation of, with Willing, 128, and subsequent rift between them, 128–129; anxiety of, to get rid of Willing, 129, 130 ff.; reports of, to Continental Congress, 129, 130; drafts on, by Robert

INDEX

Pollock, Oliver (*continued*)
George, 131; bitterness of, toward Willing, 134; Gálvez' assistance of Americans through, 136; aide-de-camp to Gálvez, 153; letter of, to inhabitants of Natchez district, 157–158; Gálvez able to be of assistance to, 252
Pontchartrain, 2, 4
Pontchartrain, Lake: boats seized on, 123; possible point for British attack on New Orleans, 150; exploits of William Pickles on, 159
Port Antonio, 244
Port Royal, most important English naval base, 243
Pourré, Eugene, 167, 168; protection of captured Englishmen by, 169; proclamation of annexation of territory in name of Spanish king read by, 169; led St. Joseph expedition, 170; seizure of boat of, by Turner, 229; boat of, met by L'Abbadie, 233; warned by Madame Cruzat, 233
Prince, Thomas, 229
Prince William. *See* Lancaster, Duke of
Provincias Internas, 5, 82, 256
Puerto Rico, 26
Putnam, Colonel Israel, 51

Rada, Joseph, 194, 200
Rapicaut, 120, 121
"Rattletrap," 105, 106, 109
"Rebecca," British boat seized by Willing, 108, 110, 113, 129, 130, 221
Recopilación de Leyes de las Indias, 32
Red River: fort on, opposite Natchez, 12; Indians of, region, 37
Religious contentions, 45
Rey, Felix del, 24
Riaño, Juan, 175, 202
Rillieux, Vizente: spectacular victory of, 161; commendation accorded to French creoles under, 163
Ripperda, Baron de, 52
Rocheblave, Pablo, 17, 18, 49

Rocheblave, Philippe de Rastel de, 94, 104, 105, 106
Rodney, 244
Ross, George, 119, 121
Rubi, Marquis of, 39
Rui, 30

St. Augustine, 171, 211, 243
St. Joseph: aid solicited from commander at, 96; small band of Spaniards sent against, 167; most important reason for attack on, 168; effect of expedition against, 169–170
St. Louis: Piernas sent to, as commandant, 33; instructions sent to, by O'Reilly, 39; fortifications maintained at, 41; population of, 53, 54; Gálvez kept in touch with Leyba in, 82; easy capture of, expected by Canadian forces, 164; information of proposed attack on, received by Leyba, 165; part played by Clark in defense of, 165–166; retaliation for attack on, 166 ff. *See also* Cruzat, Francisco; Leyba
St. Maxent, Gilbert Antoine de, 14, 17, 18; settlement directed by, 79; first to enter Fort Manchac, 155; directed landing of troops at Mobile, 176
Sainte Domingue, 3; importation of slaves from, 11
Ste. Geneviève, 41, 53, 54, 165
San Juan de Ulloa, Mexican fortress of, 253
"San Ramon," Spanish warship, 198, 201; difficulty of, to enter port, 202
Santa Rosa Island, 200–201, 206
Seminoles, 207
Shakespear, Stephen, 108, 120, 121
Sigüenza Point, Santa Rosa Island, 201, 203
Sinclair: forces gathered by, for expedition against St. Louis, 164; easy victory at St. Louis expected by, 164; significant suggestion in apology of, 166; statement of, concerning expedition against St. Joseph, 169

Smith, John, 226, 234
Solano, Josef, 208
Sorelle, Joseph, 163
Soto, Hernando de, 1
Spain: willingness of France to cede Louisiana to, 4, 5, 6; trade restrictions by, in Louisiana, 11; possession of Louisiana taken for, 13, 39; Ulloa's report to, 16; waning of defiance against, 18; continued contact with colony by, 19; enforcement of regulation under, 30; securing profitable trade for, 35; Gálvez' assistance to Americans given before, entered war against England, 85; part played by Gálvez in American Revolution while, was still neutral, 101; motive of, in assisting Revolution, 101; English reluctant to have war with, 124; took American peril lightly, 135; declared war against England, 149; formal possession of St. Joseph taken for, 167; siege of Gibraltar abandoned by, 244; anxiety of, about example of revolt set by American colonies, 249
Spaniards, efforts of Louisiana French to align Indians against, 17
Spanish: explorations, 1; reasons for discontent with, régime in Louisiana, 13; prestige diminished, 13; rebellion against rule of, 14; rule in Illinois country not interrupted, 19; insult to, honor, 20; courts available for protection of foreigners, 49; American emigration to, Louisiana, 111; victims of flood offered haven in English territory, 139; Indians caused most of, casualties, 207; Natchez-Chickasaw rebellions a menace to, control on Mississippi, 242
Stephenson, 205–206
Stuart, Henry, British Indian Commissioner, 143, 178
Sugar, 35
Superior Council, Louisiana, 6, 8, 12, 13, 15, 16, 18, 26, 31
"Sylph," English naval vessel, appearance of, in Mississippi, 114; departure of, for Pensacola, 119

Taovayas Indians, 51
Tarascon, Santiago, 163
Tauchipaho River, 160
Tawakoni, 51
Teggart, Frederick J., 167, 168
Terre-aux-Boeufs, new Spanish settlement at, 79
Texas frontier, effect of warfare on, 13
Tobacco, 34, 35, 52, 69, 77; strongest deterrent to, culture was shortage of labor, 77
Tonkawa Indians, 51
Trade regulation, problem of, 70
Treaty of Ryswick, 2
Trudeau, Zenon, 17, 18, 225
Turner, John, part played by, in Natchez rebellion, 216, 217, 218, 224, 226, 228, 229

Ulloa, Antonio: appointed governor of Louisiana, 6; life and activities of, before going to new post, 7–8; difficulties encountered by, 8 ff.; extended trip through lower Louisiana by, 12; handicaps met by, 13; possession of Louisiana taken for Spain by, 13; accusations against, 13–15; personality of, 14; demands of insurgents on, 14–15; ordered to leave by Superior Council, 15; boat carrying, set adrift, 15–16; expulsion of, 16; brought on the insurrection, 57; recognized English menace along Mississippi and Florida frontiers, 248; and the insurrection of 1768, 249

United Independent States of North America, 160

United States, issue concerning creation of, 248

Unzaga y Amézaga, Luis de: brought by O'Reilly to be governor of Louisiana, 43; previous service, 43; comparison of, with O'Reilly, 43; official appointment of, 44;

INDEX 289

Unzaga y Amézaga, Luis de (*continued*) orders received by, for defense of Louisiana, 45; stand of, in religious contentions, 46; fearlessness of, 47; attempted to establish a Spanish language school, 47; administration of justice under, 47–50; trade conditions under, 50, 70; pretense of, to stifle smuggling, 51; correspondence of, with Ripperda and De Mézières, 52; flourishing condition of Natchitoches under governorship of, 52; increase in population of Spanish Illinois under, 54; reports the lack of proper defenses for Louisiana, 55, 56; faced with problem of neutrality, 55, 85; requests for assistance by Revolutionary leaders made to, 55; request of, for permission to retire, 56; promoted to captaincy general of Caracas, 56; tribute to, 56; reconciled colonists to Spanish rule, 57; departure of, 67; had closed his eyes to smuggling, 70; Pollock's comment on association with, 86, 87; gunpowder shipped to Americans in governorship of, 87; recommendations of, concerning Pollock, 87; lukewarmness of, toward American cause, 88; despondent view of, respecting American Revolution, 135; conciliatory effect of rule of, in Louisiana, 250

"Valenzuela," 175, 177, 202
Vallé, Francisco, 53
Vera Cruz, smuggling into, from Louisiana, 34
Vigo, François, 96–97
Vilard, 18
Villars, Luis, 70, 240, 241
Villieré, Joseph, 15
Vincennes, 95, 96; Rapicaut's boats engaged in illicit trade with Fort, 120
Virginia: Grand Council of, 87; Patrick Henry governor of, 92; Clark's expeditions sponsored by, 97; money advanced by Pollock recognized as state indebtedness by, 100; Pollock named agent for, at New Orleans, 112; failure of, to send remittances for expenses incurred by Willing, 134
"Volante," 17, 18, 24, 155, 176, 202

War of the Palatinate, 2
"West Florida," 72, 123, 159
West Florida: consternation of population of, at depredations of Willing, 109, 110, 111; refuge offered to people of, by governor of Louisiana, 111; distrust of English authorities in, because of oath of neutrality, 123; British reënforcements for, 125, 138; apprehension of Willing felt in, 126; strengthening of defenses of, 133; American expeditions into, a menace to Spanish Louisiana, 136; Spain's entry into war concealed from English of, 154; plan for seizure of, advanced by Navarro, 173; surrender of entire province of, 211
Whissel, William, surrender of, to Gálvez, 206
Wilkinson, James, statement of, concerning Pollock's connections at New Orleans, 86
Williams, William L., 222, 224, 238, 240
Willing, James, 93, 98; expedition of, 102; raided Loyalist settlements along lower Mississippi, 102; merchant at Natchez, 102; agitator for Revolution, 103; return of, to Philadelphia, 103; commissioned captain in navy, 103; assertions made by, 104; import of instructions given to, 105; arrest of Anthony Hutchins by, 106, 108; arrival at Natchez of, 106–107; proposals of committee accepted by, 107; charges against, 107–108; capture of "Rebecca" and "Hinchenbrook" by, 108; hatred of settlers for, 109; depredations of, 109, 111; "seventh of March speech," 110; freedom of New Orleans extended to, 112; sale permitted of plunder of, 112–113, 118; English protests concerning welcome given to, 113–114; legality of plundering of,

Willing, James (*continued*)
  questioned, 117; Gálvez' correspondence with, concerning restoration of captured property, 119–121; one contrary result of expedition of, 124–125; surprise attack on, and recovery of post, 125; concern of, respecting control of Natchez district, 125; attempt of, to get possession of Manchac, 126; disadvantages suffered by Americans because of, 127; unable to leave New Orleans, 127; incurred displeasure of Gálvez, 127, 128; desire of, to go north through Spanish territory, 130–131; taken prisoner at Mobile, 132; return of, to New Orleans, 133; conclusions concerning, 133; important result of expedition of, 134; effect of, on Pollock, 134; final conclusion concerning, 134; flurry caused in Pensacola by raid of, 145

Winfree, Jacob, 226, 240

Yscanis Indians, 51
Yucatan, freedom of commerce with, 76

www.ingramcontent.com/pod-product-compliance
Lightning Source LLC
Chambersburg PA
CBHW021834220426
43663CB00005B/237